MW00948358

Barbara
love ha...
in my class
Barb —
4/3/2018

My Rocky Road to the Good Life

The Whole Story

Barbara Y. Hofmeister

Copyright© 2016 Barbara Y. Hofmeister

All rights reserved. No part of this book may be reproduced or utilized In any form or by any means, electronic or mechanical, including photocopying, recording or by any information storage and retrieval system, without permission in writing from the author. Inquiries should be addressed to Barbara Hofmeister, at byh@movinon.net.

ISBN 1479248495

Printed in the United States of America

This book is dedicated to my wonderful family and the many friends who have been a big part of my life. I also dedicate this to all of those who were in my Life Story Writing Classes. By helping others write their story, I was motivated to finish mine.

Table of Contents

Two Mistakes Almost Led to Disaster..........................15
Birth Through Elementary School
Violets and Pies..23
Big City..26
Tar and Samella..27
The Big House...29
Spies and Such..32
Candy Store...34
Inner Sanctum...35
Wilderness..39
The Country School...42
Skating and Swimming.....................................46
Stranded at the Dance.....................................48
Teenage Years
Back to Civilization..53
Living in the Basement.....................................55
Dysfunctional..57
Drayton Elementary...58
Oh No!..59
WTHS..62
A Success Story..64
Friends and Fun..65
Silly Girls and the Bell Hop...............................68
Three Calamities..70
Miracle Baby..72
Prom with a Stranger..73
Pencil Skirts and Maidenform............................69
Young Adult Years.
Off We Go Into the Wild Blue Yonder..................85
Pee, Poop and Blood...71
Glenda Upchurch...73
The Wild One..97
.A Bout of Defiance...101

California Here I Come....103
Finally Working....105
Facing the Music....108
Glenda's First Year....112
What Did We Do?....117
On My Own and Loving it For a Short While.....121
Trying Again....122

Early Family Years

Racing for No Reason....129
Oh Brother!....132
The Beginning of the End....134
The December When My World Fell Apart....137
Criminal Justice?....140
Al McGuire....142
Working Three Jobs....148
Dr. Jack Kevorkian....151
A Short Walk to Near Death....153
A New Smile....154
Oh My God, I Killed Her....155
New Additions....159
New Love....162
Falling in a Big Hole....165

Middle Family Years

Nearly Perfect....171
On Being a Mother....173
The Witch in Me....176
The Kitchen Makeover Caper....180
Mama Goes to College....182
George....184
The $100,000 Problem....186
Poetry....187
Music, Music, Music....191
Best Laid Plans....197
Mini Fun....201
Dirty Trick....205
Fond Memories From the 70s....208
Flapping Wings....210
Ladybugs....214
Fascinating Womanhood....215
It's a Fine Time to Leave Me Lucille....218

The Village Photographer........220
From House to Apartment........223
Another One Leaves the Nest........225
Business Was Terrific........226
Liisa was Born in Finland........228
Wonderful and Terrible........230
Falling Apart........233
The Last Straw........235

A New Beginning

I'm Alive........241
The Big Move........243
My Poor New Car........245
Counseling........247
The Crash at Work........248
Finding a New Job........249
D Day Again........250
Oh Robert........251
Back in the Lab........252
I Did it Again........254
It Wasn't Funny........255
Comings and Goings........256
Getting Fired Wasn't So Bad After All........258
A Different Tupperware Party........259

Early Love

The Best Line Ever........265
Two Awkward Situations........267
A Real Date........269
Getting to Know Him........271
Family, Football, Friends and Florida........273
Golf and Fish Hooks........275
Life Begins Again........277
My Baby Left Me........280
Cooking Over a Wood Fire........281
Jubilee........283
Move Stirred up Trouble in the Family........285
Somber Wedding........286
Bad Trip........290
Falling in a Real Hole........292
Liisa Spends a Month With Us........295
I Love Lucy........298

Train Trip to Chicago....302
Bridge and Baseball....303
Trips and Tribulations....306
Bicycling....309
I quit Smoking....311
Off We Go
A Mallard Wasn't a Duck....317
Our First Four Trips....320
A Challenge and Sad Ending....322
Good and Bad Trips....324
Sleep Naked in a Sleeping Bag....326
Talking the Night Away....328
Here and There in 1988....329
Preparing for Retirement....332
Counting Down to Our New Life....335
Movin'On
Pies Oh My!....345
"It Has Legs!"....350
A Nightmare Beginning....352
Finally We Arrived at the Beginning....356
A Relaxing Week In Felixstowe....358
Day One-Felixstowe to Lavenham....360
George, Ann and Cambridge....361
Forget Shakespeare....364
A Side Trip to Dorset....367
Back on Our Route....374
Tisn't it My Lucky Day....376
Oops Wrong Way....379
Limping to the End....384
From Michigan to Florida—the Long Way....388
He's Writing a Book....393
Limping All the Way Back to Michigan....397
Babies, Blueberries & Big Lake....399
Bathing in Hot Springs....402
Round Up....404
When Illness Struck....407
Too Much Snow....409
Going Back in Time....415
New Pull Toy....420
Volcanos, Ghosts, Glaciers and Geysers....422

Thrills....424
Flowers and Football....429
Oops—Big Time....431
Hot Off the Press....436
Revisiting England....439
Business, Family and Friends in Michigan....443
First Lobster....446
We Grew and Moved Up....450
Home on the Range Again....454
A New Book....458
Frustration then Excitement....461
Important Phone Call....465
Haunted by an Old Ghost....470
Hitting the Big Time....472
Busy, Busy, Busy....476
Stumbling Blocks in Colorado....478
A Phone in My Home....482
A Big Circle....485
Up the Coast and....487
Rafting the Salmon River....490
Good News....494
"I Can't See"....496
The American Dream....499
Plans Change Quick....503
Together at Last....505
All Things Must End....508
What a Mess....511
New Book....513
Implants, Tornados and Talks....515
Clearing the Air....517
Guess Who Came For Dinner....519
More Than a Crunch....521
The Beginning of the End Again....552
Accidentally House Hunting....531
Frustration and More Frustration....534
Don't Faint....537
Death, Dying and Rebirth....540
Spur of the Moment Decision....542
Foot Loose and Fancy Free....544
Look What I Found On-line....547

Home Sweet Home

Going Crazy With Decisions....553
How Many Square Feet?....556
The Last Trip in the Dream....558
Trouble, Trouble, Trouble....561
Ups and Downs of Life....563
We Are Not Finished Yet....569
Out On His Own Terms....570
What Did I Do?....577
Changing My Attitude....579
Thank You....581

Two Mistakes Almost Led to Disaster

Much to my horror, by June I knew I was pregnant but I hadn't seen a doctor yet. I called Duke and told him what I knew. His response rang in my ears for a long, long time, actually for months and I can still hear it today. He said, "That's your problem. You had your chance." Since I hadn't gotten pregnant when we were trying (which would have been stupid as well) I guess I hadn't worried about getting pregnant when we were together at his mother's place.

I cried a river and whenever I cried, I thought of one of the last songs we heard together. It was on the juke box at the Italian restaurant across from the base in Montgomery—*I cried a River Over You* by Julie London. The words weren't exactly what I was going through but I cried a river anyway.

Just when my life was really beginning, I felt I had really messed up. Being an unwed mother in 1956 was not cool. It was a disgrace and I dreaded having to go home and face the music.

I loved the Air Force and didn't want to leave. I couldn't tell my parents. My whole world was a mess. I remember thinking that maybe I could die somehow. In fact, I decided to take a base bus into Riverside and walk the streets until someone ran over me. Little did I know that California had a pedestrian law. Cars had to stop if anyone walked out in the street. I kept jay walking in my calf length tight black skirt (style of the day) and heels but no one would even hit the brakes fast. After walking the streets for an hour or so, I decided to give up and go back to the base. I went to the bus station with a huge black cloud hanging over my head. I was so consumed with worry and grief that I think I was somewhat of a zombie.

While waiting for the bus, a car pulled up with two guys in it. The driver asked if I wanted a ride back to the base instead of waiting for the bus. That sounded good to me so I jumped in the car. I was quiet, and did not engage in conversation with them. Soon the driver dropped off the other guy at a bowling alley and proceeded to go to the base—so he said. Suddenly I woke up and realized we were NOT heading to the base. Although I had not been in Riverside that long and didn't really know the area, it looked like we were headed to the mountains instead of the base. I started to pay attention to signs and things that would help me when I got out of the car. But the area was so remote and mountainous that I didn't see much besides the pitch blackness of the night. It seemed like we drove forever and I was constantly trying to be cool as my mind raced to how I could free myself from this dangerous situation. I saw a row of mailboxes on the left side of the road just before he turned right onto a one lane path into the woods. My heart was racing. This wasn't good. He drove slow and reached over for me while telling me what he was going to do to me. I hugged the door handle ready to bolt when the car slowed. He was near the end of the trail and slowing down when I jumped out of the car. That damn tight skirt and heels made it difficult to run; I kicked off the shoes and hiked up my skirt and ran for my life.

I heard him swearing and was glad that he didn't take off on foot after me. He surely would have caught me, but I guess he figured there was nowhere for me to go, so he could catch me better with the car. As I got towards the end of the wooded trail, I saw his headlights coming out. He probably had a tough time turning around in such a tight spot. I was thankful because that gave me a little time. But with his headlights on, I knew I'd be in the spotlight if I didn't do something drastic.

As I came to the main road, I noticed a ditch all along the road and it was pretty deep. I slid into the ditch and started crawling towards the left where I had seen the mailboxes. The ditch was partially full of water which made going pretty messy. His car came out of the path and went right. Thank God! But I didn't think he was through looking for me. I made sure he was out of sight around a curve and I got up out of the ditch and made a bee line for the mailboxes. The road by the mailboxes went straight up. I prayed I had the energy to run up the road. I had nylons on which were shredded at that point.

I was half way up the hill when I saw his headlights coming back on that main road below. I ran faster. Thankfully he didn't turn up the road I was on but went past it. I was still sure that he wasn't through with me. I kept running until I got to the top. There were three houses. No lights were on anywhere. I went to the first house and banged on the door with all my might. A dog started barking frantically. I kept banging. There was no answer and I saw that the barking dog had signaled my whereabouts to the car's driver. He was heading back my way. I ran to the second house and banged and banged. There was no answer there and with the dogs barking loudly I figured no one was home there either.

The car was coming up the hill towards the houses as I reached the final house. I banged and banged while praying that someone would be home because I had nowhere to go. It was rugged terrain all around with no other road or path from up there. I kept banging all the while the car was coming closer and closer. Suddenly lights went on in the house and at the same time, the car backed up to go away. When the door opened I literally fell inside and was hysterical for a while. They were a nice couple and after I could finally tell them my story, they called the base for me. The MPs came to pick me up. I was a mess, but I wasn't hurt.

Once I got back to the base, I had to go through some pretty tough questioning. I didn't tell anyone I was pregnant or that I thought I wanted to die. When I was faced with rape and possible death, I really did want to live.

ROUGH
ROAD

Section One

Birth Through Elementary School

1937 — 1948

Violets and Pies

My aunt Mary said the violets were in bloom when I was born on Monday, May 17, 1937, in Hornell, New York, (southwestern part of the state). But mother always equated lilacs and Lilly of the valley with my birthday. My Mother, Alice Lucille Dodd (23) and my Father Harold Weld Sayles (24) were the oldest in their families but I wasn't the first grandchild on either side. Cousin Larry was born one month and four days before I was to my mother's brother, Uncle George, and his wife Aunt Audrey. Unfortunately, his life was short as he died at the age of seven.

I had bright red hair and so did cousin Larry. I was named Barbara Yvonne Sayles and never asked my mother why she chose the name "Barbara" but because Yvonne was not a common middle name for the Barbaras I knew, I asked why she picked "Yvonne." She explained that the Dionne quintuplets were about to celebrate their third birthday just before I was born. They were always in the news and one of them was named Yvonne. Mom liked that.

Franklin D. Roosevelt was president in 1937 and the country was still in a depression but gradually coming out. Dad opened a restaurant by the train depot to try to make ends meet. He named it Salis because he said that is how everyone pronounced our last name anyway. Grandma Sayles was a terrific baker, made the pies they sold by the piece and several family members worked in the restaurant which was very small. My mother worked at the Woolworth store in the candy counter.

The restaurant was near the RR depot and was always crowded. Later they moved to a larger location and although the same amount of people came, the place being so much bigger looked empty. Dad used to say he thought the customers assumed the place wasn't that popular any more and started to go elsewhere. Dad always liked to blame others for his failures and I will never know the truth.

The restaurant at its original location

My father had one brother and three sisters. Two of the sisters, Genevieve and Mary, were teenagers (12 & 14) when I was born and they loved to baby sit and just be around what they said was such a "cute baby." My mother had five brothers but they weren't so infatuated with a baby at that time. When I was older they loved to buy me trinkets.

I guess we moved to Rochester, New York, just before I turned two because my brother was born on February 16, 1939, in Rochester. The picture on the next page was taken in New York probably shortly before we moved to Detroit.

Cousins were hard to come by since the other siblings in my parent's families did not marry right away. Long before they did marry and start having children, we had moved to Detroit, Michigan, far away from family. I was only three years old when we left New York, grandparents, aunts and uncles behind so the only family I was close to was my own immediate family. It was many years before we went back to New York to visit.

There are a couple important events in history that happened around the time of my birth:

On May 3, 1937, (two weeks before my birth) Margaret Mitchell won a Pulitzer Prize for *Gone With The Wind*. I wonder if it is a coincidence that I am such a fan of the story. I saw it at least 25 times.

On Thursday, May 6, 1937, the German dirigible, the Hindenburg, exploded while landing in Lakehurst, New Jersey. It had traveled from Germany. Thirty six died in this disaster and ended dirigible travel.

I have always been fascinated Amelia Earhart. She disappeared on July 2, 1937 en route from Lae, New Guinea, to Howland Island. The U. S. Government spent $4 million looking for Earhart, which made it the most costly and intensive air and sea search in history at that time.

Dad, me, Don, Mom

Big City

I don't remember our early years in Detroit except for a couple of very small incidents. I know we lived in an apartment building on John R (which is now a pretty seedy area of Detroit) and we were on a second, third or even fourth floor. I remember waking up one night thinking that someone was trying to get into my bedroom. I heard the sound of a wagon or tricycle on the pavement. Mom said it was a bad dream.

Mom worked as a waitress at the Famous Spaghetti Restaurant and Dad was a baker at Mayflower Donut. I remember overhearing their arguments many times and Mom talking about how hard her job was because they had seating on the second floor as well as the first and she had to carry heavy trays up and down the stairs all the time.

I remember the lady who took care of us. She lived in the same building and her name was Marge Laeffler. She and her husband were Hungarian and had two children older than us. I loved looking at the knick knacks on a shelf in her living room. She had a tiny pair of binoculars on one shelf; I doubt if anyone could even see through them. I often asked if I could have them and of course, she wouldn't give them to me. It is funny what one remembers.

Mom told of a time when I played barber shop and cut my brother's hair. Another time I played doctor and took my brother's temperature by sticking a pencil up his butt. I wonder who was watching me. I seem to remember water running and over flowing from the bathtub in that apartment. I couldn't describe the apartment; I can't remember eating there or anything else.

Tar and Samella

Sometime in the early 1940's, we moved to what I would always call my dream house. It was on West Ferry, between Cass and Second which put us a short walk from Detroit's huge Main Library and the Art Museum. We were also only one and a half blocks from Woodward Avenue (the main street in Detroit). Street cars ran down the middle of the street. Our house was closest to Second Avenue with only one large apartment building and an alley between our house and Second. There was quite a bit of traffic in the alley. Vendors would come by horse drawn carts to sell their wares such as pots, pans and kitchen utensils and even rags. I think the coal man also used the alley. There was a tall curb about two feet wide by our side door. From what I can remember, it was maybe two feet tall. I was about five years old and was standing or walking on that curb when some boys came down the alley. They had warm tar and as they walked by they smeared it all over my arm. They weren't anyone I knew—just mean kids.

At the southeast corner of Cass and West Ferry, was our grocery store called Salahanie's. I was often sent to get something from the store since it was only a half block away, but I did have to cross Cass Avenue. I don't think there was a stop light. Anyway, when I went into the store I would tell Mr. Salahanie what I wanted and he would get it for me. Everyone had to do that because it wasn't like the big supermarkets we had later. It was a small store and the shelves behind the counter went up so high that he had to use a long stick with a claw-like thing on the end so he could grab the item. Items up high were usually boxes of cereal. If I remember correctly, we didn't have many choices of brands. For cereal, we could choose corn flakes, Rice Krispies, puffed wheat and rice (they came in a large bag) and of course oatmeal and cream of rice or wheat for cooked cereals. For toothpaste we had a choice of Colgate (a paste in a tin tube), a power in a can or baking soda. I never took any money to the store;

things we purchased were just added to our bill. I don't think Mr. Salahanie sold meat. Maybe there was a meat market nearby but I don't remember. Mom and Dad didn't have a car so they had to walk or take a bus or streetcar to the store and to work. We never went to the store for milk, butter or cottage cheese because those items were delivered to us by the milk man and a bread man delivered breads, cookies and cakes. A man with a vegetable cart would often come down our alley to sell fresh vegetables (in the summer of course).

Mom didn't work at the restaurant after we moved to the big house and I think Dad worked as a draftsman. Mom was busy though because the house was also a boarding house for at least six people. And there was a two bedroom apartment in the basement. She was always busy doing laundry, the old fashioned way, which meant using a wringer washer and hanging the clothes on the lines to dry. There were always sheets hanging on the line. She was always busy and tired. She had help from a rather large but loving black woman named Samella.

In the kitchen, we had an ice box to keep food cold. An ice man would deliver a large block of ice and place it in the top of the ice box. He came regularly and I remember than he never knocked; he just came in hollering "ice man" and did his thing. The ice box was not very tall as I remember. As the ice melted, it dripped into a pan underneath which we emptied often.

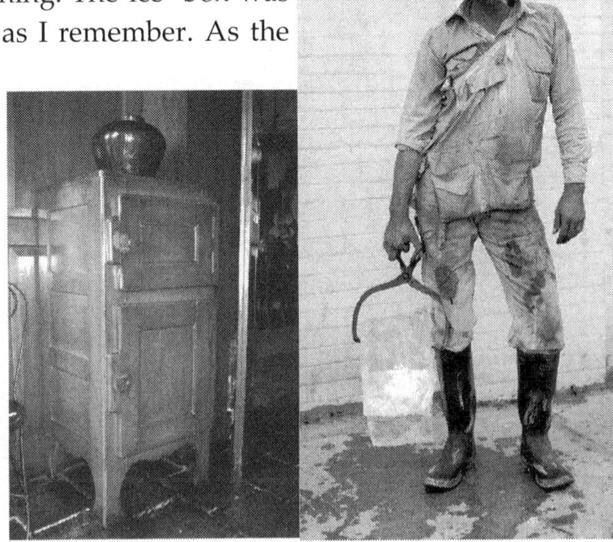

The Big House

The house was like a mansion to me. Was it because I was small that it seemed so big? Below is my humble outline of the first and second floors. Notice that the second floor was not over the sun room and back porch. The strange thing about living in this house is that we never used the second floor. The rooms there were rented as "sleeping rooms." There were also three or four beds in the attic which were used for additional roomers that came and went. The borders never ate with

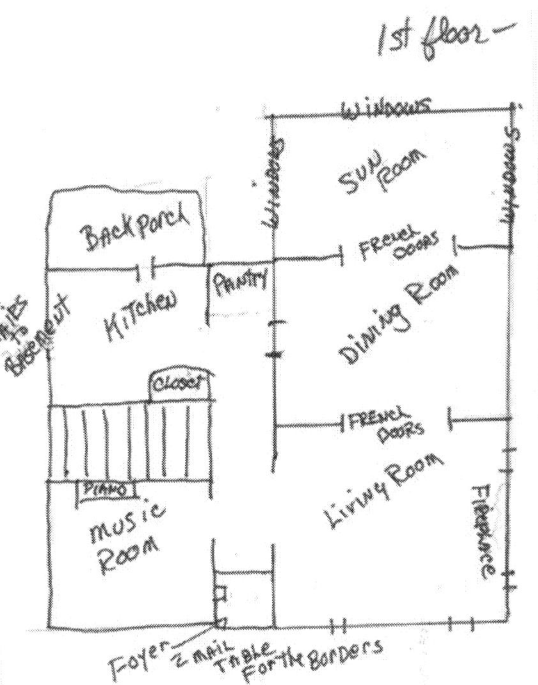

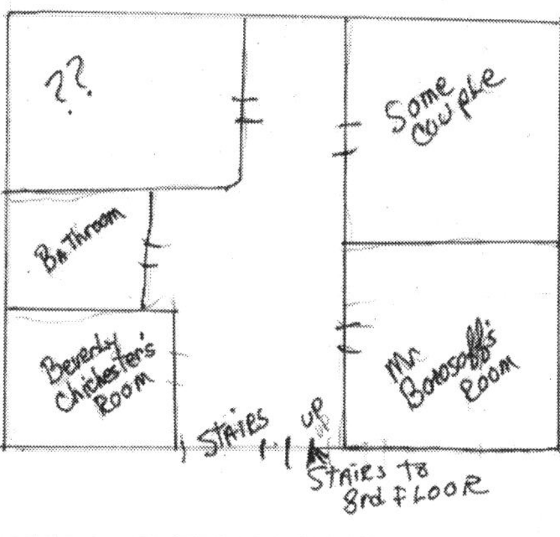

socialized with us. They had a key to the front door and came and went as they pleased. Where did we sleep? We all slept in the sun room which was a big room with windows on three sides (see diagram). Mom and Dad had a bed, and I guess we each had a bed but I don't remember. Bunnie was born on December 3, 1945, so she must have slept out there too. Beverly was born on October 10, 1947, just before we moved from Detroit. I have no idea where our clothing was kept.

Besides the two room apartment on the right at the bottom of the basement stairs, there was the small bathroom on the left by the fruit cellar, coal bin and furnace. We had to use the downstairs bathroom which was also used by the Simpson family (mother, father and two small children) who lived there. I don't remember a tub or shower. There was a big open room which ran the width of the house. Dad put a darkroom somewhere down in the basement at some time and this was the beginning of his hobby of photography and early on in his hobby he took this picture of me. I was eight years old and can't imagine mother allowing it. It bothers me whenever I look at it. Notice, I have tap shoes on and vaguely remember dance lessons somewhere. I remember standing on the kitchen table for this tacky picture. I mean, sticking that rug up on the wall between the two windows is junky. My father was like that.

The coal furnace was huge. It was much taller than I and big and round and covered in asbestos. There were large pipes that came from it and a door in the middle on the side (about half way up from the floor) for the coal. Right next to the furnace was a huge bin where the coal was stored. The bin was under a window and the coal would be delivered by the coal man. He had a big truck and he would use a troth like thing or a slide through the window to deliver our new load of coal. I remember there was never any heat during the night but Dad would go down early in the morning to shovel some coal into the furnace, then we would have some heat.

The thing that I loved most about the house was the main stairway. It was wide and went to about the top of the first floor then there was a wide landing (the width of two stairways) with a window seat under the bank of windows that was the width of the landing. I would sit for hours looking out at the city. At the landing, one had to make a hard right to continue to the second floor.

We must have moved to the big house before 1942 because I started school while we lived there. I don't remember the move, getting furniture or anything like that. I wonder if the house was already furnished. I think the piano was there. It was a wonderful player piano with lots of rolls of music. One roll was *Mare's Eat Oats and Does Eat Oats and Little Lambs Eat Ivy*. Another roll was something classical —maybe one of Liszt's piano concertos. I started taking piano lessons shortly after we moved there and my piano teacher was just across the street and down a little. I don't remember her or her name, but she was young. I do remember meeting a lady by the name of Mrs. Ford, who lived in an apartment across the alley from our house. It was a tall apartment building and for the life of me I don't know how I met her, but she loved the fact that I was playing the piano and would shower me with sheets of classical music which I don't think I could ever play. She wanted me to have the classics. Mr. Borosoff, one of the roomers, gave me a beautiful book of traditional Christmas carols with the explanation of how each song was written. I had that book stored away for a long time, but finally had to throw it away. I still have the fond memory though.

Spies and Such

Speaking of the roomers (as they were called), Mr. Borosoff was an elderly gentleman with a strong European accent. He had the room in the right front corner (when standing at the top of the stairs). My brother and I remember that maybe he was from Bulgaria and because WW II was on ,we imagined him to be a spy. Oh, the imagination of young kids! He used to bring us Switzers licorice all the time. I still love licorice. Another roomer who was there a long time was Beverly Chichester and she had the room on the other side of the stairway from Mr. Borosoff. She was a nice lady who had a severe hunchback. She wasn't old as I remember. I always wished that I had her bedroom and when she left, I did get to sleep there for a few days until a new roomer came. Both of these two were with us for a long time and the whole family got to be very friendly with them. I remember our family took a trip to Cranbrook with them (Mom, Dad, Don and I). It is funny that I don't really remember it, but there are pictures taken with all of us on that outing. That is what I remember—the pictures.

Other roomers came and went. I remember the name of Witherspoon. I think it was a gentleman and my brother and I would laugh hysterically when we saw mail addressed to him because we thought his name was funny. How silly!!

Chet and Mildred Simpson lived in the basement apartment. They were from the south and had strong southern accents. Their daughter, Sue, was just a very petite girl and I regret that my brother and I were kind of mean to her. Their son, Ronnie, was born while they lived with us. I think Mom was pregnant with my sister Bunnie at the same time. (The Simpsons remained family friends until they died. I took Ron to meet Mildred and Chet in Tampa when we had our Bounder motorhome in for repair.)

It was while we lived in Detroit that Mom and Dad met Muriel and Austin Barnes. I think they met at the Woodward Avenue

Baptist Church which we attended. The only thing I remember about that church was when the people were baptized they had gowns on and walked into a huge kind of bathtub which was behind big burgundy velvet drapes. When it was time for the event, they would open like curtains do in a theater and the preacher would help the people into the tub. I thought it was kind of neat and wanted to be baptized, but I wasn't old enough.

Anyway, Muriel and Austin became Mom and Dad's very best friends. Austin was tall and had red hair like my Dad and was a draftsman/engineer like Dad. They looked like Mutt and Jeff together. Muriel was very sophisticated. Their daughter Joanne became my best friend for a long time. She was my brother's age and fun to be with. They had more money than we did and I was kind of intimidated by that. I spent a lot of time at her house and we would play games and cards for hours. Muriel was pregnant at the same time Mom was pregnant with Bunnie and in fact, Mom named Bunnie "Muriel," but we always called her "Bunnie" because Mom really wished for a boy and would have called him Buddy which was Muriel's brother's name. Muriel had a wonderful family of sisters and brothers. They were beautiful like movie stars. I remember Ginger who was the most beautiful, and June, then Buddy who was very handsome. We always had fun with that family and we were always included in events and parties. It was as if they were family which was nice since all of Mom and Dad's relatives were in New York.

Candy Store

When I started school, I went to Tilden which was maybe three blocks from home. I don't remember much. It was a big school—probably two or three stories tall. I don't remember teachers or anything except Carol Thompson. She lived about two blocks away from our house and since it was on the way to school, I always stopped at her house and we would walk the rest of the way together. I can't remember much about her and think that is sad. The one thing I do remember is we were walking together to her house from my house one day and a boy walking towards us crossed the street and handed me a candy bar. Carol insisted that he meant it for her and we fought about it. That reminds me that there was a store across from the school and we would often go to buy penny candy after school. Our favorites were tiny wax bottles filled with colored water (we would bite into them, drink the water then chew the wax), dots on a wide piece of paper, Squirrels, Mary Janes, and Bit O Honey. We used to buy wax lips too and wear them then chew them like gum. Everyone loved them.

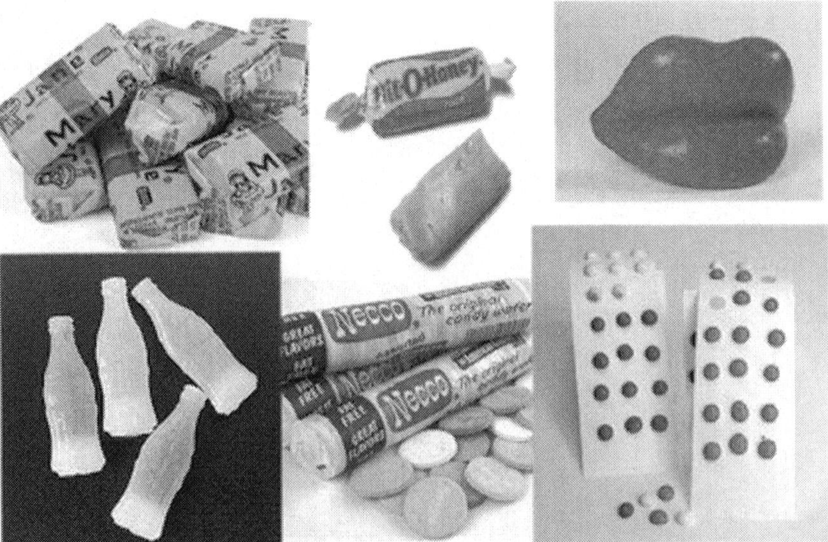

Inner Sanctum

The squeaking door scared me to death even though it was only a radio show. Of course we had been sent to bed and weren't supposed to be listening. There was a big radio (like the one pictured here) in the living room corner (nearest the French doors). After dinner, we would sit and listen to the radio just like people now watch TV. There were lots of good shows like The Green Hornet, FBI in Peace and War, Inner Sanctum, Amos and Andy, The Jack Benny Show, Lux Theater and many more. Mom listened to her soaps during the day as she worked. But the big thing we listened for was news of the war. I can remember listening to the radio one time when Grandma Dodd was visiting and she had just made a batch of her fudge. It was still slightly warm when she brought some into the living room for us to enjoy. She made the best fudge and I am glad I have her recipe.

Another time I remember was when most of Mom's brothers (Floyd, Harry, Don and Louie) and Grandma and Grandpa came for a visit. It was after the war. Grandpa went to a Detroit Tiger baseball game because they were playing the Yankees. It might have even been a World series game, but I distinctly remember the boys (minus George) and Grandpa singing barbershop. I especially remember them singing "Tell Me Why" and me crying like a baby because they were leaving. Since we had no family in Michigan, it was really special to have them there. I loved Floyd, Harry and Don a lot. Oh, Floyd brought me a lovely lacy bracelet from Italy (when he was in the war). My mother told me not to wear it to school, but I did anyway and lost it. I still feel bad about it today. In fact, I have often

looked for that kind of bracelet so I can yet replace it. It was very fine and delicate as if the metal was crocheted. I've never seen another like it.

My brother and I used to do a lot of roller skating on the sidewalks. The skates were the kind that attached to one's shoes. We didn't have bikes so skating was our fun. Of course we played hop scotch, jacks and jumped rope also.

During the war and when walking anywhere, we were warned not to pick up anything that was in a container or bag. It might be a bomb. I guess they were afraid of attacks inside the U.S.

Dad got his first car in maybe 1945. It was a 1937 or 1939 Ford. Mom put curtains on the back side windows and in the very back. That made it look dumb. During the summer of that year, we drove to New York. It was just Mom, Dad, my brother and I. We left late on a Saturday—early Sunday really. Dad always liked to drive at night and crossed into Canada. The only problem was we needed gas and all the gas stations were closed. I remember he drained the last little drop out of each hose at several stations. I think we had to wait until morning to continue after all. I stayed awake until we ran out of gas; Dad had taught me to read a map so I could help him. Mom and Don were asleep in the back.

Visiting New York was really fun. I loved my Dad's sisters, Genevieve and Mary, and they liked me too. It was fun to be the oldest niece or granddaughter. Grandma Sayles' house was just wonderful. It was all comfy and cozy where Grandma Dodd's house was neat, shiny but untouchable. Grandma Sayles was loving and would let me help her make cookies but Grandma Dodd just hollered all the time. We couldn't touch anything. I think she didn't like kids. Grandma Sayles had a nice attic and

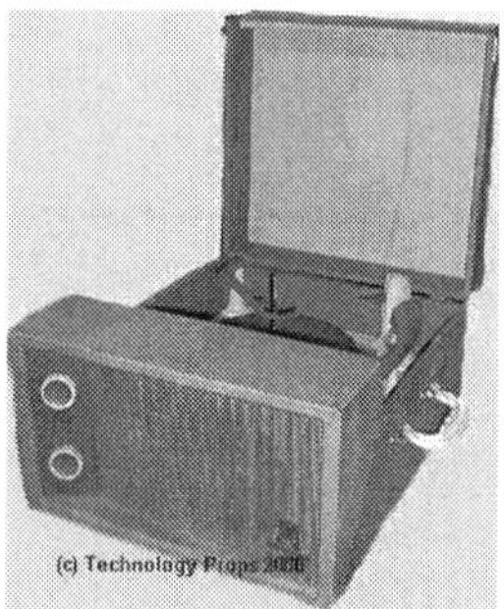

up there was an old Victrola. Don and I would go up there and listen to the rinky tinky music on those old thick records. We had to turn the crank to wind it up before a record would play. Back at Grandma Dodd's house, we listened to the big band music on Uncle Louie's portable record player. He was a teenager or maybe a little older and he didn't have much use for us kids. One song I remember (for some reason) was Bonaparte's Retreat.

Doris Kirby lived on Second Avenue one block south of our house. Her father was a violin maker. I don't think her mother was around, or if se was, I can't remember her. Doris was a little older than we were but she invited me to a party at her house for Halloween. Maybe my brother went too. There were quite a few there—all kids. She turned out all the lights and passed things around while telling a scary story. Like when she was talking about guts, the dish she passed around had cold spaghetti. Other than that party and seeing Mom, Dad, Muriel and Austin in costume for parties, I do not remember ever going trick or treating as a child—not in Detroit or anywhere. There are so many things I can't remember.

Bunnie and Beverly were born when we lived in that house but again, I don't remember. I do remember going to the hospital with my brother to have our tonsils and adenoids out. Everything was big (tables, beds and everything) and scary. I don't know what year that was.

Another thing I remember was when I got lice. Mother cut my hair very short and washed my head repeatedly with Larkspur lotion and spent hours combing the eggs out of my hair. The comb she used had tiny teeth which were very close together so it could scrape the eggs from each hair. My hair had been long but Mom cut it so it wasn't so hard to comb out the eggs. Yuk!

My brother and I used to go to the huge Detroit library by ourselves. It was only a block away. We would go for story hour. I loved books even then. Speaking of books, I remember Dad reading *The Wizard of Oz* to us in the evening. He read one chapter a night. Another big treat was when Dad would bring home a large bag of White Castle hamburgers. They were small but good.

Movies were great. I don't think we went often but they were important for the news, especially during the war. Movies, back then, ran continuously. They let people in at the beginning, middle or end. There were three or four parts to every show—the news reel, cartoons then the feature. Sometimes it was a double feature. Sometimes they had serial stories where every week was a different episode—much like our TV programs are now. One time, Mom and Dad let us go to a movie by ourselves. The movie theater was on Woodward Avenue and the movie we saw was a war movie with Van Johnson and Robert Walker. It was about dropping a bomb over Japan, I think.

Our last Christmas in that house was in 1947. I remember being nosey and finding our presents hidden in a closet. I told my brother and we played with things ahead of time.

Early in January of 1948, we moved to the end of the world as far as I was concerned. Muriel and Austin had a summer cottage near Maceday Lake in Clarkston. We had gone there in the summer and that was fun. There were always lots of people around having a good time. But in the dead of winter it would be like a ghost town. Life for the whole family would be changed drastically.

Wilderness

When I learned that we were moving to the cottage, I was told I couldn't have my piano. After all, the cottage was small and moving it there would be a challenge. But I was lucky that my father loved music. When I pleaded that I needed the piano, he agreed and it got moved. They couldn't get the car from the secondary road to our house because of so much snow so they used a sled to pull the piano to the house. It was put in the room to the back and right of the house.

The cottage was very rustic. In fact, it needed an addition for us to be able to fit in comfortably so Dad and Grandpa Sayles added a second story and enlarged the back of the house and the kitchen. Dad always built with cinder blocks and this house was no exception. The story he liked to tell was they just got the last shingles on the roof when it started to snow. It wasn't fully finished when we moved in; raw wall board with the tape strips decorated our living room and dining room. Upstairs was just one big room where we would all sleep. There was no railing around the big hole in the floor where the stairs came up. One night Bunnie got up in the middle of the night and walked right into the hole and fell straight down to the first floor. Dad always felt bad about that and in fact blamed that fall for her being a little slow in school.

It was always cold in the house in the winter. We had a potbellied stove right in the middle of the living area. Needless to say it didn't heat the house very well, especially the upstairs. After we lived there for a little while, Dad decided to build a fireplace in the living room. But the stairs were in the way. He moved them to the back of the fire place. I don't remember him doing it, but I do know when we moved from there, they couldn't get the piano out of the house; he had built it in by moving the stairs.

When we first moved to the lake we didn't have running water like we have today. We had to pump the water. I remember more than once, in order to have water when the pipes froze, we would melt snow on the pot belly stove.

I can remember a bath time when the pipes were frozen; we melted the snow on the stove then mom filled a large galvanized tub with the hot water. We each took a bath in the same water. Dad was last and he was not a small man. When he got into the tub all the water went out (so the story goes). I didn't witness it.

I never could figure out why we had to give up the big house in Detroit but somehow in my mind I know we were just renting that house with the option to buy and it was in an area that was in demand. We were only a few blocks away from what is now Wayne State University. From Mom and Dad's arguments, I heard how Dad had money to make a payment but lost it gambling so they had to move. The cottage in Clarkston was a good 60 miles from the house in Detroit and Dad worked in Detroit, as I remember. But about the time we moved or just a little after, with the war being over, he got laid off.

Living at the cottage, he started pursuing his hobby of photography. He carried his camera (speed graphic) with him wherever he went. If he came upon an accident, he took the gruesome pictures and tried to sell them to the newspapers. He also took wedding pictures and whatever candid jobs he could find. The sad thing about those accident pictures was that he made 8 x 10 glossy prints and Mom stapled them to the bare plaster board walls in the dining area of the large room. That was Mom's idea of wallpaper or paint. They were ugly to look at while eating. Those years were really difficult, as I remember. We had no money for shoes, clothes and barely enough for food.

Mom and Dad used some vacant property a few blocks away

to plant a big garden. We all had to work in the garden and Mom canned a lot of food to have for the winter. There were no stores nearby but when Dad was out working, he would stop to get milk and bread.

I mentioned before that we were really poor but I don't remember starving. We ate a lot of liver (it was cheap) but one time when Mom tried a new recipe we all complained that it was too terrible to eat. Since Mom was the last to sit down to eat, she was angrily telling us to "just eat it." Even Dad protested. We all picked at it until she sat down and started to eat. After a few bites she said we didn't have to eat it and she threw it out. The dish was some kind of creamed liver. We ate a lot of creamed tuna or tuna noodle casserole, macaroni and cheese, Spanish rice, and other casserole dishes. Those last two were my favorites.

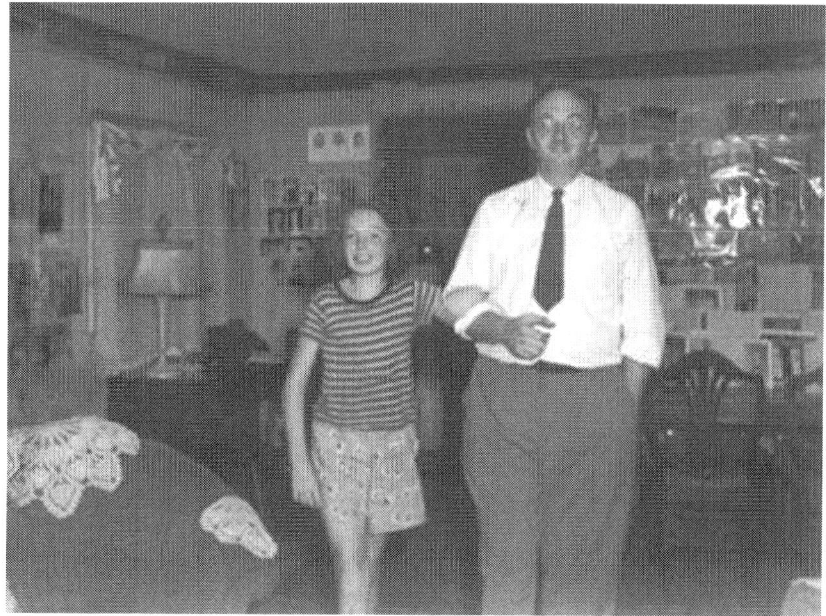

Mom was probably practicing taking pictures as if at a wedding with the bride and groom coming down the isle. Notice those photos on the wall in back of us which were stapled on.

The Country School

Hardly anyone else lived at the lake in the winter time. The only other year round person that I knew was Joan Hilton who lived with her parents out on an island which was connected to the rest of the lake area by a small bridge. The first day we went to school was probably the most traumatic day in my young life. We were supposed to walk but Joan's father gave us all a ride. The radio was on in the car and I remember the song that was playing—*Bye Bye Blackbird*.

Pack up all my cares and woes,
Here i go, singing low,
Bye, bye, blackbird.
Where somebody waits for me,
Sugar is sweet, so is she,
Bye, bye, blackbird.

No one here can love and understand me,
Oh, what hard luck stories they all hand me.

Make my bed and light the light,
I'll arrive late tonight,
Blackbird, bye, bye.

Pack up all my cares and woes,
Here I go, singing low,
Bye, bye, blackbird.
Where somebody waits for me,
Sugar is sweet, so is she,
Bye, bye, bye, bye, blackbird.

The next song was *I'm Looking Over A Four-Leaf Clover* .

There were a few other families who lived at the lake year round but they weren't nice people. Stanton Zang lived down our street and was very creepy. Then there was a whole family who lived like hillbillies but I can't think of their name at the moment. The boys were really bad (bullies) and their yard was full of junk. Come to think of it, we weren't much better. Then there was the Frick family. They were nice. I liked Jeanette. Joan Hilton was the nicest one of all and became a good friend.

The picture below is of the whole school. All grades were in one room. We had no indoor bathrooms—just outhouses out back. One was for the girls and one was for the boys. In the wintertime, we had to put on our leggings, boots and coats just to go out to the outhouse. It was a little walk from the school house too.

There were two doors into the school and both were off the front porch. One door is behind me in the picture; I can't see the other door. Just behind those two doors was a long cloak room with hooks for coats and plenty of room for boots, etc. That room was the width of the school but not very deep. The younger children sat up front and us bigger kids sat in the back. There were

four in my brother's third grade class and five in my fifth grade class.

After that first day we mostly walked. It was about one and a half miles from our house past farms. I could take that walk today and I see (in my memory) the potato farm where my brother and I worked digging potatoes for hours for only 25 cents. That was a lot of money then but there were no stores around. We missed Detroit with the candy store nearby.

The most traumatic event in my life happened in the spring when the trees around the school were all in bloom. We were outside at recess and I had these little yellow seeds in my hair (from the trees) and that reminded my brother of the time I had lice. He made sure all the boys knew that I had had lice. From then on I was called "flea bag" all the time. I was taunted with it and it hurt terribly.

Speaking of boys, they loved to go into the outhouse and have pissing contests. They would stand on the seats of the toilets and try to pee out the little vent type window up near the top. I don't know about that first hand but did see pee come out the window occasionally. Boys UGH!

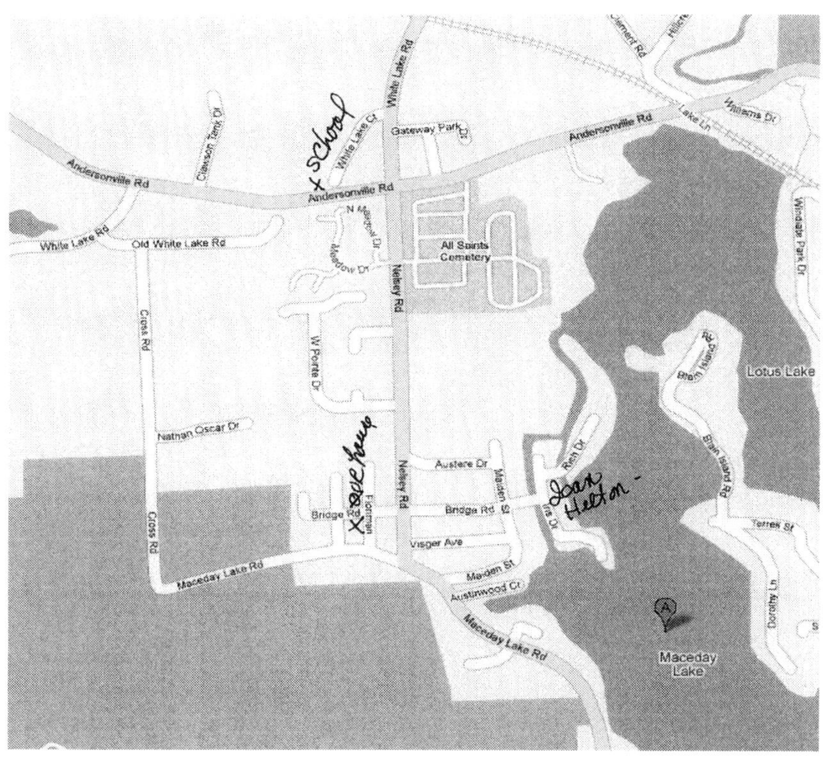

Map of Maceday Lake showing our house and the school. Where the cemetery is used to be a farm.

Skating and Swimming

We had fun in the winter after all. We would spend hours skating on the lake. One time the ice froze so perfectly that it was just like glass after we cleared the snow and as we skated we could see the fish way below the depth of the ice. Sometimes we would be out playing all day long. We also had a sled and enjoyed playing on that. It was just my brother and I mostly; at least I can't really remember many others we played with in the winter. Our sisters were too small to be out as long as we were.

The only thing I can remember about a Christmas there was Don and I were taken shopping into Clarkston and there was a dime store where we could each pick out a gift for each other. Don got me a tube of Tangee lipstick (it was very pale and more like chap stick) but it made me feel like a teenager. If I remember right, I bought him an eraser. We each only had a few cents to spend.

As winter turned to spring it seemed a little better way out there in the sticks. I remember though one spring shortly after we moved to the lake, there was a lot of rain and the creek that ran by the house overflowed. I had just gotten a new pair of shoes (and that was a big event) and had my boots on as I was walking outside helping Dad to break up whatever was plugging up the creek. I didn't know for sure where I was walking and ended up walking into the creek which was over the top of my boots. Mom was mad that I ruined my new shoes. I am sure that once they dried, I wore them anyway.

My brother and I shared a boys bicycle but it didn't have a seat on it. There is a movie somewhere where we are trying to ride it. Where the seat was, we

My 4th grade picture

had wrapped towels around the post to make a makeshift seat. It wasn't high enough and the bike was extremely difficult to ride.

Once summer came to Maceday Lake it was like a new world. All the cottages opened up and people (mostly from Detroit) came out to play. The Costa family cottage was near ours. Miriam and her sister (can't remember her name) were very rich from Grosse Pointe but they were nice to us.

We spent a lot of the summer swimming down at the beach. To get there we walked carrying our inner tubes. Or if Mom and Dad were going too, we got to ride on the running board of the car. That was lots of fun. There was a dock that was out a little way and we learned to swim to it and dive off. I didn't like diving to the back of the dock though because it was all weedy.

Please notice that while everyone was in shorts, I had on a wool dress that was many sizes too big. Why? It was a hand-me-down dress from one of Mother's friends. I probably wore it because it was nicer than anything I owned.

Stranded at the Dance

Dad got laid off sometime in 1948 or 1949 and that is when he turned his hobby of photography into a business. While we were still living at the lake he found an office building in Drayton Plains where he opened a studio (Sayles Studio). It was upstairs in the Van Weldt building right on Dixie Highway north of Frembes Street. It was just one small room but big enough for the camera and a desk.

By that fall, he got called back to work so he had Mom sit in the studio during the days to handle business. He taught her how to take a picture if she had to by putting knots on strings attached to the lights so she would know how far away from the subject to place the lights. Mom would take Bunnie and Beverly with her to work because there wasn't much business anyway.

Things changed for Don and I also. The country school was closed and we were bussed into Clarkston schools. Clarkston was a rich little community and all the kids in school looked down on us country folk. They really didn't want anything to do with us. They all wore expensive clothing and we wore hand-me -downs that often didn't fit well. Kids continued to call me "flea bag" so my hopes of starting a new life in a new school were not to be.

But I saw a boy that I really liked. His name was Jamie Alexander and I thought he was just adorable. He was one of the rich kids and popular. When it was announced there was to be a Sadie Hawkins dance where the girls ask the boys out, I thought I would ask him. We were sitting out on bleachers and I was behind him and I leaned over to ask him if he would go to the dance with me. He said "yes". I was very excited. Then came time for the dance and we were all supposed to make corsages for our date out of vegetables. Where that came from I don't know. So I made a corsage for Jamie and Dad took me to the school and dropped me off. I waited inside the door for Jamie but he never came. I was stood up. Shortly after the music started I heard a song dedicated to me. It was *Rag Mop*. I wanted to curl up and die, but I had to stay there watching my carefully made corsage wilt while waiting for Dad to come back and get me. There was no phone for me to call home.

Also one of my most embarrassing moments happened at that school. A friend of my Mother's gave me a lot of her clothing and she included bras that I could not even begin to fit into. But one day I wore a sweater to school; underneath was a bra stuffed with something (probably tissue). As I was walking down the hall someone pointed out that one of my boobs had slipped; I was lopsided. That was another wanting-to-die moment.

That next summer (1949) while Mom worked at the studio, I had to babysit my two sisters. It wasn't what I wanted to do and I am not sure how good a baby sitter I was. While the summer kids were all getting together to play, I was stuck babysitting. In October, we would move to Drayton Plains and life got better for me.

Section Two

My Teenage Years

1949—1955

The house,
Dixie Hwy looking south (top) and looking north.

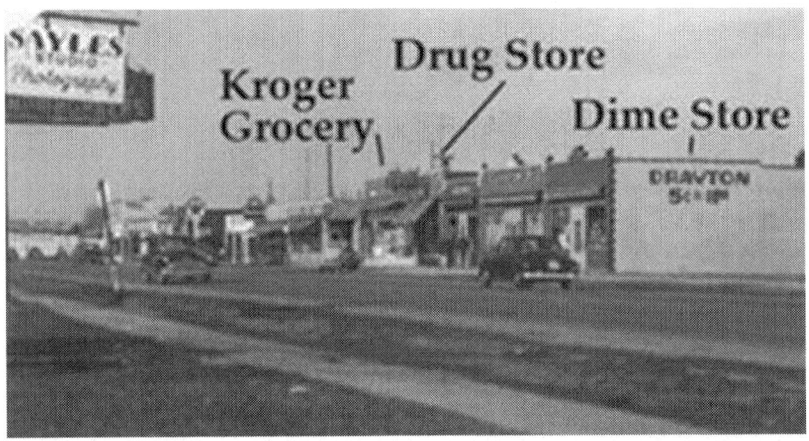

Back to Civilization

The most wonderful thing happened in October of 1949. We moved a short distance to Drayton Plains and I got to start all over again by changing schools. "Flea bag" was long gone except as a haunt in my memory. Another thing was we were back in a town. In fact, we were right in the middle of the town. Drayton Plains was only two blocks long and there was no stoplight. Next to our property to the south was a sprawling, rustic cheese market which I remember as being poorly stocked. A few doors down was an A & W Root Beer Drive-in. More about that later.

On the other side of our property was a bowling alley. Across the street was a movie theater and just north of that was the post office. Going further north there was a 5 & 10 cent store with wooden floors that creaked as you walked on them. Further north on that same side of the street was Dr. St. Louis' office (he was an optometrist), a drug store with a soda fountain and at the corner of Frembes and Dixie was a small Kroger grocery store. Across the street from the grocery store, (on our side of the street) was a factory that made trailers like mobile homes that didn't move once they were set up. Or maybe it was the lumber company. I will have to check on that. On the other corner (closer to our house, was a nice restaurant and near that was Dr. Ruva's office. He became our doctor.

The very best thing was the Drayton Movie Theater which was right across the street from our house. Movies were cheap, especially on Saturday, and there were all sorts of bonuses like newsreel, cartoons and special continued stories. There was always a double feature and you could walk in anytime. Of course you tried to get in in time to see the extra stuff before the main feature, but it didn't matter. The best part was you could sit right through all the shows again. Once you paid to get in you could stay all day. I did that once. There was a double feature starring Ann Blythe. One movie was *Thunder on the Hill*, the other was *I'll Never Forget You.*

I loved them both but especially the second one which was about going back in time and falling in love. It was so romantic and a tear jerker. I stayed right in the theater to watch it again, but my father came marching in and pulled me out and gave me a lecture about living in the present and not being such a dreamer. But I was so in love with that movie that I wrote to Ann Blythe but never got an answer. I looked for anything that was written about her and as old movies began to show up on TV, I kept looking for "I'll Never Forget You." I even went so far as to call and write to 20th Century Fox Studios to see if they wouldn't put it on tape. Then one day in 2007, I discovered a place that will get any movie you want for a price. Yep, I got it, in fact I got both of them. But watching them in today's world isn't the same. Besides I am not the same romantic little girl as I was then. I'd still like to go back into the past for just a little while to experience it all, but I would hope I didn't have to stay more than a day or two—maybe a week. I would miss too many modern conveniences.

Living in the Basement

Living in Drayton Plains was quite a change for us all. The house was made of huge stones and really not very pretty. In the back of the house the property went way back to a softball park and in the summertime, the bleachers were full of people cheering their team on. Quite a bit beyond that was an active railroad track. I loved hearing the train. It reminded me of my Grandfather Dodd (Mom's dad) who was an engineer on the Erie Railroad in Hornell, New York. When I was about seven or eight, while we were in New York on a summer vacation, Grandpa took me up in the cab of his steam engine and we rode around the yard together. Another time we were just in the RR yard, when we saw him in his engine and waved to him. I thought I was so lucky to have an RR engineer for a grandpa.

In our back yard were two huge weeping willow trees which remained there for about 10 years. Their roots got into the septic system, and had to be cut down. That was sad because they were so pretty and graceful. Also on the property way in the back but in front of the ball park was a dilapidated multi car garage. It was full of horse harnesses and other such things. Dad tore it down almost as soon as we moved in.

Inside the house, the layout was simple. From the front porch, one entered through the front door and was immediately in the living room. To the right was a small bedroom. Just beyond the living room was the dining room which was separated from the living room by French doors. Straight back from the dining room through the swinging door was the kitchen. To the right before the kitchen were two bedrooms and a bathroom. Stairs to the dreary basement were in the kitchen.

I think one of the reasons Mom and Dad moved to the house there in Drayton Plains was so they could incorporate the studio into the house and it wasn't long after we moved in that the studio moved in too. They set up the shooting room in the front room but those French doors presented somewhat of a problem so dad took them out even though they were nice. When the studio moved in, our living quarters moved to the basement except when we were sleeping which we did in our bedrooms. Dad had a darkroom down there and all too often, wet pictures and film were hanging by clothespins from clothes lines in the basement.

In the middle of the basement was a huge furnace; there wasn't much else, but we ended up doing most of our living down there because the front bedroom, living room and dining room were for the studio. Mom cooked upstairs and we slept upstairs. At first I am not sure how it worked. There was Mom and Dad and us four children. Bunnie and Beverly were three and five while Don and I were 11 and 13. With only two useable bedrooms it was difficult. Shortly after we moved in Dad enclosed the back porch which was off the kitchen and they put a roll-a-way bed in there for me. I have to mention that the bedrooms were very small and there was only one closet for clothing.

Dysfunctional

It was 1950 and we didn't have a TV; they were still new anyway. I don't remember having a radio like the one we had in Detroit either. I think we were too busy with chores to miss the radio.

I really began to know my parents about this time and what I saw wasn't good. The more they tried to work together the worse they were. Mom worked all the time; I used to think she made work just to punish Dad or us. She was usually sour and angry at something...usually Dad. Dad was easy going and let her rant and rave and did his own thing which only made her madder. Lots of times I remember him hiding in the darkroom with the lights out as a solace from her nagging but it never lasted long because she was at him as soon as he was visible to her.

Dad periodically got work again in the drafting/engineering field and then the house was quieter until he got home. But when he was gone, she was usually on us kids. I can't ever remember doing anything to please her. She would find fault with everything from the vacuuming to the laundry. I think that made her feel that she was better or we were worse.

I also can't remember my mother taking an interest in anything I did. My favorite aunts (Genevieve and Mary) told me many times (in my adult life) that they thought Mom was jealous of me and when I think about it now, she acted that way. Dad, on the other hand, always seemed to care what I was doing in school, in music, in my lessons and would work hard helping me with math or other homework. And when he was busy helping me, Mom was always angry at him because he wasn't doing something that she wanted him to do. It was never ending.

Drayton Elementary

School was wonderful in Drayton Plains. It was a short walk from the house but a dangerous one. Dixie Highway was a busy north/south highway. At the time (before freeways) it was the major route from Detroit to northern Michigan. It went right up the center of the state. It seems to me that it was a four lane highway when we moved there but perhaps it was only two lanes. It was hard to cross the street. First I would look one way, then another and just when I thought it was clear another car would be coming. Because of that highway, it seemed that we were a million miles from school. I had to have permission to cross (at first) and friends I met at school couldn't come to my house to play because their parents wouldn't let them cross the highway. Besides I was too ashamed to have friends over with our major living quarters in the musty basement.

But I loved school and my first teacher, Mrs. Garner. She was everything that my mother couldn't be. I liked the kids in school too. Everyone was fun. Somehow I was in a show early on and on the stage (wish I could remember what I was doing) and Dad came to see me do my thing while Mom stayed home and worked. I remember when we came home she lit right into him again for wasting time at that school program. Funny how those things stay with you. The Drayton Plains School was a school for all grades from kindergarten to grade 12. Classes were kind of small so we didn't feel lost there even though there were so many grades in one relatively small building.

Oh No!

In the fall of 1950, the studio business was good. Mom and Dad were both busy. October and November were busy times with people thinking of giving portraits as Christmas gifts. On December 9, Mom finished what she was doing in the house and wanted to get to the grocery store (across the street) before they closed since it was a Saturday and nothing was open on Sunday. I think they even closed early (6 p.m.) on Saturday. I remember her trying to get Dad to hurry and he was poking around so she rushed out of the front door in an angry hurry. Dad left about three minutes later telling me to watch the kids. I was 13. He no sooner left when he came back in the front door in a hurry to get his camera. There had been an accident and he wanted to get any pictures that he could. Out he went again and a little later he was back once more this time asking for blankets. Someone was hurt. I grabbed two blankets off the bed and out he went again. We stood on the porch trying to see what was going on. Dad came back again to tell me that Mom had been hit by a car and he was going with her to the hospital. He said it was bad. I don't remember if he went in the ambulance or if he drove himself to the hospital. But he was gone. I didn't know what to do other than feed the kids and try to keep them busy. I don't know if I told them what had happened. They were so young. Beverly was only three and Bunnie five. Don, of course, was 11 and he understood what was going on.

The next thing I remember was Grandma Dodd came to stay with us. Mom was in the hospital for a month or more. She had a lot of broken bones especially her pelvic bones. They were smashed and she had a concussion and who knows what else. Dad had to work at his drafting job and take pictures at night. I was even put to work. Mom had done the photo coloring for the customers (this was 30 years before color photographs) and it was a labor intensive process. The average person didn't know how to do it so I guess Dad figured I had watched Mom and would know what to do. I was told to do it as best I could. I am sure I did a bad job, but Dad kept me working. After school I would come right home and start painting pictures. Everyone ordered several "colored" ones with their order.

We all hated having Grandma Dodd living in our house. She was a very grouchy old lady even then and she wasn't that old. I think she was born in December of 1898 so she would have been 52 years old, but she seemed much older. She was a good housekeeper and cook but I don't think she liked kids. She didn't much like me. One instance stands out in my mind. I was getting ready for bed one night and in my bare feet, I stepped on something and it hurt right on the ball of my foot. I looked on the floor to find what hurt me and found a half of a needle, but my foot hurt worse than just getting pricked. Grandma heard me yelp and told me to be quiet and told me I was a "big baby". I found it hard to sleep with the pain but I guess I finally did get to sleep. The next morning when I got up to go to school, my foot was huge. It was so swollen that I could barely get my shoe on and it really hurt. She ordered me to "shut up and go to school". I wished my Dad was there because I knew he would listen to me but he was at work. I did hobble to school but it was difficult. After I was in school a while, I went in to the office crying that the pain was so much that I wanted to go home. The office found my father and he came and got me and took me to Dr. Ruva's office which was just down the street. He sent us to St Joseph Hospital where my foot was X-rayed; they found that the other half of the needle was in my foot and traveling up my foot. It had already traveled six inches from where the original puncture was. They were able to do surgery to remove the problem. I was so glad that there really was a problem and at the same time mad at Grandma for trying to make me believe it was all in my head. I am sure I gloated a bit and even sassed her, knowing me, and I am sure that Grandma was still angry at me.

A week later I went to the doctor's office to have the stitches taken out. While I was sitting on the examining table I felt something wet in my underpants. I couldn't wait to get home to check it out. I had started my period and had no idea what was happening. I equated it with my visit to the doctor and was scared. I knew I couldn't talk to Grandma about it so I talked to Dad. He told me it was okay and normal but I still didn't understand the "facts of life". Dad did come to my rescue though. He went over to the drug store, got me a sanitary belt and some Kotex and told me what to do with them.

When Christmas came that year, Mom was still in the hospital but local church groups came together to help us as a family. Santa Claus came to the house and brought bags and bags of gifts which included new clothing and toys. Actually, present wise, it was the biggest Christmas we ever had in our life. Oh, and those same people brought food all the time including a turkey for dinner.

I am not sure when Mom came home but I do remember that Dad had to rent a hospital bed and they put it in the dining room up against the windows. I guess Grandma took care of her needs.

In January of 1951, when school started after the Christmas break, there was a new high school. Waterford Township High school was a big new shinny building complete with a football field and even though I was only in the eighth grade, we were all

transferred to the high school from eighth grade up. There were a lot of kids that I didn't know because all the eighth graders from all the other small schools were now in one school. We eighth graders were kept in a separate wing (apart from the real high school kids) so we didn't get tangled up with all those freshmen, sophomores, juniors and seniors. It was very exciting to change classes and have different teachers during the day instead of just one teacher all day. And we got to go to the assemblies and pep rallies with all the other kids.

School was busy but I don't recall anything specific until my sophomore year. By then I was in a speech class and got involved in the debate team and the dramatics club. I also did a speech or two in competition. One speech I did was Patrick Henry's *Give Me Liberty or Death* speech. I also got involved in the school paper and loved that. I decided then and there that I wanted to be a journalist. But then later I decided that I wanted to be a nurse in the Air Force; I had seen too many war movies where the nurses were heroines.

Because I planned on going to college, I took College Prep classes like Latin, algebra, geometry and advanced English. I did not like Latin and didn't like science either but I loved speech, history, and English.

Things are kind of blurred in my mind as to when things happened around the house, but Dad was always building something. He closed in the front porch and built a big addition to the side of the house along with a car port so that the studio could be down stairs. He and Don had to use a jackhammer to break through the stone wall to make a hole for the door. Dad also added on to the back of the house and built a back entrance to the studio and took out the stairs that went from the kitchen to the basement so that the only way to get to the studio was to go outside either from the front or back. Finally we lived upstairs and the studio was in the basement.

Sometime between 1950 and 1953 we got a TV. It was very small and there wasn't a whole lot to watch except news and test patterns. I remember watching some of the early shows like Milton Bearle, Cid Caesar and movies. I loved movies and my favorites were zombie or scary movies. I have out grown that, thank goodness.

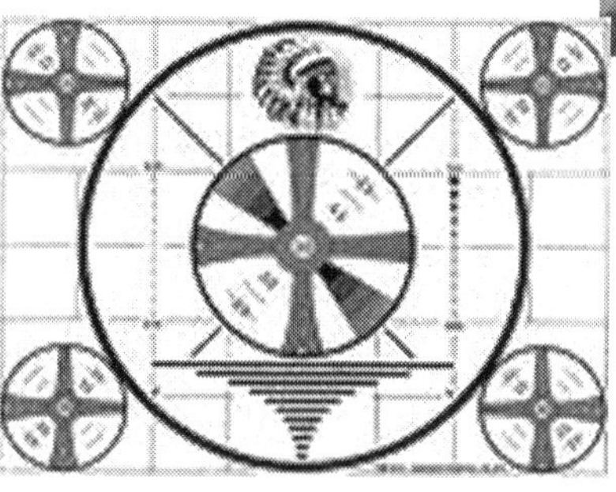

The TV screen wasn't much bigger than today's I pad maybe even smaller.

A Success Story

While I worked on the school newspaper in my junior year (1954), I had this bright idea that got me in trouble with Mom and Dad. The paper which came out twice a month had a column called Senior Sketch. This feature introduced two seniors (one male and one female) and I thought the article would be better with a picture of each senior and volunteered my parents to do the photos. Mom and Dad was still trying to get more seniors as customers but a big studio (Powell Studios) from out of state had the contract and no one else could provide the senior pictures for the yearbook.

Mom was furious with me, but I tried to convince her that it would be good publicity. Since I committed them, they had to follow through and it turned out to be a great thing. The dozen or so who had to be photographed all came in early in the year and they got their proofs and showed them off to other students and it started slowly but word of mouth got Mom and Dad a lot more business and by the time my brother Don graduated (two years later), Mom and Dad got most of the seniors and even were able to submit their photos to the yearbook. It really turned their business around.

Friends and Fun

I had a lot of girl friends in high school, especially Lucy Trevino, Sharlyn Shaw, and Elaine Stevens. By the fall of 1953 I had my driver's license and I borrowed the Pontiac station wagon a lot and off we would go usually to a drive-in to eat or a drive-in movie and in the summer we would go on picnics and so on.

I had a lot of other friends too like Dick Seaton. He was in speech class and very artistic. He was gay but we didn't talk about that. He became my very best friend. We worked together on lots of things like decorating the gym for a banquet or dance. One time we were at the school in the early evening when we heard dance music from another time coming from the gym. There were a bunch of older couples dancing to a live band. When we finished what we were working on and on our way out of the building, we went into the gym with our winter coats on and danced around the whole diameter of the gym in this bouncy kind of fox trot step from the 1930s which matched the music. We were really making fun of all of those people and all the way home we giggled about that.

Dick Seaton started working for my Mom and Dad in our junior year. He retouched negatives, while I colored and worked in the darkroom too. At Christmas rush we would sometimes have to drive way into Detroit (down river which was even further away) to pick up a bunch of wallet photos which were being printed by a big printing house. Kids in the 1950's ordered wallet photos by the hundreds. Our graduating class was over 400 so 200 wallets would be about right to hand out. Of course they weren't colored—just black and white or brown toned.

On the last day of school at the end of our junior year (1954), school ended after just one hour (to turn books in, etc.) and Elaine, Lucy, Sharlyn, Anita and I had planned a big day. It started out with a picnic, and then we spent lots of time at the beach and Edgewater Amusement Park. It was fun. I took the station wagon to school and we left from there. We went to the park and spent the whole day getting sun burned. Then we went to Ted's Drive-in to flirt with the boys in other cars. That was a big deal; it was everyone's favorite pastime. Ted's was a huge drive-in restaurant on Woodward Avenue near Pontiac. When you pulled in you drove around a bit before you parked so you could scout out who was in each car then park near one that had cute guys in it. We'd order our food and all the while flirt with whoever we parked next to. It never amounted to anything. I mean we never went out with anyone or even got out of the car, but it was fun and something everyone did.

Remember I said we were sun burned that day. We kind of remembered that vinegar was good for sun burn so we went to a grocery store and bought a small bottle. Later in the evening, probably when we were driving home from Ted's, the police stopped me. They thought we were drinking and in searching the car found the vinegar bottle. It wasn't booze. None of us ever drank anything. We were just silly girls. We didn't get a ticket or anything and were let go. What a day that was.

One time when we left Ted's, we were giggling so much when I pulled out onto Woodward Avenue that I turned left instead of right which put me going the wrong way on a eight-lane divided highway. What divided the highway was huge wide boulevard full of trees, bushes and grass. As soon as I saw four lanes of headlights coming at me (thank goodness they were a ways away) I headed for the boulevard and went up over the curb, dodged trees and made it safely to the northbound lanes.

I had my first pizza in 1953 or 1954 after a football game. A group of us went to Rocco's on Dixie Highway just north of the studio. I loved it at first bite. I really think that my first pizza even had anchovies on it and I love it that way, but never order it because most other people don't like them.

I am skipping a lot of things that happened in our junior year but basically there were plays that I either worked on or acted in and the junior class put on a Showboat variety show and I did a pantomime from Calamity Jane. The song was "Just Blew in From the Windy City." It was a big hit. Miss Looman, my dramatics teacher, taught me to pantomime and really encouraged me to work at it. I loved it and still do. We had a junior senior banquet which was something we juniors did to honor the seniors. We did the decorations and planned everything. Back then we didn't go outside of the high school for dinners or dances. Everything was done in the gym. That was part of the fun.

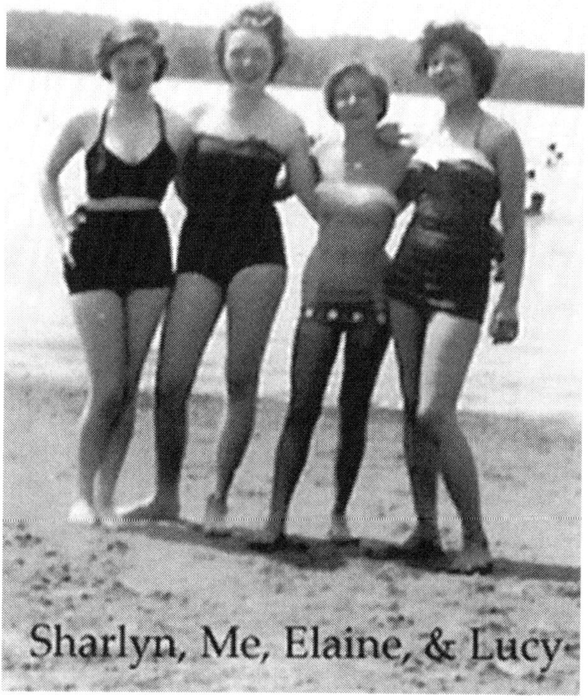

Sharlyn, Me, Elaine, & Lucy

Silly Girls and The Bell Hop

Except for that one car trip to New York before we moved away from Detroit, we didn't have any vacations. Mom and Dad worked hard and there simply wasn't time or money, but I had three neat opportunities to travel from 1953-1955.

Our family attended Christ Lutheran Church in Waterford. We only joined the church after we moved to Drayton Plains and I was about 13. It was too late for me to attend confirmation classes so I became an adult member and was baptized at the same time. I missed out on the comradery of being with a group of kids over a couple of years while learning all about our religion. But I did join the youth group which was called the Luther League. We did fun things together like go roller skating or on picnics. My brother and I were encouraged to attend the big national Luther League convention which was being held in Boston, Massachusetts. I was going to be rooming with Sally and Mary Petersen whose father would be helping with the driving. We all went in private cars and it was a long drive but we had fun.

Once in Boston, we registered at the Statler Hotel which was right down town. As a 16 year old, I was a typical giggly, boy crazy teenager and right away I noticed the cute bell hops and elevator operators. I was always a sucker for a uniform anyway. I need to explain that elevators were not self-operated in those days. Men or women wore rather ornate uniforms especially in fancy hotels and they didn't just push buttons. They had a lever which helped them control when to stop the car. It was a little tricky to get it just right.

On the way up to our floor, I was kind of flirting with the elevator operator and over the length of the trip Jerry Carroll and I became friends. After exchanging addresses, we corresponded for a year then he asked me to come and stay with his family over Easter, which I did. To get to Boston, I took a train from Detroit to Boston and that was a wonderful, grown up, exciting, ad-

venture. It was my first time to go off alone. I don't remember his family or much about the visit except that he took me to New York City to see Kismet and we went to a dog race track which I didn't like. After my trip to Boston, we kept corresponding seriously and he came to visit us over Christmas in 1954. He had asked me to marry him and I had said "yes," but after he was at our house for a while, I decided he was too wimpy. He didn't have enough backbone for me and no ambition to do any more than be an elevator operator. I broke up with him early in my senior year. But the yearbooks were ready for the printer and under my name it says "her future is well taken care of."

Our senior class took a boat trip from Detroit to Niagara Falls, New York, as our senior trip. Every class before us had taken a senior trip to somewhere but we were the first to go to New York. And we were the last class to have that trip. What the sponsors didn't know was that the legal drinking age in New York was only 18 so while in New York some kids had too much to drink. We had a ball and none in our group got in trouble. My roommate was Elaine Shaw. I hadn't mentioned earlier that she came to live with us in our senior year because her parents had moved up north and she wanted to finish school with her class. For the life of me I can't remember how we fit her into our small house. I only had a single bed. I can't remember much about her being with us that school year. We got along because we had been close friends, but there is so much I don't remember. One sad thing though is shortly after we graduated while I was in the Air Force, she died of leukemia.

Three Calamities

The Flint Tornado and Worcester Tornado

June 8-9, 1953 which was the last single tornado to kill over 100 people, struck the north side of Flint, Michigan. One hundred and fifteen people were killed and 844 injured. This weather system would continue eastward spawning another tornado that would become the deadliest New England twister on record. It smashed through eastern Massachusetts, killing 94 people, 60 in Worcester alone. Over four-thousand buildings were damaged or destroyed.

This tornado went over our house while I was sleeping on the back addition in Drayton Plains. That part of our house was not built of big thick stones like the rest of the house was and everything shook. Dad woke me up out of a sound sleep and moved me (bed and all) into the dining area. That was scary.

Big Fire and Explosion

Just a block north of our house/business at the corner of Dixie Highway and Frembes Road, there was a big explosion at the Burke Lumber Company. I ran towards the corner because I was nosey, but what I saw cured me. There sitting on the edge of the property was a bronze man, in a somewhat fetal position. There was no skin or clothing on him. He had been burned to death. It was awful. He had been thrown out in the explosion. I was so sorry that I saw it. This was early in the 50's and I cannot find anything on the internet to document this story, but I know I didn't dream it. I could have paid a monthly fee to archive the local newspaper but decided not to.

Our little world Trembled

On another day in the 50s, the earth shook with a terrible force when a freight train derailed at that same corner only a little down the hill from where the factory was. The railroad (Grand Trunk, I believe) ran behind our property. This derailment happened at an intersection so it closed Frembes Road for a long time. To see freight cars lying on their sides and twisted like pretzels was pretty amazing.

Miracle Baby

Late in 1952, Mom found out she was pregnant again. She had been told not to get pregnant because of the severity of her pelvic fractures. But accidents happen. I don't remember the pregnancy or if Mom and Dad were happy about it. Mom was probably worried about how she would deliver.

Beth Ann arrived on July 13, 1953, and she was cute but the delivery for Mom had been bad and good. Mom was in labor for a long time and the doctors finally decided that she would have to have a caesarian section. During the C section, a nurse was wiping Mom's forehead and accidently covered Mom's good eye. Mom was very surprised to discover that she could see the baby out of the eye that had been blinded in the accident. Beth became Mom's miracle baby. The story made headlines which read "New Daughter, New Sight on Same Day." And Beth Ann was forever called the "Miracle Baby."

New Daughter, New Sight on Same Day

August 5, 1953

A Miracle to Mrs. Sayles!

Woman Sees New Baby as She Recovers Eyesight

Since I was 16 I was not much interested in another baby sister to take care of. She was cute but I was busy with school and work and I left home when I was 18. It is sad that I didn't get to know her very well.

Prom with a Stranger

Except for the Senior Class Trip which I wrote about in a previous chapter, my senior year highlight was that I directed my first play. It was a curtain riser (15 minute play) which went on in front of the main curtain just before the big play. It was a cute little play (*The Lost Kiss*) with a large cast of ten. The action of the play took place in a park so the set had a little picket fence and a park bench. Just as the curtain went up, I was standing in the wings watching my actors, when to my horror the fence fell down. There was nothing I could do, but I felt bad. They were real troopers and went on with the show.

The senior prom was no fun except for helping to decorate the gym. The theme was "Ebb Tide" and in one corner of the gym Dick Seaton had made a scene with a broken boat and mermaid. The whole ceiling of the gym was covered with wide bands of crepe paper in blues and greens to simulate that we were under water. My job was to go to Pontiac to the S.S. Kresge store (prelude to K-Mart) and buy 50 large helium filled balloons. I took the station wagon but hadn't planned the logistics of getting the balloons to the high school. I should have had something to tie the balloons to because once I walked to the car (almost flying) I just had to let them go and they floated all over the car as I was driving. It was difficult to see out the windshield; I had to keep pushing them out of my way. Then when I got to the gym I had to figure out how to grab them all before opening the door. I think one or two got away but I finally made it to the gym and let them go. As planned, they floated to the top of the crepe paper and looked like bubbles floating on top of the water.

I had been engaged so was out of circulation and didn't have a date to go to the prom but I had the dress. I had purchased it when I was in Boston visiting my Jerry (my former fiance'). But then a friend of my mothers had a nephew or someone like that who agreed to take me, but I didn't know him and we never dated again. I have the picture though.

I had done a lot of pantomiming in high school and even on the class trip I did a couple of numbers. I had been on TV (The Saturday Dance Party) pantomiming to *Shake Rattle and Roll* in my sophomore year, but I never considered myself talented. But in the senior class election, I was named as *Most Talented* alongside of Jack Peter. I really thought that others were much more talented. And Patty Looman, the drama teacher, wrote the following in my year book.

> "Barb, you've sure come a long way in the 4 years. You seem to have grown so much "speech wise." Your work in pantomime is excellent, and your direction of the Lost Kiss made me proud to have you as a student. I think you'll agree with me (after seeing the plays at Central) that your production was better than some of the experienced directors' plays. Maybe someday we'll see your name on programs. Thanks very much for your help and cooperation these 4 years.
> Sincerely, Patty Looman"

Me pantomiming (lip sync) on the senior trip.

Pencil Skirts and Maidenform

All of the girls wore skirts and sweaters most of the time. We did wear jeans but not to school. Our skirts were usually full and we wore a crinoline petticoat under to make them stand out. Crinoline was just nylon net which was quite stiff and in multiple layers it was full. By 1955, pencil skirts were in. They were mid-calf, straight and difficult to walk in.

Our shoes were either saddle oxfords or white bucks which were very popular. They were suede and everyone carried a little bag of chalk so we could dust them to keep them white. Our dresses and skirts were mid-calf and yes, even the dresses were full and petticoats were worn underneath. Guys wore jeans or slacks and the same kind of shoes that the girls wore. If you notice my prom dress was very sensible and full; I was covered up. The sexiest thing girls did was wear tight sweaters that showed their pointed breasts. Yes, pointed was in and the Maidenform Bra helped achieve that. We wore girdles too and whenever we wore nylons we had to wear either the girdle or a garter belt because pantyhose hadn't been invented yet. It was all very uncomfortable. Nylons had a seam in the back which we tried very hard to keep straight.

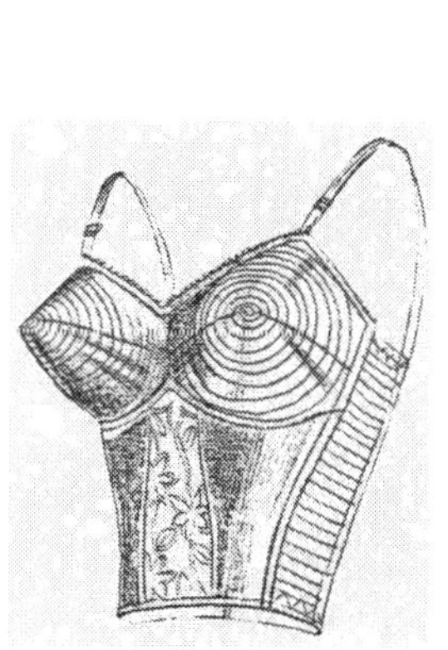

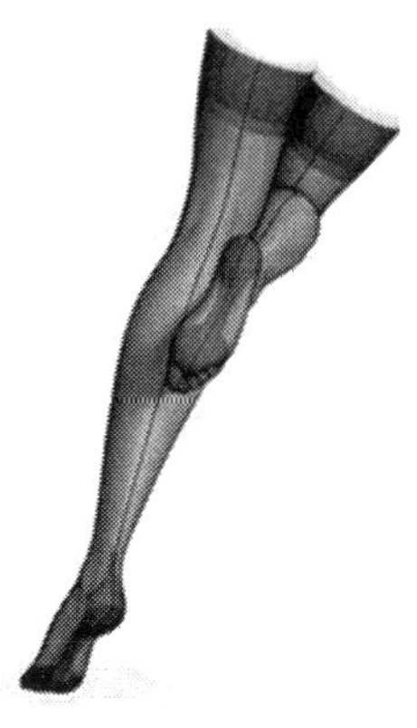

Mom and Dad on or about their wedding day in 1936.

My Mom is on the right and four of her brothers are on the car. A cousin is in the back seat and Grandma Dodd is behind the steering wheel.

Grandpa Dodd and his father (my great grandfather).

The Alan Dodd Family in the late 40s

Back: Donald, Lewis, Floyd, Mom, George and Harry
Front: Grandpa and Grandma

The Dodd Quartet. Donald, Harry, Floyd and Grandpa.

The Stephen Fred Sayles family taken in the late 40s.
Back row: Dad, Fannie, Shirley (Chic) and Genevieve.
Front: Grandpa, Grandma and Mary

Irene and Inez Weld
Grandma Sayles (left) and her Twin.

Section Three

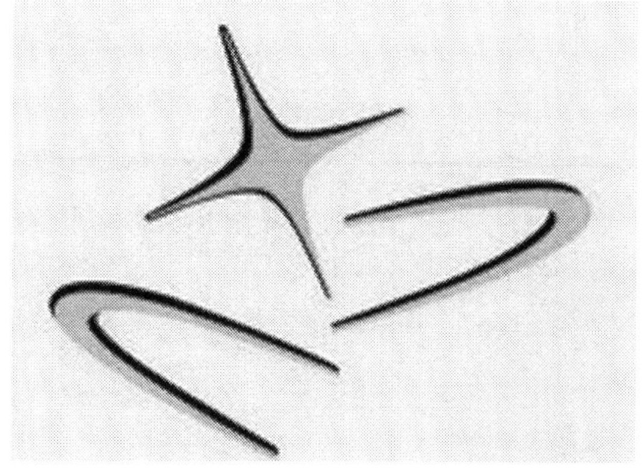

Young Adult Years

1955—1960

Off We Go Into The Wild Blue Yonder.....

I was such a romantic in high school and I still am. I loved movies then and now. When I was a teenager in the 50s a lot of the movies were about the "Big War" (WW II). They glamorized it which was a bad thing but it was a great war to glamorize. There were so many heroes; even movie actors and baseball players were in uniform and praised for their unselfishness. Glenn Miller, Jimmy Stewart, Henry Fonda, Glenn Ford, Clark Gable, Carl Reiner and many others served in our armed services during WW II. Audie Murphy was the most decorated soldier in WW II and later went on to be a movie star. There were movies about the United Service Organization (USO) and the girls who cheered up the soldiers and Rosie the Riveter who was a symbol for all the women who took on men's jobs in the factories. There were lots of battlefield scenes in movies where the nurse saved a soldier's life and I wanted to be that girl. I made up my mind early that I wanted to be more than a nurse. I had my heart set on being an Air Force nurse and to prepare for college I took college prep classes even as a freshman.

I did okay in my classes until I came to the math and the sciences. I passed Algebra—the second time I took it. Actually the first time I took it we had an old, terrible teacher, Arthur Lake. Not one person in the class passed. So he was canned but we all had to take it again. I really liked algebra once I understood it, but geometry was another problem. First of all I had another bad teacher. Mr Cuthrell, was also the assistant football coach who told jokes in class and goofed off with the guys rather than teach. I passed, but I decided that I didn't want to be a nurse that bad and quit taking science classes. But I never gave up on being in the Air Force. I figured I would do something to help my country and it wouldn't be working in an office because other than typing, I didn't take any secretarial classes.

In my senior year, the United States Air Force band came to perform for our school. They were wonderful and I fell in love with the Air Force even deeper. It might have been the uniforms or the handsome airmen. Shortly after the concert, I visited the recruiter and learned that in order to enlist, women had to be 21 unless they had their parent's signed permission. I began scheming how I would get Mom and Dad to sign.

Close to graduation time, Mom and Dad planned an open house for me. I made sure that an old friend from our old house would be invited and I called him personally and asked him to bring his notary stamp. During the party and in front of everyone, I handed the permission papers to Mom and Dad and said, "Mom and Dad, here are the papers you said you would sign." As I suspected, they didn't say a word, but just signed them and they were notarized on the spot. If my child had done that, I would not have allowed them to get away with it, but I knew Mom and Dad wouldn't want to cause an embarrassing situation. Graduation was in June and my enlistment date was August 22, 1955. I had to go to Fort Wayne in Detroit for my physical a week or so before I was sworn in.

I remember the day I was to leave. Dad planned to drop me off at the train station in Pontiac so I could get to Detroit for my induction and subsequent train trip to San Antonio, Texas. Mom and Dad would go to Detroit later in the day for the final goodby. But as we pulled up to the station, Dad gave me his parting words of advice. "Whatever you do, don't do it in the back seat of a car. Go somewhere where you can see what is getting into you." No one ever told me the facts of life and I was a virgin but this was shocking to me. It has also been shocking to every psychiatrist or psychologist I mentioned it to.

I was so excited to be going away from home and to be in the Air Force; it was a dream come true. There were seven of us gals who left from Detroit that day along with a bunch of guys. I only remember two of the gals' names. One was Nedra Rueita who was from Detroit. The other was Jaunita Spears from New Baltimore.

Our train trip was exciting. We had our own compartments

while the guys traveled in coach. We thought that the Air Force really treated the women well. We had a 10 hour stop in St. Louis and were treated royally at the USO. We were even given tickets to go see Cinerama which was marvelous. Arriving in San Antonio was a different story.

Nedra and I getting on the train.

Our train was met by a big blue bus and some guys hollering obscenities at us while barking orders like they were mad at us. "Pick up your bags and follow me." "Hurry up and get your ass in gear." It was one order after another. A couple of the gals had high heels on and couldn't move fast enough. I had on a pencil skirt (mid-calf and tight) so I couldn't walk fast enough to suit them either. Once we got to some building we were ordered to empty ashtrays, clean out bathrooms and mop the floor.

That first day was a long one. When we finally got to the barracks, it was empty except for a barracks guard. We were the last of the flight (about 75 women) to arrive. The others were out getting their uniforms. We were told to pick out a room. Each room had a bunk bed and a single bed. There were three narrow cupboards next to each other along one wall and under each closet were three drawers—one on top of another. That would hold all we owned. The mattresses were folded in half exposing the springs underneath. The walls were gray with no color in the room; it was all gray. We walked around peeking in rooms and came across one that had curtains and looked pretty. Excitedly, I exclaimed, "Look we can fix up our rooms. Won't that be exciting?" Suddenly I heard a ferocious voice shouting, "State your name, rank and serial number and from now on you will not speak unless spoken to. Now get out of here." We quickly backed away from the room scared to death. We learned later that we had just met Sargent Neif, our tactical instructor (TI). Welcome to the real world of the Air Force.

Most of us in the flight had brought diaries with us but the first day, we had to put them in our suitcases along with all of our civilian clothing and the suitcases were locked in a room so we couldn't get near them. I wrote post cards and letters to my mom and asked her to please keep them because they would end up being my diary. But somehow they got thrown away before I could rescue them.

Basic consisted of marching a lot, going to classes, testing and learning crazy things like how to breathe in a room filled with toxic gas by using a gas mask. The tests we took would help them to find out what field we would be best suited for. Our days were long starting well before dawn. There was no recreation. It was all work. I loved monkey drill—that was precision marching. Yes, that was fun. I took great pride in spit shining my boots with Kiwi shoe polish by using a tuft of cotton and a dab of water. I loved being prepared for inspection at any time. The hangers in my closet were exactly spaced and there was never an empty hanger. My clothes in the drawers were rolled tight so they could be thrown against the wall by some inspector and not fall apart. And my shoes were precisely lined up under my bed with the toes being exactly even with the outer edge of the bed frame. Yes, they were evenly spaced too. I loved starching my fatigues so stiff that they could stand alone. In order to get into them I'd have to stand on a chair or table so I could get my leg in without bending the pants. I didn't even mind picking up pebbles from one side of the walkway and putting them on the other side only to have to do it the other way around another day. It was all about learning to do what you are told without question. I loved it. Although basic was tough mentally and physically, I loved the discipline because at home no one followed through with discipline. I could get away with murder most of the time. I secretly wanted someone to care what I did; the Air Force did.

It was very hot in Texas in August so we had to wear pith helmets and take salt tablets to keep us hydrated. And look how gung-ho I was. I loved saluting, clicking my heels when coming to attention and standing at attention. I was so proud to be in the U.S. Air Force serving my country.

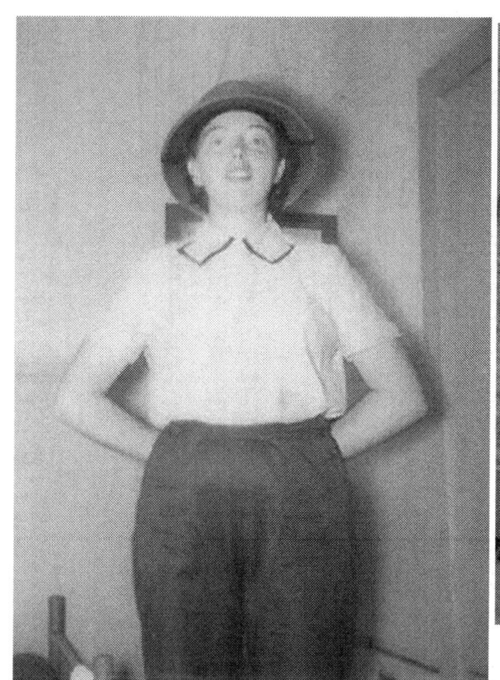

Top: winter dress uniform.

Right: summer dress uniform

Pee, Poop and Blood

When our eight weeks of basic training were over with, most of our flight headed out to schools all over the United States. A few of us though, were on hold or as it was called "red lined." Our school wasn't ready for us yet so we stayed on at Lackland with little to do. Glenda Upchurch, Joan Hanson, Moira Shiel and Neta Garcia were among those red lined.

After about three weeks, our orders came and we were all going to Gunter Air Force Base in Montgomery, Alabama, for some sort of medical training. Moira was going to the pharmacy class, Glenda, and Neta were to be in the nurse aid class and Joan and I were assigned the medical technology class. Most of the classes were four months long but ours was to be six months long.

I had a little bit of leave time and flew home on Braniff Air lines. It was my first time to fly and I felt pretty grown up. I proudly wore my uniform and was glad to be home for a little while. I was the big sister returning and I tried to show my sisters what basic training had been like by playing the role of a sergeant. I made them stand at attention while I gave them a "white glove inspection" after they cleaned their rooms and I barked orders at them. I am sure they were glad when I left again. When I left to go to Alabama, I flew again and felt very worldly.

It was late October when we all arrived at Gunter. Right away we felt comfortable at the base. Glenda and I got to be roommates. Our rooms in the old World War II barracks were small. There was barely room for the two beds with a small desk between them. But all felt a sense of freedom after basic. Except for class time, we were pretty free and could even go into town. There was an Airman's Club with dancing, a swimming pool and lots of freedom. We did have to march to class with our group but that was not bad. I liked marching anyway.

I didn't know what a medical technologist was and was surprised when I found out that it was mandatory that we learn chemistry—so much for trying to avoid that in high school. Our teacher for chemistry started out on a college level and I was lost. But there was no failing. When I got a bad grade, extra classes were mandatory. I don't know if I ever truly understood all that I was supposed to learn, but I did learn the table of elements and enough basic chemistry that I got by.

I loved all the other classes associated with medical technology and even though we were not involved with a hospital we had a lot of lab time. Each person in the class had a partner; my partner was sergeant McLeod. He had been in another field and somehow got to change fields. Sgt McLeod was a big black man and he was afraid of needles.

But we started easy with the study of urine. Since this wasn't a hospital full of samples we had to provide our own be it urine, feces, sputum or even semen. By the way, there were only four girls in this class. This was the first time that they had allowed women in this field.

When we began practicing drawing blood we were supposed to practice on each other. It was a bit scary. I drew his blood first and when he went to draw mine, he got the needle in but let go of the syringe. So there I was with the syringe dangling from my arm. I talked him back to work but he was shaking all the while. He got better in time.

Compared to today's laboratory, it was like the dark ages. All of the syringes were glass and had to be washed (which we did). The same went for the needles. Nothing was disposable. And the tests took forever to do because there were no computers or shortcuts. The fastest we could do a blood sugar from drawing the blood to finish was about 45 minutes. But frankly it was more fun to do the tests when you really had to measure, filter, add agents and read the test.

We learned the whole spectrum of the lab in those six months—everything from histology (the study of tissues) to bacteriology, to blood bank, serology, hematology and chemistry. I loved every minute of it. The Air Force had indeed put me in the field I was best suited for. And all the years that I worked in hospitals and laboratories, I dearly loved the work.

Glenda Upchurch

Funny, how after all these years, I can still picture exactly the way it was. Not only our room, but the barracks, the base and most of all the good bye. But let me start at the beginning.

Glenda, from Hickory, North Carolina, and I joined the Air Force at the same time little knowing we would meet and become close friends. In fact, we would be more like sisters. At basic training in San Antonio, Texas, we ended up as roommates. Neta (Juanita) Garcia was the third gal in our room.

During the nine weeks of basic training a bond was formed between us something akin to sisters suffering from parental abuse. We were kept busy obeying orders as well as stupid rules and regulations. We had such important tasks as spit shining boots, starching and ironing shirts and pants so stiff that they'd stand alone, scraping down the shower stalls with a single edge razor blade or cleaning the barracks steps with a tooth brush and on any task we were inspected. We were moral support for each other at 4:30 in the morning while standing at attention in the dark out in front of the barracks for reveille.

But it wasn't until after basic training that we had time to really get to know each other. Out of 375 or more girls who went through basic training the same weeks as we did and were sent in many different directions, Glenda and I ended up being sent to the same tech school at Gunter Air Force Base in Montgomery, Alabama.

Tech school was nothing like basic training. It was like going to any school (well almost). Besides marching to class in our group we had inspections, but after class we could wear civilian clothes, go into town, decorate our rooms, play records and all sorts of things. Yes, there were rules. We had an 11:00 p.m. bed check on school nights and 1 a.m. on weekends but classes were over so early in the afternoon that we had plenty of free time.

We had both been home on leave after basic and when we arrived at the base in Alabama we had a lot of good things from home with us. Glenda had her guitar, we had dressy dresses, bathing suits, a stuffed animal or two and before long our small room became crowded with junk. It felt like home.

I remember Glenda would play her guitar like an angel plays a harp. Wow! She was good. Every time she would play, everyone in the building would end up in the hall to sing along. We didn't have a day room so the hall was it. Each barracks was two stories tall and had a hall down the middle with rooms on either side.

I swear we wore out two sets of towels in the four months we were together at Gunter. We spent most of our time swimming at the base pool. That is where we met Denny and Duke. Gee we had fun.

We did as many crazy things as most teenagers. We'd sneak off base after hours to go to our favorite pizza place across from the main gate. We rode motorcycles (strictly forbidden because it wasn't ladylike) but the one real highlight was the night we decided that it was time we got drunk. At that time, 21 was the legal age; we were 18. But we dressed up (probably too much and it looked fake) and we went to a few bars but were not admitted. We were so determined to get drunk that we finally checked into a motel then ordered a bottle of whiskey via room service with no questions asked. I had never drunk before but quickly poured a drinking glass of whiskey and drank it down. I damn near died. I was sick. Glenda was smarter and didn't drink as much. Since we were almost late for bed check and Glenda couldn't move me, she called some of the guys from her class to come and help me get back to the barracks. They had to carry me to the car but when they arrived at the barracks the huge signs plastered all over the hill outside of the barracks reminded them that even the hill was "off limits to male personnel." I guess Glenda had to drag me up the hill by herself.

We helped each other a lot. She was in love with Denny and I with Duke and our love life had its natural ups and downs for which we comforted each other. Our biggest comfort was that stupid apothecary jar we found at some resale store. For some reason it attracted our attention and we bought it not knowing what we would do with it. We kept it sitting on the desk. We decided that every important thing that happened to us should be in that jar—a stub of a ticket, a piece of a flower, a thread from a dress, lock of hair, stamp from a special letter and so on. All of our good memories were in that jar, in full view and if we ever got depressed all we needed to do was look into our "happiness jar" as we called it. There was a piece of a napkin from the pizza place and that shell and a tiny bit of sand from the gulf where we all spent a weekend pass.

We became closer than sisters in those four months sharing more secrets than most close friends. Even though we knew the end was coming we ignored it. Since Glenda was in the four month long nurse aid class and I was in the med tech school which was six months long, we knew we'd be separated for two months and maybe longer. Maybe we'd both be sent to opposite ends of the states.

On the day of Glenda's graduation I was sad. In fact most of the classes were graduating that day except mine. With Glenda, Denny, Duke, Brooklyn, Neta, Moira, Kenny—the whole gang was leaving. We had a party at the pizza place. We danced to the juke box records and cried. Glenda played her guitar for us for the last time. Everyone was going in separate directions including my two closest friends. Glenda was going to Missouri and Duke to Arizona. I was engaged to Duke so I was hoping to get sent to the west coast but then that would mean I would probably never see Glenda again. It was a very sad time. And she was also sad because she wasn't going where Denny was going.

I helped her pack all the while I was crying and that would get her crying. I kept thinking that the six and a half months we had known each other was like a life time. It was time to do something about the "Happiness Jar" and we both decided that since the past was gone, we would dump everything. She didn't even want the jar. "Leave it for the next group, " she said.

The cab came to pick her up and I helped her with her luggage. She carried her guitar carefully in its case. With tears streaming down both of our cheeks, we said "good-bye." The last wave was as the cab drove away and she leaned out the window. "See you," she cried. "Yeah," I said only half believing it.

Although we planned to meet again, we never did until I got a Christmas Card from her in 1991. She was in Houston getting treatment for lung cancer. We were also in Texas so I dropped everything to go and see her. We visited for a long time that day and I asked her husband to keep me posted but he never did. I knew she must have died, but never knew when until just recently. As I was preparing to write this book (in 2008) I looked up her children on Facebook locating her daughter. She told me that her mother died on September 9, 1992, but she was not interested in sharing more. I offered to send her this story but she was not interested.

The Wild One

Duke was his name. He was about my height (5' 5") and had blonde hair. He had his own motorcycle that he rode from his home in El Centro, California, where he lived with his mother. He was kind of like Marlon Brando from the movie "The Wild One" and he loved the music from that movie. He also reminded me of James Dean the movie star who only lived long enough to do four movies. Duke was mysterious and quiet and that made him all the more interesting. I liked him the moment I laid eyes on him at the pool. He and Brooklyn were together with Denny and some of the other guys from one of the four month classes. They called themselves "Bed Pan Specialists."

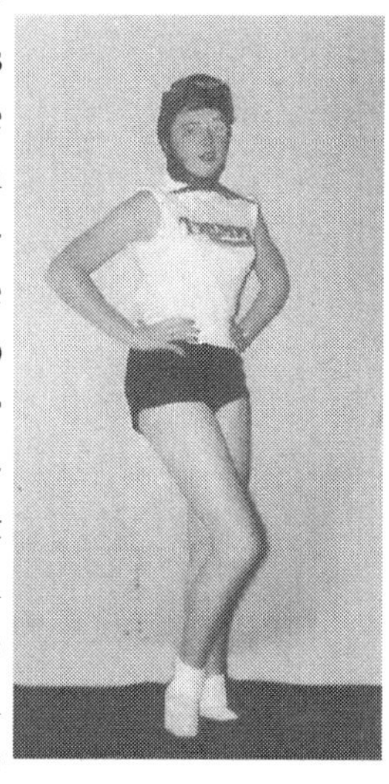

We danced at the airman's club and enjoyed pizza at the little place across from the base gate. We really enjoyed each other's company so he invited me to go for a ride. It was against regulations for us girls to be on a motorcycle and I felt like a bad girl for doing it, but that made it more exciting. I had to go off base and change into something more appropriate for biking then he would meet

me at the gas station. I loved being with Duke and I fell madly in love with him.

His bike was a Triumph T 100 and it was fun to be behind him as we rode without helmets, our hair blowing in the breeze. We rode through cotton fields and all through the country. It was exhilarating. I wanted to ride the bike by myself but I could never start it. It didn't have an electronic ignition and I wasn't strong enough to stomp on the ignition bar. But I loved being a wild one. I was always a rebel.

Duke and I became a couple. Christmas came and everyone left the base to go home. I wasn't going to go anywhere but at the last minute I decided to take a bus back to Michigan. I didn't tell anyone I was coming. Fortunately the Greyhound Bus stop was across from our house so it was easy to just walk across the street and walk into the studio. They heard the bell ring and thought I was a customer. That was fun but the bus trip was horrible. After going both ways I vowed I would never ever ride a bus for a long trip.

While in Michigan, I went shopping in Detroit for a dress to wear for New Year's Eve. I found a black strapless, sequined covered mermaid type dress. It was tight from the top to mid calf then flared out in layers of black net. I felt so sexy in it. I loved that dress.

I was glad to get back to the base because it felt like home and Duke was there. The New Year's Eve dance was wonderful and we had a great time. Duke had borrowed his friend Kenny's car and after midnight we made love for the first time in the back seat of the car. Funny but that is what Dad had warned me not to do. I will never forget what Duke said after. "You start this year as a woman."

January was the beginning of a sad time because we both knew that in February he would be leaving while I had to stay behind. I asked, "What if I get sent clear across the country from you?"

His reply was, "I will try to get you pregnant then when you find that you are, call me and I will send for you." So we were trying to get me pregnant but it didn't work. In February, Duke got his orders. He was going to Davis Monthan AFB in Tucson, Arizona. He left along with my roommate and half of the base. It was a very sad and lonesome time for me.

A Bout of Defiance

With all the other classes finished and gone, my old barracks was nearly empty so I was moved to another barracks. My new room mate was Delores Martin who was also in the medical technology class. She was a black girl from New Jersey who should not have been sent to Alabama. She was treated badly by Sergeant Rutherford who was in charge of us girls. Sgt. R. was a native of Birmingham, Alabama, and made it clear that she didn't like blacks. The year was 1956 and we were in Montgomery, Alabama.

One beautiful spring day Delores and I decided to go downtown to do some shopping. At the time, I didn't think about it being anything other than normal. We got on the city bus which stopped at several stops on the base and Delores immediately walked to the back of the bus which was not normal for her but since living in the south she had learned the rules. Growing up in New Jersey she didn't have to deal with segregation. I grew up in Michigan and had not had any experience with such treatment of blacks either. Since I was going to town with my roommate, I followed her to the back of the bus.

We weren't really paying attention at first but did begin to notice the bus driver giving me a dirty look. White girls didn't go to the back of the bus. There was not supposed to be segregation on the base so the driver kept his mouth shut for a while, but once we left the base and others got on the bus, I stood out like a snowflake in hell and people started talking. They even spoke to the driver in a demanding way; they wanted him to take care of the situation.

As we went along on our way to town the situation got more heated until finally the driver, before moving from a stop, looked in his mirror straight at me and asked, "Are you black?" to which I replied, "Yeah, what do ya want to make of it?" Delores kept trying to get me to move up to the front part of the bus to avoid a confrontation, but I refused to leave her.

When I think back on this, I realize there could have been more serious trouble on that bus. Just walking together down the streets of Montgomery and going into stores together could have started a riot. If looks could kill, we would both have died on the spot as we went from store to store. No one said anything but the tension was so thick you could cut it with a knife.

It would have been fun to include lunch on our shopping trip, but we knew better. No way could we ever sit down together in a restaurant in Montgomery. That would have been pushing our luck too far.

Just four months before, on the 1st of December in 1955, Mrs. Rosa Parks, an African-American seamstress, was arrested in Montgomery, Alabama, for not standing and letting a white bus rider take her seat.

It was an "*established rule*" in the American South (at that time) that African-American riders had to sit at the back of the bus. African-American riders were also expected to surrender their seat to a white bus rider if it was needed.

When asked to move to let a white bus rider be seated Mrs. Parks refused. She did not argue and she did not move. The police were called and Mrs. Parks was arrested.

California Here I Come

Our graduation was in April. Nearly everyone in our class was being sent to the east coast, but I was lucky to get assigned to March AFB in Riverside, California. Only one other person from our class (Stockton) was sent to the west coast and she was sent to Mather AFB near Sacramento, California. I was so excited that I would be near Duke after all and glad that I didn't have to get pregnant to be with him again.

At the airport with my sisters, Beth, Bunnie and Beverly.

I had another leave and went to Michigan on the way to California but I only stayed a couple of days. I was in a hurry to get to see Duke. I flew to Burbank and instead of going to the base, got a ride to El Centro. I went to Duke's Mom's place (I don't remember how I knew where to go or how I got there). From there his Mom drove me to Tucson where we met up with Duke and brought him back to her trailer. Duke's Mom (Mrs. Martin) was very nice to me and excited that Duke and I were getting married. She had purchased silverware for us and had a wedding dress for me as well. I started getting cold feet but didn't say anything. That to me was too much like the real thing but we went ahead and planned our wedding for July of that year and Duke and I slept together with his mother's blessing.

Almost as soon as I was processed into the base, I was thinking that now that I was like a career gal just working and not marching, I didn't want to get married. I met some people and loved my roommates who were gals I knew. Moira Shiel was from Ohio and Neta Garcia from Michigan. They were in basic with me and had been at Gunter in the shorter courses so they got there before me. The Airman's Club was fun, California was wonderful and so was the hospital where I would be working. The pool was exciting too. I waited a week or so then called Duke to ask if we could postpone the wedding for a while. I told him that I wanted the experience of working for a while. His response was "Now or never." I couldn't choose "now." I didn't really want "never" either but given the lesser of the two, I chose "never". Sadly we just said "good-bye" and I hung up.

While in California, I had a chance to entertain at the officers club by pantomiming (lip sync) to a couple of Eartha Kitt's numbers. She always had a very sexy voice and way about her and I tried to emulate her by wearing that black evening gown I wore New Year's Eve. I actually had a "stage name" too. The powers that ran the club didn't want me to use my real name since I was only an airman. So I made a new name, Bobbie Michelle. I really can't remember how I happened to have this opportunity but it was fun. Life was good.

Finally Working

When I first arrived at March AFB, I was really excited about being able to finally work in the hospital. After I was processed in, I went to the hospital to do the processing there and it happened to be lunch time so I was told to go to the cafeteria in the hospital and get something to eat first. The food was free as it would have been in the chow hall, but much better and served on real plates. I liked not having those awful metal trays and food thrown at the tray.

Except for having my tonsils out when I was very young, I had never been in a hospital. It was all so new to me. I got my tray and looked for a place to sit. It must have been an odd hour because the dining room was nearly empty but I did see one guy sitting at a table by himself. I decided to join him. He had on green scrubs. I thought everyone wore white in a hospital. I asked him, "What's the green for?" His response shocked me. In a strong Brooklyn accent he reamed me up one side and down the other for being a "stupid broad". He said something like didn't I know anything about hospitals and what was I doing working in a hospital if I didn't know anything about them. I was speechless. But one thing I did know was that I didn't like this guy and promised to avoid him at all costs.

Just a couple of days after I started regular work in the laboratory and was learning where everything was and what the duties in the lab where, the powers that be in the hospital decided that they had too many workers. So they took the newest workers from each department and put us all in a stupid class just to keep us busy for a while until some who were scheduled to be transferred left the hospital. I was so disappointed because I wanted to do lab work not just sit and listen to lectures on forms, protocol and regulations. But there was no getting around it. We had to be in this class for two weeks.

Much to my horror, one of the guys in the class was that guy from Brooklyn. Yes, that arrogant guy who had hollered at me in the dining hall my first day there. He and his buddies sat in the back of the class goofing off. They were loud and disrespectful. Goof offs! They had cough syrup bottles with them and would occasionally cough then take a swig of whatever was in their bottle. It was Elixir Terpin Hydrate with Codeine a strong cough syrup with codeine in it. Where did they get it? They had friends in the pharmacy.

Well, I learned this guy's name. It was Bob Flath and he was from Brooklyn. He had a big loud mouth but I learned that his bark was worse than his bite. In fact, those of us who were thrown into the class ended up being friends. We would go to the Airman's club and dance and have fun at the pool too. Bob was a terrific dancer. He taught me to jitterbug just like the professional dancers did. He would pick me up during the dance and swing me to one knee then the other then through his legs. Oh, we looked great together. We were never romantically inclined. We were always together in a group.

Bob was tall (about 6' 2"), as thin as a rail and wore his hair in a brush cut. He was a year older than I and had been in the service a year longer. His basic training had been at Sampson AFB in New York.

He worked as a surgical nurse in the hospital and I learned the different colored scrubs generally indicated which department people worked in. We didn't wear scrubs in the laboratory. We wore our fatigue uniforms with a white lab coat over to protect the uniform.

One night when I was on call in the laboratory, I was asked to bring some fallopian tubes up to surgery. Yes, it was Bob and his friends who thought this was something fun to do. I wasn't very smart and went around asking everyone where I could find the fallopian tubes. It was, of course, just a joke. Another time I was asked to take something to the dumpster late at night. There in the dumpster was an arm sticking up right there in the opening. They had amputated the arm that day and did that to scare me. That wasn't how they were supposed to treat amputated limbs but they did it that way just long enough to scare me. That was the last of the pranks. I finally wised up.

On a very positive note, I loved the lab more every day. One day when an order came in to make slides to look for malaria, I did that and after staining the slides I spent hours at the microscope until I found that parasite. I was pretty proud of my persistence because there was no other test for malaria.

Living and working on the base was to me like having a regular job—the first in my life. I didn't want it to end, but it did—sooner than I wanted.

Bob and I at the pool at March Air Force Base in 1956. We had tons of fun there and were great dance partners.

Facing the Music

I waited a while after my night of terror before I told any one about my pregnancy. But I finally had to admit to being pregnant and that meant I was going home. My commanding officer made me call home which was a very difficult thing to do.

On July 23, 1956, I was discharged and taken to the airport for my trip to Michigan. As the plane was about to land in Detroit, I wished that I could run away. I cried silently and walked off the plane like a zombie. Michigan was the last place I wanted to be but I had no where else to go. I had been in touch with my friend Glenda, and she told me I could go live with her in Florida, but I just didn't know what to do. I had to face the music.

Mom and Dad met me at the airport but they weren't alone. With them were their good friends, Dimitri and Florence LaZaroff who were photographers and owners of a studio in Pontiac. Dimitri had worked for Mom and Dad while I was in high school and they became friends and knew me. I was surprised to see them there but everyone welcomed me lovingly.

After the initial greetings, we all sat down (there in the airport) as they discussed what they were going to do with me like I wasn't even there. They didn't ask me what I wanted or include me in the conversation. It was obvious that they didn't want to take me home. It was a disgrace to have an unmarried pregnant teenager and they wanted to hide me somewhere.

Soon it was decided they would take me to a place called Marrilac. It was a catholic home for unwed mothers in Southfield, Michigan, and it was run by the Sisters of Mercy. I wondered why I was being taken to a catholic home but it was probably because I had turned catholic way back when I was engaged to Jerry Carroll, the elevator operator from Boston.

The home was nice and I tried to settle in. There were quite a few girls there in various stages of pregnancy. We were fed well and some of the gals were taking high school classes there so they could finish their education. We were able to enjoy the fresh air outside in the beautiful grounds and we were all preparing to give up our babies when they were born. Most of the girls were from wealthy families and they laughed at pretending they were in Europe so no one would know the real situation. They would return home as if they had just been on a long vacation after delivery. It wasn't going to bother them at all to give up their babies. It was part of the agreement. We all had to sign that we would give our babies up for adoption when they were born. I didn't like that.

The nuns were very nice and we often saw doctors. As I became more attached to the child growing inside of me I knew I could never let it go. Every hour of every day I was tormented with the thought of giving up my child.

I wrote to Glenda and poured out my feelings to her. Again she encouraged me to come to live with her. I promised her that I would if my parents would not allow me to come home, I then called Mom and Dad and gave them this ultimatum: either I could go home and have the baby there and keep it or I would go to Florida to have my baby and raise it there. They relented and said that I could come home.

I was home by fall and went right to work in the studio. Dick Seaton was still working for Mom and Dad and he was excited about the baby. He had never been around a pregnant woman and was fascinated with the movements in my tummy. He was a great friend.

The only lie I had to deal with is that my parents insisted they tell people that I was married but my husband was still in the service. I didn't care. My real friends knew the truth.

Dad took a nice head and shoulders picture of me for some reason. Maybe he was trying a new technique or something but it turned out nice. I had some wallets made and sent them out to my air force friends. Bob Flath got one because he owed me $45. I included a note telling him that I could use the money. In return I got a telegram from him asking me to marry him. What a shock! We were good friends but I don't think I had ever even kissed him and I knew that I wasn't in love with him. "Well" I thought, "why not. It would be a good way to give my baby a name." So I wrote back and said "yes".

Mom and I made plans to fly to California on December 29, 1956 right after the Christmas rush and Bob and I would be married. The doctor said that it would be okay even though that date would be a little less than a month before I was due; my due date was the end of January.

Early in December my doctor said that I had preeclampsia, a medical condition where hypertension arises in pregnancy (pregnancy-induced hypertension) in association with significant amounts of protein in the urine.

On Saturday, December 22, I was still painting pictures which were promised for Christmas delivery. The studio was closed on Sunday as were most businesses and Monday would be Christmas Eve day, the last day for delivering orders for Christmas. By mid afternoon I didn't feel well and I had some back pains. I hadn't been to any classes about birthing or anything like they have now so I really didn't know what was going on. I was in the middle of painting a picture at about 6 p.m. when I couldn't stand it any longer. I knew I had to go to the hospital. Mom and her best friend and most loyal employee, Virginia Stamp, took me to the hospital but on the way we had to take the half painted picture to Mrs. Guzeman's house (she also did painting for mom) so she could finish it. It had to be finished before the paint dried. She lived across from the hospital so it wasn't out of the way.

On the way to the hospital I was in the back seat all alone while Mom and Virginia talked the whole time trying to decide under what name they would register me at the hospital. Here I was again with other people making decisions for me and talking about me as if I wasn't there. Being in pain I had less patience than normal and I hollered out that I would check in with my real name, Barbara Sayles, and that was that. They shut up.

My beautiful baby daughter was born just before midnight and only weighed five pounds and two ounces. She was a full six weeks premature. I was so happy to have her in my arms so I could keep her forever. I named her after my best friend, Glenda Marie.

Dad came to the hospital a little after she was born but someone told him that I had had a boy. He was so excited then a bit disappointed when he learned he had a granddaughter instead.

My Dad's father, Grandpa Sayles, was also excited that he was to be a great grandfather for the first time. He even wrote me a nice letter. I wish I had saved it, but basically he just said that he was really looking forward to being a great grandpa. Unfortunately he died in November of 1956 just a month short of Glenda's birth. I remember that Mom, Dad, and I drove to New York for the funeral and to me it was sad that he never got to know of her let alone see her.

Glenda's First Year

We stayed in the hospital over Christmas and got to go home on December 26. Mom, Dad, my brother and sisters waited to celebrate Christmas until we joined the family.

At discharge time Glenda only weighed 4 pounds 12 ounces and I was trying to nurse her. Because of my uncertainty of what I was doing, the confusion of a big dinner and the commotion of gifts being opened and other confusion, Glenda was very fussy. I tried to feed her and she just kept crying and crying. By the time we had finished dinner, my mother got all excited and thought Glenda was going to starve and that made me anxious. It was a very stressful time.

Dad, bless his heart, put mother to bed. She did tend to get emotional when things weren't going smoothly. And he went to the drug store and purchased bottles, formula and a sterilizer and he made formula and fed Glenda after sending me to bed. I guess I didn't have enough milk for her. After that first rocky day and evening, we were fine.

I had to go across the street to the dime store the next day because I didn't have any clothing for Glenda. We had set up diaper service so I didn't need diapers, but I needed and bought tee shirts and little nightgowns and some receiving blankets and a plastic bathtub.

I still had some painting to do so I worked some but I was tired from getting up so much in the middle of the night. Being premature, Glenda needed feeding often and was up a lot during the night.

Bob called one night. He was in the brig. That didn't go over very big with my parents especially Dad. It got worse when Bob asked if my Dad could post a large bond for him. I was so embarrassed. Hadn't I caused my parents enough trouble? We said "no" to the bond. Bob was in the brig because he had been passing bad checks to cover gambling debts. When he got out, the county wanted him to spend a little time in their jail so he would not be able to come to Michigan for a while. I was beginning to think that maybe he shouldn't come. As I said before I didn't love him, but things got a little further complicated when Bob told me that he had told his parents that he was Glenda's father. Why would a man say that when it wasn't true? We had never even kissed. For some reason he wanted his parents to think he was a good guy. Or maybe he wanted to be a hero. I never did know the answer.

One night in March when we were in the living room someone knocked on the front door. It was Bob. He had hitch hiked from California. He came to marry me.

We were married at Christ Lutheran Church on April 6, 1957, in a private ceremony with just my parents, brother, sisters and two friends to stand up with us. Dick Seaton and Patty Cummings, both high school friends, were our best man and maid of honor. Glenda was four months old. Right away, Bob started adoption proceedings to legally adopt Glenda. I thought that was very nice. He really did love her as though he was her real father.

We moved into our first apartment shortly after we got married. It was in old Mrs. Bishop's house which was on the little street across from Mom and Dad's house. It wasn't much but it was a beginning.

We entered her house through the front door and walked upstairs. The rooms we rented used to be the upstairs bedrooms. At the top of the stairs to the left was our living room and dining room in what used to be the master bedroom. Across from the living room was a large bathroom with sink, bathtub, and toilet. To the right from the top of the stairs was our bedroom.

At the far end of the living room was the kitchen which was very small and made from what used to be a closet in the master bedroom. There was a small refrigerator and a hot plate. There was no sink or running water. The apartment was furnished with table, chairs, couch, bed and dresser. We added my cedar chest and used it as a coffee table in front of the couch. We also bought a small TV. For Glenda we had a crib.

Behind the house was the new big Kroger grocery store and after we moved we made a trip to stock up on staples. It cost a

small fortune for things like salt, pepper, catsup, butter, eggs and we didn't own any pans. That's what you get when you don't have showers and a wedding.

While we lived there, Glenda's pediatrician noticed that one of her legs turned out. He recommended that we get a thing called a "Denny Brown Splint." On a metal bar were two baby shoes to fit her. Her right foot was turned in while the left foot remained straight. We had to put her little feet in the splint all the time at first then when she started to crawl, we put it on when she was napping or at bedtime. The splint was to train her foot to go straight. She didn't like it and neither did we. We felt so sorry for her. When she was strong enough to turn over in bed she made such noise banging the brace against the wood. I noticed early on that my right foot goes out, so did my father's and my grandmother's and others in the Sayles family. So it was heredity. She wore the splint for most of a year.

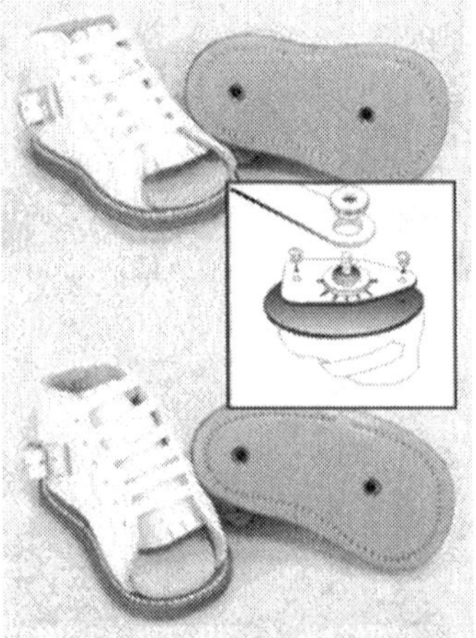

In the fall we bought my brother's Pontiac from him and moved to an apartment on M-59 across from Waterford Township High School (the school I graduated from). It was a real apartment upstairs over offices. Our apartment was in the upper left hand corner of the building pictured below. We had a small living room, small bedroom and a nice kitchen. The kitchen was quite a treat. Our bathroom was small and had a shower instead of a tub. There was a door by our bathroom which went to an-

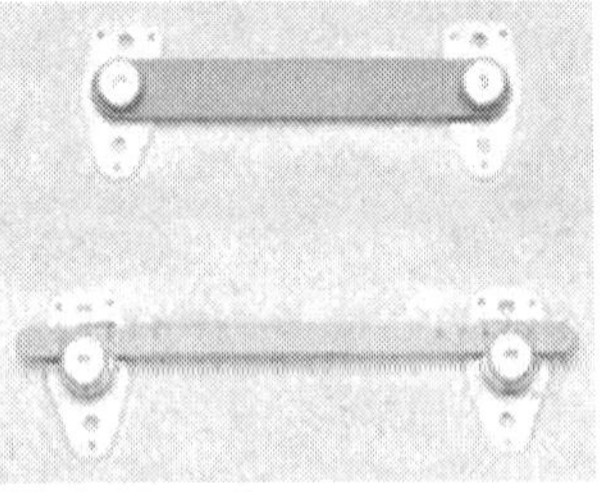

other apartment behind us. There was a couple living there who had a little girl. I forget their names, but he was a deaf mute and she didn't work. Sometimes during the day when the guys were at work, we would leave that door open and visit back and forth.

At the top of the stairs was a small area where I would paint pictures. I had a little table and drafting light that worked just fine. Bob worked at St. Joseph hospital.

In December, we heard that Bob's father had fallen and had broken his back. We decided that we should move to New York to be there to help his Mom. That decision turned out to be a big mistake in more ways than one.

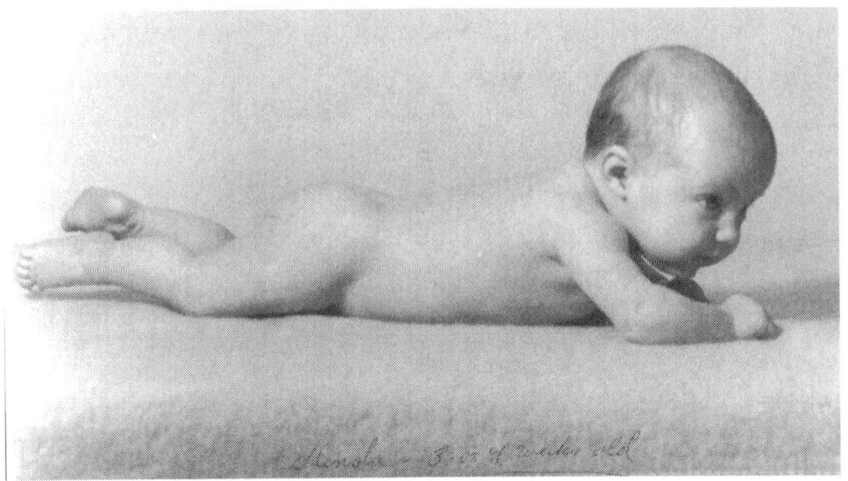

Glenda---one month

L Glenda at 6 months R Glenda almost 2 years old.

What Did We Do?

After Christmas in 1957, we left Michigan with good thoughts and high hopes about moving to New York. But on the way, things started to turn sour. That Pontiac that we bought from my brother was nothing but trouble. The battery died and we had flats. That should have been an omen.

We arrived in Brooklyn fairly early on New Year's Eve. Bob's Mom was very happy to see us and she loved Glenda. Bob's father was a grouch. Bob had explained that he always was. He scared Glenda. I tried to ignore him.

The first couple of days Bob was anxious to show me where he had worked and gone to school so we did that kind of stuff. He took me to Juan's Ice Cream Parlor where he had worked for years and we ordered hot fudge sundaes, but Bob had secretly told the guy who took our order to make my sundae with a lemon in the dish instead of ice cream. Of course it was covered with a bare minimum of ice cream, hot fudge and lots of whipped cream. They loved watching me as I tried to get a nice bite of ice cream. I didn't say anything at first and just kept trying to dig my spoon in all the while Bob was enjoying his ice cream. Then they all burst out laughing and I could have killed them all.

We immediately started looking for a place to rent. There was nothing in the city that we could afford and I really didn't want to live there. We went out to Levittown which was on Long Island and finally found an unfurnished house for $110 per month plus utilities. In Michigan we had a furnished apartment for $75 per month and that included utilities. The only furniture we had was Glenda's bed, highchair and my cedar chest. Mrs. Flath found a card table and chairs for us to use in the kitchen and two cots for us to sleep on. It was pretty Spartan living.

Levittown was built in the late 40's and early 50's for returning GI's from WW II. There were thousands of houses and they were cheap.

The Levitt ranch measured 32' by 25' and came in five different models, differing only by exterior color, roof line, and the placement of windows. Like previous Levitt homes, the ranch was built on a concrete slab with radiant heating coils. It had no garage, and came with an expandable attic. The kitchen was outfitted with a small GE stove and refrigerator, stainless steel sink and cabinets and a small front loading Bendix washer. There were over 17,000 identical houses.

One night while I was home alone (Bob was working), a group of people started walking right in through the front door. They took a couple of steps, said "Oops, wrong house" then turned around and went back out. We didn't lock doors then and with all the houses looking alike that happened a couple of other times also.

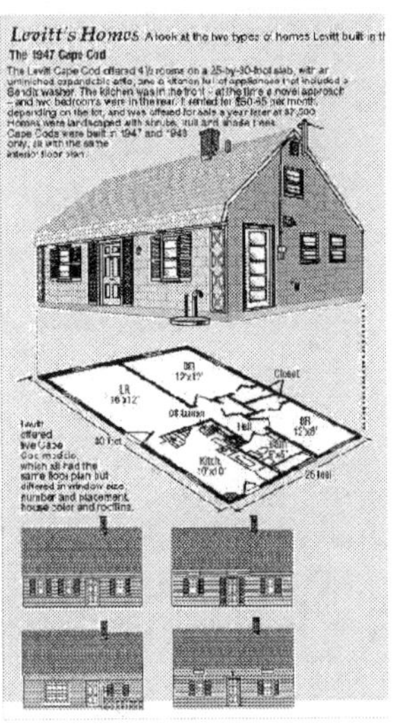

The job situation was terrible too. Oh, we found jobs right away in a nearby hospital (Hempstead General) but the starting salary was $100 less per month for each of us. Finances were very tight. There was no such thing as a credit card in the 50s or even in the early 60s or 70s. If people were running short of cash they could try to get a loan from places like Household Finance. Their interest was high and they were tough if you didn't pay on time. We did get credit from the milk man and the bread man and we lived on their products. Milk, eggs and butter were used for breakfast, lunch and dinner along with bread for such as French toast. We were able to buy the jars of baby food for Glenda.

We both quit our hospital jobs after a few months and got jobs with more earning potential. I worked for a photographer and made phone calls at night trying to sell portrait packages. Bob tried insurance but didn't do well.

While we were making a little money we purchased a house full of furniture for a cheap price (like $500 or $600) and added those payments to the loan payments. Then the car died.

I think I called Mom and Dad to foot the bill for a plane ticket so I could go back to Michigan and have Dad help us get a new car. Dad co-signed on a used Chevrolet that Dad and I drove back to New York. That was a big help but the bills were still mounting and now we had a car payment.

I had just suspected that I was pregnant about the time I had a miscarriage. That was a blessing. My sisters, Bunnie and Beverly had come to spend a couple of weeks with us and it was very difficult to feed them also. I wanted to treat them to something and had no money. One day they were playing with an old purse of mine and discovered a five dollar bill in one of the pockets. It was like finding a million dollars.

I think it was around September in 1958 when I got several bill collection calls one morning. Bob had told me he had paid those bills that the calls were about but obviously he hadn't. We had been fighting a lot over bills and money and that was the last straw. I decided that I shouldn't have married Bob even though I was beginning to fall in love with him. That morning I had a fever of 102 degrees and had had enough. I don't know how, but I got the cedar chest into the back seat of the car, packed my old trunk full of all of our clothing and then stuffed things in little spaces leftover throughout the car. I put Glenda's mattress on top of all the things in the back seat which put it only a couple of feet from the roof of the car. And to protect Glenda I put her bed sides between the driver's seat and the mattress so it was like a jail wall to keep her in the back seat. I fit every single thing of ours (even her potty chair and high chair unassembled) in that car, left Bob a note and headed back to Michigan. I had called my parents to tell them I was coming and Dad suggested I drive as far as Rochester and stay with Uncle Shirley and Aunt Lois (my

Dad's brother and sister-in-law) for at least one night before continuing on. I did just that. When I got to Rochester, I was welcomed warmly and put to bed because my fever was so high. They took care of Glenda and I was better the next morning so I continued on. I just knew things would be better once I got back home—to Michigan. As I am writing this I am reminded of Scarlett O'Hara from Gone With The Wind. She thought everything would be okay once she got to Tara.

On My Own and Loving it — for a Short While

I was so glad to get home and I found a job in the laboratory at Pontiac Osteopathic Hospital right away. I was extremely happy to be back at a hospital and loved my work there.

Things were looking up and I even got a nice little furnished apartment across from the Pontiac Drive-In at Silver Lake Road and Dixie Highway. It was very small but it worked for Glenda and I. There was a living area and kitchen combined and one bedroom. Besides working at the hospital, on my time off I would go to Mom's to paint pictures while my sisters watched Glenda. I was very happy. I didn't date or do anything exciting but I loved working and coming home to my own little place.

I heard that Bob ended up in jail for selling our furniture and not paying the bill to the furniture store. That is against the law. When he got out of jail in January of 1959 he called my Mother and told her he wanted another chance with me. She thought that was a good idea. Mom always loved the men in my life more than she loved me so she encouraged him to come back to Michigan without even telling me. When he showed up (after hitchhiking all the way) I wasn't happy but darn it, I felt sorry for him coming all that way because Mom told him to come. I said we could try to date a little but before I knew it we were together again and rented a nice basic house off of Sashabaw Road by Maybee Road.

Trying Again

We moved to 4830 Rioview Drive in Clarkston, Michigan, in the spring of 1958 after Bob returned from New York. It was a quiet neighborhood a little off of Sashabaw Road and only three miles from Mom and Dad's house. Living there was good for a while.

This picture was taken in 2009 but it looks pretty much as I remember it. There is a carport now and an addition on the other side which I tried to crop/Photoshop out of the picture.

When we first moved there, both Bob and I worked at Pontiac General Hospital. I remember having to take Glenda to a baby sitter early in the morning (like 6:30). I would pick her up out of her crib while she was sound asleep and carry her to the car and we drove to the baby sitters then went on to work. I cannot remember the lady's name but I can remember where they lived.

We first met our neighbors across the street, Jim and Judy Conway, and really hit it off with them. We enjoyed sharing a pizza and playing cards lots of evenings. It was cheap entertainment.

Next door to us were Skip (Donald L) and Lorraine Johnston.

They had two daughters. Skip and Lorraine were also very good friends and they remained friends for a very long time even many years later. Skip and I especially hit it off because we were both born under the sign of Taurus. And Bob and Lorraine liked each other a lot. To be honest Skip was strange. He sat in his room filled with books and read. He was quite anti-social. If there was a party in his house, he might go to his room and close the door to read. He didn't mind that a party was going on, but he didn't want to be a part of it. He played chess. My father had taught me to play and I really liked the game. Bob didn't play so when Skip challenged me to a game, I jumped at the chance. He beat me badly, but I went back for more. Many evenings after dinner, I would go over for my game of chess while Bob and Lorraine talked in the living room. And every night I got beaten, but every time I lost, I learned and became more determined to beat him.

Something very interesting happened to me those years when I played so much chess. I became very organized in my thinking. I planned everything I did in advance before tackling anything. I would talk to myself silently, "If I do this first, then while I am doing so and so, I can do this, then that will be ready and I can finish this and so on." After over 500 games I finally beat Skip. Maybe it was because that particular night we were playing in our house and he was out of his element, but I can still remember the great feeling of finally getting the job done. Years later after we had moved away from Skip and Lorraine, he and I still played chess one move at a time over the phone. We each kept a board set up at home and when ready to make a move we would phone each other with our move. It would take weeks to complete a game.

Bob and I had some fun times while living there. We took up square dancing and that was fun for a while. Bob would get impatient with me if I didn't learn fast enough. There were always parties after the dances and he would drink too much and I would be bored. The first couple to go home had better have a good supply of eggs, bacon and coffee on hand at home because everyone threatened that they would all be over for breakfast when the party did break up.

Bob especially loved all the extra things that went with square dancing like the western shirts and even some of the crazy games the group played. We earned patches by doing certain crazy dances. Someone might call in the middle of the night saying there was a dance in one hour. If we went and danced at least one square, we got a patch. Or if we danced on the ice in the winter, that was worth a patch. There were hundreds of different patches one could earn.

I quit work at the hospital in the summer of 1959 after I got pregnant with Mark. It was an easy pregnancy after the first three months of being sick and I liked being home. Judy and Lorraine didn't work so we girls could visit during the day most of the time. Bob worked a lot of nights at St. Joseph Mercy Hospital and tried to sleep during the day so to keep the house quiet, I would take Glenda and go to Lorraine's until I thought Bob would be up. A couple of times, I wasn't home the minute he woke up and he was furious. He opened the window and bellowed for me to come home.

Being home, I had time to make out grocery lists and do a good job of shopping. I shopped once every two weeks and had 20 dollars budgeted for groceries. That is amazing when I think of it now. I knew the price of everything. Prices were constant. A five pound bag of sugar was 39 cents. Hamburg was 39 cents a pound. A can of Campbell's soup was ten cents and so on. I knew exactly what I would be spending in the store before I walked out the door.

We were still square dancing but it was becoming more difficult for me because of my pregnancy. I would be tired and want to go home, but he was the party boy. After each dance, there were parties which I didn't want to go to. But he did so we went. The parties were usually in someone's house so I would find a spot to lie down then he would wake me up when he was finally ready to go home.

When I was pregnant with Mark, the gals in the club made cute little western outfits for the baby and gave them to me at a baby shower. I liked the gals and dancing. I just didn't like all the drinking.

One day Bob came home from work and said he had joined a booze chain. We had to call the first name on the list and ask them what they wanted. He wanted Drambuie. We purchased it and took it to their house. To show you the prices at that time there was a five dollar limit on whatever anyone could ask for. If it cost more than that, they would pay the difference. After that delivery our name went on the bottom of the list of about five names, if I remember right. Bob left me a list of what to ask for if anyone called. The calls started a few days after we delivered the Drambuie. It was really a hoot. We filled a large cupboard with different bottles of booze then even started asking for cases of beer. Not everyone fared as well as we did; I guess we were near the top of the chain.

I went to my first Tupperware party while living in this neighborhood. I think I even dated a party. Willetta Jordan was my dealer's name and she was a wonderful demonstrator. It was fun to play mother and housewife for a while. It was the 50s and the thing for women to do.

Section Four

Early Family Years
1961–1970

Racing for No Reason

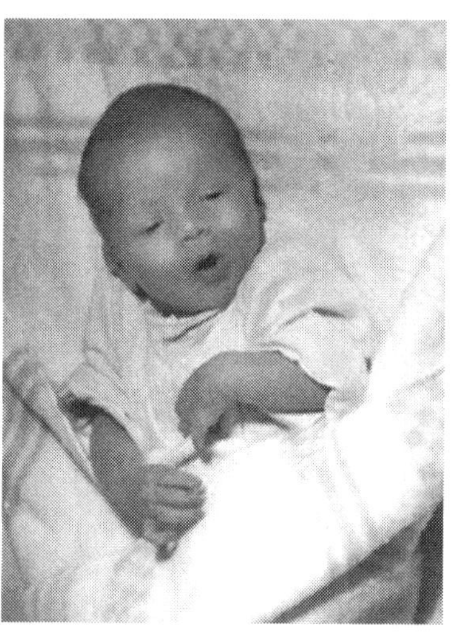

Mark Scott Flath was born on Saturday, April 30, 1960. The ride to the hospital was strange. We had been square dancing the night before and gotten home late. I woke up fairly early feeling like I was about ready to deliver. I waited a while before I tried to wake Bob. He had a serious hangover so didn't move too fast. He carried Glenda to the car while she was still asleep and I gathered my bag and some clothing for her. We were going to drop her off at Mom's so my sisters could watch her. We had just left Mom's and were only a couple miles from her house heading to St. Joseph's Mercy Hospital where Bob was currently working, Suddenly we saw flashing red lights behind us. It was a police car. When the officer came to the window, Bob explained excitedly, "My wife is having a baby." The officer went into action saying, "Follow me."

I was totally embarrassed because my contractions were pretty far apart. I didn't need a police escort. In fact my contractions were slowing down. When I explained that to Bob, he ordered, "Fake it." So when we got to the emergency room, I did an acting job at least while the officer was around. Then we waited and waited for something to get going again. I didn't know if I was going to deliver that day or not.

I distinctly remember feeling two things. First I was glad that I had my husband with me for this birth, but he was only half there. He sat in the labor room with me with his head on my bed. He needed more medical attention than I. So even though he was there, I was lonely. Mark was finally born sometime in the afternoon I believe and he was very normal in size—six pounds 12 ounces comes to mind.

I really wanted Bob to be able to be in the delivery room with me especially since he was a surgical nurse, but they wouldn't allow it even though he worked there. Dr. Warner did a good job of delivering Mark by himself. I remember thinking that Mark looked like an Indian. He was that red. The picture on the other page was taken the day we came home from the hospital.

Almost as soon as I got home from the hospital, I had a severe case of postpartum depression. I couldn't leave the bedroom. I didn't want to get up or do anything. And I am sorry to say that I didn't want to take care of my children. Bob called the doctor and he came to the house. I remember him in my bedroom. This was back in the days when doctors made house calls. He prescribed some antidepressants for me and gradually I got back to normal.

From Google Health, I just discovered this information:

> "Postpartum depression is a serious condition that affects between 8 - 20% of women after pregnancy, especially the first 4 weeks. It is necessary to seek medical attention to treat postpartum depression."

There are no known causes but a list of possible causes includes hormone changes and/or a poor relationship with one's husband. Our marriage was far from perfect. I didn't feel close to Bob. He wouldn't let me get close to him. We didn't talk much. He wouldn't share thoughts and feelings with me and wasn't interested in my thoughts, feelings or ideas.

I often wondered if part of our problem was that he was a virgin when we got married and I obviously wasn't. He didn't really care for the intimacy I sought. He acted like he didn't like sex and I always felt rejected or at least unattractive. If I put on a sexy nightgown or initiated any part of being friendly he turned away. I tried to get to the bottom of it but he never wanted to talk about it.

My depression left after just a few weeks with the temporary help of medication and life returned to normal. Bob left St. Joseph's Hospital and went back to Pontiac General Hospital and in fact started working as a private scrub nurse for Dr. Edward Gates, a very good neurosurgeon. All of the doctors loved Bob and he really was a good nurse. One group of doctors (Vandenburg, Bayliss and Brown) wanted to send Bob to medical school with a loan that he could pay back long after he finished school but Bob wasn't interested. With his off duty job of assisting Dr. Gates, Bob would often have to go running off on a minute's notice for an emergency surgery at any one of several hospitals. He actually kept a set of the doctor's instruments with him at all times.

Dr. Gates had a huge home and loved target shooting and encouraged Bob to buy a pistol and spend time target shooting with him. So Bob bought a gun and enjoyed his new hobby although he didn't have much time for it. That gun was something I hated. I have never liked guns (still don't) and was very uncomfortable having it in the house. One night Bob and I got into an argument over something and he got that gun and threatened me with it. He didn't physically hurt me but that really scared me.

Oh Brother !

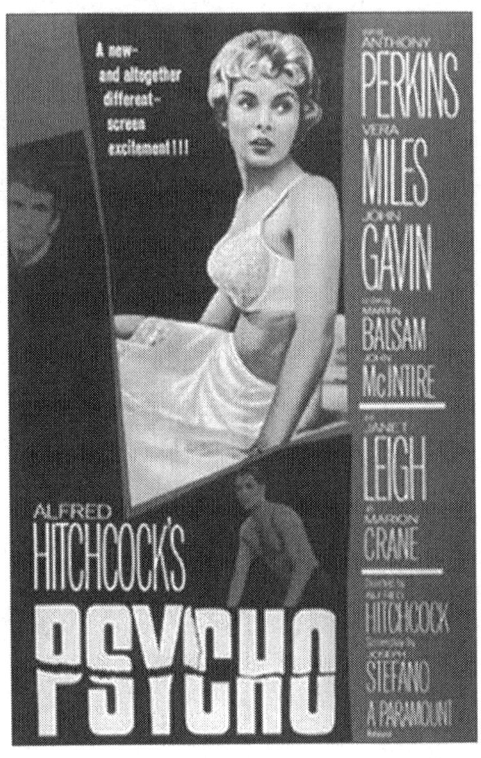

I saw the movie Psycho while we lived in this house. I saw it once with Bob in a theater. Then I took my neighbor Lorraine to the drive-in to see it one night when Bob was working the second shift (3:30 to 11 p.m.). When we came home from the movie I decided to watch TV and wait up for Bob to come home. Bob called and said he would be late because they had an emergency and would be doing surgery so I decided to take a shower and get ready for bed. I walked into the bathroom, saw the shower curtain and suddenly panicked. I couldn't get that shower scene out of my mind and with the house so quiet I was going crazy.

I called my brother and asked him to please come over and stay with me until Bob got home. He said he would but while waiting, I made sure the doors were locked. There was a side door to the laundry room and a front door. With both doors locked, I stood looking out the tiny window in the front door watching for my brother. From that position I could see the laundry room door in case he chose to come to that door. My mind was playing tricks on me. I swore I saw people moving around outside and I even thought I saw a car pull up in the driveway, but it was very dark out.

There were no street lights and we didn't even have a light at the front door. It seemed like a very long time and for every second I waited I got more nervous. All of a sudden the side door blew open and in came a man rushing toward me with his hand held high like the knife wielding murderer in Psycho. He was screeching like the music in Psycho. It was my brother. I darn near beat him to death. What a dirty trick. I have never forgiven him for that stunt.

The reason he was able to come in the side door was that I had locked the door but it wasn't shut tight. He had pulled up into the driveway in his little sports car with all the lights out. He planned to scare me and I plan to get him someday too.

The Beginning of the End

Late on a Sunday evening in October of 1960, we were watching What's My Line when Bob went into the bathroom and started getting all cleaned up as if he was going somewhere special. I asked him where he was going and he said, "I have a date. I want to see what it is like with someone else." He explained that he had a date with a nurse from Pontiac General and was to pick her up when she got off work at 11 p.m.

I was in shock, but I tried to be cool remembering something I had read recently about how you would talk to a child that was threatening to run away from home. All I said was, "Good, maybe that will be good." And as he was leaving I told him to have a good time. Okay, so he wasn't a kid and it might have been the wrong way to act, but thinking back I think he would have gone even if we had fought about it. As soon as he left, I cried.

Yes, it was true that I didn't love Bob when we married. I liked him, but being together for almost four years, I had grown to love him. I understood how arranged marriages could succeed and produce a loving relationship. So I was terribly hurt when he went on his date.

I couldn't go to bed. I couldn't possibly sleep and the more I thought about it the more hurt and tortured I was. I listened to sad music all night long making myself even sadder. As the clock approached each hour during the night, I thought sure he would be home at any minute, but the night wore on. Finally near five in the morning, Bob came home. He cried like a baby feeling terribly guilty and said how sorry he was. He assured me that nothing happened but I found out later that the reason nothing happened was because he couldn't physically do anything. He could't get it up. Was that guilt?

After begging me to forgive him, he went to work on his regular shift of seven to three thirty. I tried to take care of the kids and have a normal day also.

Bob came home from work that day, packed a suitcase and told me he couldn't stay in the house any longer. I was shocked and hurt again. We only had one car and I wondered what we would do. I hoped he didn't intend to leave me without a car. He had planned that out. His date from the night before, Ruth Schruba, pulled up to pick him up and he was gone. He moved into a dumpy hotel at the Greyhound Bus terminal.

Over the next few weeks until I changed my phone number to an unlisted number, Bob called me often to tell me of his progress at making love with Ruth. I never could figure out why he wanted to torture me so. I, of course, would hang up on him because I didn't want to hear the stories. I accepted some of the blame for trying different ways over the years of trying to be intimate with him. Maybe I pushed him out by inadvertently making him feel like a failure.

Having two children (a nearly four year old and a six month old baby) to take care of and no job left me feeling numb. I was lucky that the fall studio business was picking up and I could earn a fair amount of money painting pictures. It was difficult to do with children to take care of but Glenda was good at watching Mark and most of the time Mark was in a play pen so I didn't have to worry about him hurting himself. I had to concentrate on my work, but most of it I did at night after the kids were in bed. But that is also when I would feel the sorriest for myself.

I had horrible nightmares mostly about fish hooks. We had a record player which was called a "hi fi". That stood for high fidelity and I would play the long playing records (33 1/3) of my favorite artists. But in my dreams as I put the arm of the record player on the record to play, it would snap back and start shooting the needles at me which had turned into fish hooks. There were hundreds and thousands of them attacking me. To this day I am afraid of fish hooks and don't even like to see one.

By mid November, the painting business had picked up so much that I had to work day and evening so I hired Lorraine, next door, to watch the kids for me during the day at her house. And about that time I learned that Bob had left me a present; I was pregnant. I had all I could do to keep sane.

One afternoon, Ruth dropped Bob off for a minute. He looked so nice and I wanted to hug him and keep him. He had on a new top coat and a nice dress hat. He went over to Lorraine's house after giving me some money (the first since he left) and gave her a 20 dollar bill to help pay for the babysitting. I wondered where he got the money but thought that he might be working extra hours for Dr. Gates. In less than a month, I would find out where the money came from.

The December When My World Slowly Fell Apart

I was 23 years old and December 1960 was a very sad time for me. I was left alone with my four year old daughter, Glenda, and my eight month old son, Mark, and I had just learned that I was pregnant again. I was working in my home painting pictures for my parent's busy photography studio and that was the only money I could really count on. Back before direct color photography, nearly everyone ordered one or two tinted pictures when they placed their portrait order so I had quite a bit of work without leaving the house.

On December 15, I had a miscarriage and while silently grateful that I wouldn't have to worry about another child, I was sad that I had to go to the hospital for a D & C and that I would miss a few days of work. In the 60s, having a D & C meant staying in the hospital overnight. So I had my Mom and three sisters keep my children while I went in for my minor operation.

Bob was a surgical nurse at Pontiac General Hospital and when I woke up in the recovery room he was right there next to me. I had missed him terribly and feeling him near me I started to cry tears of happiness at having my husband with me. I heard him offer to push my cart back to my room even though it wasn't his job. He was assisted by a female nurse or assistant and on the way to my room he made a date with her. I thought I would die. That was so hurtful.

Back in my room with the curtains pulled around me, I cried the rest of the day and night. I kept wondering how anyone could be so cruel and what I had done to deserve this? I knew Bob was gone for good and I had no idea what I would do to support myself and the kids once the Christmas studio business had died down.

The next morning early, my doctor (Doctor Warner) came in

to see me with another man who turned out to be a psychiatrist whose name I do not remember. They took me to a private room, sat me down, and broke the news to me that Bob had tried to commit suicide up in the surgical suite the night before after calling the police to confess to having been a partner in an armed robbery of a grocery store not long before. His wounds (slit wrists) were superficial, probably done for sympathy and he was in a room on the first floor of the hospital with an armed guard outside of his room. I was on the fifth floor. I was discharged a short while after the meeting with the doctors and did not stop to see Bob on my way out of the hospital. It was very cold outside and I felt frozen from the inside out. I was numb, like a zombie as I headed home. Back home, I had to get to work right away. There would be no money coming from Bob.

Snow started falling early on December 24. I had purchased a few things for the kids for Christmas. I was worrying about how I would assemble the sturdy cardboard refrigerator and stove for Glenda late at night after she went to sleep. I had peeked at the instructions and they seemed very complicated. The phone rang late in the afternoon. It was an officer from the County Jail telling me that I could come down to the jail and pick up my husband's belongings. He had just been taken from the hospital and was now in jail. It was dusk and the snow was falling heavier as I drove to the jail in Pontiac. They handed me a small package containing his wallet and some clothing. I drove home in a trance. Silent Night. It was quiet out. Few drivers were on the road and I felt like I was totally alone in the world. I was glad that I had asked my brother to please come over after the kids went to bed so he could help me put things together. By the time I got home, it was totally dark outside. I fed the kids, got them to write a letter to Santa, and we put cookies and milk out then I put them to bed. I spent the rest of the night trying to put the toys together through tears. My brother never showed up, but I managed to finish the job by myself.

Glenda and Mark—December 1960

Criminal Justice?

When Bob attempted to commit suicide just after calling the police to confess to the robbery, he knew the police were on to him because the husband of one of the nurses he worked with was a detective with the Pontiac Police. He later told me that he watched for the police to arrive from the surgical suite's sixth floor window then used a scalpel to slit his wrists. He knew the police would be up there before he bled to death and that is exactly what happened.

While living at the sleazy hotel next to the Greyhound Bus Station, he had met a guy who suggested the robbery. Bob had the gun from when he was a private scrub nurse for Dr. Edward Gates, a neurosurgeon. Bob and Dr. Gates became close friends and the Dr. invited Bob to spend time at his shooting range which was behind his house so Bob bought a pistol.

Bob felt so guilty about the robbery that he just wanted to confess and take his punishment. He didn't want a lawyer; he was just going to confess in court. So just about a month after he was arrested, he was taken to court. I was there. Three other cases came before the judge first. All three had criminal records but they also had lawyers. One was even a "three time loser." All three got probation. Bob was feeling pretty good since he had no previous record. When the judge proclaimed the sentence, I thought Bob would die of shock. What a blow to get a sentence of 5-20 years in a maximum security prison.

I went to work in the laboratory at Pontiac General Hospital while continuing to paint pictures for my Mom and Dad's business in my off time. Dealing with bad babysitters and trying to make ends meet was very difficult but it made me a strong person.

I was busy working as much as I could but once a month over a four month period I drove to Jackson to visit him. The first time was the worst, but it never was fun.

After I parked the car and entered the main area for visitors, I was overwhelmed with grey. Everything was grey and cold even the people working there. I could see a jail cell like thing way over on the far wall. I was scared to death just to approach the counter to let someone know I was there. I gave them all the information they wanted and had to give them my purse. Then I was told to go to the thing that looked like a jail cell.

Before they slid the door open, I was frisked. Then the big iron gate was opened, then closed behind me with a big clang. I was caught between two cell doors and the one in front of me didn't open until a few minutes after the one behind me closed. A loud speaker told me when to move. I didn't see anyone. My nerves were on edge. When I went into the second of the entrance cells, I saw there was one more ahead of that. And each time the door clanged shut behind me I jumped. I didn't like being there even though I wasn't going to have to stay. I imagined how Bob must have felt when the door clanged on his cell the first time.

Bob had been in a special area for new prisoners; they were kept away from the general population for a while. I had gotten letters from him. We talked a little while and I left feeling sorry for him and angry at him for putting me in the position of taking care of my family alone. I don't think there were any public assistance programs for people like me. If there were, I didn't take advantage of them. I had no child support, no food stamps and no other help except my sisters.

Bob was at Jackson State Prison for a while then got transferred to a juvenile type prison where he worked as a nurse in the dispensary. There he was free to roam the grounds but he couldn't leave. He had it made. He became friends with the doctors who came to treat the kids and they would bring Bob steaks now and then. Bob cooked them over a Bunsen burner. Later he was taught bumping and painting on automobiles. I don't remember if I was even in contact with him then because we were divorced at that time. Never in my wildest dreams had I imagined him in that kind of work.

Al McGuire

Al was tall (probably 6'3") and rugged looking, with short dark curly hair. He had a square jaw with a cleft chin and reminded me of the Marlborough man. His shoulders were about 10 feet wide. That is an exaggeration but they were broad. He had a gentle southern accent (West Virginia) and a big smile. He was quite charming but also mysterious. His hands were huge like twice the size of mine and very strong.

It was a bad time for me when I met him what with Bob in prison and me supporting two children under five. As a product of the 50s where everyone was supposed to be married and have a happy home I was angry and depressed. I didn't like being alone and working two jobs. There is no support from a husband who is in prison. And it was a bad time for Al. He was hitchhiking through Michigan when he got an attack of appendicitis and had been admitted to the hospital.

We met in the hospital. He was a patient and I was a laboratory technician. When I went to draw his blood, I noticed his handsomeness and felt sorry for him. He also reminded me of a long lost love which tugged at my heart. His wrist band said he was divorced and 24 years old. I was also 24 and my divorce was pending (in Michigan you had to wait six months when there were children involved). There were orders to draw his blood several times over a three day period and I made sure I was the one to do it. Every time I drew his blood, we talked some and I really liked him.

When it was time for him to be discharged, they didn't want to let him go without having someplace to go. Since he had nowhere to go and I was lonesome, I took him home with me. I lived in a cute little house on Walton Boulevard by Sashabaw. He was very appreciative for a couple of days. It was nice to have him around, but I didn't know much about him and he wouldn't tell me much. To this day I am not sure where he was going when he got sick or where he had been. I never did know much about him. How stupid was I ?

At first I liked having him with me. He asked me to marry him after he had been at my house a few days and being lonely and stupid I said "yes." My divorce from Bob was final on June 14 (I think) and Al and I were married the same day. Shortly after, we moved to Auburn Heights.

I didn't know he had a temper until I saw him get mad at my power mower. He picked it up and threw it half way across the yard then came storming in the house. Later on and more than once, he threw me around the same way. He was especially violent after he had had a few beers.

I totally blame myself for getting into this situation and immediately after the first beating which left me with black eyes, and bruises all over my body, I started planning my escape. But it took a long time. He threatened that he would kill me if I left him. In the early 60s there were no agencies to help battered women. The beatings kept coming even when I least expected it. One night after Glenda and Mark were in bed, he came home after having a few beers and gave me the very worst beating yet then he raped me and passed out. I laid there for a while wanting to kill him and trying to figure out how I could do it. I went out to the kitchen and picked up the big butcher knife and went back to the bedroom. But on the way, I passed the kids bedroom and common sense kicked in. How could I prove self-defense if he was passed out when I plunged the knife into his chest and how could I take care of my children if I was in prison? I took the knife back to the kitchen and began seriously planning how I would escape if the chance came. Before that chance came, I realized that I was pregnant. That really complicated things.

Other complications were that I needed a job. I was painting pictures for my parent's studio but the big rush would end with Christmas. First things first. I went to a doctor and pleaded with him to please give me an abortion. He wouldn't even talk with me about it. Nor would he offer any other suggestions. I found another doctor but got nowhere with him either. There was no way that I could work to totally support myself and two children while pregnant. I was desperate.

I had a job lined up for January at a laboratory of a small hospital nearby and I knew that Al would be going out of town for three weeks with his company, the Davey Tree Expert Company. I planned to leave that job and go to work at yet a different hospital so Al wouldn't know where I was working.

I made other plans too. I found an apartment and put a deposit on it. While Al was gone, I would have the locks changed on my car and I would move to the apartment. Hopefully he would not be able to find me too easily. I was going to use a different name to get a job and I'd also get a peace bond against him. My other plan was to abort myself as soon as he left. I had heard stories about using a catheter.

The night before he left, I got another severe beating. I was painting at my painting table in the front bedroom when he came after me. The weight of my body being smashed against the six foot painting table made it come apart with me in the middle of it. That was the fuel I needed to follow through with my plan.

As soon as he left, I got the catheter that I had borrowed from the lab and threaded a coat hanger up into it. I laid down and stuck it up me several times hoping that I would disturb something. Nothing happened. I went to work and came home thinking that it hadn't worked. I saw the potty chair on the floor of the bathroom. It had some old pee in it. I made a solution of pee and water and douched with it. "A little bacteria couldn't hurt," I thought.

The next day, I left work at noon with a fever. I called my doctor when I got home and he made a house call. He thought I might have a bladder infection and gave me some antibiotic tablets. I knew different and hoped it was the beginning of the miscarriage. I thanked him and he told me if it didn't get better to call him again. I didn't take the antibiotics and the fever got higher and higher. About 7 p.m., I called the doctor again. He said he was going out for the evening but he would leave orders for me at the emergency room and I should go there ASAP.

I couldn't drive and I had two children to take care of. I called my Mother and told her that I was sick and had to go to the hospital and asked if the kids could come to her house for a while. I also asked her not to call Al. I called two taxi cabs—one to take me to the hospital and one to take Glenda and Mark to Mom's house. We lived in Auburn Heights which was a good 20 minutes from her house. From that moment on I don't remember much for three weeks.

I was in shock when I arrived at the hospital and doctors and nurses were rushing around trying to start IVs, etc. I told everyone that I had been beaten; I had the bruises to prove it. My doctor had left orders. But after a while my condition became much worse. They were losing me and couldn't reach my doctor. He hadn't left a number with the babysitter. Finally a new resident obstetrician, Dr. Packard, took charge and decided that I was hemorrhaging because my hemoglobin was dropping. He said I needed to go to surgery. He found a brand new surgeon just starting his practice. Dr. Raymond Ashare reluctantly agreed to take me to surgery. It was a brave decision on his part because I couldn't give permission. They called my parents and told them that if they wanted to see me alive they had ten minutes to get to the hospital.

They opened me up to find that I wasn't bleeding after all but in the meantime they had given me three pints of blood to replace the blood that they thought I was losing and because I was not bleeding; that overloaded my system. During surgery I went into cardiac arrest. My lungs filled with fluid. I was in really bad shape. By injecting cortisone directly into my heart, and putting me on a Bird Respirator while sewing me up quickly, they barely kept me alive. I was put in the Intensive Care Unit with odds of 1 -10 of living through the night.

The doctors and nurses told me later that I was panicky before surgery and didn't want surgery. I kept saying that I needed to move from my house to the new apartment and not to call Al and when Mom and Dad came, in my delirium, I kept telling them to move me to the new apartment.

My mother never believed that Al would hurt me like I said and so she called him to tell him that I was in the hospital. They let him in to Intensive Care once but I became very hysterical even though I couldn't talk (I had a tracheotomy). Then orders were written that he not be allowed in under any circumstances.

While I was still on a respirator in ICU, I had the nurses find a lawyer for me. I forget his name but he visited me in ICU so I could post a peace bond. Without further prodding Al disappeared and I never saw him again.

What caused all of this? The hanger/catheter scratched my liver. The douche caused an E. Coli blood infection. Yes, I did have a miscarriage while I was in ICU but at a great cost. The emergency surgery gave me a hernia (all the coughing I did) and the medicine they were giving me in a catheter which went in through a vein at my ankle and was threaded up to mid-calf on my left leg went subcutaneous and burned from the inside out. I had to have surgery on that leg to remove the burn and then it had to be grafted. I also had to have a bronchoscopy because the respirator wasn't helping enough. Eventually I had to have one third of my right lung removed. Every one of the procedures done on me in ICU gave me medical problems for the rest of my life. After I was out and healing I paid for another divorce by myself. I also paid the $10,000 hospital bill myself. It took a long time for me to heal and pay my debt but I did it by myself.

The lesson I learned was never ever again to NEED anyone. Almost to a fault, I take care of myself. But if I had been able to get a safe abortion when I was so desperate, I would have been better off. Or if I had been able to tell the doctors what I did, it would have made it easier for them to save me. I have told God that I am sorry and I firmly believe that God let me live when my chances of living were so low, so that I could support abortion rights. Unless someone has been in such a desperate situation, they have no idea what it is like. I definitely think that abortions should **not** be used for birth control, but only in desperate situations.

At 5 o'clock one morning about eight months after Al left, when I was picking up fasting blood samples on the fifth floor of Pontiac General Hospital, the operator paged me. She told me I had two calls. One was from Mom telling me that Al had just called. I took the other call which was from New Mexico. Al was on the line. I hadn't heard from him since he left me in the hospital. He simply asked if we were divorced yet. When I told him we were he said "Okay." That was the last time I ever heard from him. I am not sorry he came into my life because it taught me several valuable lessons. I was supposed to die from what he did to me, but I lived. God had another plan for me.

My brother and sisters taken in the mid 60s.
L-R: Beverly, Muriel (Bunnie), me, Don and Beth Ann.

Working Three Jobs in the Early 60's

With Al out of my life I had to start my life all over again. I had worked at Pontiac General Hospital (PGH) before Bob went to prison and was lucky that I was liked by the head pathologist, Dr. John J. Marra as well as the assistant pathologist, Dr. Jack Kevorikian. Dr. Marra was not only the chief pathologist at PGH, but he owned several private laboratories in medical buildings and he was chief pathologist at Lapeer County General Hospital as well. He helped me out two fold. He hired me to work at the Lapeer Hospital fulltime (40 hours a week) then hired me to work part time at Pontiac General (36 hours a week). Most of what I made at Pontiac went toward my $10,000 hospital bill. I also painted pictures.

Lapeer was about 36 miles from my Mom and Dad's house and since I was going to be working there five days a week, I looked for a place to rent there. I found a cute little house within walking distance to the adorable little down town of Lapeer. It was a picture perfect town with a big park in the middle of town; it even had a small river running through it. The main street in town was lined with viable stores; everything we needed was there from a dime store, to movie theater. There was even an A & W root beer stand just outside of town.

My work week started in Lapeer on Sunday afternoon. I worked from 3:30 to 11 p.m., but then I was on call the rest of the night so I had to have a babysitter who stayed all night. I didn't get called out often as it was a very small hospital but I had to be prepared in the event of an emergency. Monday through Thursday I worked regular hours (7 a.m. to 3:30 p.m.). Friday I cleaned my house and did laundry until about 2 p. m. when I packed the kids in the car and we drove to Mom's house. After dropping the kids off, I went to work at Pontiac General Hospital. I had to be there by 3:30 p.m. and worked through the night until eight Saturday morning (double shift). After work I went to Mom's to sleep until time to go to the beauty shop and get my weekly hairdo (in those days we got our hair washed, teased, sprayed with lacquer and it stayed for a week). At 3:30 in the afternoon, I was back at work again until Sunday morning at eight when I picked up the kids and drove back to Lapeer for a little rest before work that day. Yes, it was a rugged schedule but I needed to pay my bills.

A memorable time in this period of my life started on a Friday. It was my day off from Lapeer and I was cleaning house to get ready for my double shift in Pontiac when my girlfriend stopped by to give me my pay check. She asked, "Isn't it awful?" I had no idea what she was talking about until she spilled the news. President Kennedy had been killed. I hadn't had the radio on all day. It was hard to go to work that night because I wanted to be glued in front of the television to hear the whole thing over and over again.

I loved my work at Pontiac General best. There was a small shift when I started at 3:30 but by 11:30 I was all alone in the lab until about 7:30 the next morning. Pontiac General Hospital was a good sized hospital with about 500 beds. The laboratory was a maze of rooms in the bowels of the old building. At night it could be a little eerie. The largest room was a big L shaped room where most of the routine work was done such as blood counts, urinalysis and blood chemistries. A small room close to that was the blood bank and across the hall from that was our bacteriology department. I could easily get stuck in the blood bank if there was a bad accident but I seldom had an emergency that required any bacteriology work. I might have to stain some slides for the tech to read in the morning but I didn't have to read any cultures. And I didn't have much to do in the histology section. That department is where they made slides from tissues (usually from surgeries) for the pathologist to read.

Sometimes at night the lab was so quiet that I would go sit in the emergency room and visit with some of the staff there and generally see what was going on in the world. I could write a book about those stories. Other times, it was very hectic. I still have vivid memories of trying to save two boys who were in a serious accident. One had a ruptured aorta and I couldn't cross match blood fast enough. I had to scour all the hospitals for the right type of blood and had police rushing it to the lab. After sending 20 pints of blood up to surgery over a short period of time, we lost the boys but not for the lack of trying.

One day when driving between hospitals without the kids, I fell asleep at the wheel and crashed into a stump in a field. Thank God I missed the trees all around. I was not hurt nor did I hurt anyone else. But I figured that was God telling me to quit one job. I quit the two double shifts in Pontiac and enjoyed living in Lapeer.

This picture was taken just before a prom. It was a test picture before we started shooting the couples. I always went with my parents to help. Notice my crazy hair do. At the time, I had carrot red hair. During this period of my life I enjoyed getting my hair done every Saturday. I was even platinum for a little while. Between my jobs and the kids, I didn't have time for fun so my fun was getting my hair done. I never dated.

Dr. Jack Kevorkian

The assistant pathologist at Pontiac General Hospital was Dr. Jack Kevorkian and he practically lived at the hospital. I don't need to describe him because everyone has seen a picture of him in his plain blue cardigan sweater. He dressed simply and was a no nonsense kind of guy. He was single, drove a beat up van; was eccentric, yet oh, so smart. Some of my fondest memories are of those nights when we weren't busy. He and a bunch of us would sit at a table in the cafeteria for hours on end discussing everything from A to Z. One night he decided that he would invent a dripless coffee cup after finding coffee in his saucer. He even drew up the plans. One night, he told us that he was working on a grant to study the effects of cadaver blood transfusions. He had a theory that in battle field conditions (this was all before the discovery of aids) if one soldier was dead and his buddy next to him needed blood and if they were the same blood type (dog tag ID) the medic should be able to hook up a direct transfusion from the dead guy to the patient. To most people this sounds gross, but it made sense. A dead man doesn't need his blood anymore. We began studies. Normal blood is made up of four parts—the majority is red blood cells, about a third is plasma and the white blood cells and platelets make up a minor but important part. When a young apparently healthy person came in to the morgue from an accident, we would draw off his/her blood in regular blood transfusion bottles. Immediately we noticed that cadaver blood was richer in red blood cells. The plasma had decreased by a large amount. Plasma kind of waters down normal blood so to speak. We tried giving cadaver blood to patients with anemia,

but most didn't want it; when we did succeed, the results were tremendous. No cadaver blood was transfused before doing a complete autopsy to assure that the cadaver was in fact healthy prior to the accident.

The next step was that we technicians volunteered to participate by taking a direct transfusion from a cadaver without first doing an autopsy. First, if the technician matched, he/she would have a pint of their blood removed so it wouldn't overload their system. Then the technician would go into the morgue and lie down on the floor beneath the body and take a transfusion. The only bad side effect after dozens of transfusions was when a technician became drunk. It was later learned that the 19 year old girl who was DOA had an extremely high alcohol content.

Often I would have to ask Dr. K. a question about a test or something and I would knock on his office door. One time, I noticed that he was painting a picture—an oil painting. He explained that he had decided to take an oil painting class and enrolled in an adult education class at the nearby high school. The painting was well done, but understandably weird. He was after all a pathologist (they deal with death). His first painting was *Very Still Life* pictured to the right. The second painting I saw him do was titled *Motherhood* and showed a dead woman nursing a baby with a vulture on her shoulder. The next one I saw was entitled *Coma*. That was a picture of an outstretched bony hand cradling a brain, but it was seeping through the fingers. I tried to find the second and third painting on the web but they are nowhere to be found.

I loved working for Dr. K as we lovingly called him. Even when assisting him with an autopsy, he always had time to teach about the human anatomy.

A Short Walk to Near Death

While working at Lapeer General Hospital one day in the early 60s, I had a really bad sore throat so on my lunch hour I walked across the street from the hospital to the clinic where my doctor had his office. I had called ahead so they were prepared to treat me in a hurry. Dr. LePere thought a shot of penicillin would fix me up so he had the nurse do it then I left to walk back to work.

It was a short walk and I took a short cut up the grassy hill. The lab was at the north end of the building and a straight shot from my doctor's office. As soon as I walked into the door of the laboratory I started feeling strange and my boss, Dr. Marra, took one look at me and dragged me down the hall to the emergency room. He had said my eyes were glassy and he knew something was seriously wrong. Before I knew it and without any formalities, I was on a table and well, I don't remember the rest. I had gone into anaphylactic shock from the penicillin.

> **Anaphylactic shock** A widespread and very serious allergic reaction. Symptoms include dizziness, loss of consciousness, labored breathing, swelling of the tongue and breathing tubes, blueness of the skin, low blood pressure, heart failure, and death. Immediate emergency treatment is required for this type of shock.

If I hadn't been so close to the hospital and working at the hospital, I would have died. Since I did work at the hospital, I didn't have to wait to give someone my name, address, phone number and so on. Precious minutes might have been wasted. If I hadn't taken the little bit of short cut up the grassy hill, I may have passed out on my way and even gone unnoticed for too long. There were so many variables. And here I am to tell about that horrible incident. This is yet another of my close calls in which God was with me. I didn't even know Him that well at the time.

A New Smile

I was born with bad teeth. Or at least they got bad and I had lots of cavities. Even in the Air Force, I spent a lot of time at the dentist. I was tired of getting fillings and when the dentist told me that I needed gold caps on my front teeth (that was the normal way to preserve teeth at the time), I said, "That's it. Pull them all and give me false teeth." Both of my parents had dentures and Dad had said that they were no problem.

Knowing what I know today, I can't believe that Dr. Burns agreed with me. He started making the impressions for the new teeth. Then I met Al and ended up in the hospital and lost a lot of weight so I had to have new impressions.

I had all of my teeth pulled one side at a time (in the back) then on one day all of my front teeth were pulled (six on top and six on the bottom) and my new teeth were put in immediately then I went to work at Pontiac General and worked a double shift. I even enjoyed steak for dinner that night.

I was 24 years old and loved my smile. I loved my dentures. My teeth didn't hurt and I felt good. Except for doctors and nurses and of course my dentist, no one ever saw me without my teeth and until recently I never regretted this decision but that is another story.

Oh My God, I Killed Her

In the spring of 1964 Bob got out of prison early and begged me to get back with him. I had loved him, but I didn't know if I could love him again. I, on the other hand, had been working so hard between the hospital and painting pictures that I hadn't had time to play or date. I was lonely and kind of welcomed having someone around again. Part of me thought that he had probably learned his lesson and that he had changed. He got a job in Lansing while on parole and we visited a little. Bob had worked as a nurse while in prison but then was trained to do auto bumping and painting so that is what he was doing in Lansing. Glenda loved having him around, but Mark didn't know him at all. After all Mark was only six months old when Bob went away.

Bob later got a job in Lapeer working at a trailer company. He moved back in with me for a test. He was nicer—but a little skittish on some things. He didn't ever want to be behind a closed door among other little things. I let him stay for quite a while and it seemed to be okay. I knew he would never cheat on me again, that much I was sure of. I was just afraid to commit to anyone again so not marrying was just fine. One day our pastor said that in the eyes of God we were married but we had better do it legally. We did.

I continued to work at Lapeer Hospital until a horrible thing happened. I was all alone on duty when a woman came into the emergency room hemorrhaging. She was pregnant and due, I think. They wanted to give her blood immediately and requested type O (the universal donor) which is compatible with every blood type. I wanted to give her her own blood type and with nurses standing over me, rushing me, I read it to be type AB. I grabbed the bottle of blood and off the nurses went. I was doing something else not five minutes later when suddenly I was hit with a lightening bolt—I had read it wrong. She was really type O. I called ER immediately, but she was already in trouble. She died because of my error. I was wrong. My stubbornness in insisting the rules be followed caused her death. The baby lived but I wanted to die. Dr. Marra and Mr. Foote, the hospital administrator, started the cover up immediately. I was sent home in shock. It was amazing how fast things happened. The family never knew why she died. I was transferred to one of Dr. Marra's private labs in Pontiac—across from St. Joseph Mercy Hospital. I liked working there but missed the hospital atmosphere.

About the same time Bob hurt his back while working at the pop up trailer factory in Lapeer and needed back surgery. Prior to prison he had been the scrub nurse to a top neurosurgeon and he wanted that surgeon to be the one to operate on him.

He had his surgery in Pontiac and while he was in the hospital I found a cute house at the end of a street near a good school in Drayton Plains (where Mom and Dad lived). I had the doctor keep him in the hospital one extra day and my young sisters and I moved us to the new house. It took a couple of trips in a U Haul truck and I was amazed at what we four girls could do. We even managed the piano as well as the refrigerator and other heavy things with the help of a hand truck and ramps that I laid down. Before I went to bed that night, everything was where it needed to be (beds up and made and everything in the cupboards) and it looked like we had lived there forever. I was even able to re – build my painting table. The next day, I went to pick up Bob at the hospital and told him that we didn't have to drive all the way to Lapeer; we had moved. He was surprised. As I turned off Sashabaw for the two block drive to the house, he was very unhappy because it was a dirt washboard road. His poor back took a beating even though I practically crawled those two blocks. Once in the house though he was okay, that is until the new parole officer visited us. His parole officer in Lapeer was very nice, but the new one was the worst. He told Bob that any time there is a robbery, he would have Bob down there in the lineup and he better not violate curfew or leave the county. Poor Bob was in the dumps for a while. It turned out that the guy liked to scare his new parolees which he truly did. He didn't bother us as long as Bob checked in weekly.

Bob couldn't do the work he had been doing when he got hurt

so the state rehabilitated him by sending him to on the job training in a commercial photo studio in Detroit. Bob was given a choice of what kind of field he wanted to be trained in and chose something he had wanted to do for a long time. Bob had been fascinated with photography since coming to Michigan and becoming acquainted with my parent's business. He had even learned to help them with weddings and other candid work but he was not crazy about portrait photography. Besides I had told Bob that I would divorce him if he ever became a photographer because I hated the business I had to grow up in. But commercial photography was different and the state found Jim Ransier, a commercial photographer in Detroit, who was willing to teach Bob on the job. The state paid Jim and he in turn paid Bob so it was a good deal.

Bob loved that kind of work because it was so varied. One day he may have been photographing a huge machine, the next day he may be on a girder 25 stories up taking pictures of the men placing the last girder in place, or he might be taking pictures of furniture for an advertising brochure.

In the meantime, Dr. Marra moved me to his other laboratory which was across from Pontiac General Hospital.

I loved this house and we even had a dog, a collie named King who was a stray we decided to keep. He didn't like men and he barked incessantly when the kids were out playing because he wanted to play with them. We finally had to give him to folks who had a farm way out in the country.

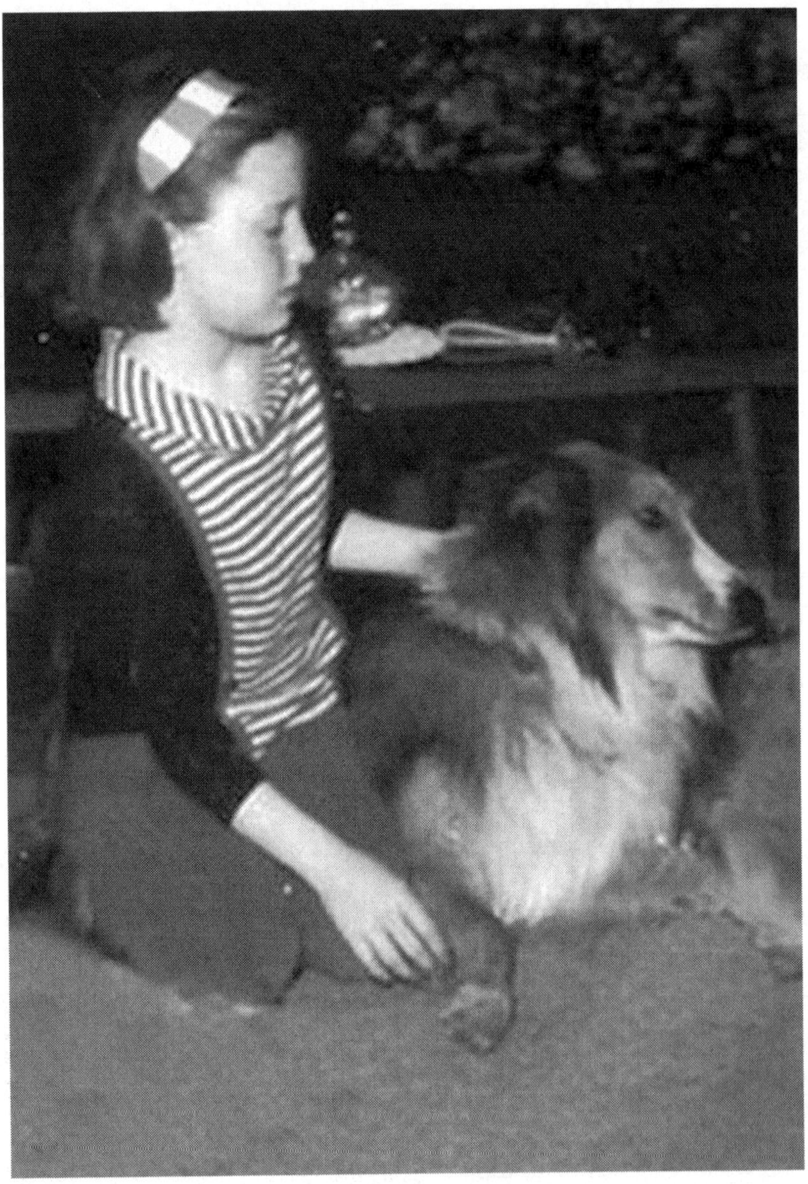

Glenda and King

New Additions

When I became pregnant for Robert I decided to quit smoking immediately. It was over the holidays and I ate instead of smoking. I gained 60 pounds with that pregnancy. I felt like a blimp.

Robert Allen Flath was born on August 2, 1965 and he was an adorable baby and very good too. Just after Robert was born, we were told that the landlord wanted his house back. We were lucky to find and buy a house only a block or two from the one we had been renting and during the move, I got pregnant again. I didn't

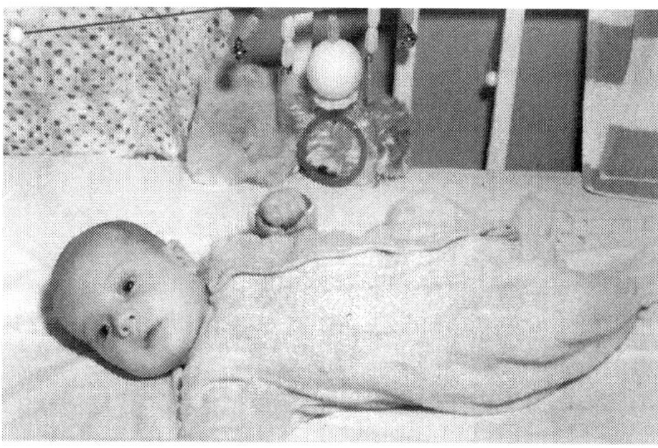

even know it because I had been so busy with work and moving. One morning as I was getting ready to go to work, Bob said, "I think you are pregnant. Better do a test when you get to work." I laughed but decided to catch a urine sample anyway and take it with me to work.

When I got to work, Mary Kay, the other technician was in the office. I went to set up my pregnancy test (the test took two hours back in that day) and noticed another test tube was set up. I didn't think anything of it. Even though we weren't open yet sometimes patients stopped in early to drop off a specimen. When the time was up I noticed the other test as well as mine were both positive. I asked Mary Kay who the other test belonged to and she said, "It is mine." I said, "Dr. Marra won't like this. We are both pregnant." She just about fell off of her chair and we spent the morning commiserating about our situation. And since we were the only two who worked in that lab, we also worried about what the boss would say when he found out. We would be leaving him in a fine mess. We figured we were both due on August 15. Robert would be just one year old when the new baby arrived.

I changed doctors and the new doctor ordered me to lose 25 pounds during that pregnancy, which I did.

I went into labor for Jim on June 26 and because my other chil-

The house on Seebaldt was the first house which was totally ours and I was very happy there.

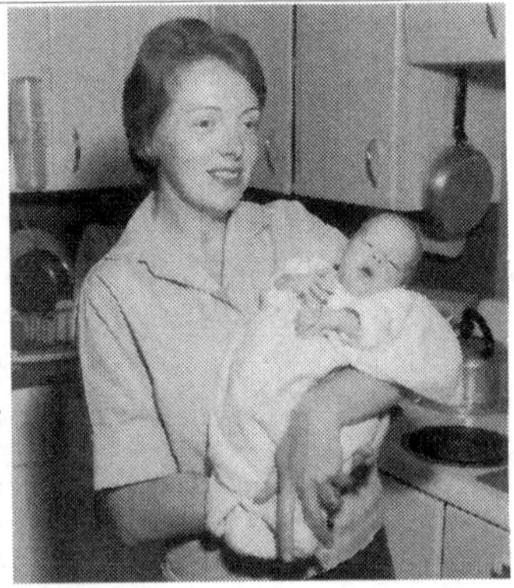

dren had come fairly fast, they broke my water and then the contractions stopped. I laid there for two days trying to complete the delivery. James Edward was finally born on June 28, 1966, which was six weeks early. The two boys were only ten and a half months apart. I had the doctor tie my tubes while I was still in the hospital. My family was now complete. Glenda was ten, Mark was six, and the two young ones under one.

Having two in diapers, on different schedules and neither walking was a challenge. A few months after Jim was born, I quit working in the laboratory and found a new career with Tupperware which would allow me to be home during the day. Bob watched the kids at night.

I loved my family very much and loved being home with them.

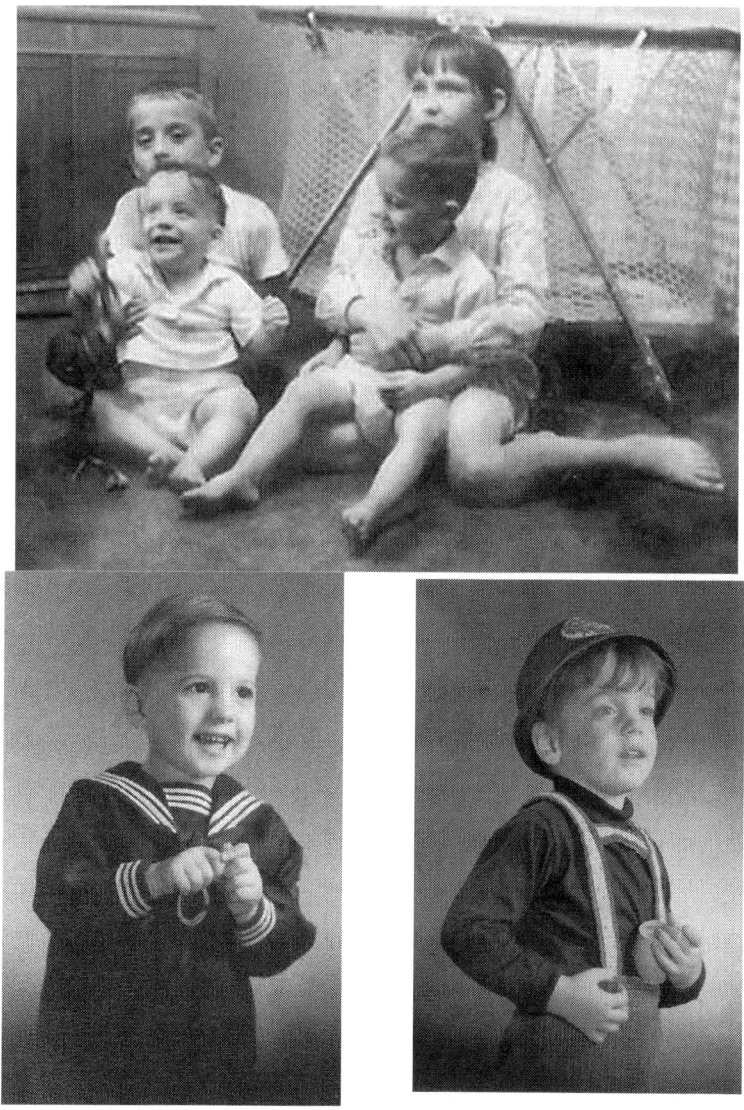

Top: The four kids—James with Mark
and Robert with Glenda.
Bottom formal portraits of Robert and James.

New Love

I loved Tupperware from the very beginning. First of all, I loved the product and I was eager to be the best. I loved the concept that I could get a raise any time I wanted just by working a little smarter or harder. Every Monday morning I drove to the distributorship (in Pontiac) for the sales meeting. People who sold a lot got special recognition and I liked that. That kind of recognition motivated me to do more and more. We were given hints on how to have better parties and how to recruit dealers in order to become a manager.

When they presented the rewards and prizes we could earn, I wanted them all. After I did my first parties, I knew that I also wanted to be a manager. The reward (besides monetary) was a company station wagon. I went to work on that goal right away.

On the way to becoming a manager, I was not only earning money but gifts as well. For every campaign, we were given a booklet full of things we could earn if we did this or that. I would bring the brochure home and the kids would look at all the stuff and say, "I want that. Get it Mom." The first prize I earned was an English Racer bicycle. In fact I earned two—one for Glenda and one for Mark. Yes, I had to really push to get these gifts, but the kids helped by helping to fix meals, packing Tupperware, answering the phone properly and watching the younger boys. For the next contests, I earned living room furniture, lamps, beds and lots of neat appliances for the kitchen. I earned a movie camera, tenting equipment and on and on. It was fun. While earning prizes, I became a manager and got my Ford station wagon. Then I worked at promoting other managers and got an even nicer car—the Ford LTD wagon with retractable head lamps and other extras. It was the ultimate.

Once I became a manager, I was working day and night. Between having my own parties, I was recruiting and training new dealers and managers, attending manager meetings, and I had to hire someone to help with the kids. I found an angel who lived a couple of blocks away. Elsie Adams walked to our house every morning and took care of everything while I was on the phone which was a big part of the job. She would often start supper, fold clothes that I had washed and just loved the kids especially Robert and Jim who were not in school yet. She was the sweetest person and we all loved her.

In August the gals from our distributorship were all going to Orlando, Florida, for Jubilee at Tupperware headquarters and we had big goals to reach in order to get big prizes. I wanted to be among the top recruiters and did recruit 13 new dealers. I was recognized in front of thousands and we got to run out into the field and choose a present (all large) from hundreds scattered on the stadium field. My present was a large box of Sirocco bathroom things. I was very disappointed. The gals in the top sales category got bigger gifts like freezers, refrigerators, washers, dryers, and more. For the next Jubilee (a year later) I made sure I was in the top sales category and did in fact earn a big upright Westinghouse freezer.

Besides the gifts we earned at Jubilee, we got lots of good training and recognition. At my second Jubilee in August of 1968, I was recognized for being in the top 10 of managers in our region in the United States. Our region included about 10 states in the east but I can't remember them all.

Tupperware gave me a self confidence that I could never imagine. I had loved speaking in public in high school but this was even better. I felt that I was truly helping others to a better life by helping them become dealers and managers or even by showing them a better way to manage their kitchen.

After Jubilee, Sandy Lane (one of my promoted out managers), Bob and I went to Freeport in the Bahamas for a couple of days. That was lots of fun.

In the fall of 1968, I had to have surgery (gallbladder) which got complicated. Many little stones went into my bile duct and I was in the hospital a lot longer than normal. Recovery was long too.

Because I couldn't do parties and train dealers, I gave up my Tupperware managership and even quit being a dealer.

When I quit, I had quite a record. I had promoted out dozens of managers and yet still had 65 of my own girls under me. It had been a lot of work but I loved seeing others succeed and grow. I would miss Tupperware a lot. I would end up going back to Tupperware two more times, but it was never the same. I didn't have the energy or the drive that I had once had.

Bob and I at a Tupperware Jubilee. I was just announced as one of the top ten managers in our region. It was a very exciting moment and something that made me proud.

Falling in a Big Hole

The year 1969 is a blur to me. I really missed Tupperware but didn't want to go back and start all over. My self-esteem was dwindling. Bob had a tendency to put me down all the time and the longer it went on I began to crumble. By March and after all the dreary sunless days of winter, I was depressed and began to believe I was as bad as he said I was. Also he did little to help around the house. If I asked him to fix something, he ignored me until I ended up doing the job. I had sought out counseling through the county because I couldn't pay and if Bob knew I was getting counseling help, he would be angry. The counselor put me in a nice group and we met once a week. It was good for me, but I was still fragile for some reason.

I usually had dinner on the table within a few minutes of Bob's coming home from work. We always ate supper together and I always fixed nice dinners. On weekends it was a little different. We ate breakfast and lunch at odd times and dinner was more casual too. One evening in March of 1969 (I think it was a weekend night because he was home all day) after I had been busy all day, the time got away from me and I didn't have dinner ready at the usual time. He simply asked "What's for dinner?" while he was sitting watching TV. I felt that I was being blamed for not having dinner on the table at the right time. I did not answer him but proceeded to prepare dinner while crying. No one knew I was hurting; they were all in the living room. When dinner was ready I called the family. It was on the table. They sat down and started eating while I went to get some things from the bedroom and bathroom. I gathered up all the pills I had (pain killers) from surgeries, etc., took a book, some paper and a pen, a nightgown and my purse, walked out the front door, got in the car and drove. I wanted to die. There was a motel nearby. I checked in and asked to have a room in the back so I wouldn't be bothered by the highway noise. That wasn't the real reason. I didn't want anyone to see my car.

I stayed up a good part of the night. I read a little, cried a lot, wrote my suicide letter, listened to music, cried some more and took all the pills and went to sleep.

I don't remember how anyone found me but the next thing I knew I was being taken by ambulance to the hospital. I don't really remember that fully. But they did pump my stomach and put me in intensive care for a while, and then I was transferred to the psychiatric ward. That was where doors were locked and everyone walked around like a zombie. I was there for 45 days. I saw my psychiatrist weekly. Once he asked me how the "barbs on Barbara were." He also called me a "castrating bitch" and I fought back. I was supposed to be able to go home for that weekend, but he didn't want to let me go. He said I was too combative. Bob argued for me by telling the doctor I was like myself again instead of the quiet brooding person I had been. I did get to go home but I was so heavily medicated that I don't remember much. I do remember that Bob had purchased season tickets to the Masonic auditorium and I really enjoyed that.

When I got out of the hospital, we were told to go to group therapy together. Bob didn't want any part of that but he had to go. I remember walking into the group and giving my first name and saying I was there because I tried to commit suicide. When it was Bob's turn he told the group that he was only there for me and that there was nothing wrong with him. Boy did the group light into him. I silently chuckled.

I did get better and so did Bob. He even talked to me a little which was a big improvement over the previous years and the sun came out which also made a big difference.

Section Five

Middle Family Years

1971—1980

Nearly Perfect

The early 1970's were among my best years with my family. I dearly loved being home with the kids and Bob had a good job making enough money that I didn't need a steady job. I still did some art work on photographs for my Mother (Dad was out of the business since their divorce) but that work didn't amount to much since direct color was in. The only work I had was on the restoration of photographs or corrections on the new color photography.

I delighted in fixing good meals and having dinner ready when Bob came home from work. I loved being involved with the kids in school. Yes, I was a room mother. I felt a little guilty because Robert and Jim were getting the benefit of having a Mom at home, where Glenda and Mark didn't.

I loved having time to read, play the piano and even joined a once a month all girls pinochle group. I felt quite normal. I even had a lovely garden that flourished.

At least once a week I would prepare something new for the family for dinner. I had a new rule that would apply when a new meal was served. No one was allowed to look at something new and say such things, "Oh, that doesn't look good" or "Do we have to eat that?" When a new meal or new dish was presented no one could say anything good or bad. They simply had to try it then when the meal was finished, I would take a vote. When I counted to three, everyone would show a thumb up or down. The majority vote would hold and either it would never be made again or would appear on the menu as often as the cook felt like preparing it. This worked like a charm and almost everyone abided by the rules.

I said almost everyone abided. Bob hated squash therefore I never fixed it. I, on the other hand, loved squash so I thought it was time for the family to see if they liked it. One night mashed butternut squash was prepared and I warned him ahead of time that it was part of dinner. I asked that he take a small spoonful without saying a word. He agreed. Everyone sat down to the table and as always Bob was the first to dish up his plate; I was still bringing stuff to the table. He took a small spoonful of squash and put it in his mouth, but the texture was too much for him; he spit it all over everything and everyone. At that point no one was about to touch the squash except me.

Many weeks later I tried a new frozen Bird's Eye product which was sweetened carrots; they tasted nothing like carrots. Everyone ate them, liked them and wondered what they were. I lied and told them all that it was squash and from that time on the kids, at least, ate squash any time I fixed it. Bob never did.

From playing so much chess, I became very organized. Before I went shopping, I made my list based on specific menus for the week. I posted a monthly calendar on the side of the refrigerator and filled in the menu for each day of the week. I did not cook on the weekends. With the menu posted, Bob, the kids and myself could warm up (thank you microwave) whatever leftovers they wanted when they wanted to eat. The posted menus would refresh their memory on what was available. Weekends were wonderfully free. We slept late, ate late and I got to rest a bit.

Glenda had asked me to get her the things she would need when she started her period and I told her I would, but I couldn't quite bring myself to believing that she was growing up. I wanted to keep her as she was. One Christmas morning she told me she had started her period and I felt bad that I wasn't prepared. I jumped in the car to go to the drug store, but I was crying so hard, I didn't see Bob's car behind me and I smashed right into it. That was a bad day in more ways than one.

On Being a Mother

Okay, I had been a mother since Glenda was born in 1956, but at first I didn't know what I was doing. Like most of us, I learned from my parents, grandparents, family friends and so on.

My parents used corporal punishment a lot and most of the time they didn't follow through. As a kid, I had jobs to do (besides the painting) but I could get out of them easily. For example, I was supposed to do dishes when I was a teenager, but if I didn't do the job fast enough, Mom would scream and holler and I would tell her that I was going to do it, but if I stalled long enough she would do the job herself.

In the Air Force I learned responsibility and what it meant to follow orders. I felt secure knowing exactly what I could and couldn't do especially when it came to doing my job or details. I felt that was a better way to be a parent too. But it was a bit extreme for children.

So for Glenda and Mark, I insisted the rules be followed and that if they weren't there would be consequences—mostly spankings with a belt. I wasn't the mother I should have been. I was working so much that most of the time babysitters or my sisters did the parenting.

But in the 70s with time to try different things, I read a lot on parenting. I used to get three magazines a month, *Good Housekeeping, McCall's and Reader's Digest* and all had great articles in them. I had a stack of self-help books on the end table next to my chair in the living room. There were a lot of good shows on TV but some like Monday Night Football did not interest me at all so I would sit and read my helpful books and get good ideas on how to be a better mother. Often I would announce a new procedure or rule to the kids after I thoroughly investigated something new.

One day my daughter, Glenda, gave me a novel to read. I seldom read a book just to read it, but she said she thought I would really like it. The title was *Suffer the Children*. I put it on the top of my pile of books thinking that maybe someday I would read it.

The very next day, I was in the kitchen when I heard my three boys talking. It sounded like they were plotting something and their voices were coming from the living room. I snuck into the dining room just to the edge of the wall so they wouldn't see me and I eavesdropped. They were saying things like, "We have to do something with this." One said, "Let's burn this one." Finally they walked away without doing anything and I went over to where I knew they had been. What they had been looking at was that new book *Suffer the Children.* They thought I was going to learn how to make them suffer.

Lying was something that would get someone the most punishment. I always promised the kids that if they *fessed up* right away, they might get a lecture or at least a talk, but nothing more. On the other hand, if I had to use my lie detector to get the truth, there would be a punishment. The lie detector was an orb like thing that hung from a chain. It had come with an Ouija board that Glenda got for Christmas one year. I would hold the chain very still over the hand of the one charged with the misdeed and if the orb started swinging up and down, they were telling the truth, but if the orb swung left to right, there was a lie. I swear that I did not move the chain. I held it very still.

Most mothers have a sixth sense and know when someone is lying. I am sure they pulled a few things over on me, but when I was home most of the time, I knew what was going on. The lie detector worked most of the time. There is one time I remember though where I am not sure.

Someone wrote with crayon or some colored markers on the kitchen wall. No one would admit to it. I threatened with the lie detector and still no one confessed. I got the chained orb and still no one confessed. Usually the sight of it brought out the confession. I can't remember if all three boys were suspect or just Robert and Jim. I honestly didn't have a clue who the guilty party was and I think the lie detector picked the wrong person. Will one of you please fess up? It is much too late for punishment now. Maybe I deserve the scolding. I quit using the lie detector.

The above picture was taken in the summer of 1971 at my sister Beverly's wedding.

The Witch in Me

I barely remember Halloween as a child. The only thing I do remember is that I was dressed as Uncle Sam once when we lived in Detroit. I also remember going to Doris Kirby's Halloween party and a picture of Mom and Dad with their best friends, Muriel and Austin, dressed as cannibals for some party they were going to. I do not remember ever going trick or treating.

When we lived in Clarkston and even in Drayton Plains, there was no such thing as trick or treating for us. At the lake, few lived there in the fall, and in Drayton Plains we lived in the business part of town and our parents never took us out to the neighborhoods.

So maybe that is why, when we lived on Seebaldt and I had children in the local schools, I really looked forward to this holiday. I also had more time since I wasn't working fulltime.

One year, I bought a black light and made a ghost to hang from one window. With the black light on it, it looked great. I also bought a tape of spooky sounds and music and I hooked up our tape player to a large speaker which we put outside. With the house dark, the ghost in the window and scary sounds being broadcast, the house looked ominous.

I went to the butcher shop and got some long leg bones and planned to lay them in the driveway along with tombstones I had made out of white board. A couple of the head stones had stuffed work gloves coming over the top of the tombstone. And I added a little blood splatters under the glove like it dripped onto the tombstone.

We had an old dresser without the mirror in the garage and I got the bright idea to make the garage into a mad doctor's laboratory. I covered the dresser with a blanket so it wouldn't look like a dresser and I had a lab coat and a wild wig. That would be my outfit. I found a Frankenstein mask and a great out fit for my daughter Glenda (pants and a jacket which were too short in the legs and sleeves and big boots). Added to that I had a sheet to put over the monster, rusted chains, flasks and beakers borrowed from the laboratory and dry ice.

As the kids reluctantly walked up our driveway with the spooky music, the ghost flying, dodging the grave stones and bones, they met me in the garage. I gave them their candy first then in a scary voice with a European accent, I asked them if they would like to see my monster. They did. So I went to the head of the dresser and slowly removed the sheet. There was the Frankenstein monster looking dead. His arms appeared to be chained to something. The kids would cautiously move closer and the monster didn't move or breathe. But suddenly Glenda broke the chains and sat up. The kids turned and ran while screaming only to meet the headless man who had moved from his hiding place in the outside corner of the garage. More screams.

Mark was the headless man. He was tall and had put football shoulder pads on his head then covered his head and body with a man's overcoat. He was scary.

The funny thing about that Halloween was that the kids kept coming back again and again especially the young teens. They loved it. The little kids wouldn't come near. The music scared them too much. If I wasn't busy with other kids in the garage, I would run candy out to them. My two young boys were out trick or treating themselves with their father. That was the best year.

Almost every year, we used the black light and the music, but I don't remember that we ever did that big of a production again. Sometimes I would dress as a witch with makeup (big ugly nose, warts and greenish face) and when they rang the doorbell I would open the door to see scared kids. Another time I found a great skull mask and made myself a hooded sheet dress. I decided to just sit on the step with an elegant ornate candle holder and my big bowl of candy. I didn't say anything as the kids came up. They came cautiously as usual and reached into the bowl but immediately I would put my gloved hand on the top of their hand and just keep it there for a minute. I looked at their eyes and still didn't say a word. They didn't last long and went screaming off.

My kids always came home for lunch from the elementary school. We lived about three blocks from the school. On Hallow-

een they had to hurry home so I could get them made up. They always wanted make up rather than have a "store bought" costume. Maybe I was the one who influenced them. It was safer for them when walking and the theatrical part of me enjoyed doing it. Dracula was always fun and a hobo was simple to do. Glenda was a witch once (my favorite). This picture of Robert and Jim is the best though.

When we moved to Ortonville just before Halloween in 1977, I was mourning the fact that we couldn't do Halloween fun anymore. Our new house was an apartment up above a store on the main street. No one would come there for trick or treating. Robert, Jim and I got the bright idea that we could go out to the neighborhoods dressed in costume and give candy away to all the kids that were trick or treating. I dressed as a witch, Robert was the headless man and Jim was

Frankenstein. We looked good together. So off we went to the neighborhood in back of the business district. But every time we walked up to some kids they ran away. No one would come near us. We stood on a street corner and they would cross the street so they didn't have to pass us. I don't think we gave much candy away the whole night. But we laughed and had fun.

Even now, I love to dress for Halloween especially if I am going somewhere new with new people. And I am in my glory as a witch and I still like to shop in costume shops for fun things for a Halloween party.

Don't you love the nose?

The Kitchen Makeover Caper

In 1974, I decided to re do all the cupboards in our kitchen. When we bought the house they had many coats of paint on them. It was time for a change. I had purchased some product that would strip off the paint so I took one door off a cupboard to try it out. Working in the garage, I stripped the inside of the cupboard door easily. I didn't realize until much later that the reason it was so easy was there were fewer coats of paint on the inside than on the outside. Because that one inside door was so easy, I decided to do the whole job and to prepare took all the doors off and set them in the garage to deal with later. First I would tackle the fixed part of the cupboards.

The ends, stiles and underneath were terribly difficult. What I thought I could finish in a short time took over three weeks of working constantly and I am not even talking about all the doors and drawers. I ended up renting a hand sander to finish removing the paint and did so by laying on my back underneath the cupboards so I could sand. It was terrible work. Because of the sanding dust I put big wet sheets up at both entrances to the kitchen and worked alone.

Bob was not a handy guy. After I realized that the job was bigger than I could handle, I appealed to him to help. His answer was, "I didn't want it done." I finished the job but all the while I was angry with him and angry at myself for trying to do it all alone.

Bob finally did decide to help one day and came in the kitchen with his hand drill which had a sander disk attachment. He started working on the scalloped nick knack shelf that surrounded the window over the sink. In less than five minutes of working on that, he managed to completely mess up the design so I kicked him out. Did he plan that?

Without a kitchen to work in for that length of time, everyone's nerves got on edge. Bob wouldn't even help by going to get pizza or anything. So every day I had to quit at a decent time to fix dinner. We ate in the dining room instead of our normal kitchen table.

Once the cupboards were all sanded, I started on the staining and antiquing. We went without cupboard doors for months but it all looked really nice when I finished. I had always done all the painting in the house so it was only natural that I would do something like that also. I always mowed the lawn too until the boys got old enough.

My kids in 1974—Mark, Glenda, Robert and Jim

Mama Goes to College

In the summer of 1974 while I was finishing up on the kitchen, Neta, a friend from the Air Force stopped by. She was one of the seven who joined the Air Force at the same time. We had been in basic, tech school and at March AFB together. She was living in Florida and had come home to visit her parents so included a visit with me in her trip. She saw that I was not working and asked, "Why aren't you going to school on the GI bill?" I answered that I didn't know that I could. She went on to explain that I had two years' worth of school due me and it was going to run out soon. I was astounded because I had only been in the Air Force a little less than a year. I checked with the VA and sure enough, I qualified. I had two years of college coming to me but it expired in two years. Right away I registered at Oakland Community College and signed up for classes that fall.

With four children in school (two in elementary, one in junior high and one in high school), I knew it would be a challenge but I was feeling good enough about myself by then that it was exciting. I signed up for a full load (16 credit hours or four classes) that first semester. I wanted an easy class along with three harder ones so I took typing. I also took social studies, psychology and literature. I planned my classes so that I only went on Tuesday and Thursday and on Monday, Wednesday and Friday I went to a health club that my mother and I had joined. I felt terrific. I loved everything. Besides feeling great about myself, the Veterans Administration was paying me about $700 per month to go to school. That really helped our family situation and also made me happy.

After dinner on Tuesdays and Thursdays, I sat right down to do my homework. My kids thought that was neat and I think they did more homework too. The hardest class I had was the one I took because I thought it would be easy—typing. I had so much homework with typing that I just barely got it done every night.

I maintained a four point average. I just couldn't get enough.

When it was time to sign up for the next semester, I signed up for four more classes. I can't remember what I took when but I did take several psychology classes, and even had to volunteer in the state hospital one semester. That was an education in itself. I took American government and really loved it. I thought that strange because I had hated government in high school. I took several literature classes, English classes and several drawing classes. I started with basic drawing and ended up in figure drawing where all our models were nude—both male and female. Drawing the human body was a challenge. I really loved creative writing even though I balked at writing poetry. Another great class was the acting class I took. We were doing the *Wizard of Oz* for some elementary school during our class hour. I was cast as the Wicked Witch of the West. I loved it, but on the actual play day and in order to be ready in time, I had to put my make up on prior to my Psychology class. It felt silly sitting in class with my ugly witch face (big nose, warts and all) while taking a psychology test.

In order to get my two years in, I also had to go full time in the summer but that wasn't hard because a full load in the summer was only eight credit hours or two classes. I always had one regular class with an easy one like physical fitness or canoeing. I was scheduled to take World Civilizations in the summer of 75, but complications from a hysterectomy made me drop that class. Instead of being in the hospital for one day, I ended up being in for weeks.

I was proud to be on the dean's list and my kids were proud too. I was physically fit and felt great. I was also active in the PTA at the elementary school. But all good things must come to an end and they did when the benefits of the GI bill ended for me. It was a wonderful two years and I learned a lot.

George

One of the semesters in college in 1976, I took an advanced psychology class that required that we work two hours a week for the whole semester at Pontiac State Hospital which was a hospital for the insane. I did not look forward to that at all. After all I had been in a mental health ward at Pontiac General Hospital for 45 days after trying to commit suicide some years before and I didn't like the zombies that we all became. The State Hospital was scary looking just by its foreboding looks from the outside and I didn't like the thought of even driving into the parking lot there.

Pontiac State Hospital was on the corner of Telegraph and Eliz-

abeth Lake Road in Pontiac. I had passed it many times. For one thing it was right across the street from the Pontiac Mall and whenever I went to work at Pontiac General Hospital I had to turn on Elizabeth Lake Road to go to the general hospital. Even though it was set back from the road, the large collection of Victorian buildings was spooky. Built in 1878, the name had changed several times.

I summoned the courage to drive to the hospital and park then cautiously walked up to the main door. Just after I entered I found myself in a huge cold room with marble floors. It was strangely quiet and almost ghostly. There were a few offices off of the main area and I found the volunteer office easily. I forget the coordinator's name but she told me that I would be working with the patients during craft time and gave me a little information about what I would do.

I was taken to the basement which was dungeon-like. It was very cold, gray and empty of patients for the moment. I learned that I would be working mainly with a patient named George.

When the small group arrived for their craft time, I was pleasantly surprised that they didn't look like the zombies I had expected. They were normal looking elderly men. I'd guess they were in their mid-50s. George wanted to work with clay so we started molding and talking. He seemed so nice that right away, I felt at ease. George did most of the talking. He told me that he was a spy during World War II and had been with Glenn Miller just before his plane crashed. He went into great detail and I listened intently because I was such a fan of Glenn Miller. After about a half hour of this, the supervisor called me over and told me that when George started talking like that, I had to tell him that it wasn't true and encourage him to come back to reality. I felt sad because I liked listening to his story. So when he started again on some fantastic tale, I would say to him, "George you know that isn't true. Let's just talk about today and what we are doing." He would be okay with that for a while then suddenly and quite innocently he would almost suck me into another story. But I caught on easily.

I liked George and enjoyed my two hours a week there. On my last day as I was preparing him for my going away, he looked straight at me and said, "You ought to be in movies." I was flattered and thanked him, then he said, "I know Cecil B. Demille and I can get you in the movies easily." I knew he had gotten me again, but since it was my last day, I let him ramble on. We only had another minute or two together anyway. I chuckled all the way home.

The $100,000 Problem

I went on a diet once where I was really counting calories. Yes, it was a pain but I worked hard at it. I gave up any sweets even though I baked desserts for my family all the time. I even gave up the sugar and cream that I had used in my coffee. I felt great and I looked good.

One day Glenda brought home a $100,000 candy bar and told me that I just had to try it. I wasn't interested and put the candy bar on the top of the refrigerator. I didn't even think about it again until several weeks later when Glenda noticed that I hadn't eaten it. She broke a piece off and made me taste it. I did and it was good, but that was as far as I was going to go. I stayed off sweets for a long time.

In the fall of 1975 while attending Oakland Community College full time on the GI Bill. I was also going to Vic Tanny's health spa and still avoiding sweets. But I had an English class that was terrible. I like English but this class was the pits. And I had to spend an hour in a lab, speed reading after class. To get to the lab, I had to go through the book store. One day when I was dreading the lab even worse than before and as I was going through the bookstore, I noticed a bunch of $100,000 candy bars on the counter. I bought one and took it with me to the lab. Eating that delicious candy bar full of caramel and chocolate made lab tolerable.

So for the whole semester every time I went to the lab, I had a candy bar. Then I got used to eating a brownie or anything else sweet. I was like an alcoholic going off the wagon—no control.

Poetry

Written for a Creative Writing Class in 76

Time

The clock is ticking your whole life away
And never will you have this moment again.
Yet you let time pass you by like the birds
In flight, and say that tomorrow will be
A better day. But when this moment melts
Away, it cannot be recaptured. Live
This moment, love this minute, don't deny
This instant. This is the only moment you
Can be sure of. So grasp this minute, caress
It, live it. Tomorrow may be too late.

Total Woman

The advocates of Total Women
say you should be ready
at a moments notice
pamper and baby him
no matter what your day was like.

Greet him at the door when he comes home
be fresh and feminine
in a thin negligee
make sure you're alluring
no matter what your day was like.

A gourmet dinner must be prepared
you'll eat by candlelight
then you must seduce him
love him passionately
no matter what your day was like.

The Weed

My life is controlled
by a small white paper cylinder
stuffed with tobacco.
there's hardly anything
I can do without
needing that pacifier.

I hate cigarettes
their greasy film covers all things
windows and furniture
and especially me.
sure I'll quit sometime-
when I'm dead.

Ice Storm

When the giant transformer
                    sizzled and died
It took our house to the grave also.

The icy silence was everywhere
As cold and motionless as a dead body
                    in the morgue.

Too Long

You say you must fix that door, but
not today. When the sun shines brightly
and warms your bones
you say that'll be a better day.
So when the sun beams dance
as if at play,
you decide to wait for a cloudier day.
It's been this way
for many suns and clouds
and moons and stars
and rain and snow.
Soon there'll be no door to fix
it will have rotted from its hinges
and the same for me for
I also have been ignored
too long.

P.S. 2010: This poem really epitomizes my marital life at that time. Except for a brief good period, we were nearing the end and did divorce four years after this.

The next poem is pretty much how it was then also.

Family Dinner

It's so much fun to be a mother and wife
But who said life was to be fair.

It never fails–that if I spend hours
like a gourmet chef
Slicing, stirring, chopping and baking
A delectable dinner for my family.

Then one child blows in through the door
I hear him shout–"Ma, gotta go
I'll grab a sandwich on the run."
That's ok–there'll still be four for dinner.

But another strolls in and announces
"I ate hamburgers at Martys"
Three out of five still ain't bad.
Until another phones to say
"I'm working late. I'll eat here."

Oh well now's my chance
For a quiet dinner for two
Just Bob and I by candlelight.

As he enters the room he squints and says
"What's wrong–blow a fuse?"
Then he turns on the light.

He sees what's for dinner
"Ate that for lunch today
mind if I eat the cold chicken?"
No I don't mind
I like eating
Alone.

Music-Music-Music

My father loved music and wanted all of us kids to have the opportunity to play a musical instrument. Early on in that house in Detroit, I had that wonderful player piano that eventually got accidentally built into our house at Maceday Lake. But when we moved to Drayton Plains, he made sure I had another piano. Even though it wasn't a player piano, it was nice to have.

Dad had played a French horn in high school and I remember a picture of him with his horn. He never was very good, but he kept trying. Poor Dad would have played more but Mom never let him. I mean if he started to practice, she would say, "Don't you have something you should be doing?" Then she would rattle off all the things that he should be doing. She couldn't sit and relax so she thought that no one else should either.

When my brother was old enough, Dad bought him a clarinet. I wanted one too so Dad got one for me. I never did learn to play it very well and gave it up for the piano. My brother did very well with the clarinet and added a couple of saxophones. Then he started a band, *The Blue Notes*. It was a big band of high school kids and they played the big band stuff from the 40's which was my Dad's favorite. My brother even rented a hall by the high school, remodeled it and made it into a teen night club. It was called the *Blue Note Teen Club*. His band played for all the dances. They played the Glen Miller style of music and there were lots who would come to dance. This all took place while my brother was still in high school and Dad was in his glory.

When I came home from the Air Force and got married, the piano stayed at Mom and Dad's place but in the early 60's after Al left, I moved the piano to Lapeer and from there to the two houses in Drayton Plains. Glenda and I took lessons for a while but as hard as I tried, I just didn't like reading music. I wanted to play easier and sound better. It seemed like an organ would be better than a piano.

Meanwhile, my father gave Mark his first musical instrument—a trumpet. It was a real one even though Mark was only two years old. Mark dragged it around but never appreciated it. It got beat up which to me was a waste. When Mark was in the fifth grade he wanted to join the band and found one of my brother's saxophones in Mom's house and started playing that. He took lessons in school and played beautifully.

About that time, Mom and Dad divorced and Dad moved to California so my sisters didn't get musical instruments. That was sad. Beth Ann did pick up the clarinet that was in the house and played in high school and college marching bands.

Back to the piano: It was in the basement of our house in Drayton Plains. In about 1973 or 74, I bought an organ. It was a small Hammond without pedals and only one keyboard. I got bored with it right away. It was too easy. Grinnell's music store where I bought the organ had a great deal and offered that if you traded up within 30 days of buying an organ, they would give you full credit towards the next one. I traded up five times and finally fell in love with the Hammond B 3 that I ended up with. Then I added a huge external Leslie speaker which really gave the organ a special sound.

I took lessons from a great organist and learned how to play with chords. It was so much fun and I was happy that I could play popular music easily and sound pretty good.

I put the organ in the dining room against the wall that was between the living and dining room. But early on I realized that playing the organ in the evening was out of the question; the family was watching TV. I got the bright idea to buy a set of drums and found a good used set. I put the drum set in the dining room behind the organ and something magical happened. Whenever I sat down to play (even in the evening) everyone made a mad dash for the drums. First one there got to accompany me first. It was such fun. I had also purchased maracas, a bongo drum, a tambourine and set of spoons so everyone could play something. And whenever my father was in town he would bring his horn and sit in with us. Mark, of course, had his saxophone and I loved playing with him. He was such a natural talent.

Early on Mark, earned top honors at the state solo competitions for high school musicians. I could work for days trying to play a song and Mark would sit down at the organ and play it beautifully without any music. I envied his ear and talent.

Robert and Jim were also great musically. Robert started out with a trumpet, but ended up with a French horn. Jim started with a baritone horn and ended up with a tuba. Both were excellent and always got the top honors at solo competitions. The thing I liked best about Jim's tuba though was I could always pick his playing out in a band concert. It was harder to pick out the individual sax or horn because there was more than one of them.

Top :
Glenda on the drums.

Right:
Mark's senior picture.

Left:
Robert's
senior
portrait.

Below:
Jim and
Robert in the
Haslett
Marching

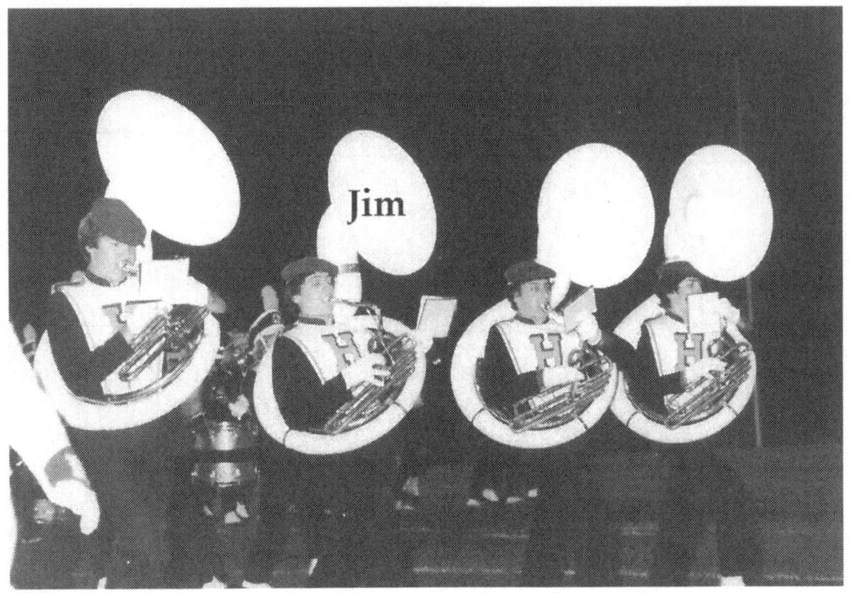

Jim and the tubas at Haslett High School.

Pictured here is Jim in the 5th grade with his baritone horn which was almost bigger than he was. And he complained every day that he had to carry it to school but he did it.

The Best Laid Plans...

In 1975, I was still taking classes at Oakland Community College. Because I was going to college on the GI bill, I had to take a full load and often I made one class easy like I did in the spring of that year. That easy class was physical fitness and no matter what I did, I had a bladder problem. I would make sure I was empty before we would do our exercises but the jumping jacks would really get me. I went to the doctor to see what could be done.

Doctor Warner said that I needed bladder repair and with my tipped uterus (always a problem) he suggested that they do a hysterectomy at the same time. It was fine with me. My tubes had been tied nine years before and I didn't care if I had periods or not. So the surgery was scheduled for the Monday after Glenda's graduation open house. I do not remember the date but it was probably in May of that year. The doctor had said that it would be a simple procedure (done vaginally) and I would be home the next day.

When I planned Glenda's open house I forgot one minor detail. I had to check into the hospital late in the afternoon of the day before surgery which was the day of her open house. I told my family that I would be disappearing from the party and not to make a big deal out of it. I had parked the car at a neighbor's house behind our house and already had my suitcase in the car. I didn't want to upset the party. I also told Bob and my family not to bother to come to the hospital that night, for the surgery or after and I would be fine. I had already registered for the summer class and took my "World Civilization" text book with me. I would be missing the first two classes and wanted to be on target.

On that Monday, I had surgery and all night I kept thinking that I was drowning. I told the nurses that I knew I was drowning. No one paid any attention to me. In the morning, I called Bob from my bedside phone and told him to call the doctor and tell him that something was wrong. Finally the doctor came and discovered that I had been hemorrhaging internally all night and I had lost at least two pints of blood. Right away they got me ready for surgery. This time they had to do the fixing through the abdomen. Goody! I would have a scar on top of scars. In the operating room they fixed the problem but before they took me off the table, they noticed that I was bleeding vaginally. More repairs. Then I got pneumonia and a bladder infection. I was in the hospital for about 10 days and missed my class.

I had lost 20 pounds and only weighed 109 pounds—the lowest in my life. Slowly I recovered at home and I don't remember how it came about, but we planned a vacation. Glenda and Mark were working so it would be just Bob and I and the two young boys, Robert and Jim. We planned a vacation to please each of us—Disneyland for the boys, the Grand Canyon for me and Vegas for Bob. It was a most wonderful vacation. We flew to California, rented a car and drove to Arizona on the way to Vegas then drove back to California. We had only had two other vacations in our whole married life so this was a treat.

Disneyland and California were fun, but I really fell in love with the Grand Canyon. We only had one night and part of one day, but we did the most exciting thing there. When we checked into the lodge, we noticed a sign about an early morning horseback ride with breakfast. We signed up. We were the only ones in the group besides the guide who was a real cowboy. He told us that he rode his horse from southern Arizona all the way up to the Canyon without once crossing private property. He carried everything he owned in his bedroll. That was neat.

It was quite brisk when we ventured outside that morning but the sun was up and promised a warm day. It was late August but we were at over 7,000 feet in elevation. We rode for about half an hour then at 7:30 a.m. we rode into a big clearing where Clarence, the chuck wagon cook, had our breakfast ready. We each picked a log to sit on and ate so much that no one was even the slightest hungry until after 7 p.m. that night. Clarence had fixed, eggs, bacon, ham, hash browns, biscuits, gravy and toast, and we were encouraged to eat all we wanted. Oh, there was hot chocolate and coffee too.

We had fun in Vegas too; the whole vacation was terrific.

While I was sick and recovering, Bob's brother and wife (Allen and Marilyn) who lived in Long Island, New York, wanted to help by keeping Robert and Jim for a while. I guess Bob flew them out and back. I don't remember. What I do remember is that the boys thought it was neat that they were at both oceans in one summer. I never saw Jaws but I think the boys did while they were in New York. That scared them from swimming in the ocean.

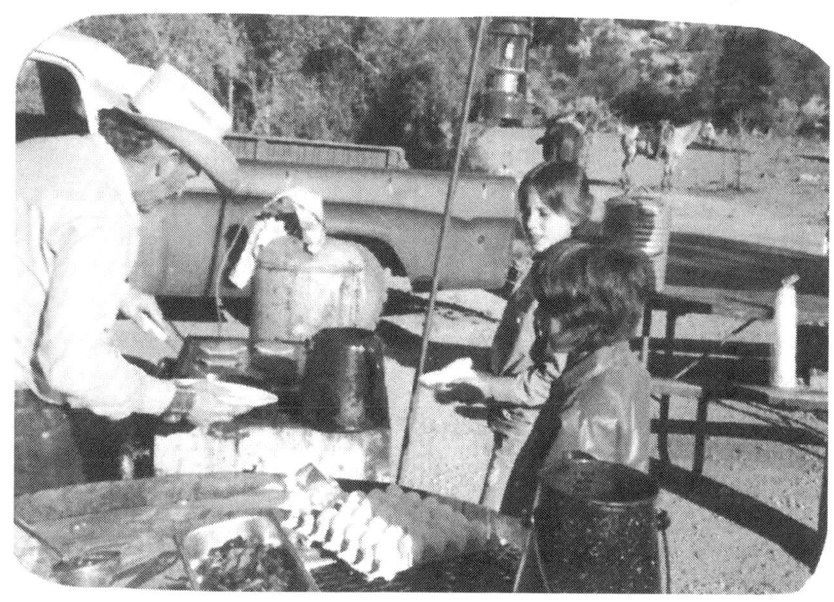

Robert and Jim at the Canyon
(our horse back ride)

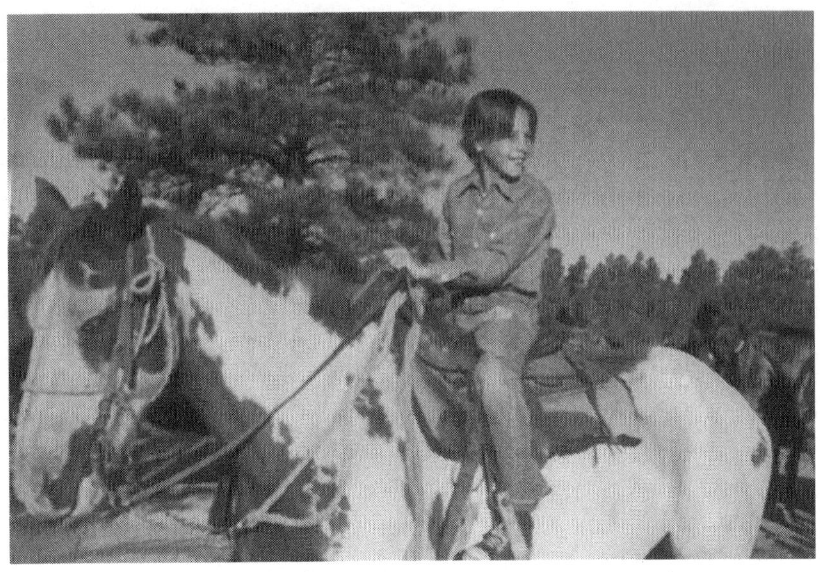

The kids at the Grand Canyon and with Bob at the ocean in California.

Mini Fun

My son Robert's Godfather, Clayton Roth, was my brother's best friend when he was in high school. He and his wife had a little motorhome and had invited us to join them for a trip up north in Michigan to go canoeing.

Bob and I had been canoeing once and it wasn't fun. We had gone with our neighbors, Duane and Kay, and canoed the Pine River in the spring of the year. Neither Bob or I had ever canoed before and we made a lot of mistakes. We ended up overturned in the icy cold river many times that day. It was scary.

We decided we would go with Clayton and Karen because the river we were going on wasn't as wild as the Pine River. The thing that was most fun was riding up in their Mini Midas motorhome. That was a great way to travel. It was a sunny bright day and we thoroughly enjoyed it especially because Clayton was a knowledgeable athletic guy and he gave us some hints that helped us canoe better.

I think we went twice with them in their motorhome and one day, he called and asked if I would be interested in buying the motorhome. They were going to get a boat or something else. I jumped at the chance. I don't remember the price but I was able to afford it.

Our first camping trip was to Washington, DC, but the whole family did not get to go. I think it was just Robert and Jim and I especially remember that while we were in the Washington Monument I noticed that Robert had a lot of red itchy spots on his arms. Yep, it was chicken pox; he was just breaking out with it. We felt sorry for all those that we accidentally infected.

We really had fun camping and even though Bob had never wanted to camp, it was different in a motorhome. We had all the comforts of home, beds, toilet, sink, stove and refrigerator.

In the 70s camping was really fun because no one had their computers or televisions with them. Everyone was out to enjoy the out of doors and the people camped next to them. Kids loved it and found many friends at each new campground.

Somewhere around 1974-76 we decided to plan a big canoe trip for adults and we would use the motorhome to transport the food, beverages and wood for cooking. We would also sleep in the motorhome while everyone else would bring tents.

We picked the Pine River in the spring which meant it would be wild. And we reserved a group campsite at a primitive campground (no hookups for the motorhome) near the starting point for the canoe trip. If I remember right we had about nine couples for the first trip.

I did all the planning and shopping. Since we wouldn't get up there until late on Friday night, we planned to have hamburgers, beans and chips. For Saturday morning, I planned scrambled eggs and bacon, plus coffee and juice. For the canoe trip, I purchased lunch meats, cheese and bread. For Saturday's dinner, I bought steak and potatoes which would be baked and Sunday's breakfast would be pancakes and sausage. It was fun going to the grocery store to buy everything. We also carried up firewood because everything we were cooking was to be cooked over an open wood fire. Oh it was fun and I was in my glory. I loved organizing everything and cooking.

Art and Jeanne Saunders were both active in Cub and Boy Scouts with us and Art was an inventive kind of guy. Knowing we would need hot water for our sponge baths and for washing pots and pans, he took an old water heater and cut it in half and rigged it so copper tubing went from the bottom on the tank and coiled around under the fire then up to the top of the tank. We filled the tank with cold water and by gravity the water would run under the fire and get hot. Then because it got hot, it would move up to the top. In a short period of time, we had a tank full of nice hot water and it stayed hot as long as we had a fire. All we had to do was dip a pan in the top of the tank and take out what we wanted. It was such hot water that we had to mix it with cold so we could put our hands in. It was a fun weekend and it grew. The last time we did it, we had 15 couples.

One time our motorhome came in real handy when we had a horrible ice storm. Because the house had no electricity, we had no heat and I couldn't cook on our electric stove. We could use the bathroom because we had city water and a gas hot water heater. The motorhome had a furnace and a gas stove so I could fix meals. We all slept in the freezing house then went out to the motorhome to get warm. I think we were without power for at least a week and it was bitter cold. We managed just fine. I was in college then and I remember doing homework in the Mini.

In August of 1976, I was mad at Bob and wanted to get away all by myself. I wanted to go anywhere but thought that maybe I could talk Mom into going with Robert, Jim and I. The only way I could get her to go anywhere was to suggest we go to Texas and see my brother, Don. So we did just that. We took our time stopping in Kentucky and other places along the way. We took local roads rather than freeways and had a god time. We visited a horse farm, a plantation, went to New Orleans and I loved the whole trip.

The boys had been watching the Olympics and were especially intrigued with platform diving before we left. They thought jumping off of the big platforms looked like fun. I tried to tell them that once they were up that high, it wouldn't be easy. They didn't believe me so on the trip, I kept looking for a campground which might have an Olympic pool and diving boards. Sure enough I found one in Decatur, Alabama, and we camped there. They climbed up the big platform, then climbed back down. But I talked them into going back up and just jumping. Jim was 10 and Robert was 11 and they finally made it off the platform. No way would I ever do that.

We did a lot of camping at two nearby campgrounds in Holly and took it to Cedar Point, an amusement park in Ohio at least once. And I remember that we used it to take Mark to drum major camp in Indiana, and/or band camp and when he left for the Air Force we drove him to Detroit in the Midas. Steely Dan was playing on the eight track player and I cried all the way home.

Dirty Trick

Because of things I was learning from my self-help books, I had been petitioning for the family to go without TV for a month. My biggest obstacle was my husband, Bob. He liked football and I guess that it was probably fall when I first suggested the ban. Every time I mentioned it he said, "No."

I seldom actually watched TV. I sat in the living room with the family, but I usually had my nose in one of the books that were on the end table by my chair. I would hear bits and pieces of shows and maybe paid more attention to some of the variety shows like *Laugh In* or *The Carol Burnett Show.* I really didn't like the cops and robbers shows but preferred public television or things that were educational. I had seen commercials for *Roots* which was to air on January 23, 1977. I mentioned to the family that it would be a good show because it was a true story and I was looking forward to watching it.

It debuted at 9 p.m. and five minutes to nine, my husband turned to me and said, "I think that your idea of no TV for a month is good and we ought to start it right now." I wanted to kill him or at least punch him out. Now that the football season had ended with the Super Bowl on January 9 that year, he could give up TV for a month. But I really couldn't say a word. Everyone had heard me plead for no TV for a long time so I went along with it even though that was the only show I really wanted to see. In our bedroom later, I told Bob how very mean he was and all he said was that he would buy me the book which he did. I think I finally saw the series many years later.

We played games and did other activities for that month and it was really fun. The only time anyone could watch TV was when Bob and I were out and we allowed them to watch public TV. I can't remember how we controlled that. Maybe we took the turner knob off the TV and hid all the pliers in the house. I don't know. What I do know is that the kids were more than happy to let us go out so they could watch something.

After the month was up, we decided that we would go through the TV guide and highlight programs the kids could watch. We picked comedy and educational programs and that worked out fine. After the two months were over, it was back to normal. But I remember those months fondly.

Fond Memories From the 70s

Besides the things I have written so far there are more fun memories from those days in Drayton Plains.

Mom and Dad were divorced in the mid 60's but Mom was doing great in her business and she had a swimming pool built in her back yard. That was always a fun place to spend a week-end day in the summer. Everyone would be there and Mom loved having the family around. She had it built for that very reason.

I got very active in the Drayton Plains Elementary School PTA and bingo. In fact, I ran the bingo for one year and enjoyed that. The high-light of that year was when I suggested that we who worked the bingo and all from the school put on a variety show and invite the bingo patrons to come. We called it the Fools Follies and I produced and directed it. The admission price was only ten cents and it was like a Vaudeville show.

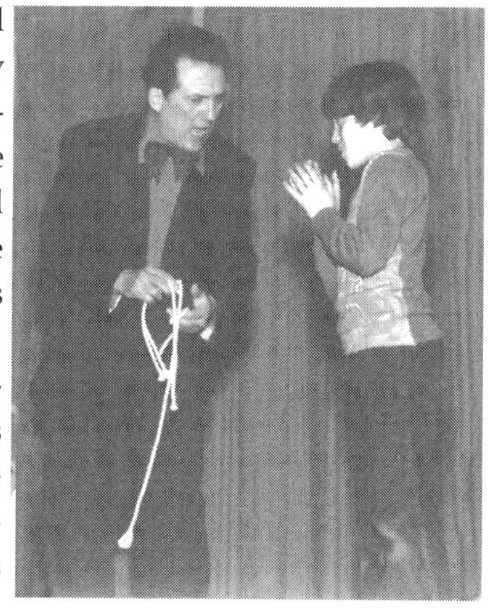

We had such great talent between the teachers and parents that it was the best show I have ever done. Robert and I pantomimed to Barbra Streisand's

Blind Date. Bob was a funny magician and was real good. Bob even sang with three other guys but he got to laughing so hard that he ruined the song. It was all in fun.

Christmas was always fun. I would bake cookies and make fudge for weeks before the holiday started. I liked to give a little box of cookies, fudge or divinity to teachers and neighbors. I made the following cookies: cherry coconut drops, chocolate snowballs, pressed, frosted cut out, noel nut balls, and more. I would spend whole days just making cookies and candy.

If Dad was in town, he and his wife, Frankie, would come over a day or two before Christmas for the evening and we would exchange gifts. Because my Mother and Dad didn't get along at all, my sisters would come to our house to visit with Dad.

On Christmas morning, Clayton (Robert's Godfather) and Karen would come over early and have breakfast with us. After they left, my Mom and my sisters would come over for dinner. Bob always cooked the turkey and dressing.

My neighbor had a garden and it looked like fun so I looked for a place to have one. We had half of a lot on the north side of the garage that I thought would work but there was an apple tree right in the middle of the section. We never used that part of the yard so I had the tree cut down. I only used a small section the first year and Bob prepared the soil buy using a rented garden tiller.

What a thrill it was to see everything growing so nicely. We didn't have rabbits or other critters so there were no big problems. Early every morning I would go out and walk the rows admiring all that was growing. We had beans (yellow and green), beets, radishes, carrots, corn, melons, peppers (two kinds), cucumbers, onions and tomatoes. I read the seed magazines and learned what to plant where. For example, I planted melons in the corn and they did fine there.

The second year I doubled the size of the garden and it was more wonderful. My corn was seven feet tall before it fully tasseled out. I even bought ladybugs and praying mantis so I didn't have to use any insecticide. I sure did a lot of canning and freezing of the wonderful vegetables.

Robert and Jim were in cub scouts and I was their den mother. It was great fun once a week planning stuff for the kids to do. Bob was also active in the pack and later when Robert went into the Webelos. I always felt bad that I was still working when it could have been Mark's turn to be a scout. He didn't have the same opportunities that Robert and Jim did. The younger children in a family often get more than the older ones. My sisters had more opportunities and so did Ron's. It is just a fact of life, but I still felt bad.

Flapping Wings

In 1973, I began noticing that Glenda and Mark were growing up. Glenda was in high school and working. She talked of travel when she graduated but wanted to keep working with her Grandmother at the studio. Unlike me, she loved working there and being with her Grandma. Mark was very active with music and the band and when he went away to band camp I missed him. I hated to think of them leaving home in a few years.

Glenda was in her sophomore year in high school and liked some of the exchange students in school. She really enjoyed being around them. They were often at our house too. I remember Yuko from Japan and Anikka from Finland. One day Glenda asked, "If I can save enough money to go to Japan or Finland will you let me go?" Bob and I talked about it and decided to agree to her going if she saved enough money. I didn't really think it would be possible and honestly thought that I would never have to deal with it.

In 1974 (Glenda's junior year), she had enough money to go to Finland. So she made her plans to go for the summer and she would be staying with Anikka's family. We corresponded with them and got her ready to leave.

I remember going to the airport. She was so excited about the trip and I was missing her before she even got on the plane. Back then you could watch your loved ones board the plane and stay and wave goodbye to the plane as it taxied away from the gate. I cried so hard when she got on that plane and for days after that I thought I could never have any tears left for any other event. I had to face the reality that soon she would be leaving home for good.

She was such a fantastic daughter. She never gave us a moment's problem and we were proud of her, but letting your first bird fly is tough. At least it was for me. She wrote letters often and was having a great time. As the summer wore on, I went on with the rest of the family and looked forward to her coming home.

I was so excited the day we went to pick her up, but when she got off the plane, she was crying. She didn't want to come home. She said, "When I got to the airport in Helsinki and heard English, I started crying and I can't stop." You see, Glenda had fallen in love while in Finland. She not only fell in love with Erkki Pekka Paunonen, but fell in love with Finland.

She was like a love sick puppy for days and weeks. One Christmas we had gotten her her own telephone in her bedroom. She had to pay for the long distance calls and at first there were many.

Bob was not happy. He definitely did not want her to be in love with someone that could possibly take her far, far away. I kept telling him to say nothing. "If you keep protesting, you will make her go to him. Just listen to her and support her. This affair will dwindle and die." And that is exactly what happened. The calls dwindled down to a few, then none. We were pleased that she appeared happy while getting involved in her senior year in school and still working at the studio.

Glenda graduated and although she remembers that she was accepted into a college, I don't remember that. She continued to work at the studio and truly felt that Grandma intended for her to run the studio someday since no one else in the family was interested in the business.

But in the spring/early summer in 1976, my sister Beth Ann, dropped out of college and wanted to work in the studio. Suddenly Glenda was not the top dog any more, the miracle baby was. So she made other plans.

She joined the Air Force with a departure date of late summer and planned a three week camping trip with her girlfriend for the time just before she was supposed to go off to basic training.

Just before she left on her trip, Glenda got a phone call from Pekka saying that he was coming to the United States to study restaurant management in St. Louis, Missouri, and he wanted to stop by on his way to school. He did and that was all it took to start the romance again. Glenda did go camping to the Smokey Mountains as planned but after a very short stay, the girls drove to St. Louis and spent the rest of their time there.

Glenda was so torn when she came home. She wanted the Air Force, but she was afraid that Pekka would have to go back to Finland and she would never see him again. She vacillated all night and nearly talked my ear off. I couldn't tell her what to do, but I did think that the Air Force wouldn't let her out. After all, she had already been sworn in. By morning she had made her decision. She was moving to St. Louis and the Air Force did let her go. In fact they gave her an honorable discharge which she framed and it hangs in her business today.

She completely emptied her room and I couldn't go into it for weeks. I cried every time I went into the room. It echoed in its emptiness. My heart was broken. The boys were chomping at the bit for me to make the room ready for them. They had been in bunk beds and were anxious to each have their own room. It took me at least three weeks to be able to get that room ready.

A few months later she called or wrote and said she and Pekka were getting married and wanted the wedding to be on December 22 (her birthday) at my sister, Bunnie's house in Farmington Hills. It would be a small wedding and she and I planned it via the telephone and mail.

The wedding was very nice and not at all expensive. She borrowed a wedding dress and my sisters and I did most of the food. There were only about 30 of our closest friends and family at the wedding. Glenda and Pekka went back to St. Louis.

Six months after the wedding (June of 1977), Pekka and Glenda announced that they were moving to Finland. Bob was right to have worried in the first place and I was so sad at losing her but I was glad she was happy.

My first bird had completely left the nest and I realized that the most difficult part of motherhood was letting go. I guess I did a good job as a mother in raising her to be independent but losing her to another person and country was very hard. I missed her terribly and at the same time hated the side effects of motherhood. It just was not fair.

A side note: Notice my hair got curly. Mark had gotten an Afro permanent and it looked so terrific on him. I loved it because it looked so touchable. At the same time I was tired of going to the beauty shop regularly and hated doing my own hair. So I got an afro in the fall of 1976. It was so wonderful and easy to take care of. Plus I liked the look. Sadly as soon as I got my perm, Mark straightened his hair. Mine is still curly. I get a perm every 4 or 5 months and can't even think of changing my style. It was and is liberating.

Ladybugs

After having a very successful garden the first year, I decided to be a better farmer by trying to be organic although that is not what it was called back then.

The garden was growing nicely with the help of a compost pile next to the garage. I had noticed a few aphids in the garden and wanted to get rid of them without pesticides so I browsed the seed catalogs to see if they had any gentle solutions. They did. Ladybugs and praying mantis were for sale. I promptly ordered both.

I was very excited the day by good bugs arrived. The mantis came in a tiny hive. I was told where to place it and that they would hatch and get to work in due time. The ladybugs came in a small box which was about four inches square. The instructions were to wait until dusk then open the box a tiny bit in one corner and shake the bugs out into the garden. I can't remember but I think I had ordered 1,500 of them.

They were packaged with wood shavings and even though I shook for quite a while, I wasn't sure they were all out. I left the box in the garden, figuring they would all get out eventually and went inside to watch the evening TV shows. While sitting in the living room, I swore there were bugs crawling all over me, but I put it to imagination and tried to concentrate on the show. But I kept feeling like bugs were crawling so I jumped up to run to my bedroom. Darn, the curtains hadn't been pulled. I didn't want to take time to close them, so I went into the closet, turned on the light and closed the door. This wasn't a walk-in closet; it was very small. But I pulled down my pants and sure enough, my legs were covered with lady bugs. I screamed through the door for someone to come to carry the bugs out to the garden. They did and the garden prospered minus the bad bugs.

Fascinating Womanhood

Through the ups and downs of our marriage, I always tried to learn how to be a better wife. In most marriages there are good and bad times. Ours was no different. My nervous breakdown and lack of self-confidence was one of those bad times. Bob's drinking had progressed. I remember the night strangers brought him home. They found him passed out and hanging out of the driver's side of his car on the side of the road at 5: 30 in the evening. By checking his wallet they found out where he lived. One guy drove Bob home while the other followed. When the doorbell rang I was surprised by the stranger but not by the circumstances. That time was the worst. They got him in the front door with great difficulty. He was dead drunk. I let him lay half in the foyer and half in the living room the whole evening. We just stepped over him as we needed to.

Bob got sober after he went to work in the photographic department at K-Mart. Those were better years, but the same old problem was there. We didn't make love and he wasn't very loving. I needed someone to cuddle with and he wouldn't let me be close to him in bed or in conversation. With the help of many self -help books and articles from magazines, I had tried everything. Then I heard of *Fascinating Womanhood*.

My neighbor, Judy Benscoter, told me about it. Judy and I graduated from high school together and her husband was big in Boy Scouts. We also attended the same Lutheran church. We signed up to attend classes at a local community church. We got our book and workbook and started to learn how to be subservient. The promise was that our husbands would love us more.

Derived from a set of booklets published in the 1920s and 1930s by the Psychological Press, the book seeks to help traditionally-minded women to make their marriages "a lifelong love affair." According to *Time Magazine,* Mrs. Andelin wrote *Fascinating Womanhood* when "she felt her own marriage going sour." The book's self-published edition sold over 400,000 copies, and since being published by Random House, the book has sold an additional 1.6 million-plus copies. The book serves as a touchstone for those of the anti-feminist persuasion as well as those seeking to live in a system based on patriarchy.

The first thing we were told to do was sit down with our husbands and tell them sincerely that we have made a serious mistake by trying to take charge of our lives and his life. I added, "From now on you are the leader of this family and I trust in any decisions you make. My job is to make this home as comfortable and pleasant as possible and I promise to do my best."

We were told to organize the house and make sure it was clean and tidy when our men came home. I did that or at least I tried to. I started boxing up things in the basement but ran out of room to store them neatly. My Mother had a pull down stairway to her attic storage and I thought that if I had something like that, I could get rid of the boxes. I only mentioned it and one night a few weeks later, when I came home from bingo (I was the bingo chairman for our elementary school bingo game), the stairway was in. He had his friend Art Saunders help. "Wow," I thought. No way would he have cared before.

We were told to have dinner on the table shortly after our husbands came home. Now that Bob was working at K-Mart that was easy because he was always home at five. I also made sure I was bathed and dressed for him when he came home and that the kids had their things picked up and put away.

Another thing we were told was that we should keep our bodies fit. I was jogging in the morning but my shoes weren't good. My feet hurt. I slightly mentioned this to Bob and in a couple of days, he had purchased a nice pair of good running shoes for me. Double Wow!

We had to be careful not to nag about anything. An example was if the roof was leaking simply put a bucket under the leak and keep the bucket emptied. Nope, we couldn't say a word. He had eyes; he could see what needed to be done and if he chose not to do anything about it that was okay. As I type this all now and realize how well I played the game, I shake my head in wonder. I must have been desperate because I am one who had burned her bra long before.

But I did see a change. One evening stands out in my memory. Bob came home as usual, I was dressed nicely, dinner was being kept warm and the table was set. He kissed me passionately in the kitchen then dragged me to the bedroom but on his way past the living room, he told the kids to keep watching TV for a while. We made mad passionate love.

It was then that I realized that Bob could only love me like I wanted to be loved when I was weak or appeared weak. Suddenly I remembered coming home from the hospital once after some surgery and as soon as we got home he wanted to make love. Hmm, that was something to think about. The trouble was I was basically a strong person. He had made me strong when he first left me. But I continued to try to be a Fascinating Woman.

One day it all came back to bite me, bad. For all our years of marriage I had told him that if he ever became a portrait photographer and wanted his own studio, I would divorce him. I didn't care that he was a commercial photographer which he had been for a number of years. Working with K-Mart was no problem. He took all of the pictures for the advertising pages in the newspaper. But I had hated Mom and Dad's business and how it affected our family and never wanted that for us.

In May of 1977, Bob came home from work and announced that he had quit his job and was going to open his own studio. My world caved in. "What?" I thought. "How could you do this to me?" But I didn't say it, at least not right away. Yes, I had given him permission to make all the major decisions, but he knew how I felt about the studio. I grew up in one and didn't want what happened to my Mom and Dad to happen to us. Mom and Dad fought constantly in the studio and I knew Bob and I would be at each other's throats too. Besides, he had had a steady job and now we would be pinching pennies. We didn't have anything saved. I thought he was being irresponsible. The other thing I thought about was I would be expected to help in the studio and that would be against Fascinating Womanhood. I said to myself, "Screw Fascinating Womanhood."

It's a Fine Time to Leave Me Lucille

Even though I felt that *Fascinating Womanhood* betrayed me, I tried to keep up the persona. We went driving around looking for a location for his studio. He liked the area of Ortonville which was just a little north of Mother's studio. I didn't think that was nice to be a competitor to her, but he thought there was enough business up there.

There was an old mall there that was basically empty. That wouldn't do as far as I was concerned. The main street of Ortonville was only two blocks long. There was no grocery store in town just a few little businesses that didn't look very prosperous. There was a bar, feed store, farm implement business which was going out of business, a hardware store, library and a few other stores. The biggest part of the town was the town offices, library and fire department. I noticed a dry cleaner that Friday. I said, "That's funny, a dry cleaners would not be closed on a Friday." He didn't think it was strange but I got him to stop the car so I could go look in the window. There were very few clothes hanging on racks and not much else. There was no sign stating their hours or if they were out of business or whatever. I pushed Bob to check around to see what was going on.

The building was for sale. Wow, we didn't want to buy a building. We only wanted a place to rent. But we ended up buying the building which was an old grange hall building without a proper bathroom. It had a chemical toilet (outhouse) inside located in the rear of the building.

Bob got all excited about fixing up the building. He had to raise the ceilings and build a dressing room and a few other things. I had to walk away. I packed the motorhome and left my family. I took my typewriter and went to a nearby campground. I simply wanted to be alone. I had been working on a project with the elementary school and I wanted to write some articles about education from a parent's point of view. As I was working, I had the radio on and it seemed that at least five times a day or more, Kenny Rodgers was singing "It's a Fine Time to Leave Me Lucille." After about five days of hearing that song, I packed up and pulled out of the campground. I went to a garden supply place where I bought petunias to plant in the flower boxes outside of the studio. On my way home I stopped at the building. Bob was nowhere around. I planted the flowers then went home.

I had made a promise to myself that I would stay four or five years which would be long enough to see to it that the business got in the black then I would leave. The Village Photographer was going to live.

The Village Photographer

It was the summer of 1977, and it took all the strength that I had at the moment to jump into getting the studio ready, mainly because my only daughter had just moved to Finland with her new husband, Pekka.

Getting the studio ready meant raising the ceiling so Bob's lights could go up high enough for proper lighting. One night at dinner Robert asked why the ceiling had to be raised. Bob told him with a very straight face that the cleaners used to be for midgets. Robert believed it and told his friends and Bob kept the joke alive. Bob loved to be the joker and Robert was gullible.

Because we had to buy the studio, we had no extra money for anything let alone supplies for the studio.

The studio location was perfect. It was on Mill Street at the corner of Cedar Street. The Village Offices and the pub, bank and hardware store were close by and with a side walk we thought that maybe we would have traffic by our window. Although the village itself was and is very small, the surrounding area is very rural and large in area. The homes in the surrounding area tended to be large and expensive. We thought that would be good for business.

We had a nice reception area, a shooting room, and our work room. There was also a good sized area to the right of the front door that we didn't use so decided to rent those rooms out to two lawyers. They made a nice looking office.

We had our grand opening during the weekend of Ortonville Days. Prior to the opening, I had the bright idea to send Bob out photographing people at work in town. At first he balked at the idea because it would cost money, but I persisted. I said it would generate curiosity and bring people in to see their neighbor's pictures. It did just that and our opening was very successful.

Our first paying customer was a man who needed a new passport picture. Bob had purchased a Polaroid camera specifically for passports without talking to me about it and it didn't work. It cost us ten times the $7.50 the man paid for the job. Well, that was a lesson.

Our next customer had a picture that she wanted framed. But we hadn't bought a staple gun yet to shoot in the nails, and we didn't even have any Elmer's glue which we needed for the backing. While Bob was in the back room and the customer was in the waiting room, I ran to the hardware store to get things we needed. Again, that job cost more than we made. We made a trip to Mother's studio and borrowed some supplies. She was very helpful that way.

Gradually business grew and we were doing well. Bob was a good photographer and I did the art work on the finished prints when they came back from the lab. I also took care of most of the customers and developed a great method of delivering proofs and taking orders. I used what I learned in Tupperware which was a lot and applied it softly to the customers we had. I was great on the phone and with the customers. Bob was a little rough with his Brooklyn accent but that made him a unique photographer. He didn't do as well in the selling area and in my mind the selling should have started the minute the customer walked through the door. That's what I wanted—subtle selling.

I took an active part in the business but I knew I had to keep to my territory. If I made suggestions on poses in the sitting room, he let me know that I over-stepped my bounds.

We were doing okay, but driving from our house to Ortonville every day was not my idea of fun, especially at the beginning. We maybe had one customer a day, if that, and nothing to do but twiddle our thumbs. I kept saying that I needed to be home, but Bob wanted me there. We played cards in the back room but I wanted to be home. I spent the day thinking of all the things I could be doing at home. Before I left for work in the morning, I had to have dinner ready so that Mark could put it in the oven at a certain time and that was no fun. I missed being home with all three boys. And without much money coming in, we started talking about selling the house and looking for a place to rent in Ortonville. I was about to face another loss.

Both pictures were taken after the studio had been open for several years. Above —Sheila Sinks (helper), me and Bob in the reception area. Below—I am painting pictures out in front as part of Ortonville Days.

From House to Apartment

By the fall of 1977, we had found an apartment in Ortonville. The location was perfect; it was next door to the studio. It was also next door to the Village Pub which worried me. Bob hadn't been drinking for a while and I wondered if the temptation would be too great.

The apartment was huge. It had four bedrooms, one bath, and a large living/dining/kitchen area. It was nice that while the boys were doing dishes they could be with the rest of the family and watching TV. There was a nice bar/counter which we often ate at and there was a built in curved booth across from the kitchen. There were only five of us to eat meals then so it was just right.

The only problem with the apartment was the 22 stairs we had to climb to get there. At the base of the stairs was our laundry room so those stairs made doing laundry a bit difficult too. But with three boys, I could always send one down to put clothes in the dryer or bring them up to be folded. Below our apartment was the Village Sweet Shoppe and the owners were very nice people.

The boys weren't happy about changing schools and we felt bad about that. Mark was entering his senior year so we talked with the old school and he was able to finish his senior year. He had to drive the 15 miles to and from his school. But it was important for us and him because he was the drum major of the marching band. That was something he had worked toward for years. One good thing was that if he had to go back to school in the evening, he could spend the time in-between at my Mom's place. Robert and Jim were 11 and 12 so they weren't in high school yet, but it was still an adjustment for them.

After our house sold, we had a big garage sale. We had so much to get rid of but one good thing was there was some storage space in the studio. My big freezer which I had earned through Tupperware went in the studio.

Although the organ was going to the apartment, the drums had to be sold. I remember that day so well. I was sitting at the card table in the garage when a man came up to me and said, "I'll take the drums," and handed me the exact amount of money. I started bawling like a baby and ran into the house crying. I couldn't take his money. I didn't want the drums to go. A friend was helping with the sale and she took care of him. He probably thought I was nuts, but it was very sad. All those fun musical times would only be a memory from then on. Tears well up in my eyes even as I write this 35 years later.

The piano which had been in the basement all those years we lived in Drayton Plains had to go too, but I didn't cry about that. In fact, we gave it to my sister, Beverly. The organ made it up the 22 stairs into the apartment and I enjoyed it there when I was alone.

To get ready for the actual move, I would carry a couple of boxes of things to the apartment every day when we went to work. Since I wasn't that busy in the studio, it gave me something to do to put shelf paper in the cupboards and drawers and store linens and dishes that we weren't using at home. One day I took my hanging plants and placed them in the apartment; another day I took all the wall pictures and hung them. On moving day we rented a truck and asked a few friends to help. It was easily done in a day and we had company that night; everything had been put away, the beds were made and we were home.

Only it wasn't home. In one of my psychology classes, I remembered learning that losses can lead to depression. In a very short time I lost my ability to be a stay-at-home-mother, lost my daughter to another country and lost my home. I was almost ready for a breakdown.

Another One Leaves the Nest

Mark graduated from high school in 1978, and a few weeks later was off to see the world via the United States Air Force. I cried once again and I cried for a long time. I wanted my whole family back. I wanted to be back in Drayton Plains and have my life back. I remember so vividly his leaving. We drove him to Detroit in the motorhome and all the while his eight track tape by Steely Dan was playing. Even today, when I hear Steely Dan I think of that day and cry.

He came home for a short visit after tech school and before going to Germany. Yes, Germany. Okay, so suddenly half of my children were overseas. It pained me that they were so far away. I couldn't touch them. Glenda wrote weekly and I so looked forward to her letters. Mark seldom wrote and I really missed hearing from him.

Life went on. I really enjoyed the work in the studio after all, but trying to come home with enough energy to fix dinner was a chore. We ate simple things that didn't need much preparation and I missed those new dishes I used to prepare. Bob was spending a lot of time at the Village Pub and drinking again. I went to Al Anon meetings with my friend, Brenda Pyle. Her husband was the town drunk.

Business Was Terrific

The old entrance to the lawyer's offices at the side of our building was now where my little restoration room was. It looked pretty at night.

One of the two lawyers who had rented our extra space from us moved out and we included those rooms into our studio. I decorated one of the rooms to look old with antique look-alike furniture and when people came into the studio inquiring about restoring an old photograph, I would take them in there. I loved that room.

The room that was just off the hallway in the main part of the studio was used as the room where we took orders and that was great because it was more private. Everyone had to make an appointment to place their order and I was ready for them.

Because of techniques I had learned with Tupperware and my Mother (she was one terrific salesperson), I was able to make the customers comfortable. From my observation of people, I learned, early on, that most people were uncomfortable about being photographed. So, we directed everyone who worked for us to make notes on the customer's envelope. Little notes helped us pretend we remembered all they had said the first, second and third time they came in. They became like good friends. As Bob was taking their picture, he was supposed to make notes too, but he seldom did. I had big ears though so I wrote the notes.

We belonged to the Michigan Photographers Association and the Detroit Photographers Association. Mom and Dad had also belonged to this group. Once a month they had a meeting and had speakers on various things like how to take glamour pictures or how to make weddings more profitable. There was something new every month. At the same time the photographers were meeting, the color artists had their own meeting. Although we were a very small group, we also learned something new at each meeting.

During our fellowship with the photographers at the meetings, word got around about how well our studio was doing. I was asked to be a speaker at one of the upcoming meetings. I agreed. My talk was about all the little things we did which led to big orders and big business. My secret was that people want to be someone and feel important. We let our customers be important. I had involved the audience by asking rhetorical questions. I must say it was one of my best speeches ever. It was organized, and everyone was totally attentive during every minute of the hour I spoke. That in itself was unusual because past history showed that when a speaker talked about anything other than F stops and lenses, the photographers weren't interested. They stood in the back of the room and talked amongst themselves. I got a standing ovation which was also unheard of and people rushed the stage with more questions than we had time for during the program.

My Mother had done a program once. I tried to help her with it by organizing it a bit. At first she was all over the place. Mom was a character and everyone loved her, but she wasn't a good speaker. In her speech, all she talked about was herself. She was patting herself on the back the whole time. When I finally finished with the people who had rushed the stage, I went back to where Mom and Bob were sitting. Just as I got to the table Mom said, "Wasn't as good as mine." Did I really expect her to be complimentary? I should have been happy because it was the first time she ever saw me perform but I wasn't happy with her. I was happy with me and so was Bob. And I gained quite a reputation for my sales techniques.

Liisa Was Born in Finland

My first granddaughter was born in Finland on April 15, 1979, and I wasn't there. It broke my heart that I couldn't have been with my daughter and new granddaughter.

My mother offered to go with me to Finland and offered to pay the bill too. I knew Mom wasn't a big fan of travel but she loved Glenda dearly. More than once Mom told me that she was so glad that I didn't give her up for adoption like they originally wanted me to do.

Things were bad at home. Bob was drinking more and I just did not feel close to him. In fact I was sleeping in Mark's room. I would often cry myself to sleep with music that Glenda and Mark loved–the Beetles for Glenda and Steely Dan for Mark.

I had written Mark and told him that we would have a three hour layover in Frankfurt and asked if it was far from him. He either called or wrote and said he would meet us at the airport. He asked if I could pick up a couple of tapes—preferably jazz. I remember going to the record store and being overwhelmed with choices but I picked the Moody Blues and I fell in love with it myself. I especially loved, *Nights in White Satin*. I secretly thought that if it wasn't for Robert and Jim, I would stay in Finland with my daughter and granddaughter.

I enjoyed our two weeks in Finland. Liisa was beautiful and I loved holding her. Pekka's parents were very hospitable and we enjoyed good food and sauna at both their year-round home in Helsinki and their summer cottage. Since we were there on June 21, we got to witness the longest day of the year and honestly the sun never set. We sat up all night watching the sun glide along the horizon, never dipping below the horizon.

Glenda and Pekka owned a little restaurant in Helsinki and I was impressed with it. The name of it was Kokkipoika which translated to Chef Boy.

I enjoyed shopping in Helsinki and was taught this Finnish sentence: "Mina puhu vain Englantia." which means I speak only

English. With that phrase I was easily able to go anywhere in Helsinki because most spoke English quite well. I really loved Helsinki.

The saunas were a treat and they relaxed their normal rules for us. Normally everyone takes a sauna together and all are naked. It doesn't matter if you are related or not. It is somewhat sacred and understood that it is for health not lust. For us they had women first then the men. After the sauna then everyone jumps into an unheated pool (which is really cold) or into the sea –still naked. Then after the pool, towels are provided while everyone sits at tables around the pool to have a beer and sausage.

Mr. and Mrs. Paunonen had a beautiful pool in the lower level of their home in Helsinki. There was a walk to the back yard from the pool and I learned that in the winter after the sauna they ran outside to roll in the snow. My mother was a good sport at her age (66) and joined right in. Even at the summer cottage she ran outside stark naked and jumped into the Baltic Sea.

I didn't look forward to leaving Glenda and Liisa and coming home to Bob, but I did miss Robert and Jim. It was a wonderful experience though and I thanked Mom for paying our way.

Wonderful and Terrible

My darling daughter, Glenda and granddaughter, Liisa flew to Michigan around the beginning or middle of November 1979. Liisa was about seven months old and the most adorable child I had ever seen. It was heavenly having them both with us. Of course, I had to work and it was the busy time of the year but since I was next door they came over and I went home often.

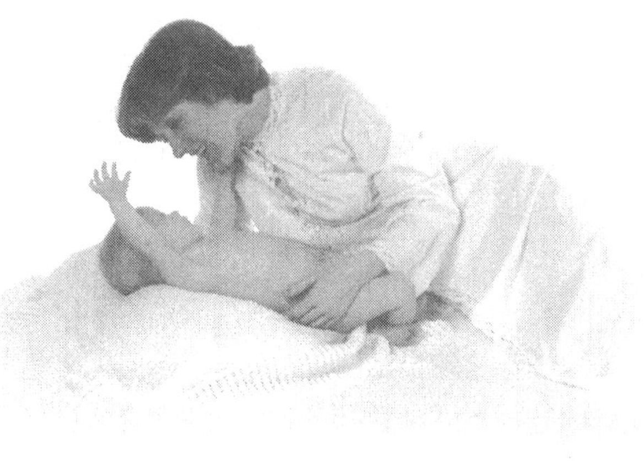

We planned a huge party in the studio for all of our friends from Drayton Plains and the new friends in Ortonville. I wanted everyone to meet Glenda and Liisa.

While Glenda was home, I went back to Bob's bed because I needed the bedroom for them. We actually got along that month or so maybe it was because I was so happy having Glenda around that I didn't care what Bob did.

Christmas was coming and Glenda planned to stay through Christmas and Pekka and his Mom were flying in just before Christmas. We were going to have a full house. I prepared Robert and Jim to double up in one bedroom with a sleeping bag for the one without a bed.

We got wind of something that made Bob furious. Bob didn't like surprises at all. We heard that Mark was going to fly in from Germany and be at my sister's house on Christmas Eve playing Santa Claus. Bob wasn't excited that Pekka and his mom were coming either.

Pekka arrived a few days before Christmas and immediately Bob turned sour. In fact, he either stayed at the Pub or in the bedroom. He wouldn't talk to Pekka and actually he was cold to everyone in the house. It was a very uncomfortable time. And as it got closer to Christmas Eve, Bob even threatened to stay home from the family party at Bunnie's. I could have strangled him. I was excited that my family would be together again and he was trying to ruin it--in fact, he was ruining it.

At my sister's house, Bob continued to be a grouch and he wasn't nice to Mark when we all discovered that he was there. That night, back at home, I think it was Jim who got sick. Since he was sleeping on the floor, he didn't get up fast enough and he ended up throwing up in Robert's shoe which wasn't funny.

Just after Christmas my sister, Bunnie, took Robert and Jim skiing up north and brought Jim back early with a broken arm. He needed surgery. The whole Christmas holiday was becoming a bad nightmare.

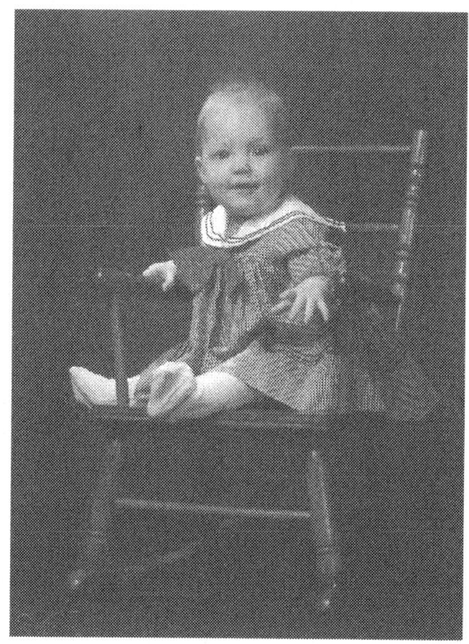

Bob took these pictures as well as the one on the top of the previous page.

It seemed like we were running to the airport all the time. Pekka and his Mother went home first and Bob got happier. Next was Glenda and Liisa and I got sad. Then it was Mark's turn to go. As each one left, Bob got happier and I got sadder.

One terrific thing happened with everyone home. We had made arrangements to go to Windsor, Ontario, Canada, to our friend's studio and have a family portrait made. The Hebert's were great photographers and this portrait is a testament to their fine work and my beautiful family.

The last Family portrait. Within a year the family would be no more.

Falling Apart

Our marriage struggled through the first half of 1980 and we kept very busy with the studio. The following event would set us on a course toward the final divorce.

I was on the board of directors representing the artists for the Detroit Association. Bob was asked to be on the board but he didn't want to. When I agreed to be on the board without asking his permission, he was very angry. But I had made a commitment and felt it was important. He didn't like me going to the board meetings but I went anyway and we always argued about it.

The problem with this board was the president. Joe Kubek was a night owl and totally unorganized. One night late, during the summer of 1980, he called to say there would be an emergency board meeting the next day at noon at the Holiday Inn which was located at Eight Mile and Telegraph so we could look at a new meeting place. He wanted me there to look over the facilities and see if the room for the artists would be sufficient. I knew I had no appointments the next day so I said that I would be there.

As soon as I got off the phone, Bob lit into me. I don't remember if he had been drinking or not, but that didn't matter. He was possessive of me anytime. He wanted me to be in the studio and I knew I didn't need to be there.

We had an exchange student staying with us at the time and I was totally embarrassed at his ranting and raving. Paivi, from Finland, was a sweet little girl and even though it was late at night, it must have disturbed her. I even remember that Bob got physical with me and I got mad back.

I went to the meeting and on the long drive there and back, I was fuming. The minute I got home I went in to see Neil Wallace the lawyer who was still renting space in our studio. I told him that I wanted a divorce right then and there. Of course he calmed me down but said he would start the process. But Bob was his good friend as was I, and he said that he wanted us to get counseling and that he would help us.

Neil met with us once a week and I can still remember one time when Neil, when trying to get Bob to open up, asked him what kind of bike he had as a kid. Bob hollered at Neil and threw out some expletives and said that had nothing to do with anything.

At one time Neil ordered us to take our lunch break together up in our apartment. And we were to talk and get to know one another again. So we tried it the next day. As soon as we got to the top of the stairs, Bob said, in an angry tone of voice, "What do you want to talk about?" I wanted to hit him, but I tried. I could see clearly that it wasn't going to work.

The heat was off for a while though and we took a nice trip in the motorhome with Paivi, Robert and Jim. We went all the way up to the Upper Peninsula and we were getting along okay. But it wouldn't last.

The Last Straw

Bob and I had still been working with our lawyer friend Neil Wallace to try and get our marriage back on track. We had even gone to Las Vegas over the New Year in 1980. The whole time we were there was like we were each there separately. We hardly did anything together and we never made love. So much for the second honeymoon. Come to think of it we never had a honeymoon unless I counted that time he and I went to the Bahamas after a Tupperware Jubilee.

It was March 1981 and the State Photographers Convention was coming up. We were working on getting our prints ready to submit for competition. I was entering prints to be judged by the artists. I was also on the program to do my program about selling like the one I had done in Detroit.

Bob had picked the four prints that he wanted to enter into the competition and had them printed and mounted. The next step was the art work which is what I did. Normally (on customers' work), I just knew what should be done, but competition prints were different. The photographer is being judged not the artist so I asked him what he would like fixed or changed on his prints. He said, "Just make them look good." "I'll be in a no win situation," I replied, "If they lose because of the art work I'll be blamed." We had both sat in on many judgings and knew that the judges could really pick apart a print. Again I asked him to please tell me what he wanted done and I added that I would fix it. He wouldn't tell me. This went on for a couple of days as the deadline got closer and closer. I stood my ground and would not work on his prints at all; they just sat there. Meanwhile, I shipped mine on to Traverse City.

I didn't even want to go to the convention after days of fighting but I had to go. I was on the program. So I took off by myself to drive up to Traverse City and checked into the hotel. On the four hour drive to the convention, I did a lot of thinking. I was now ready to go my merry way. I had finally had it. Our business was in the black and the four years that I had promised myself was up (remember "It's a Fine Time to Leave Me Lucille").

As soon as I got checked in, I went to the registration area and posted a note on the message board. "If you need a right hand in your studio, I'm the gal. I am available immediately to relocate anywhere in the state." I had a couple of things going for me. I was known because of my Mother who was a well-known Master Photographer and I was known in my own right because of the program I was about to do at that convention.

The next day I had three possible offers. One seemed more promising though and I liked the area. Packer Studio was in East Lansing, Michigan, and from what he said it was a nice new plush studio that wasn't living up to its looks. It sounded like it looked like Sax Fifth Avenue but with Wal-Mart presentation and prices. We talked a bit about what I would do and he liked my ideas but we both agreed that I should spend an afternoon there in the studio and we would work out a deal. Salary would be discussed when we met again. I made an appointment to visit Don and Betty Packer in mid-April.

I came home from the convention and told Bob and the lawyer that I would be leaving even though I didn't know if the job was a done deal or not. I knew that I could find a job somewhere if that one didn't work out.

When I visited Don and Betty at their studio, I fell in love with it. It had such potential. He wasn't the best photographer but he wasn't the worst. I agreed to begin on May 18 1981. I was excited. The day I went up for the interview, I looked at apartments and townhouses and found just the one I wanted in a nice area called Lake of the Hills. The school district was one of the best and I liked that they had a great music program.

When I came home I told the boys and Bob that I was definitely moving out. I told the boys that they could stay with their father or come with me. I wasn't going to force them to come with me, but I told them how much I loved them and wanted them to be with me. I think I took them to the townhouse and school. Robert was all for going but Jim was balking. I worried that he would stay behind.

I sold the motorhome and had the boys come with me while I looked for a car. We picked out a white Ford Escort with red interior and bucket seats. It was pretty.

On the weekend of my birthday, May 17, 1981, I moved away from Bob for the very last time. The boys would stay in Ortonville for about two weeks until school was out then I would move all my furniture up. But on this little move that I made, I took very little with me because I didn't want to strip the house of things they would need. My townhouse had a stove, refrigerator and dishwasher; I didn't need a TV. I took a good bunch of my clothing, my painting table, and little sauce pan, frying pan, a radio and Mark's Futon. That is all I needed for the two weeks.

I didn't cry; I was happy. It was a new beginning and I felt like I was soaring like an eagle.

Section Six

A New Beginning

1981–1989

I'm Alive

My town house was very comfortable. I loved every square foot of it even though it was empty of furniture. Lake of the Hills in Haslett, Michigan, was a nice collection of condos and apartments surrounding a little man-made lake (more like a big pond). There was a nice swimming pool and an executive golf course included in this apartment/condo community.

My town house was the center unit in a five unit section. Downstairs there was a large living room/dining area, kitchen and half bath. Upstairs were three bedrooms and a full bath. There was also an unfinished basement. It was perfect. I put my painting table in the basement. I had moved it so many times that I knew exactly how to put that monster together. It was six feet long and only made out of plywood, but with its slanted workspace, it was perfect for the work I did on photographs. It was functional without being the least bit attractive. Dad had built it for me many years before and had used over 100 screws in the building of it. It was very sturdy.

Packer Studio was only a few miles away in East Lansing and it was an easy drive to work. I met and liked the other two employees. Dianne Lange did just about everything and had worked for the Packers for a long time. Rod Gleason was a photographer who did most of Don's work. He was very talented and in fact did a beautiful job on anything he photographed. They both accepted me right away and we became friends. My first week at work consisted of getting to know their operation and I started to work on a new price list.

Don and Betty had owned a studio in East Lansing for a long time. I remember that my brother worked for them part time in the early 60s while attending Michigan State University. From what he said the studio wasn't that special. Shortly before I got the job at Packer Studio they had just moved into a very plush stand-alone building that was huge. The entrance with its high ceilings and thick carpeting was impressive. It looked like an art museum with large portraits hanging on the walls. Everything was first class except the prices. They were even cheaper than K-Mart or Wal-Mart.

When I started work on the new price list I had a couple of hurdles. Betty was scared and so was Don but he was more supportive and reminded Betty that that was why they hired me. With my confidant air, I pushed ahead raising the prices by 200% or more. They had charged five dollars for a sitting fee and I was raising it to a minimum of $25 for a very basic sitting which I still thought was too cheap for a photographer with Rod Gleason's artistic ability. And when I first started presenting the new prices to customers no one batted an eyelash. Don and Betty were happy. With the new prices and my sales techniques the average total sale went up tremendously. I was selling huge prints that were very expensive and everyone was happy.

But I am getting ahead of myself. Those first two weeks by myself were very relaxing. I was finally free of tension 24/7 and I loved just being alone. At night after work, I searched out the area finding what was near by. The restaurants were varied and many. There was a lovely mall near my townhouse and I frequented furniture stores looking for a kitchen table because I would need one. In our apartment in Ortonville, we had a built in booth which couldn't be moved. It was much fun acquainting myself with the East Lansing area. I felt at home.

I found a beautiful white round table with soda fountain chairs for the kitchen. The cushions on the chairs were a yellow and white check and I had a little white vase with yellow flowers for the center of the table. I loved the look because it was fresh and clean looking which I felt represented my new life.

The Big Move

It was early in June I think when the Boys were out of school. I had made plans to rent a U Haul truck and I asked my three brother-in-laws to help with the move. I had driven to Ortonville on Friday and we planned the move for Saturday. Bob and I barely spoke that night but we had previously talked about what I would take when I moved. Neil (our lawyer) had made us discuss the division of furniture and things long before the actual move. Bob was very generous and insisted that I take most of the furniture because he wanted to make it easy for the kids and I. I appreciated that. All he asked for was something to sleep on, the stove and refrigerator (since my apartment had one) and some dishes, silverware and pans.

I had moved a lot of times prior to this move. While Bob was in prison, I moved to at least four different places and did it all myself or with very little help. The one time that I moved with Bob, my sisters and I did all the moving while he was still in the hospital and Bob and I had moved a couple of times. Every time, everything was in place that evening and it was very orderly. This move from Ortonville would be my worst move ever. First of all I hadn't been in Ortonville during the previous week to start packing and organizing everything. We needed to do everything in one day.

When Mike, Jerry and Tom arrived, they started loading things into the truck. I was trying to keep one step ahead of them and did, but it wasn't at all organized. They had a pretty tough job. Some of the things were very heavy and bulky like my organ. And since we lived in an apartment up 22 stairs, carrying stuff down wasn't that easy. They did a super job.

One funny thing I remember from that day is all the girls coming by to say "good-bye" to Jim. Even Mike, Jerry and Tom were amazed. To understand why this was so strange I have to explain that Robert always looked like he stepped out of a fashion magazine. His hair was always neatly combed and since he was very good looking he looked like he would be someone every girl would be attracted to. Jim, on the other hand, didn't try to attract girls. He was very handsome but often his hair was uncombed and although he wasn't a slob his clothes were often wrinkled or sloppy.

Robert and Jim were just short of 15 and 16 when we made the move. Their birthdays are the first of August and the end of June. Jim didn't want to move and was moody before the packing started. He had decided to go but wasn't happy about it. Robert was excited for the new environment and school.

The boys helped with their own packing and carried some things down and they rode in the car with me once we had everything loaded. It was about an hour's drive to the new place.

When we got to the town house, Mike, Jerry and Tom carried everything from the truck into the house and kind of put it where I wanted it or just set it somewhere. But there were boxes everywhere. We could hardly walk through the house. Somehow we made beds and early Sunday morning I had to take Jim to nearby St. Johns for a Lions Club All State Band rehearsal.

After I took Jim to St. Johns, Robert and I spent the day working our butts off unpacking and getting the house in order. It was a very hot day and I remember that periodically we would walk the short distance to the pool and jump in to cool off then go right back to work with damp bathing suits on. He was a big help that day.

By Monday and time for me to go to work at noon we were all settled and thus began our life in Haslett.

My Poor New Car

One Monday morning shortly after we moved (maybe early in July) I needed to take Robert somewhere in Lansing before going to work. On Mondays we didn't start until noon. I clearly remember that before I left the house, Jim and I had an argument. He had been hard to live with from day one in Haslett because he didn't like our situation. I distinctly remember that I told him, "I have had it with arguing with anyone and I am not about to put up with your grouchiness." I also told him he was welcome to go live with his father. I had enough to deal with. Work, and taking care of two teenage boys and not having enough money were enough to deal with and I and didn't need to fight with him.

Lansing has some one-way streets that I wasn't familiar with and the place we were going was on one of those streets. Cedar Street was a three lane southbound street. My mind was still on the argument with Jim when I turned onto Cedar Street. I knew I had to turn left into the business so I got in the center lane forgetting that I was in fact on a one way street. When I was ready to turn, I put my blinker on and since there was no traffic coming toward me, I turned left. Immediately I was broadsided by a big old boat of a car like an Oldsmobile or Chevy. She had been in the left of the three lanes when I turned in front of her. I didn't have a seat belt on (since there wasn't a seat belt law) and that was probably a good thing. She smashed in my door but good and I was pushed over on to Robert's lap. Bits of glass were everywhere even in my hair. What a shock that was. Not only wasn't it a good way to start the day, I hadn't even made the second payment on that car yet.

The car got fixed and I kept working but Jim was still giving me a hard time. I found a counselor (psychologist) I thought might be able to help. Bruce was wonderful and we had family meetings once a week, but Jim persisted in being obstinate.

Then horror upon horror checks from work started bouncing.

Dianne and the other workers at Packer Studio had the same problem. We were all complaining as it was causing everyone but Dianne a hardship. Trying to figure out how to handle Don and Betty was the topic of conversation whenever we had a moment together.

Counseling

I don't remember how, but I found a counselor (psychologist) that I thought might be able to help. Bruce was wonderful and we had family meetings once a week, but Jim persisted in being obstinate. My most peaceful times where when Robert and Jim went to Bob's every other weekend.

Bruce was great in trying to help us resolve the problems. I clearly remember one specific time. Bruce had asked us to plan a vacation for the three of us. He wanted to see how we went about working through a situation. The rules were simple; agree on a place to go with time and money being no object.

I started, "Hey guys, we can go anywhere we want. Got any ideas?"

Robert came up with a couple of suggestions. Jim sat with his arms folded tightly in front of him and kept his mouth shut tight.

I said, "That sounds great Robert. What do you think Jim?"

Jim said, "I don't want to go anywhere."

It went on that way for a while but we never got anywhere with Jim. I think Bruce counseled with the boys separately and still Jim was not a happy camper.

Once school started in September things got better. The boys were on the swim team and that meant getting them up in what seemed like the middle of the night. Swim practices were a couple of hours before school started. I felt sorry for the boys because they had to get up, pack their duffle bag and go to school and jump in the pool before they were even awake. It was tough for me too but it was a good thing.

The marching band was great for the boys too. And school was good. They met friends and things calmed down a lot. Life was good again.

The Crash at Work

My paychecks were often late and they were not only late for me but for Dianne and Rod as well. When we did get our checks, they often bounced and that was very difficult for both Rod and I. Dianne had a husband to support her so she wasn't destitute, but she had worked for the Packers long enough to start getting fed up. We spent many working hours getting more and more upset as we talked about how things were or were not going.

About once a month the Packers held a breakfast meeting at Coral Gables (a restaurant) in East Lansing. When the October meeting was scheduled we decided that it was time to challenge the Packers at their own meeting. Dianne was the one leading the charge. Since Dianne had become a good friend and since I felt the same frustration as she did, I promised her that I would stand up with her when she read the list of complaints at the meeting.

The meeting started out as usual until Dianne got up. We could tell she had built up a good head of steam and she really let them have it. Don and Betty were shocked but Don hit Dianne right back and they had a big argument. Suddenly Dianne said, "I quit" and right away I jumped up and said, "I quit too." We gathered up our purses and walked out of the door. We went to my place and had a glass or two of wine and then the reality hit me. She had a husband to support her while I was on my own. When the boys came home from school they couldn't believe what I had done but I assured them that we would be okay and I would get another job right away.

Finding a New Job

The job market was pretty dismal in the fall of 1981. Reagan was president and even college graduates couldn't find a job so my prospects were dismal. I still had my photo art work to do but that was spotty and not dependable. I tried promoting it to other studios in Michigan and got a couple more jobs. I needed a job though.

Just after I quit at the studio while talking with my daughter, Glenda, who was living in Florida she suggested that I try Mary Kay make-up. She was being quite successful at selling the product and even had a company owned pink Cadillac. I wasn't into make up but thought I could try, after all I was a sales person.

The problem with Mary Kay was that to get started one had to buy the product and keep stock because when people were at a party you would sell them what they wanted on the spot. This was more complicated than Tupperware where everything was ordered and shipped later. Keeping the stock up was even more difficult because of all the different shades. Lipsticks came in dozens of colors and what you bought you got to keep although they would take them back if you didn't have your name label on the different items. Instead of making money, I lost close to $500.00 and ended up giving all of my stuff to Glenda.

We did okay though because I had enough art work to do. We were heading into Christmas and the studios were sending me lots of work. We had enough food to eat and a comfortable place to live.

D Day Again

On Wednesday, August 5, 1981 I drove into Pontiac to the Oakland County Court House. I had to appear in court to get the final divorce papers. On the one hour plus drive to the complex, my mind was replaying the road I had traveled to get to this place in my life and planning ahead for what lay ahead for me. I was sad that it had to end this way but I knew there was no other way. I felt good that I had really tried hard to make the marriage work and there was nothing left to do.

I was surprised that it was over so fast without any fanfare. I remember feeling somewhat empty like Peggy Lee's song, *Is That All There Is.* My lawyer wasn't there and I knew Bob wouldn't be there because he wasn't contesting the divorce. I was all alone and it was over in just a matter of minutes.

As I drove back towards Lansing (over a one hour drive) I mentally left that part of my life behind. That part of Michigan that had always been home to me., but it no longer was. I hadn't planned to stop in to visit Mom or anyone else in the area but driving up M-59, I suddenly saw the sign for Tipisco Lake Rd and on the spur of the moment, turned. I wanted to stop in to visit with Dad and Frankie. They were packing for their move to New Mexico and would be leaving in a few days. Frankie's mother had lived in Silver City and when she died, she left it to Frankie.

I didn't visit long as it was sad saying good bye to something else. I just wanted to get to my new place and continue my new life.

Oh Robert!

Bob was in prison when I had been divorced before so any decision I made I made for myself. I never had to think about visitation rights and other such things. Right away the boys were going to their father's every other weekend but when I thought that it would be fun to go to Florida for Christmas I didn't think to ask Bob if it was okay. I just went ahead and made the plans. Since we had already made plans, he allowed us to go, but I learned a lesson.

We planned to leave the evening of the boys' last day of school and I was rushing to finish up the last of the art work I had to get finished. It was a typical cold, evening with a little bit of ice on the road in spots when I sent Robert up to the corner to pick up a pizza. He didn't return as fast as I thought he should and I began to worry. I was looking for him when I saw him drive in and he spent a little while looking at the front of the car. I knew there was trouble but at first he denied that anything was wrong. I always knew better though. Finally he told me what happened; when he applied the brakes to stop the car it slid sideways in the store parking lot sending car sideways over a curb. The tie rod was bent. So much for leaving that night.

I don't know how I found the bump shop to fix the tie rod on a Saturday which was less than a week before Christmas, but I did and we were finally able to leave for our 24 hour drive on Saturday, December 19. The hard part was the money it cost to get the car fixed. I am sure I charged it and would worry about it later.

With three drivers we were able to drive straight through and arrived in Lake Worth on Sunday December 20th. It was so good to be with Glenda, Pekka and little Liisa. The nice weather was a bonus.

We spent a lot of time at the beach and Robert and Jim enjoyed the sun and surf. I was extra happy at being able to be with Glenda on her 25th birthday and their anniversary.

Back in the Lab

When we came home from Florida I started looking for a job. An ad in the newspaper caught my eye. A doctor's office needed a medical technologist. "That's me," I said to myself. But I was a little rusty. The last time I had worked in the laboratory was 1966 and it was 1982; a lot had changed. Hospitals had changed the most with computerized testing machines but this doctor only wanted someone to do routine blood work such as blood counts and I knew I could do that easily. The interview went fine, and she asked me to stay to work half a day so she could evaluate my work.

Dr. Carol Beals, (a Rheumatologist) was about my age (45) at the time. Donna, her RN had been doing the lab work but the office was getting so busy she couldn't help the doctor as much while doing lab work. Donna showed me their procedure for diluting the blood so the counts could be done and I went to work for my half day. I diluted the tiny amount of blood (in a pipette especially designed for white blood counts (WBCs), then added the diluent, mixed the two then applied a tiny drop to the counting chamber and looked in the microscope to actually count the cells. The next step was to do the math but something kept bothering me. Donna had said, "Take the total cells counted, add seven then add two zeros." That just didn't work in my mind; the "add seven" part bothered me. I kept wondering, "Why seven?"

After doing the blood work for several patients and when Donna wasn't around, I found the little instruction booklet that came with the test kit. There it was—my answer and a dilemma at the same time. The instructions read, "Count the number of cells in the chamber then add ten percent then two zeros for the total WBCs per cc. For example, if you count 70 cells, add seven then two zeros. Your answer will be 7700." The dilemma was that Donna had been calculating wrong. I would be doing the WBC's for these same patients and now their numbers might change drastically just because of the calculation. If for example I had counted 150 I should add 15 instead of 7--- 16,500 wbcs/cc is a lot different than 15,700/cc. I finally decided that I should let both Donna and the doctor know even if it meant that I didn't get the job. I did and the doctor appreciated my telling her, she also gave me the job, but Donna didn't like me from that moment forward.

Donna was an old busybody type nurse. She had to watch and stick her nose into everything. If I was in the bathroom or out to lunch, I would find her in the lab changing things around. I finally told her to stay out of my lab and that got her even madder. We were silent enemies. And I knew since she was very close to the doctor that she was always tattling on everything I did or didn't do. I was always on time, did my work accurately and kept my nose out of her business but I felt the tension. I liked having a steady pay check so I said nothing. I really liked the job, the patients, the doctor and getting up to go to work every day.

I Did it Again

Dianne was still my friend even though we weren't working together and she thought I needed to start being with other single people again. She told me about a local singles group—Graduate and Professional Singles (GAPS). They had regular meetings with speakers on many different subjects then on Fridays they would meet for TGIF. I started going and loved the people and met a great gal, Dee Brown. We became friends. It was great to have someone to chum around with who was also single.

Then I met Dick Long. He really came on to me and that felt good considering all the years I felt I was unattractive to men (especially my husband). I liked the attention and he was oh so good sexually. Maybe I was part nymphomaniac because I just couldn't get enough of sex with him. He was so ready and willing anytime and anywhere. More than once when he took me to work early in the morning, he walked in with me (no one else was there yet) and we "did it" standing up with me leaning against the refrigerator in my lab.

But he was a drunk. Yep, I had hooked up with another bad apple again. And when he was drinking he treated me very badly and it was driving me crazy again. We would be okay for a while then he would stand me up and I would find he was with another woman. I kept asking myself, "Why do I do this?"

I figured I needed counseling so I made regular appointments with Bruce, the counselor who had helped with Jim when we first moved to Haslett. That was the best thing I ever did. He was great and he helped me to see a lot of things about myself that I had ignored. It took a while because I didn't want to give up the sex, but I finally broke it off with Dick once and for all and I decided that I did not want any men in my life except my boys. I finally felt really terrific about myself and comfortable in my own skin.

It Wasn't Funny

Mark had been in the Air Force for a long time and typical of so many boys; he did not write letters. I missed talking with him and didn't know a lot about what he was doing, but I think he was mad at me besides just not liking to write letters. He was mad because I split up the family and divorced his father. He did communicate that much.

I wrote to him often and asked questions which never got answered. I wanted to know what kinds of things he was doing in Germany. One time I made a multiple choice answer sheet and sent it to him complete with a little golf pencil and a self-addressed envelope so he could send it back to me. I had statements like this.

I am__________.
a) fine
b) just okay
c) having a ball
d) working hard and having no fun.
E) other

I never got that letter back and I kept begging for a letter. One day in my mail was an envelope from Mark and I was so very excited that I ripped it open. Inside were two pages of yellow dog paper and writing was on both sides of each paper. I grabbed a cup of coffee and sat down eagerly to read, but I couldn't read a word of what was written. He had written the whole letter in German. I sat and cried. It seemed like such a cruel joke.

I tried very hard to find someone who could read German but I couldn't find anyone. Too bad we didn't have computers back then.

Comings and Goings

Mark came home from Germany after his discharge in November of 1982. I felt sorry for him because he couldn't come "home" to the place we had lived when he left. Not only had I moved, but with Bob and I divorced, he had moved too. It had to be hard for Mark. He couldn't stay with Bob because his apartment in Ortonville was tiny. So he came to Haslett and I didn't even have a bedroom for him. Robert and Jim each had their own bedroom; the best I could offer Mark was the couch. It wasn't a perfect situation.

I told Mark that he could have two weeks, but then he needed to try to find a job. I was having a hard time making ends meet with two boys and very little child support; I would need help.

Mark and I had often clashed when he was growing up so I knew I would need patience. I was working at Dr. Beal's office so I was gone during the days Monday through Friday.

When the two weeks were up he still didn't try to get a job. When I would leave for work in the morning he was still sleeping and I would call at noon to see what he had lined up for interviews but I could tell that he was still on the couch and that I had probably awakened him with my phone call although he denied it. After several weeks of this, I decided to drive home at lunch time and catch him in his lie. I never tolerated lying. I caught him, but nothing changed. He would stay up until very late at night then sleep till late and not want to eat dinner with us saying that he wasn't hungry. It was disrupting our happy home and I had vowed when I left Bob, I wasn't going to let anyone make me miserable again.

We got into a fight one night at dinner time and I kicked him out. I felt bad but at the same time I felt that I had to do it. Mark went to stay with my mother (his grandma) and that was fine with me. In fact, I felt this tough love was good for him although I am sure he would not agree. He finally got a good job in California with the FBI.

Robert took an early graduation from high school so he could go and help his dad in Ortonville. Bob had had heart problems and Robert had missed Ortonville. So in January of 1983 which was shortly after Mark left, Robert moved to Bob's. He came back to Haslett often, but the comings and goings of both boys were sad. I still had Jim with me and he finally liked living in Haslett and was enjoying school and the band that he was a part of. He played tuba or during marching season, the sousaphone. Jim had a lot of friends and they were often at the house.

Getting Fired Wasn't so Bad After All

On Monday, February 14, 1983 I went to work as usual and at 5 p.m. the doctor called me into her office and handed me a check for two weeks' pay and told me I was fired. She said that she couldn't stand the tension in the office any longer.

I had never been fired before in my life. Yes, it hurt my ego but I didn't have time to dwell on that. I had to find a job. And this was at a time in our history when even college graduates couldn't get a job not even in the fast food industry. Ronald Reagan was president and the economy was bad.

As soon as I got home that evening, I made a list of all the places I would go to try and get interviews the next day. I had decided that I had had enough of "secure jobs" with bouncing pay checks and getting fired. I wanted to be back in sales where I could control my success. On the top of my list were companies that sold office equipment to big companies. At the bottom of the list I had written, "If all else fails, there is always Tupperware." On Tuesday, I went out trying to get interviews and got nowhere. So when I came home in the late afternoon, I called the nearest Tupperware distributor and said, "I want to be a Tupperware Manager." I had my kit by Thursday and 5 weeks later I was a manager complete with a company car. No one had ever gone from dealer to manager that fast. I knew what to do and how to do it.

I had heard that a few months after I was fired Donna was also fired. She was the problem not me. But if I hadn't gotten fired, I never would have ended up back in Tupperware and I never would have met my husband, Ron, but that is another story; keep reading.

A Different Tupperware Party

At one of the GAPS happy hours I sat at a mixed table. Next to me was a handsome man I didn't know well. His name was Jim Neve. He was an engineer who worked at the Michigan Department of Transportation. We got to talking and he asked what I did. "I am a Tupperware manager", I answered, proudly. He replied, "Gee when my wife left me, she took all the Tupperware with her."

Right away, I thought, "There is a market here" and proceeded to talk to him about having a Tupperware party just for guys. I explained how easy it would be to invite a few guys over for beer and snacks then I would do a short demonstration on how Tupperware could make a bachelor's life easier. He set a date for his party. He said, "I've done some dumb things in my life, why not." The date for his party was set for July 6, 1983.

I arrived for the party early as I always did. Jim lived in a nice apartment in East Lansing and he was ready with snacks. Then his friends arrived. Dick Long was there but since we had recently broken up for good, I just treated him like a customer. There was one other guy I knew from GAPS, Dick Erickson, and a couple of other guys from the department of transportation (DOT) that I didn't know, but I was very professional, did my demonstration, took their orders and left so they could continue their get together. I felt it was a very successful party for everyone.

One of the Highway people at the party was Ron Hofmeister. He came because he wanted a lettuce crisper. He lived in the same apartment complex as Jim and they worked together. When Jim told Ron he was having the party, Ron jumped at the chance. Ron's son, Kurt who attended Michigan State University, had moved in with Ron for a little while and came with a lettuce crisper that he had acquired when he and other MSU students were renting a house together. When Kurt moved out, he took the crisper with him. Ron also bought some sandwich keepers so he could take his lunch to work.

I was not interested in any of the men at the party. I was just doing my job, but Ron told me later that he was impressed with my professionalism and my self-confidence. Ron was seeing another woman at the time so this was just a professional meeting. He remembered me more than I remembered him.

After the Tupperware party, Dick Long called to say that he noticed Ron really looking me over. I poo pooed that, but Dick persisted and said that Ron was one of the nicest guys he had ever known. I still wasn't interested but thanked him for that information.

In September of 1983, I had to have surgery. I had a cyst on my ovary and the doctor suggested I have the ovaries removed. My uterus had been gone since 1975 so it didn't matter to me. Ron's girlfriend, Betty who I didn't know, was in the hospital at the same time. She had had a hysterectomy but I didn't know that. Ron told me later that he noticed me walking the halls like all good patients do after surgery. But he didn't say anything to me and I didn't see him.

Section Seven

Early Love

1983—1984

The Best Line Ever

One of the problems with being self-employed as I was with Tupperware was being sick. Not being able to work hurt the budget. I didn't have time to lay around and lick my wounds so shortly after I came home from the hospital I was back at work. I remember the night clearly. It was a Thursday, September 22, 1983. My party was in the evening in the south part of Lansing and it was a small party so I was finished by nine or a little after. On my way home from the party I decided to stop at the Red Rail (a country western bar with a big dance floor) where members of the GAPS met on Thursdays for socialization, dancing and a beer or wine.

The Rail (as we all affectionately called it) had a terrific band and I loved the music and atmosphere. I didn't see anyone I knew so I took a seat at the far end of the bar and ordered a glass of wine. My friend Dee Brown had been there but had gone home with her friend George. I was just going to enjoy the music and my wine then go home when Ron Hofmeister came in and sat next to me. He and his friend Jim Neve had been to an Oktoberfest party in Lansing and on a lark decided to stop in at the Rail on their way home. Jim was a frequent visitor to the Rail but I had never seen Ron there until this night and I didn't really remember him from the Tupperware party.

We started talking. He was surprised that I was working so soon after surgery and I was surprised he knew I had surgery. I explained that no work meant no money so I didn't have a choice. He was impressed with my tenacity. His friend Betty was not progressing as well in her recovery.

Ron asked lots of questions about me and seemed sincerely interested and I asked lots of questions of him. As I think back on this we acted like we were the only two people in the building. It was very intense. The Rail could have burned down and we would have still been sitting there talking. We weren't even drinking, just talking.

After a couple of hours of our talking, Ron said, "I think you need some cuddling. Why don't you follow me home and I promise that is all we will do." Wow, I never heard that line before but somehow it didn't seem like a line. I believed him and was really feeling the need to just be cuddled and loved—no sex—so I agreed to follow him home. And that is exactly what we tried to do but being in his arms as he held me so tightly was heavenly. We even talked more and hugged more. Then one thing led to another. We made love and it was tender. We went to sleep and woke up a few hours later wanting more and well, it was just a beautiful night.

Two Awkward Situations

From the moment he walked into the Rail and through the night it was heavenly. I had never spent a night like that in my entire life. Certainly not with Bob as he didn't like to be close. I liked Ron a lot and felt that he liked me too.

Ron's phone was out of order that night. It had been reported to repair service the day before, but still wasn't fixed. Ron was a high level employee in the Department of Transportation and was going to be late for work because we slept late and played a little more. He wanted to fix me breakfast but he couldn't call his secretary. This normally conscientious man didn't fret about getting a call in to work. I felt he truly wanted to play hooky as long as he could. That was flattering. I had never been with anyone who wanted to fix me breakfast before so we just kept talking and enjoying the morning without thinking of the consequences.

Ron actually fixed a wonderful breakfast of eggs, bacon, coffee and toast and we kept talking until we had to go our separate ways. But before we parted, Ron asked when we could have a "real" date. Although I had a few daytime parties, I basically worked nights and almost every night. So we left it that if a party canceled at the last minute, I should give him a call and we would go out for dinner. I didn't like parting that way but there was no other choice.

When Ron finally got to work, his secretary, Teresa, was a panic because he had never not shown up for work before. He always called if he was going to be even a minute late. She was looking all over for him and even called his old girl friend Betty, who was still recovering from her surgery at home. Well that was not good. Ron had told me that they weren't steady but he hadn't really broken the relationship yet; he had ignored dealing with it. The cat was out of the bag but good.

On Wednesday, October 5 in the afternoon, my evening party canceled. Normally I would be upset, but this time I was excited and nervous at the same time. I didn't want to call Ron and put him on the spot in case he didn't mean what he had said. I hadn't heard from him at all so my self doubts were working on my subconscious. What if it was only a one night stand? What if it meant more to me than him?

Thank God that part of my brain was working; I thought of a reasonable solution. I called Jim Neve at work and told him the situation and asked him to let Ron know that my party was cancelled and added that if he was free, he could call me. Almost immediately, my phone rang and it was Ron. I had butterflies in my stomach because I didn't really expect him to call. I really liked him a lot and this meant that he really liked me too.

We agreed on dinner but he sheepishly explained that I would need to drive. His car was in for repairs. That was no problem because I had a company car. We set a time for me to pick him up. I was very excited to see him again and relieved that my doubts were only in my imagination.

A Real Date

Our first date started out a little rough. I picked Ron up and asked him to drive my car which he did and he drove to the Elks Club where he was a member. They had a special meeting going on and lucky for me the restaurant was closed. That was a God-send because thinking quickly on the spur of the moment he decided we would go to The Knight Cap in downtown Lansing.

The Knight Cap is a very small intimate restaurant with exceptional food. I had never been there before and immediately I was impressed with how quiet it was even though there were other diners and how dimly lit it was. It was a most heavenly evening. I had never felt so pampered and romantic before. Knowing what I know now, I wouldn't have felt that way at the Elks Club which was open and noisy with ordinary but adequate food.

Again, even though we were in a public place we felt that we were all alone and talked the night away again. Ron was so easy to talk to and so sincerely interested in everything about me. He wasn't boisterous or filled with ego and I loved learning about him, how he got to the DOT and what he did. I was falling in love even though I didn't want to. My goal at the time was to work hard in Tupperware and get hired on staff in Kissimmee, Florida. I didn't want to fall in love but it was happening anyway. And Dick Long had been right when he said that Ron was a "really nice guy". He was kind, thoughtful, considerate, and sincere.

We dated a lot that fall and winter, although it was difficult. Money was short and weekends were my only free time. Ron was paying high child support as well as the house payment on their big home on Lake Geneva in DeWitt, a suburb of Lansing, as well as his own apartment. Good thing that we didn't need a lot to entertain us. We both liked cribbage, backgammon, gin rummy and just talking which didn't cost anything.

Ron had two children at home yet (David and Susie) and got them every other weekend. He wanted to save those weekends just for himself and the kids which I certainly understood. On the free weekends, we might go to a Michigan State Football game, or go out for dinner somewhere or just watch TV together. We talked a lot on the phone which I really enjoyed and we continued to get to know one another.

Getting to Know Him

Every time Ron and I talked about anything, we were amazed at how similar our lives had been. He grew up not more than 10 miles from where I had lived a large part of my life. We both went to different country schools which were only a few miles apart and our families were both very poor in our young years. Our families were very much alike in structure also. Ron was the oldest and so was I. His next sibling is just 22 months younger (sister Gail) and my brother Don is also 22 months younger than I. There was quite a gap before the next siblings in both families. My sisters, Bunnie and Beverly are 9 and 11 years younger than I and Ron's sisters Jean and Linda are also that much younger than he and Gail. And we each have a baby sister that was born when we were in our teens. My sister Beth Ann was born when I was 16. Ron's sister Norma was born when he was 18. Both families are made up of five children with one boy and four girls.

We are both Missouri Synod Lutherans although Ron was raised in that religion from birth. My family didn't join the Lutheran church until I was a 13.

As we made other comparisons, our paths had crossed many times. I had worked in Lapeer and so had Ron. Ron went to Wayne State University in Detroit which was only a few blocks from that big house I lived in when I was a young girl. Although he didn't go Wayne State until my family had moved away, we knew the area well and could talk about that part of Detroit.

We had both been married for over 20 years and we both left our spouses. Ron's wife Martha had requested he move out and I left on my own. But the really ironic thing was that we both moved out of our respective homes in the same week of May in 1981 although we didn't know each other at the time. That coincidence nearly blew me away.

Ron and Martha had owned a business together as had Bob and I. Ron and Martha had a bakery while Bob and I had the studio. We had so many of the same life experiences it was easy for us to understand the difficulties we each had to overcome in running a business with a spouse.

We both had children that were about the same ages or at least close. Ron has five children (three boys and two girls). I have four children (three boys and one girl). Our oldest children were born within a few months of each other and it goes on from there. We just kept being amazed at the similarities.

We both loved camping and had similar stories about trying to camp with our former mates only to find them not happy about the experience. Bob was a heavy drinker and so was Martha and we had both tried counseling while our mates didn't cooperate.

We both joined the military. I joined after high school and Ron enlisted (rather than being drafted) after college. We did often kid each other about our choice of military branches. Ron was in the Army. I always thought that my choice (Air Force) was a cut above the Army. We still jokingly argue that point. He insists that life in the Army was much harder than life in the Air Force.

There were some obvious differences. Ron grew up in a very loving home and I didn't. His parents didn't divorce as mine did and I had been married three times where Ron only married once.

Family, Football, Friends and Florida

Ron and I had been meeting when we could which was not as often as either of us wanted. I hadn't met his kids yet. One night we were sitting at a table in the Red Rail (the country/western bar where we met the night that I ended up going home with him). Ron's son, Karl, came in with his wife, Donna. Karl came right up to me and said (in a very serious tone), "What exactly are your intentions with my father?" I was dumbfounded and stammered a bit I am sure. I'll bet I looked and sounded like a blabbering idiot. Then he said he was joking and that is how I met Ron's oldest son.

Living in a college town as we did, I had always wanted to go to a college football game. Ron's best friend, Jim Neve, had tickets so Ron and I were invited on more than one occasion. I loved it. I have never liked pro football but college sports were different. We took sandwiches and snuck in with a thermos bottle filled with Southern Comfort. Jim's friend Norma joined us and that was the beginning of a wonderful friendship. The four of us became fast friends and spent a lot of time either playing cards or cooking up a meal. Jim loved to make homemade soup.

Jim had rented a cabin up north (near Boyne Mountain) for New Year's Eve of 1983-1984 and invited us to join them. It was cold and snowy but with the fireplace and great friends we had a warm, wonderful time. We cooked together, played cards and just had fun. That started a tradition that we continued for many years of always being with them or at least talking to them on New Year's Eve if we weren't in the area.

I made plans to go to Florida to visit with Glenda, Pekka and Liisa in February of 1984. I don't remember the exact dates. I think I stayed a couple of weeks and when I came back, Ron was at the airport to greet me. What a treat that was. He said he had really, really missed me and I had missed him too. From that time on we were as inseparable as we could be with my job and his weekends with Dave and Susie.

Ron and I New Year's Eve 1983-84

Liisa and I on the beach in West Palm Beach, Florida in February of 1984

Golf and Fish Hooks

I had always said that golf was a stupid game. I mean who in their right mind would chase a little white ball around a huge expanse of green grass with hills and sand traps and trees galore? Ron was a golfer and I liked him so much I decided that it was about time I learned especially since I lived on a golf course. The golf course at Lake of the Hills was perfect as it was only nine holes with most of them being short. There were two par fours and even they were short. It was a very well maintained and pretty executive course. In the spring of 1984 I called my friend Dee Brown who was an avid golfer and asked if she would teach me a little about the game. She did.

It took me a while to get the knack of hitting the ball and then learning the underlying rules of conduct but I liked it. I especially liked it when my five iron connected with the ball which sent it sailing far landing right on the green next to the hole. That did not happen often; mostly my ball only waddled a few feet from where I hit it and I would have to do it again and again. Every time I played I got a little better and it was more fun. I especially loved being outside, enjoying the grass, gentle breezes and a good hit once in a while.

Ron was thrilled that I had learned a little and we got to play once in a while on the weekends when he didn't have the kids. It didn't take long for me to get really hooked on the game. I loved it and wanted to play a big golf course someday so was excited when Ron suggested that we go overnight to a course he liked in Lewiston, Michigan.

Early in July of 1984 Ron planned the weekend trip to The Garland Golf and Country Club in Lewiston. It was very nice and there was a pretty lake nearby. We golfed one of the days and it was wonderful. I still have the score card which indicates Ron beat me pretty bad but I was still learning and it didn't matter. I just loved being out in God's country. I remember one of the holes way back which skirted the woods and just as I got to the tee box I looked to the flag and there was a deer standing near the green. It was just beautiful.

Ron noticed that the marina at the lake rented row boats and he wanted to go fishing. I told him that I was scared to death of fish hooks from when I used to have nightmares about them attacking me. He promised to be careful. So he rowed out and when he got to a place where he felt the fish were, he flicked the line but it didn't go in the water. The fish hook caught on my sweater on my left shoulder. I firmly said, "That's enough, please go back". I should have learned a lesson right then and run far away from him. I can't tell you how many times he has promised me that something will be okay by saying "just trust me" but then it turns out to be not the way he promised.

I don't remember if it was that trip or another one but sometime in Michigan we had to go to urgent care or a doctor's office and framed for all to see was a huge montage of snapshots of people who had fish hooks through fingers, lips and all sorts of body parts. I remember being more than uncomfortable while sitting in the waiting room.

Life Begins Again

Ron gradually introduced me to the rest of his kids. David and Susie were the youngest and the ones I would get to know the best early on. David was 15 and Susie was 12 (13 in August). Karl was 27 (Glenda's age) and married to Donna, Kurt was 24 (Mark's age) and married to Oneida who was Donna's sister, and Marty was 22 (23 in October) and married to Bryan. At the time none of them had children.

Things really progressed in our relationship and we started talking about his moving in with me. We were in love and both struggling financially so it made sense to share one place rather than have two to pay for. Although we hadn't talk about marriage yet, we knew we wanted to be together as much as possible and so he moved into my town house on April 27, 1984.

I loved getting up early and making his coffee before he went to work and having dinner ready when he came home. I had plenty to keep me busy during the day what with working with new dealers, taking care of hostess planning, manager meetings, recruiting and lots of telephone work. Yes, I usually had to run out right after dinner to do a party but it worked out fine.

Once Ron and I were together in what had been my house that meant that Dave and Susie came there every other weekend. I tried to make them feel at home. Jim was still at home, but often he was visiting his father so it was easy to have the kids there. At first our times together were strained a bit. David and Susie still lived at home with their mother who didn't like me at all. I remember the first time the kids came to my house, I fixed a dinner and we played pinochle after. They were polite, but I knew they would have rather been with Ron alone.

Sometimes Robert was at my place and that was fine with David, but Susie didn't like the teasing Robert did and complained to her mother and she in turn asked Ron to keep Robert away when the kids were there. When Ron had the nerve to tell me what Martha wanted it did not go well with me to say the least.

After all we were in what had been my house and he was my son. No way would I tell him to stay away. So the tension began. But I truly thought the weekends were fun. We planned things for the kids and I really enjoyed them. I especially liked the card playing.

I had all of Ron's kids over for Father's day in 1984 and that worked out fine. I liked all of his kids. Since we weren't really merging two families like the Partridge family did, it wasn't really a big problem with getting along. Mark and Glenda (since they have lived out of state) have never met Ron's older three kids. Mark hasn't met any of them and Robert and Jim were seldom around anymore.

L-R Karl, Donna, Susie, Bryan, Marty and David. Kurt and Onida were missing.

My Baby Left Me

Jim graduated from high school in June of 1984 and I had an open house for him with most of my family attending. Mark couldn't come as he was working a new job in California and my brother Don was still in Texas. I remember it as a wonderful day. Ron had to leave the party early to attend some function with his family but it really didn't matter.

Almost immediately after graduation Jim left on a long journey with the Oldsmobile hot air balloon team. He was a chaser and loved the whole adventure. As I remember he was gone for the rest of the year.

Ron and I settled down to a routine of work and some play. We played golf often after work if I didn't have to work. One thing we really enjoyed was Friday evening. After work, Ron and I would go to the Elks Club for a fish fry dinner which always began with a martini then to top off the evening we went to the Harley House (hotel) in Lansing. The lounge there was very plush and relaxing. A trio headed by Brian Grinnell on piano played perfect soft jazz or at least soft lounge music. We would talk the whole time and it was as though we didn't have a care in the world. Life was good.

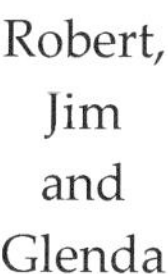

Robert, Jim and Glenda

Top:
Me, Jim and Ron

Bottom:
The balloon team.

Cooking Over a Wood Fire

I earned a nice cabin tent, Coleman stove, lantern and more in a sales contest from Tupperware. We were going to go camping and hoped the kids would come with us. I didn't actually get the tent until fall in 1984 but the weather was still great for camping. We planned a weekend at Holly State Park near my old stomping grounds of Ortonville. I spent all day Friday getting everything ready so we could take off as soon as Ron got home. I am not sure Dave and Susie were that excited about going but I was prepared to make it a fun weekend. I had the fixings for S'mores, and grilled pies and the menu was easy with hot dogs and hamburgers. We had a baseball and gloves plus games and cards. What we didn't plan for was the rain.

When we got to the park, we got one of the last sites. It was in a bit of a gully and quite small. David had brought his own little pup tent which he set up. Ron and I got the cabin tent up and it wasn't easy. Then we moved in with our sleeping bags etc. We managed to eat just before it rained. I tried to make the campfire pies by sticking my arm out a slot in the tent to reach the fire but it didn't work too well. We snuggled in our sleeping bags and let the sound of rain lull us to sleep.

When we woke in the morning we were all wet. Everything was wet and David's tent was floating. Not being deterred, we packed up everything and threw the wet sleeping bags in the back of the car. Before we left the campground we found another site, not far from where we had been which was now vacated. It was very large and on higher ground. We moved the tents to the new site as well as our cooking gear then took off to locate a laundromat. While the sleeping bags were drying we read or played a game then we were back in the campground in time for lunch. From then on the rest of the weekend was fine.

But it appeared Susie was never happy. Dave was fine even floating in his tent but we just couldn't get Susie to enjoy anything even weekends at our place. We tried though. Pinochle, backgammon and cribbage were fun for her so we did a lot of that.

As our time together grew, we did more camping and even included a canoe trip on one of Michigan's fun rivers. I especially remember the AuSable River trip with all of Ron's kids and spouses. Marty and Susie weren't looking forward to a day without their curling irons and hair dryers and I think that Donna and Oneida weren't that excited either. It was, after all, a rustic campground. My buddy in this was Bryan. He jumped on an idea I told him about—the huge water tank that worked with the campfire to heat water (page 199). Bryan had that thing built in no time.

I remember that weekend as fun and exciting. I cooked everything over an open wood fire and we even had soup cooked in a big kettle hanging from a tripod over the fire the first night. We had steaks for dinner another night and pancakes and eggs for breakfast along with a fresh coffee.

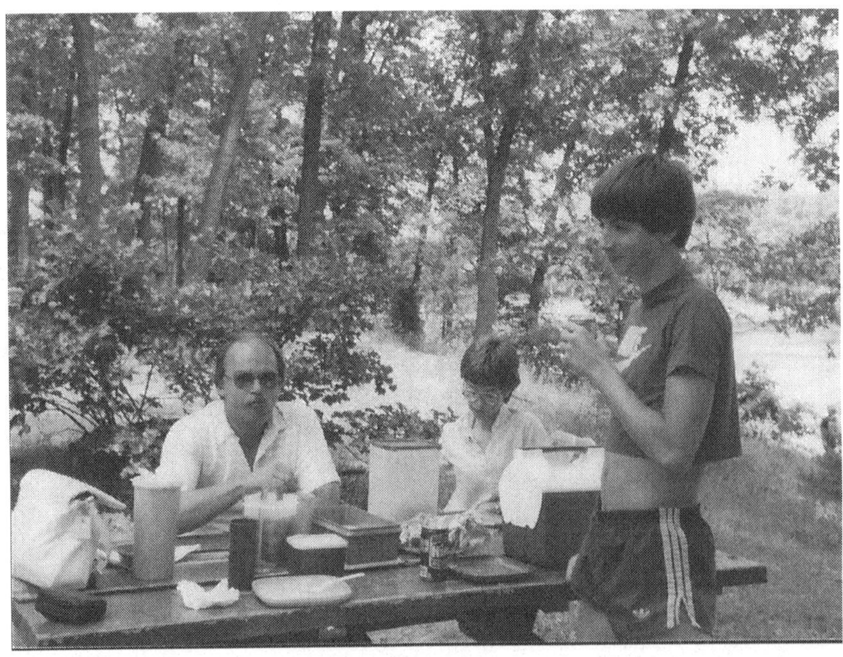

Jubilee

One of the highlights of the year in Tupperware was the huge week-long event called Jubilee. It was held at Tupperware headquarters in Kissimmee, Florida, (near Orlando). Tupperware had five or six Jubilees (one for each region) every August to reward high achieving managers and dealers and to get everyone excited about the fall selling season. There would be upwards of three or four thousand attending and every night was unbelievable. During the day there would be seminars and at night in the huge arena which was larger than a football field Tupperware put on a show and gave gifts like cars, freezers, furniture, trips around the world and more. It was a lot like Let's Make a Deal and Queen for a Day only on a much larger scale. It was something that could not be easily explained to a novice. All I can say is I wouldn't have missed it for the world. I had worked hard from the beginning of the year to recruit dealers and build my unit (Success Express) so I could be recognized and I knew I was due for some big gifts.

Ron's parents came up from their home in Winter Haven, Florida, to visit family in July I believe. I don't remember how long they were there. I didn't get to meet them because they were staying with sister Gail (I think) and I was busy with parties. I do remember that Ron's dad got sick and was even in the hospital for a little while because he was taking too much of a medicine he had been prescribed. The family was afraid for him to drive back to Florida so Ron offered to drive them knowing that I was driving to Florida about the same time and he could get a ride back with me. The plan was made.

I drove with Diane Fish a dealer of mine who I had recently promoted to manager and she was very excited to be attending her first Jubilee.

Ron had no concept of Jubilee like so many non-Tupperware people. His idea of conventions was to skip out of as many meetings as possible whereas none of those attending Jubilee would ever consider missing a meeting. Ron wanted me to spend time with him, but I just couldn't except I did agree to drive from Orlando to Winter Haven to pick him up the day before Jubilee was finished. That was hard to do because our programs were packed night and day. When I picked him up, I was introduced to his parents but we didn't spend any time at all because I wanted to get back.

Once back at Jubilee, Ron attended a couple of the meetings and one general meeting and after seeing the hype he finally understood why I didn't want to miss anything.

Ron spent the last night of Jubilee in my hotel room which I shared with one of the managers (there were two double beds in the room). I tried to keep him from being horny but it didn't work. I hoped we were quiet enough but I am sure we weren't. I wasn't very comfortable knowing my roommate was a few feet away.

The next morning Diane, Ron and I drove back to Michigan and resumed our normal routines.

Move Stirred up Trouble In the Family.

Ron had been dating a woman for a couple of years before he met me. Betty was a lovely woman by all accounts and Ron's family liked her mostly because they didn't see the relationship going anywhere. With me it was another story. Whenever Ron's ex (Martha) referred to me in talks with Ron and others I was "THAT REDHEAD". So for that reason, when Ron moved to my place, her radar sensed danger. But remember it was Martha who kicked Ron out of her life.

A few months after Ron moved in, Ron's children called a meeting with just Ron. Ron reluctantly went to the meeting and when he came home he told me that they had demanded that he move out and nix the relationship with me. They wanted him to go back to Martha who by the way was not at the meeting. Ron came home and told me the whole story. He stood up to them telling them in no uncertain terms that he would never go back to their mother and he professed his love for me loudly. We hoped that was the end of the animosity but it wasn't. In fact it kept getting worse. Good thing we loved each other so much. It was a bit hard for me to truly like his kids knowing they didn't like me at all, but I tried to credit their animosity to negativity from their mother.

Somber Wedding

Ron and I had never talked about marriage. I think we both thought we would eventually marry but neither one of us spoke about it. We felt like we were married except for the legality of it all.

One night in November, I think, we were sitting on the bed just talking and I surprised myself and Ron by asking, "Are we ever going to get married?" Ron wasn't shocked and he didn't stammer or anything. He simply began to talk about when a good time would be. Since Ron operated at home like he did at work, his thinking was in terms of finance and accounting. The end of the year was coming and meant a tax advantage if we married yet that year. So we looked at the calendar and picked the date of Saturday, December 22.

In talking about the date, we decided to pick the weekend his youngest children would be with us so they could be involved. And we decided the only other people we would invite would be the rest of our kids. We didn't want our sisters and brother there or any other friends because we thought it would be good to just be an immediate family affair. If we had to do it over again, we would never have done that. We would have eloped to Vegas or anywhere and enjoyed the day to ourselves or we would have invited everyone.

First of all our siblings were miffed that they weren't invited. My only child in attendance was Robert as the rest lived so far away. Mark was in California, Glenda in Florida and Jim was in basic training in Texas. Also in attendance was our best man, Jim Neve (the man who had the Tupperware Party where I first met Ron) and Carolyn Branch (my former Tupperware manager) was my matron of honor. Jim's girlfriend Norma and Carolyn's husband were also invited.

Secondly Ron's kids were not at all happy. We could tell they didn't want to be there. It showed in their faces and actions.

After the ceremony, we all came back to our place for some refreshments which included a cake. It was just okay. We took the time to open Christmas gifts then everyone left except David and Susie. The next day after we took them home, we headed to Grand Rapids and a motel there with a nice inside pool. Ron had come down with a cold though so he didn't feel great. We only stayed Sunday and Monday coming home on Tuesday.

On New Year's Eve, we went out to dinner early with friends then went to the hot tub place. The hot tubs are in private enclosures which are outside of their private rooms but it was sleeting out. Need I mention that it was cold, but the hot tub was warm so we enjoyed that then back into our private space, we had a little wine after which we drove home. The roads were getting icy so it was a little hairy driving. Once home we turned on the TV to watch the ball come down in Times Square then went to bed.

When we woke up New Year's Day, we noticed the electricity was out and it was cold. Everything outside was covered with a coat of ice and branches hung heavily. Luckily we had city water and a gas stove and hot water heater plus I also had plenty of candles. To warm up the kitchen a little I put pots of water on the stove to boil and we filled the bath tub with water in case our lines froze. Our phone worked and we got a call from Jim Neve. He invited us to come to his place for chili and cards with Norma.

We remained without power for five whole days and we were perplexed because the news in the paper said everyone's power had been restored. I decided to call and see what was wrong. It turned out that no one from our community had even reported the power was out. It got fixed right away and everything was fine.

Above:
The portrait Ron and I had made a few weeks before our actual wedding. We drove to Ontario, Canada, to the Hebert's studio as they were good friends of mine.

Robert, Ron and I

Top: Carolyn Branch, Me, Ron and Jim Neve

Bottom: Marty, David, Me, Ron, Karl, Kurt and Susie

Bad Trip

While Ron was married to Martha, he always took his kids to Florida for spring break or sometime in the spring. But he hadn't made the trip since they separated in 1981. Once we were married, I think Dave and Susie hoped we would take them to Florida and we did. We wanted to make the trip special and planned to include Disney World and the ocean over on the east coast near where my daughter lived.

Easter was on April 7 in 1985 so we probably left a little before that. I know we drove straight through to Georgia before stopping at a Howard Johnson Motel. We had a bad experience there—mainly with their restaurant and have never been to one again, but once we stopped at the welcome center just inside the Florida state line, all problems with the hotel were forgotten. The kids ran around like it was Christmas and enjoyed lots of fresh orange juice.

We stayed with Ron's parents who were very excited to see us and especially the grandchildren. I loved Ron's parents and they showed a lot of love toward me. Of course we went to church on Easter and the kids enjoyed the pool in their complex for a couple of days before we drove to Disney World for the day. I love Disney and so did the kids.

We planned a trip to the east coast so they could play in the ocean and I could see my daughter and family. I had rented a very nice room in a hotel on Sanger Island and invited Glenda, Pekka and Liisa to come and visit which they did. The ocean was fun, but Susie didn't like sharing our time in Florida with anyone like Liisa and Glenda. She pouted and was not pleasant to be around. She just couldn't understand that Glenda was my daughter and Liisa my granddaughter whom I hadn't seen for a while. Her attitude ruined the trip for me and I am sure she was not at all happy either. I even caught Susie making gagging motions in the back seat of the car whenever I talked about Liisa. My visor was down and I could see her in the mirror.

Oh well, we tried to have a good trip. Once we left the coast, Susie was better but I felt bad that my visit with Glenda and Liisa was ruined. Susie was an angry little girl whom I felt needed counseling.

As much as I loved Ron and he I, dealing with his kids was becoming a big problem. Ron and I argued about how to handle the situation and we were at opposite poles. Handling kids was one area of our lives where we were one hundred degrees apart. Because of Ron's strict Christian upbringing in a German family his guilt over the divorce contributed to his going overboard with the kids. He kept trying to keep the peace and the more we tried, the more it didn't work. They were never happy.

Falling in a Real Hole

We got into a nice routine. Friday night dates or cards with Jim and Norma were the norm. When the kids were over, we played games and watched TV or movies. Of course we went to church on Sunday. The rest of the week was work. Saturday, I usually delivered my Tupperware. Back then we dealers and managers had to deliver our parties' purchases to the hostesses.

In May Ron and I gave a conformation party for Susie at the club house in our complex. It was a large room and all of Ron's sisters were there and of course Ron's kids as well as Martha along with neighbors from where Ron used to live with her. Robert was my only child in the area. It was a very nice party and I think Susie appreciated it.

In June Ron and I flew to San Diego so Ron could attend a conference there. During the day when he was at meetings, I would drive around and explore the area and when he was finished for the day, I would show him what I discovered. I fell in love with that place and travel. I couldn't wait to do more.

When we came back from the conference, we were playing golf at a local golf course not even two miles from home and on the fifth hole, I hit a good shot which landed just to the right of the green. Ron's ball went to the left so we parted and I walked to my ball. Although it was no longer on the fairway, it wasn't in long grass and I figured it would be an easy shot. Walking to the ball though, I stepped into a seventeen inch deep hole which had been camouflaged with long grass combed over it. Inside the hole was a broken irrigation tile which tore into my chin badly. I was bleeding profusely. Ron dropped what he was doing and came to help me off the course. Since we were straight back from the starter's shack, we stopped in for a second so the young girl could see what the problem was. I was dripping blood all over everything. We asked her to tell the owner and left our phone number. We then went to the local urgent care facility which was a little more than a mile away. At urgent care they tried to clean the wound which had a lot of grass and whatever in it then stitched me up and sent me home with an antibiotic and crutches. Well it got infected and we never heard a word from the owner of the course. Robert and Ron's son Kurt went to the golf course with camera and tape measure and sure enough the hole was still there hiding in plain sight. There had been no attempt to fix it. They measured its depth and the width and we were surprised how large it was. After hearing their news, I then got mad. I called a lawyer. Ron didn't think it was necessary but I felt violated and was missing a lot of summer fun. The fact that the course owner hadn't bothered to call or fix the hole told me he didn't care so I figured I could hit him where he might care—in his pocketbook. Well, I didn't get much mainly because Ron wouldn't support me; he thought I should just get over it.

Their lawyer came to the house and pressured me to settle for six thousand dollars. I should have demanded more. The lawyer wrote me a check on the spot and I'll bet he was laughing all the way back to the office.

Even though I was still steaming over the above incident and in fact, still on crutches, I planned a surprise birthday party for Ron's fifty second birthday early in July. I had heard about a charter bus company which took people to the Detroit Tigers baseball games and provided sandwiches and drinks on the way to the stadium and back. That sounded like fun and Ron lived for baseball (still does). I invited his kids and their spouses, people Ron worked with and our close friends Jim and Norma. The surprise worked and it was a fun trip. I think the Tigers won too which made it even more special.

Liisa Spends a Month With Us

I had asked my daughter, Glenda if she could send Liisa (who was six at the time) up to visit for a month and she did. It was late July and August and we enjoyed our time with her. I took her to my mother's place once or twice. She had all the other grandchildren over often to play in her lovely swimming pool. I also took her to see her grandfather (Bob) for lunch one day.

I distinctly remember while on our way to Mom's one day we were going past farm after farm and I pointed out all the corn that was growing. I figured that she wasn't that familiar with farm agriculture living in Florida.

She asked, "Why do they grow so much corn?"

I replied, "To feed the cows and pigs".

"Why don't they let them just eat grass?" was her next question.

I should have known I was getting into dangerous territory.

I answered, "They feed them corn and grains to get them fat before they take them to the market."

She asked, "Who do they sell them to?"

When I told her that they sell them to the meat companies so they can make hamburgs and steak she was appalled and screamed,

"You mean they don't just let them die naturally?"

I felt like a really bad Grandma to have to break the facts of life to her. The fact that she became a vegetarian is not surprising because her mother, Glenda never liked meat and would pick at it or not eat it. This all started after she had a biology class where they talked about parasites in animals.

We really enjoyed having Liisa with us but she was a bit lonely since no other little children lived in our complex. I taught her how to play Jacks and to jump rope and took her shopping for back to school clothing at a very nice resale shop nearby.

We also took her to the zoo at Potter Park which she dearly loved and camping to Holly State Park. Robert came out to camp with us too. She liked camping. She found an acorn on the ground and Robert told her to plant it so it would grow into a tree. So she did and we watered it. When she wasn't around Robert put an eight inch weed in the ground where the nut had been buried and told her that it grew already. She was so excited.

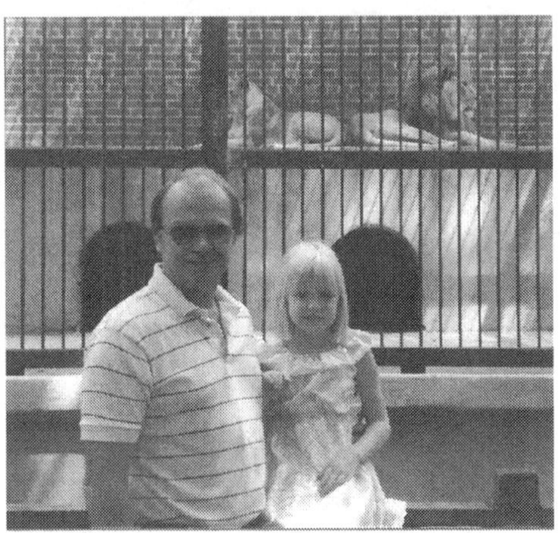

But the same old problem reared its ugly head any time Susie came over. Susie couldn't share the stage with Liisa. This was becom-

Top: At the zoo — Bottom: at Mom's pool with second cousins. L-R Holly, Jason, Kathleen, Liisa, Coleen and Allison.

ing a big problem. I wanted to like Susie but it was getting increasingly difficult. I wished Ron and/or Martha would do something but they didn't.

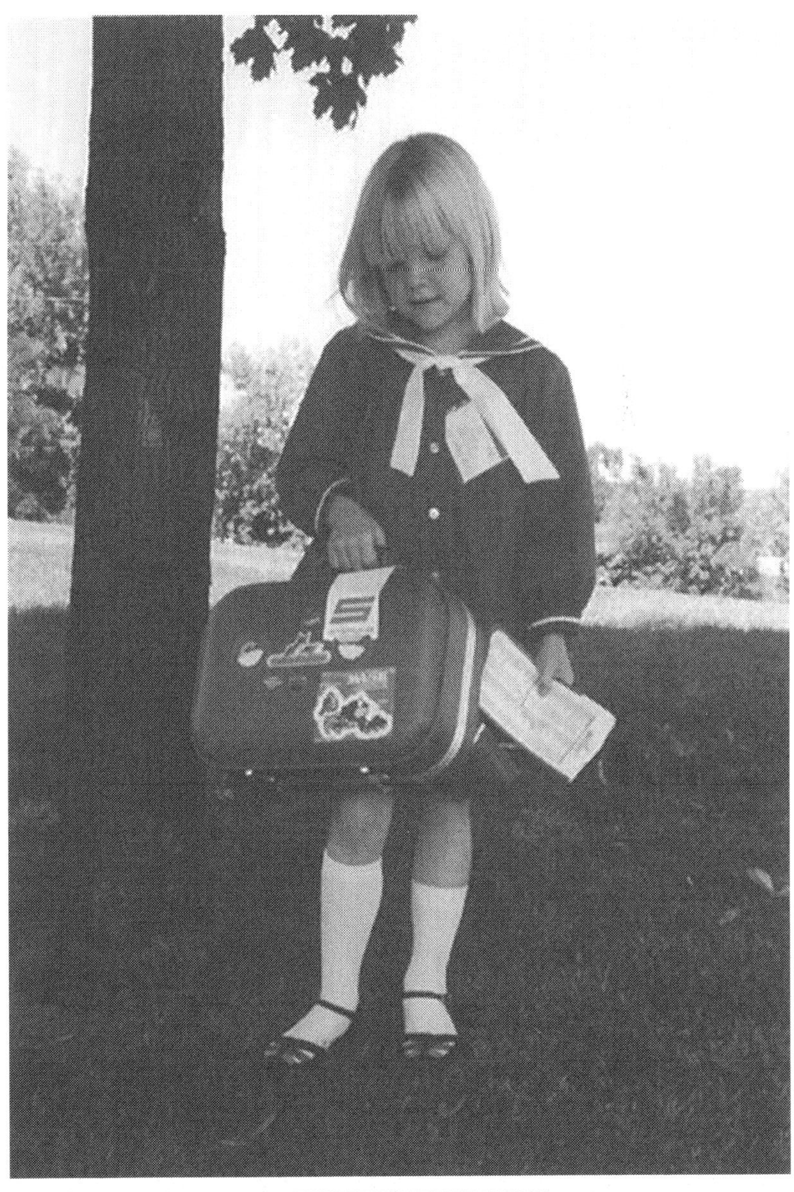

Liisa ready to go home in one of her new (used) outfits.

I Love Lucy

It was Friday, November 1, 1985 and I felt alive and wonderful. My love, Ron, and I were nearing our first wedding anniversary and it was a glorious fall day. The sun was shining brightly making the leaves sparkle in their fall radiance. The red, brown, gold and orange leaves were as brilliant as I had ever seen them. The beauty of it all nearly took my breath away. The sun was warm and there was a gentle breeze just barely tickling my skin when I walked confidently up to the door of the lady who was to be my hostess that day for a Tupperware party. I loved my job but was looking forward to my vacation with Ron in a couple of weeks. We were going to Freeport in the Bahamas over Thanksgiving thanks to the settlement I received from falling into the hole at the golf course.

That afternoon I was wearing a red corduroy suit and felt sharp and confidant as I started the party. There were easily twelve to eighteen women in attendance and they sat in a half circle around the room. After introducing myself to the group I asked if they would please go around the room stating their name and adding why they liked Tupperware. All of them had glowing things to say about our product or listed their favorite pieces. It seemed that each one was more enthusiastic than the one before. Dead center, directly in front of me, the next lady said, "I am Lucy and I hate Tupperware; I don't even know why I'm here." Everyone's body language told me they were embarrassed for Lucy and to try to take away Lucy's comment those who came after Lucy had more wonderful things to say about the product than the ones before. I wondered why indeed she had come if she didn't like Tupperware, but I went on with the demonstration.

At the end, I told everyone I was going to the kitchen for a drink of water and I invited them to come up to my table to actually examine the product and when ready to bring their order to me in the kitchen. Lucy was first as she hadn't bothered to look at my display and as she laid down her blank order form, she simply said that she wasn't buying anything. With that I thanked her for coming anyway. Several ladies booked parties and scheduled them within the next week or so.

The next party from that group was held in the evening. I got there early as usual and who did I see come in the door, but Lucy. I started the party the way I always did and the introductions came to a screeching halt when they got to Lucy. She stated (without any embarrassment) "My name is Lucy and I still don't like Tupperware." Comments were wonderful after Lucy's statement but I still wished she had stayed home. I wondered if maybe she didn't understand the product or warranty. I changed my plan for the evening's demonstration and decided to cover the basics including the warranty.

After the demonstration, Lucy approached me and asked if the warranty was really true. She went on to say that she had bags of cracked, or sticky Tupperware in the basement. I told her to please bring all of her bad Tupperware to the next party and it would be exchanged for brand new pieces at no charge to her. Her face brightened and she let me know that she would do that. She didn't trust me enough to place an order though, but I thought I was getting closer to making Lucy a friend.

At the next party, Lucy was the first one there with her two large grocery bags of Tupperware and after I examined them I told her that there was no problem; the company would replace them all and the new pieces would be delivered with all the orders from the party. I didn't dare try the same introduction game though. I did the one where everyone uses an adjective that starts with the first letter of their first name along with their name for example; I was "bashful Barbara". At the end of the demonstration, Lucy came to me and dated a party of her own. Her party would be just a few days before we were leaving for the Bahamas.

Lucy's party was huge. She had already received all of her replacement Tupperware and she was extolling the virtues of Tupperware to everyone. She had $500.00 in orders before I even got to her house, and she had a large group at the party who placed big orders. Lucy was happy and I was happy. I set her delivery date for the week after Thanksgiving.

We left for the Bahamas on November 21. Thanksgiving was on the 28th. We had a wonderful time. The resort was beautiful, we enjoyed sitting under thatched umbrellas drinking exotic drinks while watching the waves play on the beach. We enjoyed dressing up for gourmet dinners at different restaurants and we did a little hang gliding. I had always wanted to try snorkeling so we signed up to do that too. Every evening we dressed up and went to one of the casinos and played a while.

The day we had scheduled the snorkeling adventure turned out to be a little rough but the boat went out to the area where we were to do our thing anyway. We were warned to stay close to the spot where we went in so we wouldn't get swept away. Ron and I were together at first but then I got completely hypnotized by all the beautiful looking fish and forgot to pay attention to where I was. Suddenly I was upon a lot of dead coral and I panicked. I couldn't stand up without stepping on the sharp coral and it was scraping my stomach which was exposed because I had on a two piece bathing suit. I screamed for help between gulps for air but there was absolutely no one around. I screamed again and again but I didn't see anyone. I thought I would drown because I was all alone wasn't getting anyone's attention. The others were on the other side of the island. I was also getting very tired. Miraculously I ended back at the beach with all the others and I really don't know how. I was totally puzzled at how I got back but I was thankful. Back on the boat, I enjoyed the Bahama Mamas which were provided by the captain and after we got back to the hotel I put ointment on all of my scrapes which were many.

We flew home on Thanksgiving day and had a little layover in Chicago. During the layover we went to a restaurant in the airport and had a mediocre Turkey dinner. Once home we got into our routines. I packed the Tupperware orders and went to make my deliveries as scheduled. When I got to Lucy's she was a panic wondering if I was all right. I was, of course, so I assured her that

I was fine. But she went on to tell me this story. She said she was taking a nap on a certain day (the same day we were snorkeling), and she woke up shaking from the vision she had seen. She had seen me in trouble but didn't know the details. All she knew was that I was in deep trouble and she prayed hard for me to be okay then saw a bunch of angels circling around me. Now I knew how I got back to the beach. I had known that Lucy was a deeply religious woman but didn't really understand how powerful that could be. I have often wondered what would have happened if I hadn't tried really hard to make Lucy a friend?

Train Trip to Chicago

I have always loved trains and thought it would be fun to treat Dave, Susie and Robert to Chicago near Christmas to take in all the wonderful Christmas decorations in the store windows.

The train trip itself was wonderful and the kids enjoyed it. I had reservations at the Drake hotel in Chicago which is a very old but nice hotel.

We spent one full day at the famous Museum of Science and Industry. What fascination. Colleen Moore's Fairy Castle was something that Susie and I really enjoyed. It is totally mind boggling to see everything. It was huge. They have a coal mine, and lots and lots of amazing exhibits. They are only open from 9 a.m. to 5:30 and there is no way on earth that one can see everything in that small amount of time.

We took the kids to Gino's pizza place. It is world famous for their deep dish pizza. People who visit this place write their names on the wall. We didn't have anything to write with so I had Susie use my lipstick tube to write her name and the boys did the same.

We went in some of the shops like Gucci's. A doorman in formal dress stood at the revolving door to greet everyone. I remember looking at a nice sweater for Ron in there and almost dropped dead when I asked the price. It was over $400. We did not belong there at all. I was uncomfortable. It wasn't even fun looking at things in those expensive stores. We more enjoyed Marshall Fields and Macy's. It was a fun trip for all of us.

Bridge and Baseball

About this time we were getting vibrations from Dave and Susie that they resented having to come to our place every other weekend. None of their friends lived near us and there were few kids in our area so we offered them their freedom if they wanted it. We told them they were free to stay away but welcome to come whenever and as often as they liked and we sincerely hoped they would. As soon as we granted freedom, they flew the coop. All in all even though we missed them, it made our lives easier and we hoped theirs was easier also.

We had been hearing that Ron's dad was failing a little so we decided we would drive to Florida for a couple of weeks in March of 1986. We didn't take Susie and Dave this time (much to their chagrin) as Ron really wanted to devote all our time with his Dad.

Earlier in the year, knowing that we would be there to visit in the spring, Ron's Mom had written and asked if I would please learn to play bridge before coming down. She also sent me a book on the basics of the game. I love cards, but there are so many rules with bridge that I was a bit overwhelmed. Ron already knew how to play. I kept the book handy and read it whenever I got the chance, but I learn best by doing so I wasn't progressing very much.

Both his Mom and Dad were very excited to see us and we were excited to see them too. First of all, Ron and I did a few chores for them and planted some flowers on their patio. We had a ball picking out the plants we thought they would enjoy.

Ron took his dad to a Tiger baseball game which was a highlight for his dad especially. Ron was able to get two box seats that someone had just turned in. They were right behind the dugout and his dad was totally delighted. Mr. Hofmeister was a die-hard baseball fan.

At night we played bridge. Dad Hofmeister was so excited that he kept us playing until very late at night. He sure loved playing cards. They let me keep my book handy and also allowed me to ask questions. I did okay in fact I loved bridge because to play well one had to think and plan to make the goal. It was my kind of game. They really enjoyed helping me learn and playing with us. I couldn't wait to find groups to play with in Michigan when we got home.

We took them out to eat a few times and helped with meals there at home. One time we took them to the nice dining room at the Elks Club and Mom Hofmeister was really impressed. It generally took very little to impress her. Sitting in the dining room, she saw other couples dining together and they seemed very alive and vibrant. She could imagine them planning trips and doing things together while her own husband was on the way down. He had retired when they moved to Florida, but she kept working. She taught piano at home. At that time, she had just quit teaching and now realized that they wouldn't have retirement together after all. She and I went into the restroom together and out of the blue she said, "My mother warned me about this." She was talking about their 12 year age difference. I hugged her and reminded her of their wonderful years in Florida but I felt so sorry for her.

When it was time to come home, Ron hugged his parents and on the way out of town, Ron said, "That is the last time I will ever see my dad alive." He was right.

Shortly after we got home (April 10 to be exact) we got a phone call from Ron's sister, Gail, saying he had died at home. They had had Bible class in their home that morning then he laid down to take a nap. That was the end.

His body was flown back to Michigan and Ron's Mom flew on

the same plane. Ron's brother-in-law, Tom, handled the funeral arrangements since he was (and still is) a funeral director.

Of course, Ron and I were at the funeral home for the visitation (several days before the actual funeral). The Hofmeister family (most were from the thumb area of Michigan) was there most of the time also. And so was Ron's former wife, Martha. She was there just like she was still a member of the family. That was very uncomfortable for both Ron and I. Ron was trying to introduce me to his aunts and uncles whom I had not met but they were already conversing with Martha. I think that some in the family didn't even know they were divorced and it was very uncomfortable for Ron to introduce the new wife while the old was there. Divorce was not common in the Hofmeister family which was very "old school", staunch German Lutherans. I felt like I didn't belong so I just sat still and out of the way and couldn't really be by Ron's side where he would have liked to have me. Ron was terribly angry at Martha for parading around like she did. Martha was a very vibrant and fun lady. Everyone loved her but I was intimated by her. Funerals are no fun anyway and I was glad when it was over with.

If Martha had simply paid her respects then attended the funeral it would have been fine but to be there representing the family all during the viewing was wrong in our opinion. I really felt bad for Ron.

Trips and Tribulation

I don't remember exactly when I gave up my manager ship and fell back to being just a Tupperware dealer but it was about this time. I wanted more time for us and more freedom to be with Ron when he was off work. Because I had to give up my company car, we searched for and found a used van which I could use for Tupperware as well as for camping.

In May of '86, I learned that my son, Mark was going on a cross country bicycle trip from southern California to Boston with six friends. Once I knew of their route, I determined he would be closest to me when he reached Tennessee so I volunteered to go down and ride across the state with my four wheels being a SAG wagon (support and gear) for the group. I forget what town I met them in but it was somewhere in the western part of the state. It was such fun to get to meet the group and I couldn't believe the distances they rode each day rain or shine. Most of their rides were well above one hundred miles.

They had the hardest time eating enough for breakfast to keep them going on the day's ride until I introduced them to Shoney's restaurants. They had a breakfast buffet which was huge and one paid one fee and could eat all they chose to eat. Shoney's lost money on those guys. They wiped out the buffet in the flash of an eye and were very happy. I was having such fun with them that I called Ron and asked him to fly down and ride with me in the van for the rest of the trip. Basically I carried supplies so they wouldn't have so much to carry on their bikes. He did and we left the group in Rogers, Tennessee, after a nice group dinner. The group went on to finish their trip in Boston after covering 3, 864 miles in 42 days.

In June, Ron and I went to Baltimore. He was attending an Association of Government Accountants convention there and Robert was there with his new girlfriend, Elizabeth. They showed us around a bit and we went out to dinner with them. That was a fun time.

Ron's Mom had come up to Michigan for a visit with her girls who all lived nearby. We invited her to come and stay at our house for a couple of days so she could be there for Ron's 54th birthday. The fourth of July was on a Friday and Ron's sister Gail had a big party at their place on the lake that Sunday. There was a lot of food and drinking and hard game playing. Ron played a lot of volleyball and when playing with the younger nephews it was no easy game. He really played hard.

We brought Ron's Mom home with us and Ron had to go to work on Monday as usual, but we planned a nice dinner for his birthday on Tuesday. When Ron got to work they immediately had a fire drill and he had to walk down several flights of stairs and up again. He didn't feel well. He had tightness in his chest and decided to come home. When I suggested that I take him to the urgent care which was nearby, he said, "No it would go away". I tried hard to get him to go until finally the pain was so bad that he gave in. Stubborn German. The minute we got there they had him in a room and called an ambulance. In no time he was hooked up to all sorts of monitors and IVs and on his way to the hospital. I went home and told his mom what the situation was and we decided that maybe she could call one of the girls to come and get her. This was only three months after losing her husband and I didn't want her sitting there alone worrying about her only son. She didn't want to come to the hospital.

They kept Ron in the hospital for about five days. Before they released him we met with a dietitian then I went home and threw out everything that was a no-no and promised to cook healthy from then on. The other order we had from the doctor was to get active. We planned to work on that right away and bicycling came to mind because of recently being with Mark.

But when Ron came home he was very weak and could hardly walk to the end of the sidewalk, but I pushed him a little every day and gradually he got better.

Shortly after his return home Liisa came for her summer visit again and I distinctly remember him wanting to go out and dig up a few worms to take her fishing. He went out with shovel in hand but just couldn't dig a hole and he felt like a failure. He sat and cried. I made up my mind that he would get strong and we worked on it.

Ron used to smoke cigars but ironically he had given them up on the past New Year's Eve. I was still smoking cigarettes and I felt terribly guilty especially since I was trying to cook healthy meals while polluting the air with smoke. I started making plans to quit by first talking to myself to reprogram my thinking. All day long I would think and even say out loud, how I hated cigarettes. I was working on it but still smoking. Long time habits are hard to break.

Bicycling

It had been a long time since I had ridden a bike. In fact the only bike I ever rode was the one my brother and I shared in 1948-1949. It had no real seat; we wrapped thick towels around the seat stem to try to cushion our butt. But we were never high enough to ride normally. So when we went looking for a bike, I was skeptical about trying to learn to ride at my age (49). We went to a local bike shop, rode different bikes in the parking lot and settled on 3 speed Raleigh bikes. I had a girls bike probably because I thought all girls had the female version. I was expecting coaster brakes so had to get used to handle bar brakes. We were excited. The bikes were fully outfitted with water bottle racks complete with colorful bottles and I had an odometer on my bike.

The first ride I took was around our little lake in the complex. It was a small lake with condos on both sides and a nice blacktopped road all around. I think it was only seven tenths of a mile but it tired me out. I encouraged Ron to do part of the ride and he did. We went slow while still getting used to shifting and the bike itself.

Every day we rode a little then after a couple of weeks I suggested we ride around the nearby neighborhood at Lake Lansing. My odometer indicated that it was 4.4 miles from our house and back. Wow, we felt like a million dollars and thought we were doing great which we were. The Lake Lansing ride was perfect and it was a fun ride. Each time we rode, we completed the ride in less time and pretty soon we decided we needed to do the loop twice in each set. We were riding a lot and enjoying every minute of it. We even started riding up to the nearby frozen yogurt shop just to get a cone.

Then we heard of a bike group that met nearby in various spots for rides at all times and days. The biggest was the Wednesday night ride from the Campus at Michigan State University. They had rides of all lengths and for all types of riders. We joined in a beginners ride one week and were hooked. We kept expanding our rides by taking longer and more challenging rides and felt like we could conquer the world. Between biking and golfing we were getting in good shape.

The middle of August Ron went to the cardiologist for the final checkup and blew the doctor away with the treadmill test. He was then released from the heart doctor's care. Good thing, because we had the van all loaded for a camping trip to Mackinaw City. We had our bikes and planned to take them on the ferry over to Mackinaw Island so we could ride all around the island. What fun we had. We biked up and down the hills and all over the island. We had been there many times but never covered the area as thoroughly as we did that trip.

The only concern during our camping trip was following a fat free diet. What I would normally cook while camping wouldn't be healthy and restaurant eating was iffy. I wished I still had my little motorhome.

During every single bike ride I kept saying to myself, "My name is Barbara Hofmeister and I weigh 128 pounds. I feel great especially because I don't smoke and I exercise regularly. I hate the taste of cigarettes and what they do to my body etc...." I was using self-hypnosis while I had a pack of cigarettes in my pocket but the day was coming when I would no longer be chained to those coffin nails.

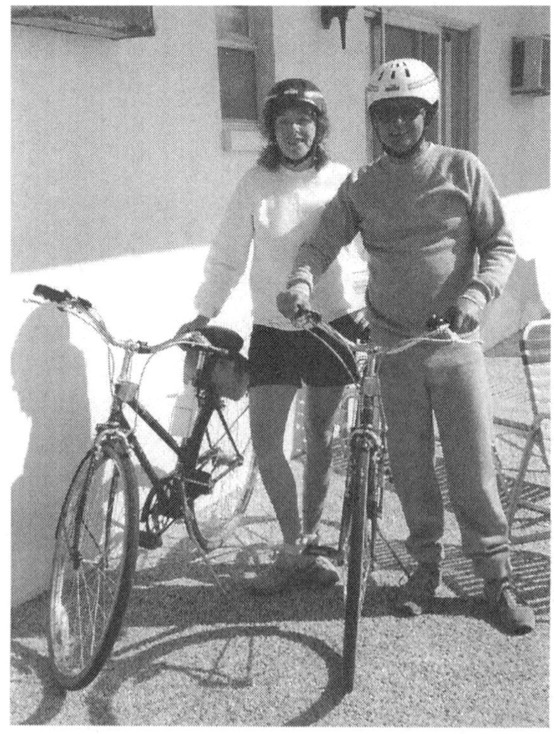

I Quit Smoking

It was November 4, 1986 at 2:30 in the afternoon and I was in my basement working on photographs. I did photo color corrections and photo restorations for my former boss, my former husband and sometimes my mother. That day I was working with a portrait that needed a lot of work and in between the applications, I had to spray the photo with lacquer so I could put another coat of art work on top of what I had done. Yes, I was smoking as I usually did, after all I was a heavy smoker at three and one half packs a day. I never went anywhere without my cigarettes and often carried several packs in my purse. God forbid I ever ran out like I did one day long ago when I got stuck (all alone) on a broken elevator. I had been smoking since I was eighteen and that added up to thirty one years.

Suddenly I couldn't take it another minute. I couldn't breathe. I walked up stairs with my cigarettes, my beautiful (and expensive) leather case and my gold lighter which was a gift from Carolyn my Tupperware manager and best friend. I grabbed the brand new carton of cigarettes from the top of my refrigerator where I always kept them and walked out to the dumpster. I threw them all away. Then I went back to work in my basement.

I am not going to lie. It was the hardest thing I ever did but I was determined. I had purchased some Nicorette gum earlier in preparation for that day. It didn't take long before I put a piece of the gum in my mouth. It helped but after a day or two of that I had all sorts of sores in my mouth. It was a listed side effect. I decided to buy some regular gum and picked up a pack of Wrigley's and put a half a stick of gum in my mouth with a half of the Nicorette square. That helped a bit and gradually I weaned myself off of the Nicorette gum and to this day still have a half of a stick of Wrigley's Extra Winterfresh gum in my mouth most of the time. It still wasn't easy. I am surprised that Ron didn't divorce me on the spot. I was a moody, crying, cranky woman.

We were heading to Florida to spend Christmas with Ron's

Mom since this would be her first Christmas alone. In preparation for the long drive I bought some yarn and got out my crochet hook. I had made several granny square afghans before and decided it would help me pass the time in the van if I was crocheting. The funny thing was I was never able to use the squares; they matched my varying feelings on the trip; some were tight and some were very crooked, but it did help keep me busy. Ron says that he would look over at me while he was driving and tears would be rolling down my cheeks. I really missed my best friend (those stinking weeds) because they were always there when I needed them. If I was happy I needed a smoke, when I was sad I needed one, when I was nervous, anxious or whatever, my cigarettes were always at my side. How sick now that I look back on it.

For that whole trip to Florida I had my times when I was very touchy or I cried but gradually it got better. I got so I couldn't stand to be around others who smoked and at the time the restaurants in Florida catered to the smokers. We often had to wait a long time for a non smoking table in a restaurant.

On Christmas Eve we went to the Mall by Mom Hofmeister's house and right in the middle of the mall was an ear piercing stand. I had always said I would never have pierced ears but that night I walked right up to the stand and said, "Do it" much to Ron's surprise.

Section Eight

Off We Go!

1987—1989

A Mallard Wasn't a Duck

All the while we were in Florida we struggled again to follow a healthy diet. Yes, we were biking a lot every day, but eating out was the problem. We did all right, but on the way home, I started talking to Ron about maybe buying a small motorhome so we could go camping that way and with my own kitchen on the road, I could cook healthy stuff. And, I added, that we could take our bikes with us on weekends and buy ten or even twenty degrees in temperature in the spring and fall each year by heading south to southern Ohio or Indiana. He was quite responsive to the idea.

I remembered that January was usually the month for the big RV show and made a note to find the date and put it on our calendar. When the day came to go shopping for a motorhome, Ron basically left it up to me since I had more experience in this area. I knew I didn't want to have to make up a bed every night as I had to do in my old mini motorhome. So we started looking. There were hundreds to look at and it was basically tiring going up and down stairs all day. Ron was quite impressed with what was available. Rather quickly we narrowed down our choices. We both wanted a Ford 350 engine not a Chevy. We decided on a length of twenty four feet. Once we came up with those two decisions it was just a matter of aesthetics.

We loved the twenty-four foot Mallard motorhome but there was another by a brand whose name I forget that was equal except for the price. We compared everything and really liked the Mallard best but wanted the price to come down. Ron didn't want to dicker for price so I suggested he find a nice place to rest and I would see what I could do. I had done this kind of thing many times when buying a car. All I had to do was get the two dealers to fight for my business.

I told one that I really liked the motorhome but the other motorhome had this or that and was cheaper so he came down to meet the price. Then I went to the other dealer and did the same thing which led him to come down in price. I did that three or four times and knowing what I knew about shows, I felt sure they would bargain down to near cost to make the sale during the show.

We got our price and a couple of things thrown in like a bike rack on the front grill. The price was $26, 300 and it had everything we wanted. The cab was just like any other van/truck cab but there was a bed over the cab which had a mattress. It was the equivalent of a double bed and came complete with a ladder. In back of the cab area on the street side was a dinette with two bench seats which made into a double bed when the table was taken off of the pedestal. Behind the dinette was a small but tall closet then came the bathroom complete with tub/shower combination. It had a nice sink and potty. This was a lot better than my old motorhome. Across from the bathroom was the bed. I used to joke that we rolled out of bed and hit the toilet but there was a little bit of floor space in between. At the foot of the bed was another closet that was quite short but perfect for shirts and jackets. Heading towards the front of the motorhome was the stove with an oven underneath and cupboards above. Closer to the entrance door which was pretty much in the middle of the motorhome on the curb side was a sink. And on the other side of the entrance door was a comfy barrel chair that swiveled to any direction. Besides all of that it was pretty inside. The colors were mauve, pink and blue. We wouldn't get the motorhome home until the second week in February.

We were excited and kept busy while waiting by talking about where we would go. I couldn't wait to show Ron how comfortable camping could be.

The first week we got it, I spent a good deal of time shopping for towels, dishes, silverware and pans. I didn't want to be carting stuff from the house all the time and I wanted real dishes not paper plates. For dishes I picked a pretty pattern in Corelle. I delighted in playing house in my new little doll house. I wanted it to be a perfect home away from home and it was.

Our first trip in the motorhome was March 6, 1987 to Hueston Woods State Park in Oxford, Ohio. It was luxury and fun all in one.

I wrote in my diary that we biked Saturday morning, came back to the motorhome and ate a sandwich for lunch and rode more for a total of thirty two hilly miles. I also wrote that we had spaghetti and a salad for dinner Friday evening, cereal for breakfast Saturday and I was fixing meat loaf, baked potatoes and green beans for dinner.

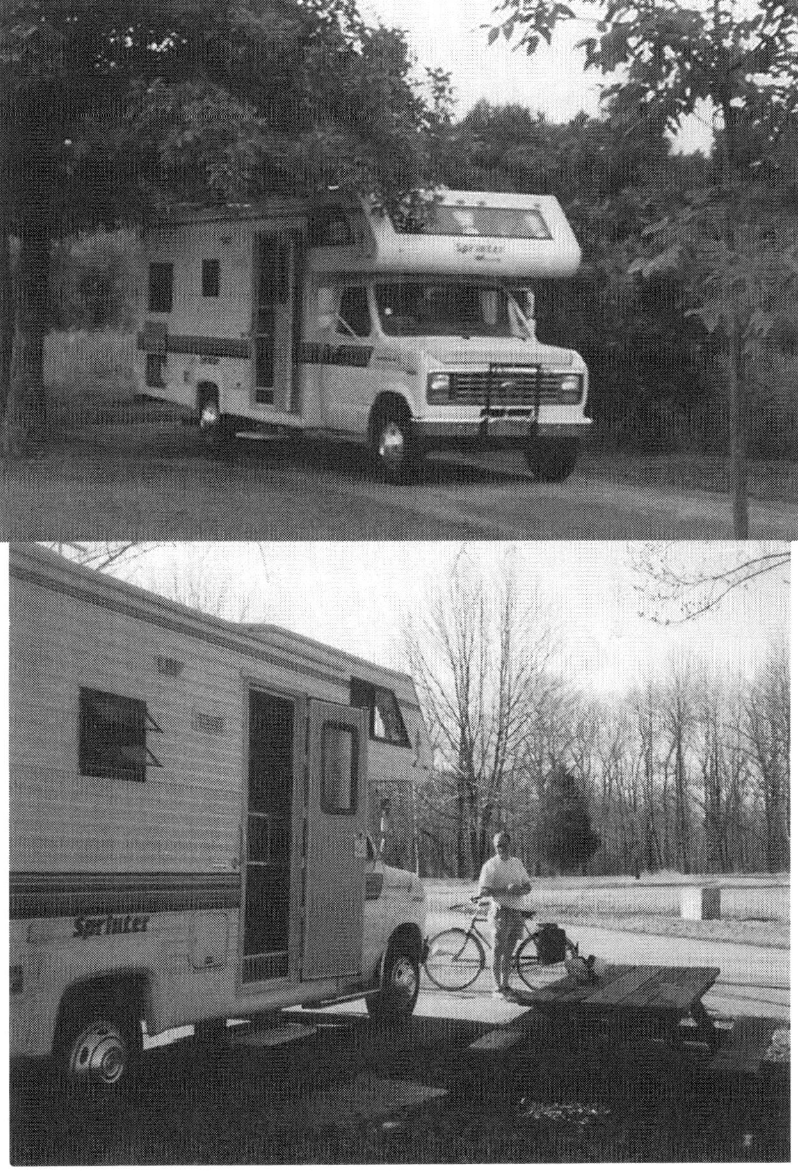

Our First Four Trips

That first weekend (March 6-8, 1987) we were way south in Ohio (near Cincinnati) and it was almost perfect weather wise. The park didn't have water at the sites yet because of winter freezes, but we could carry it in those big green cans we had. We didn't dare fill our water tanks yet or use our toilet because of freezes to come back in Michigan. By any Michigan calendar it was still winter.

We skipped the following weekend and on March 20-22 we were in Northern Indiana at Pokagon State Park in Angola. It was beautiful and we biked close to fifty miles that weekend. I remember one ride was into town and I was scared because we had to cross railroad tracks which weren't parallel to the road; they went on an angle and I was afraid of my tires getting caught in between the rails.

March 27-29 we went to Chain of Lakes another Indiana state park in Indiana. Besides biking we took a two hour hike and loved every minute of it.

On Thursday, April 2, 1987 we took our first big trip and that was east. We had stopped in a rest area in Maryland and everything was covered in heavy wet snow. Twelve inches was predicted. My son, Mark was going to be at Quantico in West Virginia for some classes for his employer (the FBI) and we wanted to spend the weekend with him and hopefully do some biking together. He had his bike with him. Unfortunately it rained and rained the first night. We had picked Mark up at the FBI. Since it was raining all night, we stayed in and played Yahtzee. Mark slept where the dinette was and said it was quite comfortable. Saturday we rode our bikes to Quantico. It was a cold but fun ride. Mark adjusted my seat for me and that helped a lot. Sadly it rained again all day Sunday so we talked and played cards which was fun. After dinner we took Mark back to Quantico. Monday Ron and I drove the motorhome to Mt. Vernon and toured the house. While there we discovered a bike path all the way into DC. We rode that on Tuesday. It was only 16 miles one way and before we knew it we were at the Jefferson Memorial. After riding around and visiting all the memorials and sites in the area we rode back to Mt Vernon then picked up Mark one more time. We decided on Pizza Hut for dinner then said "good bye" to him for a while.

On the drive home we talked about how adventurous traveling in the motorhome had been so far and we couldn't wait to do more. Oh and the biking was super terrific even in cool, rainy weather. What fun!

A Challenge and Sad Ending

Clifty Falls State Park in Madison, Indiana, easily became my favorite of all the campgrounds after we spent a week there (May 16-23 in 1987). This park was heavily wooded and had lots of wildlife which was exciting to watch. No there were no bears that we saw, but many deer, rabbits galore and everything else from skunks to snakes. Riding was easy and our eyes and ears were treated to sights and sounds like we had never seen or heard before. Or was it that while out in nature we were more tuned in to everything around us? There's no fragrance to even come close to the way that woods smelled early in the morning while wet with dew which was gradually warming up to the sun's rays. And after a rain the scent was even more heavenly and with the rushing water going over the falls it was as if an orchestra was playing.

On one of our bike rides around the park, we noticed a nature center and inn which we investigated then we saw a road which was signed "south entrance". Since we hadn't been there yet, I took off and Ron was right behind me. It didn't take long before I realized I had made a mistake. The road went straight downhill for three quarters of a mile. Oh it was steep. During the few minutes it took to fly to the bottom I was thinking, "Oh God, how will we ever get back up". At the bottom, we looked at each other knowing we had no choice but go back up. We didn't have any money with us so we didn't want to leave the park.

We started to ride up but in just a few feet we had to quit. Our lowest gear wasn't low enough to get us up that hill. We walked pushing the bikes but an uphill push was no fun in fact it was nearly impossible and exhausting.

After we got back from Clifty Falls State Park, we went shopping for new bikes. This time, we got eighteen speed bikes. That made a big difference because you could shift as you were moving where with the three speed bikes one had to stop to shift. We felt positive we could do that hill at Clifty Falls with ease.

On June 21, we took our little motorhome to Nashville for an

American Association of Governmental Accountants Association conference. We wouldn't use the motorhome in Nashville but thought it would be more fun to ride in. We had a one night stopover on the way there. When we bought the new bikes, we knew we were going to the conference so I looked at a map to see where Clifty Falls was in relationship to Nashville. We planned to make that our stopover on our way home from the conference.

We didn't get to Clifty until 6:30 p.m. on June 25. Because it was kind of late, we thought we would just "do the hill" then worry about dinner. On our way to the hill we did the perimeter of the park and I was excited to see all of my old friends—the rabbits and deer. The smells were just as I remembered too; I was in heaven. At the hill, we went down without a care in the world. Coming back up was difficult, but we didn't walk at all. The new bikes were worth it and we felt great.

When we got back home and walked in the door, I knew something was wrong. Just inside the door, I had a wall hanging and under that was an adorable child-sized park bench on which sat a little teddy bear. On the bear's head was Jim's hat which he left at home when he went in the Air Force. The hat was gone. Upstairs our bed was messed up. Ron's son David knew where the key was and it looked like he had a party while we were gone. I was furious especially since the hat was gone, but Ron would not talk with David to ask what happened. After several weeks with me stewing, he did bring the subject up, but very lightly. I never got the hat back. Ron was afraid to rock the boat with his kids. I felt he had guilt issues to work on. We both needed help with his kids. I suggested counseling and he agreed. We met with Bruce for a little while.

Jim and the hat that disappeared.

Good and Bad Trips

We did a lot more than bike and camp the summer of 1987. We still had family fun what with David's graduation in June, and of course Father's Day and a Hofmeister Family reunion and at least once we met up with Marty, Bryan and their little daughter, Erika for bike rides around the campus of Michigan State University. Those rides were always good for an ice cream cone and just good times.

We also included my family on a couple of camping occasions. Once, my sister, Bunnie and her family joined us at Holland State Park and they bought Mom along. She stayed with us in our motorhome. Another time, my sisters and their families camped with us at the Sleeping Bear Dunes at Silver Lake. We always had great times there. They didn't have bikes so on Saturday morning we went for a bike ride (sometimes for a breakfast) while they played with their kids.

Not all trips were fun. We took Susie, a girlfriend, Bryan, Marty and Erika to Cedar Point which is a fun amusement park in Ohio. That is for sure one of my favorite places. The Blue Streak Roller coaster is to die for but that weekend was way too hot and crowded. We drove to the park which is in Sandusky on Friday and got a campsite with full hookups. We sure needed the air because of the heat. All day Saturday and part of Sunday we waited in lines for rides. I wrote in my diary, "Yep, we all squeezed into our closed up air conditioned, motorhome. Ron was a little grouchy. It was awful. I won't say anymore." Sometimes it is good that we don't remember all the details.

In August, Mark flew home with two friends who were going to bike the Tour de Michigan with him. That wasn't our kind of biking. They were racing at breakneck speeds and so close to each other that it was scary just to watch. We saw many accidents.

We had camped eighteen times (three were longer than a weekend) from March 6, 1987 up until Labor Day when we were back at Mill Creek campground in Mackinaw City. We were celebrating Ron's recovery from his heart attack. We felt like we had made great strides in our health and we were mostly having a great time. We still worked, of course, but weekends were a blessed reward for working.

Even after Labor Day, we kept going with five more weekends taking us up to the middle of October. One trip was five days long when we took a bike tour with the American Lung Association. We chose the trip that was the farthest away from our house at a weak moment when we weren't thinking. Houghton/Hancock, Michigan, is as far west as St Louis, Missouri, but because it is in Michigan, we forgot it was so far away. It was a fun trip even though the weather was crappy. It was cold and rainy and when the sun did come out, the black flies were biting badly. We biked well though and did fifty miles the first day alone.

To finish out the year in the motorhome, we drove to Glenda's in Florida for Thanksgiving and Robert who was on leave from the Coast Guard joined us then rode back with us.

In December we flew to San Diego so Ron could attend a conference and I went with him. We stayed at the luxurious Del Coronado Hotel and that is when I definitely began to think about us living in the motorhome after Ron retired. There was too much we wanted to see in this great country of ours and in my mind's eye, the motorhome was a perfect home for sightseeing. Of course retirement was a long way off so there was no immediate planning yet.

Sleep Naked in a Sleeping Bag

We couldn't wait to take the motorhome out again. We missed our little home. We planned to camp in Ohio the first weekend in March and were watching the weather. A big winter storm was predicted but by Friday morning, everything looked brighter and better in our area although not very warm. After talking with the ranger at Hueston Woods State Park, he said that the roads in the park were ice covered, but they were salting and everything would be fine in two hours. Since it would take us longer than that to get there, we decided to go.

There was absolutely no one else in the campground but shortly after we had dinner, we saw three cars pull in and start to set up tents. They were all young girls with two adults. We thought they might be girl scouts but since it was freezing out we also thought they were crazy.

From the warmth of our little house we watched as they tried to start a fire. They finally got it going but it was a pitiful excuse for a fire; the leaders didn't have a clue what they were doing. When we went for a little walk later, we were nearly ambushed by the girls as they begged us to let them come in our motorhome. They said they were cold and wanted to sleep in the motorhome. I told them I would tell them something that would keep them warm for more than just that night. They were all ears.

I told them when it was time to go to sleep to take all of their clothes off and climb into the sleeping bag. I added that they should wear a hat to sleep and promised they would be toasty warm. The minute I said, "take all your clothes off" the girls made nasty sounds like that would the most disgusting thing in the world. I figured I had to explain why that worked so I went on.

"Your skin is a thermostat and will keep you cool if you are hot or warm when you are cold but if you have a lot of clothing on, your skin will be telling your body that you are hot or at least warm and your body will work hard to make you cooler. With nothing on and simply covered with the sleeping bag your skin will know exactly what to do and that is generate heat. Oh and the reason for the hat is that 90% of your body heat escapes through your head." One girl listened and said she would try it while the others still thought it was nasty to sleep without clothes on.

In the morning when we went for another walk, I asked how many were warm that night and only one raised her hand. She was the only one who slept naked in her sleeping bag.

Talking the Night Away

Early in 1988 Ron's boss, Charlie Chambers died while in Georgia shopping for a new home for their retirement. Charlie was the Deputy Director of Finance for the Michigan Department of Transportation and he had been there a long time. He was well past retirement age. Ron never thought he would have a chance at that top job because it looked like Charlie was never going to retire but suddenly the job was in his lap.

Ron had always loved his work at the department and he had a very high position under Charlie and at first he was thrilled until he started actually doing Charlie's job. It was very political and Ron didn't like that. What he had liked were the day to day operations; he didn't like having to kiss legislator's butts to get anything done. Instead of coming home happy, his shoulders started drooping. He had more senseless meetings which drove him crazy; he missed the real work.

A couple of months into his new position, the department started an austerity program and were promoting an "early out" program to clean house. And about the same time, Ron came home from a week long retreat of department heads and he was beat. We talked about it a bit, went to bed and when I got up at 2:30 in the morning, I noticed he was awake in bed. When I asked if he wanted to talk, he said yes and got up. We went downstairs and got comfortable on our huge sofa and talked. We talked until morning. Ron hated his new job. Even though he was going on 56, he was ready to retire. His new position would give him a bigger pension. We also talked about how we loved the motorhome and we even talked that maybe we could just live in it for a year or two and do all the traveling we wanted to do. What we did decide was that he would give nearly a years notice and we could retire on March 17, 1989. He would have the benefit of helping to pick his successor, and prepare him or her for the position and we would have the benefit of the "early out".

Here and There in 1988

In April of 1988, we got word that my father was very sick in New Mexico. My sisters, Bunnie and Beverly, wanted to go see him so I volunteered to take the motorhome and we would drive straight through. We got caught in an ice storm in Amarillo and pulled over to wait until the sun melted some of the ice and we made it safely to Silver City where Dad lived with his wife, Frankie. We were shocked at the house and his so called studio as they were both a disaster. What an unkempt mess. He and Frankie had been married for a long time by then and apparently she had kept things tidy but now was failing so it just went to hell. Oh and his ideas of photography were horrid also and he seemed to have no respect for anything or anyone. I had always thought he was so smart and suddenly saw the light. I had a hard time dealing with what he really was.

When I heard my dad stating his ideas of life, politics and women, my stomach churned. One time he said, "Turn any woman upside down and they are all the same". Oh, my God I thought. I couldn't wait to get away and was thankful that I had my bike on the front of the motorhome. I just had to take off and go for a hard ride and I did but we didn't stay long. I kind of pushed my sisters to leave early.

Ron and I had lots of good weekend camps that year and many included family. Bunnie and Jerry joined us in Holland and Kurt and Oneida camped with us at Holly more than once. Marty and Bryan spent time with us and so did Jim and Norma. In June we went on another Lung Association bike tour up at Houghton/ Hancock again. This time the weather was much better but the black flies were even worse.

From the end of June to the July 4 weekend, we went to the Smokey Mountains. Bunnie, Jerry, his mom and their kids were there as well as Glenda, Pekka and Liisa who drove up from Florida to camp with us. They had tents or pop ups while we had our little house. We hiked with everyone, and rafted some pretty serious white water where Jerry and I got knocked out of the raft at the same time—right in the rapids, but we were okay. We also toured the interesting visiting area in the National park. It was beautiful, but the big event was that Ron and I biked up the main road in the park to the top. It was a very steep climb up 13.5 miles. When we got to the top, Ron said, "I guess I don't have a heart problem anymore." I laughed because he had been fine for a long time. We didn't follow through and go to the other side because that was all down hill and we would have had to climb back up to get back to camp so we left it at that, turned around and tried not to break our necks coasting down the hill at 35 miles per hour. We both kept our hands on the brakes most of that way too otherwise we would have even gone faster. We were ahead of all the cars.

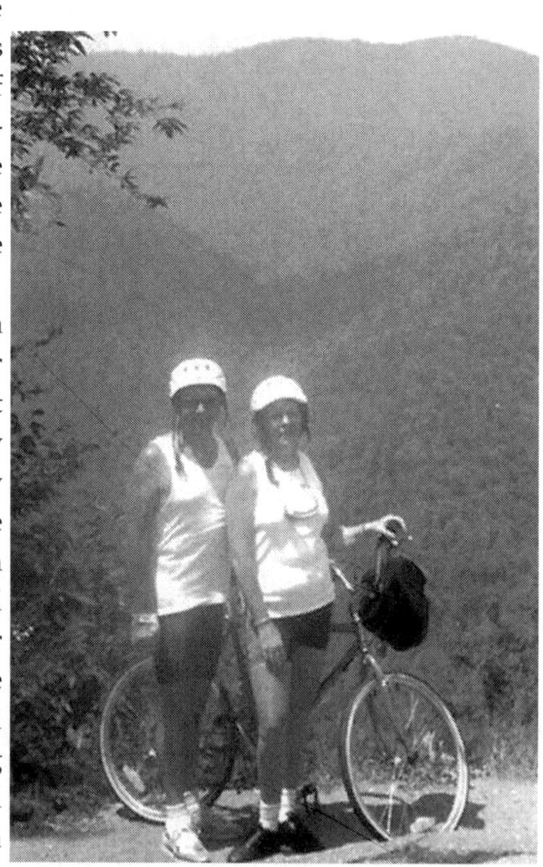

At the top of Route 441 in the Great Smokey Mountain National park.

Later in July Liisa came back for her third summer visit and we were very happy to have her. By now she wasn't the only grandchild in the family. Marty and Bryan had a daughter who was nearly one year old (Erika) and Marty was expecting again in the fall. Karl and Donna had a daughter, Mary, and a son named Richard.

Top Bryan, Marty and Erika at their cabin.

Left Erika and Marty

Preparing For Retirement

We had a lot of planning and preparing ahead of us and we actually looked forward to it. Ron gave his notice almost immediately after our all-night talk. But first it was time to continue our weekend adventures. Besides enjoying the bike riding and camping many weekends, it gave us an opportunity to really talk about what we envisioned life on the road to be like. We brainstormed what problems we might encounter and we made a ton of notes.

In all of our motorhome camping so far, we never took a car. At first we talked of doing the same when we took off for that year or two. But it really was a hassle at times to have to move from the campground just to go to a store and you couldn't always plan ahead.

One weekend, we were sitting outside of our little house, when we saw a couple pull in with a small motorhome and they were pulling a small car behind the motorhome. They unhooked the car, easily, set up camp and took off in the car. That opened another possibility.

We never got to talk with that particular couple and we wished there was a book on RVing where we could learn these things. After searching we found one and read it cover to cover, but it didn't answer our questions entirely. In fact the couple that wrote the book traveled in a trailer pulled by a truck. We didn't have that combination so we kept looking and talking. Anytime we found an older (retirement age) couple camped near us we talked with them and got lots of helpful information. Remember this was all before the internet or Google. We researched the old fashioned way.

Ron investigated which cars could be towed and how and found the best choice was a manual transmission, but we didn't check all makes. Our Horizon seemed to fit the bill. So then we researched how to hook it up. Our RV dealer helped.

Yes, we had nearly a year to prepare but we had a lot to learn.

Around every campfire and while driving, we asked questions of each other and brainstormed more. What would we do about banking, medical care, mail, family, with no phone how would we keep in touch, what would we do with our stuff, where would we go first and it went on and on.

My first thought was just getting ready. I searched out storage units and checked the prices. We even discussed simply selling everything but discarded that thought almost as fast as the idea came up. We both thought we would want to own property in northern Michigan eventually and build a small house up there so we would need a lot of the things we had. Buying all new would be expensive.

Our living room furniture would not look good in a cabin so that could be sold and the same regarding the washer and dryer, but we would keep my organ, bedroom furniture and all the dishes, pots and pans. As far as clothing went, we would pare down. Ron wouldn't need so many suits nor would I need all I had. We would have a large moving sale when it was time to go.

I had a large box for each of the boys containing treasured bits of their school life which I had saved so I could make a scrap book for them when they each got married. Now was the time to make each scrap book and be done with it. I saved that project for winter days and evenings. Another project that I would do when the days grew shorter and colder was go through all of my home movies which had never been organized, sort them, put them in order and make a master VHS tape. The DVD wasn't available yet and PCs were in their infancy.

I first had to search out a professional to help with the movie project as I wanted it to be narrated and with music; it was a big project. This work of love took hours and hours especially when it came to searching through my old records to pick just the right music to go with each section. The video ended up being two and one half hours long but not boring at least to the family.

Speaking of records, I decided to get rid of them all as well. I had LP albums that went back to the 60s and even some 78 speed records like the one I had of Tommy Dorsey with Frank Sinatra and the Modernaires. Frank only sang a tiny bit in the middle of the number which was titled Buy War Bonds. It was a wonderful record and I figured it would be worth something to a collector.

I planned to sell all of our wonderful Atari games and other games which we had enjoyed as a family. They would go with the moving sale. It was fun to plan and I am glad I had the greater part of a year to work on it.

One thing that complicated our plans was my son Jim who was now stationed in eastern England was planning to get married. They picked March 18 as their wedding date and Ron was retiring on March 17. There was no way we could go to the wedding with all we had to do so get ready to leave our town house by March 30 so I promised them that we could make a special visit to see them after the wedding—in June of that year. We reasoned that weddings are a busy time and we couldn't visit and get to know Sue and her family in such a short time so a longer trip would be good and we could take our bikes.

Counting Down to Our New Life

By the time the holidays were over, we had already accomplished a lot in getting ready to move on. I had finished the video tape from the old movies and even mailed them to the kids as a Christmas present. Once finished, I pulled all of the film out of the reels and threw them away. That actually felt good. I was finished with the memory books also and had mailed them out. I had also gone through all of my cookbooks looking for those stained pages which told me it was a recipe I used often. I typed up the recipes that I would want to use in our travels and packed all of the cookbooks for storage.

By this time, we were into serious planning for the rest of our life. We had a countdown with projects to be completed weekly. It seemed monumental. Ron spent hours thinking about how we would handle finances on the road. Remember this was before on line banking, and many of the conveniences we enjoy in 2012. Ron's pension would be direct deposited into his credit union and we planned to use credit cards and pay by check for most services. We were blessed with his medical insurance from the state of Michigan. But Ron still worried if we had enough money to live like nomads. He made budget after budget and still was not sure.

I was concerned with getting medical care on the road and decided to get our medical records from our doctors so we could carry them with us. That was a great idea.

My other worry was getting mail and after searching RV magazines I chose a mail forwarding service in Denver, Colorado, that sounded good. All our mail would go there and she would hold it until we called and told her where to send it. She said she would put it all in a large priority envelope and send it on. We planned to have mail sent to general delivery in a small town near where we would be. We wanted to get mail once a week and it would be an expense we had to budget for.

We had no cell phone; they were big, bulky and expensive and tended to work only in big cities which we didn't intend to be near. Our option for telephone was to get a message service from the same company which would take care of our mail. We also had to have a phone calling card so we could make long distance calls from pay phones. We kept telling ourselves that it wasn't the best option but we were better off than those pioneers who left home in wagon trains years before. The families they left behind were lucky to ever hear from them again.

Our plan was to leave on March 30 and head south to Huested Woods State Park in Ohio and had picked the next campgrounds along our route to Florida. We poured through RV travel magazines and maps planning our route south. We planned to travel U.S. red roads (they are major routes usually red in color on maps) instead of freeways and as often as we could stay in state parks. We planned to go to West Palm Beach then over to Ron's Mom's place and spend a little time in Florida before heading back to Michigan for Susie's graduation and our trip to England.

Besides getting ready for our new lifestyle, we had to research (without Google remember) bicycling in England because we were definitely going to take our bikes. After visiting with Jim and Sue we wanted to bike across England, Wales and Ireland. We had a lot to learn about that and it was easier to shop for supplies while we were close to our bike shop. We would need panniers (those saddle bags that hook on to the bikes) and maps. My favorite bicycle catalogs were a big help.

Besides a retirement luncheon at work, we wanted to have a retirement party for Ron so invitations had to be ordered a menu planned and the club house in our community had to be reserved.

We wanted to give everyone our new address and phone number so they could keep in touch so I made a flyer showing a cute drawing of our motorhome towing our little car. Notice we had discovered that a roof rack on the car which would hold our bikes would enable us take our bikes away from the campground should we want to. That was a very smart move.

Here is a synopsis from my diary which details what went on from February 1, to March 30, 1989.

Wednesday, February 1, We are really counting down. Ron said this morning, "I can now say that next month I'll be retired.

Thursday, February 3, Mailed out change of address forms to all our travel magazines.

Saturday, February 4, Well, the couch is gone, as well as coffee table, lamp, drapes etc. Robert was so excited to have these things for his apartment. He also took my painting table (for photography work) and all of Jim's boxes to his father's. Played pinochle with Jim and Norma in the evening. Fun!

Monday, February 6, Picked up stuff from Speedy Printing (invitations and moving notice. They look good.

Thursday, February 9, Picked up the business cards, addressed the invitations and packed the downstairs wall hangings (pictures). The place looks naked.

Saturday, February 11, I cleaned the basement while Ron was at the spa. We shopped at Gordon's Food Service for stuff for the party. Went to dinner with Jim and Norma then came home and played cards. I didn't feel good—tired.

Monday, February 13, at 4 a.m., Ron took me to the ER. Fever chills—-hurt all over. I thought I had pneumonia—they said bronchitis. Came home and slept all day.

Friday, February 17, One month from today, Ron retires. I've spent this week resting and resting. Haven't even been outside. Lungs still scratchy. I'm crabby—-want to exercise and resume normal activities. Yesterday, I cleaned out the desk and that tired me out.

Saturday, February 18, Felt much better.

Monday, February 20, Ron is off—President's Day. We took the car to Dennis Trailer to have the tow bar put on. Ate breakfast out. We priced some of the stuff for the sale.

Wednesday, February 22, I bought Jackie a nice scarf and pin and took them to her as a thank you for teaching me to do my nails (acrylic). We cried as we hugged goodbye. She's my first goodbye. I know I'll cry a river when the time comes to actually leave.

Friday, February 24, E Gads!! Three weeks to go. Ron has a cold and I'm tired. I wake up early every morning and can't go back to sleep for thinking. I'm worrying that our full-time life will be awful—that I'll miss not having a home to come home to. I suppose this is normal.

Monday, March 6, It was a slow week. I didn't do any big thing. All our pictures are down and packed. I took a bunch of our clothes to the cleaners. Now they're packed in a wardrobe box—for storage. Couldn't pick up the motorhome as planned on Saturday—ice storm. We will wait till next Saturday. It will be warmer. Meanwhile we wait.

Friday, March 10 We got the motorhome. They completed the hookup for the tow bar. Ron drove the motorhome and the car home. I followed in his state car. It looked so cute to see the car being pulled. Right away we took down the sheets that had been covering the windows and made a clever box for a narrow slot under the bed to hold shoes. We put the new mattress (special ordered) in place. Wow!! It's a thick wonderful mattress.

Saturday, March 11, We filled the pod. Can't believe it holds so much. Fantastic! I've been planning cupboard storage—put towels (rolled) under the bathroom sink. Jim and Norma came and took the big hanging plant from the kitchen. Kitchen looks empty now. Went to Jim's for chili and pinochle after we shopped at the mall for two more milk crates. Took the mattress from the cab bunk out of the motorhome and will use that space as is for six milk crates filled with clothes (stuff that would normally go in drawers which we don't have) and an under-the-bed-type box which is filled, too.

Monday, March 13, Wow—did I work! Food—cupboards—clothes—cleaned off my dresser and Ron's too—just did a bunch. Also returned the cable box. Ron cleaned off the desk

Sunday , March 19, Ron's retirement luncheon on Thursday the 16th was great—150 were there, and when it was over, we felt a little lost. Then the next day was his last day at work. He said people filed into his office all day long. I picked him up at 4:30 (no more state car). It was the beginning of an ice storm. We came straight home. I had been shopping and cutting veggies, etc., all day and we did more at night. Woke up to ICE—thick and everywhere. It took Ron a long time to chisel the ice off the car to get in. Then he got to the club house and that door wouldn't open. Once we got going though, things progressed nicely. The party was a big success and his sisters and brother-in-laws stayed overnight and slept on mattresses on the floor.

Monday, March 20 Packed all day. Tired.

Tuesday, March 21 The movers came at noon and were done by four. Now we only have one day to get ready for the moving sale. We are sleeping on the floor in our bedroom There is nothing much left in the house, but it is too cold to sleep out in the motorhome.

Tuesday, March 28 The sale was a big success and we sold out in two days and we spent a couple of days cleaning the town house. I made a new recording for our answering machine. It says, "Hi, this is Barb. Ron and I are home, but home now is our motorhome parked out in the parking lot. So if you'd like to see us—come on over—we'd love the company. Yes, we are un-winterized and everything is moved in. We had filled the motorhome so full that I was worried we were over-weight. But Ron took it and had it weighed and we can still add 1,500 pounds. Yes, but there isn't a speck of room.

Wednesday, March 29 Poor Ron has the flu. Since Ron is sick, I made the last trip to the storage unit. We were scheduled to go to dinner with

Jim and Norma and did, but Ron left early and went home. I cried when we hugged and said "goodbye". Oh, I checked for messages on our voice mail today. It is so fantastic. I love it. It will make full-timing easy.

Thursday, March 30 It's cold and yucky. We got our business done (car loaded, bikes on top). Ron went to the credit union while I went to the laundromat. That done, we put water in the motorhome fresh water tank, hooked up the car and walked over to the office to turn in the keys to our town house. I cried a little saying, "goodbye" one more time when leaving the house. Then I was fine. Ron seemed so relaxed. It was good to finally be starting our new life.

This picture was taken just minutes before we took off for good. We were very excited and ready for our new life of living and traveling full time in our motorhome.

Section Nine

Movin' On

1989—2003

Pies Oh My!

Mother Nature wasn't helping much as we started out on that grey day the end of March. Our spirits were high though. We were on the road and free. That felt good. Our plan was to spend a few days at each campground so we could explore the area on bike and by car then move on. We did not have reservations anywhere and that in itself was quite liberating. There was no timetable. Except we were looking for the sun and it never showed it's brilliant light for several weeks.

At our first stop, which was the familiar Housted Woods, near Cincinnati, Ohio, we even experienced snow. Thankfully it did not stick, but it was downright cold and grey. We stayed in the motorhome except for taking the car to find a fitness center so we could exercise a little. We belonged to a fitness group that had other centers across the country. Our motorhome didn't have a built in TV so we had purchased a little one, but there was no place to set it that was convenient. We finally gave up and just read. The nights were downright cold and we were glad we had electricity.

We only moved a little at a time which was our plan. The whole idea of this mode of travel was to not tire ourselves out like we had done so many times on vacations. We wanted no part of the "hurry up and get there" routine. So the second leg of our trip to Florida was only 150 miles away and we stayed three days. It was a little warmer at General Butler State park in Carrollton. We even took the bikes off the car and set up our chairs outside and while there we biked and hiked.

By Thursday, April 6, we were at the Mammoth Cave Campground in Kentucky and planned to take a tour of the cave as well as explore the area. As is usually the rule in the national park campgrounds there are no electrical hookups which presented a problem at night. It was bitter cold (near freezing) and we couldn't run our furnace; it ran down the battery. Thank God we had a wool mattress cover between the bottom sheet and the mattress which I had discovered in my research ahead of time would keep us cool in the summer and warm in the winter. We also had a nice down comforter. Even though it was cold, we were warm in bed. Yes, it was cold when we got up, but running the engine a bit allowed us to run the furnace and we were toasty in no time. Lesson learned: Spring even south of Michigan isn't always warm 24/7.

The tour of the cave was not what I had expected. It was just a giant hole in the ground. There were no stalagmites or stalactites which I thought all caves had. It was a four hour strenuous tour. We met a man on the tour who would impact our life. I don't know his name. He was behind us in line and we got to talking. He was deaf but spoke well enough that we understood him. He asked where we were from and we told him we were just starting full-timing. He did that too only in a van and by himself. Although a great grandfather and alone he had been traveling and seeing the country for five years. He told us that we must plan to visit Yosemite National Park in California and when we do, we should stay at least a week. He said every time he goes there he cries; it is that beautiful.

We had to keep moving south because it was just too cold but on our way to Nashville, we wanted to stop and visit our daughter-in-law, Donna and the kids (Mary and Richard) who were visiting her parents in Russellville, Kentucky. We arrived in the town proper around lunch time and didn't want to arrive at her house at lunch time so we stalled by walking the town square and reading the historic signs. We smelled food but couldn't see an eating place so we went to the court house and asked where people ate in town. We were directed to a large building which housed a furniture store. Strange. But yes, the restaurant was in the back of the store. You see, the building used to be a Kresge store and when they closed the furniture store moved in. Everyone petitioned for the furniture store to keep the lunch counter which they did. We sat at the counter and ordered a sandwich, but what caught my eye was this huge piece of peanut butter pie I saw displayed in the glass pie cage which sat near the counter. Oh my it looked good but I resisted because I just knew Donna's mother, being a good southern wife surely would have pie or some decadent dessert for dinner. It turned out she didn't cook or if she did it was very basic. I kept seeing that pie and thus began my five year search for pies which added a few pounds to my weight.

We did learn about tobacco farming because Donna's father had a big bunch of land devoted to tobacco. It was very interesting.

We were in Nashville by April 9, and our motorhome tanks even froze there. In the morning when we woke up our water hose had frozen solid. We had to bring it in the house and put it in the tub to thaw out. Lesson learned: Listen to the weather forecast and prepare for a freeze. We did the normal touristy stuff in Nashville including Opryland which we weren't crazy about.

The next stop was Lynchburg, Tennessee, and a tour of the Jack Daniels brewery. Interesting fact: That county is dry so there were no samples of the bourbon. It was a cute town though.

By April 12 we were at a new favorite park, Fall Creek Falls State park but the way there was tough. The road was narrow and winding and at first we were lost. We stopped at an Exxon gas station. While Ron got gas, I went in to look for a map on the area hoping it would have more detail than our United States Atlas. There on the counter were fresh homemade pies labeled "Janie's Pies". There were regular sized pies and small tart sized ones. They looked good and it was if they were saying "take me home." The pies had unusual names which I had never heard of relating to pies. One was labeled Japanese fruit, another chocolate chip and then there was a chess pie. I couldn't pick just one so I purchased three little ones–one of each flavor. After dinner we cut each one in half so we could taste them all and we ate them in one setting. They were the best–no doubt.

We stayed a week at the above park and did many different things. We basically had the campground to ourselves except on the weekend. The park started filling up so on Saturday we took a long sixty mile ride in the car (it was nice having other transportation besides the motorhome and bikes) and as I was the navigator, I just happened to direct Ron so we just happened to pass that Exxon station on our way back into the park. We stopped and I got more pies and put them in our little freezer for later. We got mail twice while in that area, hiked a ton, biked more and just had a wonderful time. The pie story continues later.

Our next stop was really two locations both near the Great Smokey Mountains National Park. We hiked and biked in really remote areas and as I rounded a corner on a lonely gravel road one day there was a black bear. Well, he didn't want to encounter me either so in a split second he was back in the trees and we continued on. Our campsite in the Elkmont campground was just above a fast moving river and the sound of rushing water lulled us to sleep each night. The nights were warm enough that we left our windows open. It was so heavenly. I wrote "Had hobo's for dinner (old campfire trick to cook meat, potatoes, carrots and onion wrapped in a tinfoil package over a wood fire), nice campfire a drink and pies for desert. Perfect day in a perfect place."

We decided to move a little faster to get to Glenda's in West Palm Beach, Florida, so we could spend a little time there before arriving at Winter Haven where Ron's mother lived. We wanted to be with her for Mother's day. Glenda's place was perfect. I mean visiting was nice, but her pool which was surrounded with jasmine bushes which gave off the most fragrant smell was a delight to our senses. Being able to jump in the pool or hot tub at any time was a treat too. We golfed a couple of times, walked a lot and biked too. I loved walking the beach and Lake Worth has a very nice beach.

We drove to Winter Haven in a storm. Yes, a bad storm of love bugs. Another lesson learned; never travel from east to west or visa versa in May in southern Florida. The love bugs mate and commit suicide on the windshield, and the front of the motorhome. They were packed in so deep in that cab-over section of the motorhome it took Ron three days of scrubbing like crazy to clean out the stinking mess. It was especially hard because we were parked in a parking area next to her apartment and we weren't close to a hose—just buckets of water. We took Ron's mom to Cypress Gardens for Mother's Day and had a delicious lunch and enjoyed the walks surrounded by gorgeous flowers.

From Winter Haven, we started heading north. My birthday treat was three whole days at Disney World and we camped right in the park at the Wilderness Campground which is a five star resort. We didn't have to drive anywhere; we simply used the monorail. I felt like a kid in a candy store. While there we ate at three special restaurants—Norwegian, German and for my birthday at the Moroccan for a really different birthday. When we had finished eating there, the server sprinkled rose water on our hands. One sad thing happened on the Space Mountain ride. I lost the gold bracelet that Ron got me for our third anniversary.

Hiking at Fall Creek Falls State Park in Tennessee.

With Ron's Mom at Cypress Gardens.

"It Has Legs!"

On Thursday, May 23 we were back at Housted Woods and it was just like we left it nearly two months before—cold and rainy. Yucky! Mid morning Ron went to get a newspaper and was back in no time. The river had completely flooded and we were trapped in the campground—couldn't get out if we wanted to. Later the sun came out and we did ride a bit but in order to get the bikes out we had to take them on the car. While temporarily stranded we met some other campers. There was a newly wed couple who were in a tent (didn't sound too romantic), a guy I called Diamond Jim who was quite a character but best of all we met Nancy and Grant Joy. They were on their maiden trip with a new Winnebago motorhome. Right away I liked her a lot and we wrote for years and met them on the road lots of times.

We were back in Michigan to begin the round of visiting with family and friends. While we were at Holly State Park, Jim and Norma came to visit with their pop up trailer. I was standing there talking with Norma while picking at a mole on my finger when she noticed and said that I should have it burned off then she added "especially that one on your neck". I hadn't noticed anything but she described it as black. I felt it and sure enough there was something there. Ron didn't notice (but I was learning that is normal for him) so I asked him to check it out. He agreed it had to be burned off. A day or two later we were at Mother's pool and I was again picking at my finger when my sister, Beth, asked what I was doing. I told her that I had a mole especially one on my neck and was going to have them burned off. As I was telling her that I lifted up my hair to show her the one on my neck. She looked closely and screamed, "It has legs". Then I was a panic. Ron was absolutely no help so I was thankful that my brother-in-law, Mike, was there. He was a medical technologist and knew what to do. He took a cigarette and burned it off. It was a tick. It bothered me a lot that I had been "petting it" for a couple of days. Yikes! We had been to ranger programs about them at the Smokey's and were told to check each other for ticks all the time. Ron was oblivious. I was mad at him for a couple of days but living in such a tiny space, I had to get over it. He, of course, promised he would try to be more observant which never happened by the way. No one is perfect especially me.

We had a lot to do once we were back in Lansing and then there was graduation, the open house after graduation, Erika's birthday party and errands to do. We went to the storage unit because we had to get some dressier clothing to send to Jim and Sue in England. I added a front rack for my bicycle to hold the front panniers which were on order, I got a new permanent, and Ron got a hair cut. We were busy which in reality was too busy especially after our nice, leisurely trip to Florida. I couldn't wait to get on with our life.

Sunday after the birthday party we went home, hastily stuffed our panniers as full as we could get them so we could make a trial run then went for a twelve mile ride. It was a piece of cake. We knew that adding thirty pounds in pannier weight would not be that big of a problem. It just felt so remarkable to be on our bikes and zipping along with the breeze on our bodies. We were ready to really pack.

We had read about others who had biked England and their advice was that when packing the panniers everything should be in Ziploc bags so they are protected against rain. Yes, we waterproofed our panniers, but double protection couldn't hurt. We had two gallon, one gallon and pint sized Ziploc bags and used a bunch. Everything was rolled tight and put into a bag. The bags when packed were heavy—probably 30 pounds. We were ready. Here is a picture of the panniers on our bikes from later in the trip, We boarded the plane in the morning.

A Nightmare Beginning

We were all set for our trip to England and felt we had thought about everything. We took ourselves and our bikes to Detroit Metropolitan Airport. We had researched and found a long term parking lot which was not right near the airport. We can't remember for sure but I think, Ron dropped me off at the airport and unloaded the bikes and our panniers then went to the parking lot while I stayed with the bikes. I think the shuttle might have delivered us bikes and all but can't be sure. Anyway we got to the airport okay.

The gal at the ticket counter wanted to charge us for the bikes to the tune of about $75 each but I held my ground. She checked and agreed that boxed they went as luggage. She gave us the boxes (one for each bike) and a third box for the helmets, pedals and water bottles. They were checked through along with the rear panniers from each bike which when snapped together made one piece of luggage. We hand carried our front panniers (snapped together) and a small handlebar bag as our only other luggage.

Inside our bags we each had the following: two pair of the lycra bike shorts, two tops, bike shoes, sandals for when we weren't biking, a pair of jeans each, two pair of socks, rain gear, and a couple pair of underwear and a bra for me. I might have even had a shorty nightgown and lightweight robe in case the bathrooms were shared and down the hall in a Bed and Breakfast. We planned on hand washing our bike shorts, socks and undies nightly. We would find a laundromat when needed. It was funny to us that as full-timers we had simplified our life a lot; this was taking another giant step in simplification.

Our flight to London was quite typical except we didn't get to sleep. The lady near us was watching a funny movie and laughed out loud a good part of the night. We were punchy when we arrived but we got through the preliminary procedures (passport) then got our luggage. We were only a few steps from the customs check but first we had to put the bikes back together. Ron did that in full view of a customs guy who wasn't busy. It didn't take long. Once we were set we rolled our bikes up to the gate and he waved us right through. Pushing a bike which was loaded with panniers through the very busy Gatwick airport was not easy. We had to get some pounds (British money), and inquire about getting into London.

We had chosen Gatwick because it was a multi modal station meaning they connected with many other forms of transportation. From my research back in Michigan, I learned that we should take the train to Victoria Station in London and from there we would need to take the circle line (subway) to Liverpool street then take the train to Ipswich from there we would change trains again and go to Felixstowe which would be the end of the line.

At the airport, after we got pounds, I went to the train information booth. When I told the man what we were told to do, he said, "You can't take bikes on the circle line." I asked, "Then how do we get from Victoria Station to Liverpool Street?" Very curtly, he said, "You got wheels on those bikes, ride them." Oh No, I thought. We don't have a clue where to go and are not acclimated to riding on the left side of the road. No, we just couldn't do that. I didn't like his answer so I went to the terminal information booth and that man was very nice. He called someone and said we could take the bikes on the circle line. Back to the train man I went and he just wouldn't sell me the tickets if I was going to try to go on the circle line. Back and forth I went until we decided we would wing it. We bought the tickets just to Victoria Station and figured when we got there we would figure it out. And that is what we did.

Remember we had missed a whole night's sleep, it was morning and we had to go quite a ways before we could even think of resting. Once on the train it was a nice 30 minute ride. Our bikes were in the baggage car so we just enjoyed the view and rode in comfort. When the train stopped at the station we had to hustle to get back to the baggage car and get the bikes before it took off again. We had been warned that the stops are only long enough for people to get on and off.

Once we got to Victoria Station the fun really began. It was hard to try to get around this very, very busy terminal while pushing bikes which were loaded with panniers. We found a place that was a little out of the way and Ron guarded both bikes while I went to the ticket window. I learned that the circle line is a subway not unlike the NY subway. You had to go down stairs, stand on a platform and wait for the train then since it only stopped for a minute push on. Now imagine doing that with loaded bikes. The other problem was the only gate we could get through was a big wide one and that put us on the wrong side of the tracks. While being on the wrong side of the tracks wouldn't be so bad it did mean that instead of going just two stops we would have to go the other way in the circle and therefore travel the majority of the circle.

So we headed to the stairs. It would have been nice if we could have helped each other down the large, long flight of stairs, which was congested but leaving a bike unattended at either the top or bottom was not wise. Try again to imagine pushing a heavy, bulky bike down the stairs. It was difficult to say the least but we made it. Getting on the train wasn't so bad but like any busy subway train there was nowhere to sit. We stood holding on to the bikes (didn't have a free hand to hang on to anything else) while the train hurried then stopped abruptly. We were jerked, pushed, and were in everyone's way for the trip that lasted what seemed like an eternity. And to make matters worse all that jerking and jostling made me have to pee really bad. There was nothing I could do but hold it.

Getting off of the train was okay, but pushing our bikes back up another long, busy stairway was worse than pushing the bikes down. We moaned wondering if this day would ever end, but first I had to find a bathroom.

Liverpool street station is where the big trains came in. I found the bathroom okay and left Ron to guard the bikes while I ran. Inside the bathroom I saw that all the stalls required change in order to get in to go. I ran out to get money from Ron, but all he had were bills. I ran around like a chicken with my head cut off trying to find someone who could give me change. I should have learned their currency before we left Michigan. What's a pence? I needed ten pence to use the toilet. After what seemed like forever, I had the coins I needed and finally was able to get relief. Then I went out and gave Ron a lesson on British currency so he could go visit the loo or toilet also (a bathroom is where you take a bath in British speak) .

Once on the train that would eventually take us to Felixstowe it was easy and relaxing. Our bikes were once again in the baggage car and we could enjoy the ride through the beautiful English countryside. Unbeknownst to us we had one more hurdle.

Finally We Arrived at the Beginning

When we got to Ipswich we watched with horror as everyone getting off the train walked a bit then went up two flights of stairs to a platform that went over the tracks and then down into the station proper. There was no other way to get across the tracks. Even though the ride from London was relaxing, we were overly exhausted. Even walking was a challenge. Now we had to do the stair bit again. I don't know where we got the strength but we did it. We may have even helped each other because we were in the country instead of the big city.

The train station in Ipswich was very old yet charming to me. I loved it. We went to the window to get our tickets for the short ride to Felixstowe which is as far east as we could go from that point in England. Any further and we would be swimming in the North Sea. We were ecstatic when we learned that we didn't have to do any more stairs. We purchased a sandwich to eat during our short wait for the train and I called Jim to let him know we were almost there and the time the train would arrive.

When we arrived we couldn't believe that we had finally come to the end of our long travel. We made a mental note: if we ever do this again, we find someone who can pick us up at the airport. Jim and Sue were there to greet us and we actually got on our bikes to follow him to the bed and breakfast which he had reserved for us. We almost lost Ron as he started riding on the wrong side of the road. It's hard to learn new tricks.

Our room at the B & B was on the third floor but they had a nice area on the first floor for our bikes. All we had to do was carry the panniers up (no elevator). We took showers (in the bathroom on the second floor) and felt terrific after. We had a nice dinner at Jim and Sue's house and fell in love with our new daughter-in-law. Jim brought us home early as he had to work at midnight. We had gotten our second wind by then so we went to the pub on the corner and enjoyed a drink.

I loved the pub; it was a lively place and everyone was singing the song that goes "I'm Henry the eighth I am." I was so excited to be in England and experience the uniqueness of it. Now I was sure it was going to be a fantastic adventure.

A Relaxing Week in Felixstowe

We spent a week in Felixstowe resting up and getting acquainted with things British like walking and biking on the left side of everything. Even going up and down stairs is opposite of our way. We spent a lot of time with Jim and Sue and her parents Jan and John as well as her brother Pete.

Jim took us to the base the first full day there and got us some British currency. Things were more expensive in England at the time and I could see that Ron was a bit concerned whether we would be okay for the whole six weeks of our trip. I am more of a free spirit than Ron is and I would always say if we start running out of money we could stay at hostels instead of B & Bs.

We did two touristy things from Felixstowe. We toured Colchester Castle (built between 1069 and 1076 but not finished until 1100) and eavesdropped on a school group that was learning about castle life. We learned a few things too. Another day, we took the train back to London and did some of the touristy things there like walking over the London Bridge. We went to a museum which showed all the different and horrible methods used to torture in the medieval days, went to the Tower of London (saw the crown jewels among other things), and walked to the Parliament building.

When we got back to Felixstowe, Jim picked us up and took us to their home for a lovely dinner that he cooked (he is a good cook). After the goodbyes Jim took us back to the B & B and we gave him that box of clothing so he could ship it back to Michigan for us. I'll never forget the lovely walks along the promenade, the beautiful flowers all over the town, nice drives in the surrounding countryside, small villages, fun in the pubs, and good food too like chicken pie and vegetable soup. And best of all were the visits with Jim and Sue. I wrote in my diary: Its been wonderful. Now we must pedal.

Top: Ron, Jim and Sue in a pub. Bottom: Colchester Castle

Day One
Felixstowe to Lavenham

It was Wednesday, June 21, and we were so excited to get on the road that we were up early, dressed for biking and had eaten a good breakfast. Everything was ready to go. Ron went to get our bikes. While I was waiting, I noticed the wind; it was very strong. Oops that was not what we wanted. We hadn't had wind all week so that was a shock. Right away I noticed my front tire was flat. Ron tried to fix it and ended up having to replace the inner tube—the old tire had a bad valve. Good thing we had a couple of tubes with us. We were off.

It was tough going for the first ten or twelve miles as we had to travel with trucks, busses and fast moving little cars on a major road but once onto the little lanes we intended to use for the bulk of the trip we were fine. Those single lane roads really didn't have route numbers. We learned to travel from village to village by these "finger signs". One needed to know all the villages on the route because they didn't direct one to the farthest town—only the next one.

Being in the country and seeing the neat farms and villages was like going back in time. If cars hadn't been parked on the town streets I would have felt like we had indeed traveled back in time at least five hundred years. I loved the thatched roofs and the

timbered buildings in Lavenham were amazing. It is a fifteenth century town with lots of interesting buildings. We stayed in a room upstairs at The Angel which was a pub and the floors were so slanted that if you laid on the floor you could easily roll to the wall. The buildings are still standing and used even though they were built in the thirteen hundreds or earlier. We walked around after our bath and were hungry but no one served dinner until 7 p.m. We decided we would have to plan differently. But we really felt good after our 33.6 mile ride.

The crooked house, built in 1395 is now a gallery in Lavenham, Bottom; Many buildings in Lavenham look like this.

George, Ann and Cambridge

Since Felixstowe and Lavenham had bed and breakfasts everywhere we thought finding a place to stay would always be easy. Halfway into our second day, we realized that that would not always be the case. We hadn't seen a single shingle out for a B & B. in a long time. When we arrived at Balsham where we thought we would end the day, we inquired as to where we might find a B & B. We were directed to the post office; the man there said there was none in town but suggested we try the pub. There was a pub in every village. The gal there gave us two numbers to call but the first was booked. When we called the second lady I told her we were an American couple biking across England, Wales and Ireland and asked if a room was available. She was very cautious and instead of answering, she asked questions like, who we were and if we were married also if we smoked. We answered correctly so she gave us directions to their place in the town of Linton.

It was about three miles away and as we were biking, we laughed that she asked if we were married. We decided to make sure they knew we had nine children and we were going to let them think all the children were ours together. Maybe we thought that it would make us seem more married. There was no shingle outside as it was a regular neighborhood and might not have been licensed but we didn't care.

When we arrived they were very friendly after seeing we were not young kids. We figured they probably had been a bit suspicious when on the phone I told her we were Americans bicycling the country. Ann and George were gracious hosts and we just loved them. She had tea and biscuits ready for us when we arrived and was interested in our adventure. We told them that we would like to stay for two nights so we could bike to Cambridge and back the next day then continue or travels. That was fine with them. After our bath (few had showers) we rode to the small village for dinner.

In Cambridge we were in bicycle heaven; everyone rode bikes—old, young, students, professors–everyone. Other than the very old, large and beautiful buildings, it reminded us of a US college town complete with musicians on the corner playing for a little change to bookstores, lunch shops and couples holding hands while strolling in the park. But the buildings were the most impressive. The University of Cambridge, founded in 1209, is massive and made up of different colleges. It is the second oldest university in the English speaking world. We enjoyed every minute of the day and right away wished we were staying there for the two days rather than having to bike to and from Linton. There were plenty of lodging places after all; another lesson for another time.

When we got back to George and Ann's she volunteered that I could use her washer to do a load of wash which I did. When it was done I came downstairs just as she was taking the clothes out of the washer. She noticed there wasn't any underwear in the load and asked me where they were. I told her that we don't wear underwear with our bike shorts and I showed her the padding inside at the crotch area and explained that sitting on seams from the underpants would be painful after a while and I explained that the padding was a chamois which wicks away moisture so we don't get chapped there. I think she probably thought that we were naughty not wearing undies until I educated her on cycling wear.

We became pen pals with George and Ann and continued to correspond with them for years and even went back to their place several years later on another bike trip.

Forget Shakespeare

While we were yet in Michigan and just after buying a huge map of Great Britain, Ron marked the map with a yellow highlighter. He drew a line from Felixstowe to Fishguard as the general route including some special spots like Cambridge and Stratford on Avon.

From Linton we were off again and still heading east. We stopped mid day in the town of Saffron Waldon and toured the museum and a huge manor house called Audley House. While in that town we went into a big church and it so happened that the organist was practicing; we sat and listened for quite a while. It was very moving to be in such a beautiful place listening to an organ like I had never heard before. Or maybe it sounded best because of the setting. At any rate I shed tears listening.

We finished biking and ended up at a farm house B & B. When we arrived we were greeted by a large peacock which was beautiful. Our room was huge and even had a tea kettle and tea bags. It was a short walk to a pub for dinner and it was nice not to have to ride the bikes for a little bit.

The next stop was not so pleasant for two reasons. Sandy was only fifty miles north of London and a new, busy town I will call a suburb; there were no B & B's so we stayed at a motel and because it was Sunday the only place we could find to eat was a Texaco station (pubs don't serve an evening meal on Sunday). Lesson learned: plan to be in a little village on Sundays and eat early. We did go to a pub later to have a drink and nice conversations with people there. Back at the motel Ron expressed his worry that we would run out of time. We had plane reservations on July 28 for our flight from Shannon, Ireland, back to the US. I tried to calm him down saying that we could always take a train if it looks like we can't bike the whole thing in time. Ron was also worried about hills in Wales. I mentioned the train idea again.

Our next planned stop, Milton Keynes, was still too close to London and busy. We tried to reserve a B & B ahead of time from the Tourist Information but they didn't do that. She did give us phone numbers. Many were booked and the explanation was when tourists come to visit London they stay on the outskirts. It was summer tourist season. One of the roads we had to go on to get to our stop was many lanes wide; it was a big city main road full of heavy traffic and roundabouts. I wrote in my diary that night, "I just want to get out of England; I don't like it."

The next day was easier especially because as we were off of that busy main road. I discovered a bike lane which led us to the town we wanted to go to and the predicted rain did not happen for a while. But it suddenly got cold, windy and did rain. We ducked into a pub for lunch and while eating decided that we would stop in each new village asking for a local B & B. The third town we stopped at didn't look too promising but we went into the post office to inquire. The postmaster was very helpful looking in the yellow pages and even suggested a few to call. As I was making a list a customer who had kind of overheard our dilemma, offered her home and some tea to warm us. Even though she was on her way to go shopping she delayed her trip and had us follow her home. Both Pat and her husband were wonderful as was the tea and warmth. Ron made a call to the inn in Blakesley. They had a room and it was only five miles away. We could brave the windy cold rain for that long.

The next day was another cold rainy day but it was easy riding. We were thankful to be in the country. Our rain gear kept us dry but Ron's panniers weren't repelling the rain. Good thing for the Ziploc bags. I made a mental note to look for more waterproof spray for his bag. He had another problem though. His bike was making strange noises. He looked at it and discovered he had a bolt missing from near the derailer. We didn't find any help at the hardware store but I spotted a woman using a bike to deliver mail. We asked her if there was a bike repair shop nearby. She didn't know of one but suggested a garage saying, "He's ever so helpful." I love the way Brits speak. Well he tried but he just did not have anything that would fit. We decided to wait until we got to Warwick. As we continued on the way, a beautiful red fox ran across the road and into the hedges. I was excited to see the fox but I don't think the sheep in the field were.

We had planned to stay two nights in Warwick and thoroughly enjoyed our time there. Besides touring the beautiful castle, we visited a library to see if my ancestral castle was listed and still standing. It was but it wasn't on the way. My hope was that maybe we could find a way to take a train to the south, visit the castle then come back to continue our ride. Ron wasn't excited about that because he was still concerned that we didn't leave enough time to get to Shannon.

Finally we got to Stratford on Avon. The whole trip I had been looking forward to visiting this town where Shakespeare was born. What a disappointment. The place was mobbed with tourists and to add insult to Shakespeare there was a McDonald's just down the street. I went into the tourist information place and came right back out. It was full of rude Americans from New York. I didn't want to be around them. I told Ron, "Let's keep riding." which we did.

Warwick castle was built by William the Conqueror in 1068 and is considered a fine example of a medieval castle.

A Side Trip to Dorset

Before we left Michigan my sister Bev, suggested we should be sure to include a visit to our ancestral castle. I didn't know we had one. My father's mother's maiden name was Weld and this castle in southern England (by the English Channel) was built by a Weld. I told her I would check into it but it wasn't really on our route. After our visit to Warwick castle and learning that castles are really protected in England I started looking into how we could get there and back in a day.

Our B & B in Cheltenham was only two miles from the train station so as soon as we checked into our lodging, we took the short ride to check out the departure times. That was easy. We planned to leave in the morning and did.

The train trip was pleasant except for changing trains in Bristol. We had to do stairs again and realized that coming back to Cheltenham would mean the same. On the last leg of the train trip we visited with two couples who were very interested in our trip. They wanted to know where we were going and I explained that I wanted to see my "ancestral castle". They asked the name of the castle and when I mentioned Lulworth, one said, "Oh that's Colonel Weld's place". You could have knocked me over at the mention of the Weld name. The lady went on to explain that Colonel Weld was the Queen's representative for all of Dorset and that he often had visits from the Royal Family. That was impressive too.

When we arrived at the small village of Wool, we got off and went looking for a place to stay. There were several B & B's and we picked a cute pink house with a thatched roof. The shingle on the front of the house labeled the house as Sexy's Farmhouse. We later learned that it was supposed to be Saxy's when first named but the mistake in the title from long ago remained forever. We arranged for a room with the owners, Sophia and Malcom Haas, and told them we were just going to drop of our panniers for now and ride down to investigate "my castle". Sophia asked,

"You're a Weld?" I must add a little bit about how we were dressed. When we left Cheltenham in the morning we were dressed as we were every day we biked. We had on lycra bike shorts, a very casual top, shoes and socks and our hair was a mess from having ridden with helmets. I had very little make up on and in other words did not look at all like the Welds they were thinking of.

We easily rode the five miles to the castle because we were minus the panniers but we couldn't find it right away. I think our mistake was we were looking for a big castle. As we would soon learn, Lulworth was never a fortress. It was in fact built as a hunting lodge. We were finally directed to a lane and told to look for the little gate house at the road. We found it and told the lady at the gate house what we were after. She was very helpful, directed us towards the castle and added that we should be sure to visit the church on the property. Very soon we came upon the church and investigated it. It was open and looked very much like it was still in use. In checking the cemetery, we did not discover any Welds and thought that strange. We continued on to the castle and walked all around. We couldn't go in as it was covered with scaffolding because it was being repaired by the English Heritage organization which protects and promotes England's historic environment and ensures that its past is researched and understood. Lulworth Castle was pretty but not as large as I thought it might be. We went back to the gate house to thank the lady. She asked if we saw the church and we answered that we did and told her it wasn't locked as she had said it would be. "Oh no," she replied, "You went to the wrong church. The church you need to see is the one that doesn't look like a church and it is very close to the castle. After you see it I will tell you about it." We went back and peeked in the windows. Yes, it was a church, but it looked like a mausoleum from the outside.

The story is best written on a web site I found recently: Http://gouk.about.com/od/englandtravel/ss/lulworthchapel.htm

> Catholics were officially persecuted in England from the time of Henry VIII until the late 18th century. During the reign of Elizabeth I, Catholics could be hung, drawn and quartered for harboring priests or practicing their faith.
>
> By the 17th century, things had relaxed somewhat, but Catholics were still prohibited from worshipping in public and were subject to various other restrictive laws.
>
> The Weld family, owners of Lulworth Castle, supported a priest at the castle - disguised as the family tutor - and held clandestine services in their private chapel - within the castle - to which other Catholics were welcomed in secret.
>
> In 1786, when freestanding Catholic churches were still banned in England, Thomas Weld determined to build a Catholic chapel - in the guise of a family mausoleum - on his estate. King George III and Queen Charlotte visited Lulworth in 1789 after recovering from his first bout of madness. According to family legend, the King gave Thomas Weld permission to create the Catholic chapel. "Build a family mausoleum," he is said to have declared, "and you can furnish the inside as a Catholic chapel if you wish." Soon, Masses were being served, openly on the Lulworth estate. Thus, with the King's permission, two years before Catholic's were legally entitled to worship in public (1791) and 40 years before full Catholic Emancipation in England, in 1829, the chapel became the first freestanding Catholic church in

> England since the Protestant Reformation.
>
> Masses are still held in the Chapel and Catholic wedding ceremonies are conducted there.
>
> In the early days of the United States, Catholicism in the former thirteen North American colonies was organized under the hierarchy of the Apostolic Vicar of London, a kind of Papal emissary in the days before full Catholic emancipation in England.
>
> In 1790, John Carroll became the first Bishop of North America, charged with setting up the Catholic hierarchy there. He was elevated to Archbishop in 1808. Carroll is also credited with founding Georgetown University, the oldest Catholic university in North America.
>
> Before taking up his position, Carroll was consecrated Bishop in the Weld family's private Catholic chapel, The Chapel of St. Mary, on the Lulworth estate. Later, he commissioned Benjamin Latrobe, architect of the United States Capitol, to design America's first Catholic cathedral, the Basilica of National Shrine of the Assumption in Baltimore, MD. Some of design elements of that Cathedral can be directly linked to the Chapel of St. Mary at Lulworth Castle.

When we reported back to the lady at the gate house, she told us the above story and suggested that we go visit with Colonel Weld himself and directed us to his house. Ron was very hesitant especially in light of our looks. I mean with bike shorts on and chain marks on our legs we didn't look properly dressed to visit someone as important as the Colonel. We bicycled to the house and Ron stood out way far away while I knocked on the door. I was shaking but knocked and a very stately gentleman answered the door. I said, "My name is Barbara and I'm a Weld from the United States. My husband and I are bicycling across England. May I speak with Colonel Weld." He said he was the Colonel and invited us in. Ron and I were both shocked but we did go in. Right away he introduced us to Lady Weld and asked if he could get us something to drink. He offered scotch or sherry. Ron had a scotch and I had a glass of wine and we sat down to talk. The house appeared very very comfortable although a little ornate. They were both very friendly and answered every question I asked.

Early on in our conversation, I inquired about the Catholic Church on the property. I told him that I was raised a Lutheran and that my grandparents were Methodists and Presbyterians. He explained that there were many who left England to gain religious freedom in the United States. I always knew that I was a nonconformist.

I asked if there were any books or portraits of the ancestors in the Weld family. He showed us to his dining room where the paintings of Humphrey and Thomas Weld hung. They were rescued from the fire that happened in 1939. I took a picture of the Colonel and Lady Weld in front of the ancestral paintings. All in all it was a very enjoyable day.

From there we went back to our bed-and-breakfast then out to the pub for dinner. When we laid down to sleep that night and looked up above we could see the straw that the roof was made of. I'm so glad we took the side trip to Dorset.

Left Picture: Colonel and Lady Weld
Bottom left: The Catholic church

Top: Lulworth Castle as we saw it.
Bottom: Lulworth now.

Back on Our Route

The train ride back to our route was about the same as our ride down. Except that in Bristol we had to wait an hour and a half for a train. We got off the train in Gloucester and found the cutest bed-and-breakfast ever. The lady reminded us of one of the old ladies in Arsenic and Old Lace. She was so sweet and lovely and her house was also very nice. We walked into town to try to find a place to eat and all we could find was more British food. I was tired of such heavy food and really just wanted a salad. They didn't do salad in England—not the way we do anyway.

We were in Wales and noticed the difference right away. Everything seemed a little grayer, perhaps dirtier, but the hills were thankfully not as bad as we thought they would be. All of England was experiencing a heat spell and drought; it was very hot in our B & B in Hay on Wye. There was no air-conditioning anywhere. Hay on Wye looked like a book buyers paradise. I think it was the used book capital of the world because of all the used bookstores in town. Books were crammed three deep on the bookshelves in the very old stores and they were in piles everywhere. It was even hard to walk around the stores looking for a book because it was so cluttered.

Ron had a lot of trouble with his bike gears during the ride. So far we had covered 382 miles but his bike needed fixing before we went much further. My knees needed fixing too but there was no help for that. I was glad Ron's worries hadn't come true about the hills being so bad in Wales. We found a good bike shop in Brecon and Ron's bike was okay for a while after that.

The biking wasn't as bad as trying to find food that was good for us to eat. We had to eat late because the pubs didn't open until seven. We tried eating a bigger lunch but then it was hard to pedal with such a full stomach. We had both gained weight even though we were exercising all the time. It was about that time that we decided to buy fruit and yogurt and let that be our dinner. Good choice.

We had our best day biking to Haverford West. We covered forty six and one half miles in two and one half hours. We got there early and spent the day shopping. I had fallen in love with the duvet covers which we had enjoyed since we were in England and wanted one for our bed in the motorhome. I spent the day looking through many beautiful ones until I found the perfect one. They had so many different choices of fabric that it was hard to choose. Since we couldn't carry it, I had it shipped to my mother-in-law in Florida. It was really my only souvenir of our whole trip because we couldn't carry anything that was not necessary.

Our last day of biking in Wales was horrible. We had planned an easy day (only fifteen miles), but we had a headwind the whole way and the hills were steep enough that it was hard to bike. At times we were only biking four to five miles per hour.

We were looking forward to getting to Ireland the next day. What we didn't know was that Ireland wasn't going to be easy to bike either and we would have problems there that we didn't even think about in England.

Tisn't it My Lucky Day

The ferry to Ireland was made more pleasurable because as we were boarding we met a neat couple – Jane and Mike. We spent the whole trip talking with them.

From our first bed-and-breakfast in Ireland which was at Rosslare we were heading to New Ross. The only road to New Ross was a major one, heavy with traffic, and it was rather lonely. There were no towns, no place to eat and no place to stop and it wasn't particularly pretty. Right away we missed England.

From the beginning of this trip we had enjoyed the villages and the quaint cottages and old stores. The people and the roads for the most part were good too. Each part of England was a little bit different. In the East there were lots of cottages with thatched roofs. The Cotswolds were picturesque with their yellow stone houses. And Wales although not so pretty had a lot of character. So far in Ireland we hadn't seen anything but roads, trucks and cars. And we were hungry.

We decided that we needed to find a village and promised each other that if we saw a sign for a village we would make a short detour. We saw a sign and turned off but it was a horrible, winding road. After going a little ways it went uphill very steeply. We were covered with flies ---nasty flies, and at that point we gave up trying to find a village, turned around and went back to the big road. But something happened to my bike on that ride; my rear tire was not riding true.

We traveled quite a few more miles when we finally saw a sign for an inn. It looked rather upscale but Ron said we should go in and try it anyway. There was no menu which should have been a clue. But the man that greeted us said they were making salad which sounded good. He gave us the choice of ham, beef or salmon and some other kinds of meats; we chose salmon and sat down to wait. It looked like the whole restaurant wasn't open yet so we sat in a pub like area. When the salads came they looked good and we enjoyed them. That is we enjoyed them until we got the bill. We hadn't thought to ask ahead of time how much these salads would cost. The cost for salads and soup were twenty six pounds which was equivalent to forty dollars. Outrageous! That ruined the day for us and we were not liking Ireland very much at that moment. After lunch we still had at least ten miles to go which would've made a forty mile day and I was getting tired because my bike was riding so hard. I asked Ron to stop if he saw a bed-and-breakfast sign. He was ahead of me while I just kept trudging along. When he stopped at the top of a hill, I saw the bed-and-breakfast sign and it listed that they served evening meals. I thought that was perfect and we wouldn't have to bike into town to get something to eat after we had cleaned up. There was a lady mowing the lawn at the entrance and I asked her the price. She said, "Ten dollars and fifty cents with a full breakfast and five dollars for the evening meal." Her smile captured me. She wanted to show us the room first and said, with a lovely Irish lilt that I can still hear today, "'Tisn't it my lucky day now that I was pushing the mower as you rode by or else you mightn't have stopped." She gave us the room she was born in

which was quite charming and explained that the farm had been in the family for four generations. After the simple dinner of ham, beans and carrots she took me out to see the lambs because I had told her that I'd seen lots of lambs out in the pastures we had passed and they had these red marks on them. I wanted to know about the marks but more importantly I had never touched a lamb and I wanted to. They looked so soft. I forget what she told me about the red marks but I did enjoy petting the little lambs. I even got to hold on to the goat that the little lambs suckled from. She explained that the goat made a better mother than a lamb does. Our hostesses name was Kathleen Devereaux and we enjoyed talking with her about a lot of things. She started the bed-and-breakfast because she was poor since the farm was not able to make it on its own. She said the people of Ireland were very poor. Our stay with Kathleen was very pleasurable and kind of undid the unpleasantness of the earlier part of the day.

Oops Wrong Way

We got to New Ross in short order and found the bicycle shop but it was closed. A gentleman came by and told us that Paddy always closes on Wednesday. There was a phone number on the door so I went to the florist shop to use their phone. I talked to Paddy and he said he would come right away which he did. He fixed the broken spoke and righted the wheel (it was crooked) and we were off just a little later than we planned.

It was difficult to find the road we were looking for and again there were no places to eat lunch until we finally got to the town of Graigiguenamanagh. We were very disappointed in it. It was a nothing kind of town with nothing to do and hardly any place to eat. The pubs did not serve food. If people are poor they can't afford to go out and eat. We found the bed-and-breakfast but it was so dirty I didn't want to stay. We had no alternative though. It was either stay or bike all the way back to where we had come from. We finally found a little grill in town and ate a hamburger and fries and then went back up to the B & B. Later for dinner we went back to town and to the same grill and had mediocre spaghetti. There were several pubs in town but none of them were busy. We went into the Anchor pub and were the only customers. I like to meet the town's peoples so we went to another pub and couldn't believe the characters there. The postman was blitzed but there was a young boy and a nice man from South Lampton. Ron and I figured out that the men in that town come to the bar late at night (an hour before closing) for their one pint of Guinness; they can't afford to drink anymore than that. It's probably their one pleasure in a day.

Ron and I talked. We had to change direction and head to more civilized areas—not that this wasn't civilized, it was just too poor and too remote. We needed to head west.

After breakfast (served in dirty dishes) we were scared that we would come down with some strange disease. We ate only the toast. I reported her place to the tourist board as the dirtiest I'd ever been in.

It was a nice ride to Carlow even though we had to deal with wind and we easily biked twenty-five miles getting there in time to have a fantastic lunch at the Lone Owl pub. We had roast pork, stuffing, veggies and potatoes; the best part was it was only three dollars and fifty cents. We found a bed-and-breakfast that was a great big house with beautiful grounds and it was only ten dollars. For dinner we ate at another pub. It was also terrific. We each had a chicken sandwich with cheese and tomato which was very tasty and we added an apple tart with cream for dessert with coffee. The whole meal was under six dollars. It appeared to us that we made a good choice in changing direction. We really liked the scenery in this area better too.

On Friday, July 14, we arrived in Kilkenny and planned to stay for a two-day rest. Oonagh Egan, a sparkely young woman, owned the bed-and-breakfast where we stayed and she suggested several different places to eat and they were all good. Between eating and walking we investigated the whole town and made our plans for the next day which would include visiting the castle in town. Even though it was very hot there we found a cool spot in the woods behind the Castle to sit and read. I wrote in my diary that I was missing having my own place on those days when we weren't moving. I longed for my own refrigerator, my own games to play, a radio to turn on and I added that I felt a bit displaced. For dinner one night we ate at Kyteler's Inn. It dates back to the 1300s and the owner was accused of witchcraft but escaped hanging for some reason. Riding to Clonmel the next day was just plain beautiful. There were mountains and tall pine trees. We rode past a castle ruin and other lovely sites. It was a good road with little traffic and we were able to get in 33 miles. The mountains surrounding the house were breathtaking and we walked into town for lunch and dinner.

Because we wasted a couple days at the beginning of this part of our trip, we had to make up a little time. We had decided to look into taking a train to get us closer to Shannon.

As we were riding into Tipperary Ron's bike was acting up again. I kept hearing his gears slip over and over again. We found a bike shop and Ron took his bike in while I found the bed -and-breakfast. I found the train station too but it was locked up tighter than a drum and there were no notes posted about how to get in touch with anyone. We went to several other businesses and finally found that the tourist information was where we could get the train tickets.

The train trip was better than any in England and we found that the guards/porters on the train were very friendly and helpful. That was a relief.

Galway was a zoo with hundreds and thousands of people at the beach. The beach was disappointing though because it was all stones instead of sand. We got through that area fairly easily though and stayed out of town at a bed-and-breakfast. This part of Ireland was so different from the eastern part.

The next day when we were about seven miles out of town on our way to the next stop Ron's bike started acting up again. We were almost in the middle of nowhere. We pulled over and looked at his bike; it was the derailer again. We had no choice but to keep going. We nearly got lost though because all the signs were in Gaelic. We stopped at the Texaco station where a nice guy there fixed Ron's bike again. Continuing on we couldn't help but notice how different the landscape was in this area. Four foot-high stone fences (walls) marked the edges of all the farm properties and sometimes there were stone fences in the middle marking off squares or just areas. We saw a farmer sitting on a stool in his field milking a cow. There was no barn. We guessed that when it was milking time the farmer walked out to the field, found the cow and milked her. Life was simple out there. We saw another farmer digging peat and we stopped to talk to him. He told us they use the peat to burn in their fireplace so they can keep warm. After it's dug up it dries fast and three lorries (trucks) full is enough to last him for the winter.

We rode forty three miles the next day even though it was very hot and windy. After we got to our bed-and-breakfast we added another ten miles to bike up to and on the Sky Drive up high. The view was spectacular. We looked out on the Atlantic Ocean and could imagine we were seeing America from there. For dinner that night we took a bottle of wine, some cheese and bread and sat on a park bench watching people. We saw a guy we called "the politician". He was making one phone call after another acting like he was very important. Another couple was waiting to use the phone but the politician just kept talking and making one call after another. How rude. We just had to laugh. We met two cyclists from Austria and two couples (one was from Illinois and the other was stationed in Wales).

The following day was fantastically beautiful. Mountains all around us were draped in various shades of what looked like green velvet. It was oh so refreshing to our eyes. It was very quiet as we biked. There was no one around---just the beauty. And all of a sudden out of the corner of my eye I saw a clearing and a jewel like I've never seen before. It was a huge Abby set way back in that sea of green. I just had to stop my bike and stand and look at it so I could soak it up and remember it forever. But the bad part about this part of the trip is Ron's bike again. I felt so bad for him and there was nothing I could do. There was nothing he could do either. Basically his bike was like a three speed bike now and that made pedaling up the hills difficult.

Sunday, July 23 was going to be an easy day just to Galway

City but when we got there we realized it was just a big tourist area. We did eat lunch at McDonald's and Ron was happy about that. We decided to go to Kinvera which was a harbor town; I thought Ron would like that. So it was another thirty-five mile day. For dinner we got wine, cheese, bread and yogurt — oh and cookies too. We visited the little Dunguaire Castle and met two nice girls who took our picture in the banquet room. After dinner we went to a pub and it was the most fun. Three local musicians played and everyone was singing. The two girls came in and we talked with them a lot especially the one from San Francisco. We didn't leave until late.

Limping to the End

Monday, July 24, was not our best day. Ron's bike was giving him fits all day. He was grumbling and I didn't blame him. I was dying from the heat and burning sun. My arms and knees were very hot. We found a bike rental place and the young guy there made the most sense. He said it couldn't be fixed. When that bolt was lost and the replacement was the wrong size it threw the gears out of line. So with that "good" news Ron decided he could limp along.

We ate in an mediocre pub with one-inch thick cigarette butts under the bar and a bathroom that didn't work. Back on the road the heat was just awful and there was no shade or relief. The coastline was strange —all limestone gray. The ocean was clear and blue though. Then we came to a very bumpy road which was awful and Ron got a flat tire to make matters worse. There was no traffic on the road so we stopped along the side. It was blazing hot and there was no shade—just cows and flies. Ron tried to fix his tire (while the cows just stared at us) but it wasn't just a leak, it was a valve problem. I was glad we had picked up a spare inner tube way back in Cambridge. But the bad part was Ron's pump wouldn't work on the valve which was English. Why did there have to be differences? We decided to walk to the next town even though it was so hot. I didn't want to leave him so I walked but I got to thinking that that was silly. I could be riding. It was no fun pushing a perfectly rideable bike. After about a mile of pushing and walking, I decided to flag down the next vehicle that went by. So when a van approached from behind, I flagged it down and they stopped. It was a nice family from Pennsylvania. I asked them if they could give my husband a lift. The lady asked if he was tired. I laughed and told her about the flat tire and the wrong inner tube. They told Ron to climb in the back of the van with this bike and off they went. It felt strange for me to be riding without Ron but at the same time it was far easier than worrying about his stupid bike. When I got to the gas station his tire with almost ready so that worked out good.

The town was Lisdoonvarna— a pretty name for a falling down town. We went downtown and found a hotel for ten pounds but oh what a dump of a place. Believe it or not we ate in the Ritz (the real name) which was worse. This town which is famous for its springs and baths didn't look very prosperous. At the hotel for the whole evening we didn't have any water so we couldn't even flush the toilet.

As we started out the next day it started to rain but it was a pretty short and easy day. The first few miles were the worst. We were riding into a driving rain which pelted our face all the way uphill. When we got near the Cliffs of Moher it cleared up a bit but the wind was still blowing strong. The Cliffs were an amazing sight (they are very famous) and we enjoyed coffee and carrot cake in the coffee shop there. From the Cliffs it was downhill with the wind on our back the whole seven miles to the coast town of Lehinch.

In Lehinch we got some laundry done, ate dinner then went to a little pub to watch the local characters. There was a fat old drunk who had his young daughter with him and he was on his third Guinness. After dinner the tide was coming in so we decided to walk by the sea. We both thought we were feeling the mist from the ocean when in reality it was raining again; we got soaked before we ended up back at the bed-and-breakfast.

The next day we had another easy ride downhill with the wind on our backs. It was only 20 miles so we were done in a hurry. Once we got away from the ocean the wind had died down a bit. We inquired as to where we could stay when we got to the airport and settled on the airport hotel because it was right there and we wouldn't have any trouble getting to the terminal.

The last ride in Ireland was only 15 miles long and it especially seemed very strange to be biking into the airport which was a fairly busy road. I kept imagining us trying to bike into something like Detroit Metropolitan Airport or any other big city airport. There it was a piece of cake. When we checked into the hotel they gladly offered to put our bicycles in a storage room so we didn't have to worry about them. That was a nice treat. Since it was our last night in the U K, we decided to splurge on dinner in the hotel dining room. It was very nice and relaxing. Ceremonially Ron threw his well worn tennis shoes into the waste basket in our hotel room. Then we packed and were ready for the flight back to the United States.

We had ridden just short of one thousand miles, met a lot of wonderful people and had a ton of memories. A lot of bikers, like my sons, would have scoffed at our thirty-mile days but that was how we wanted to do it. Our goal was not to see how fast we got anywhere, but stopping along the way to meet the people and see as much as we could. Biking is the best way to see any area because (unless you are a young kid) you can go slow enough to see the sights around you. This was the trip of a lifetime.

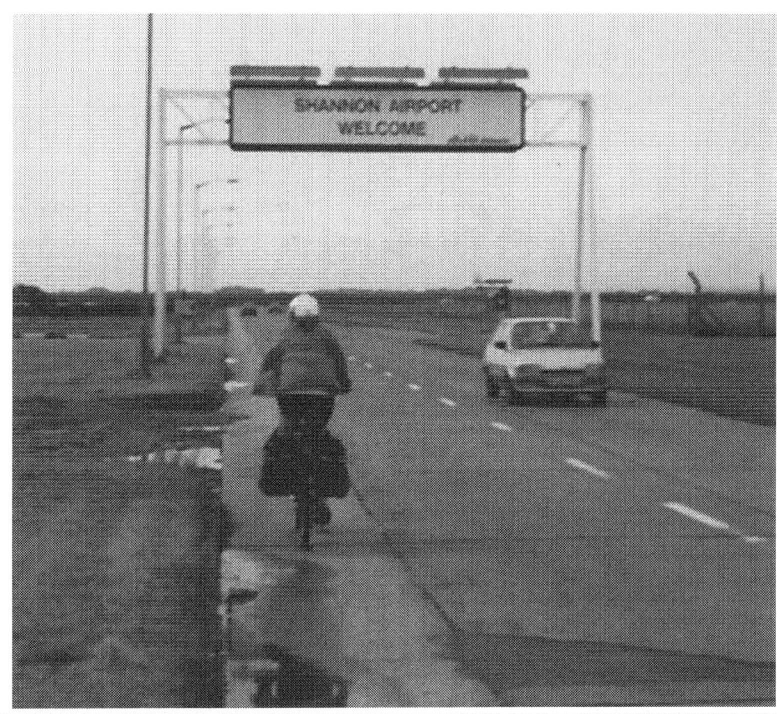
SHANNON AIRPORT
WELCOME

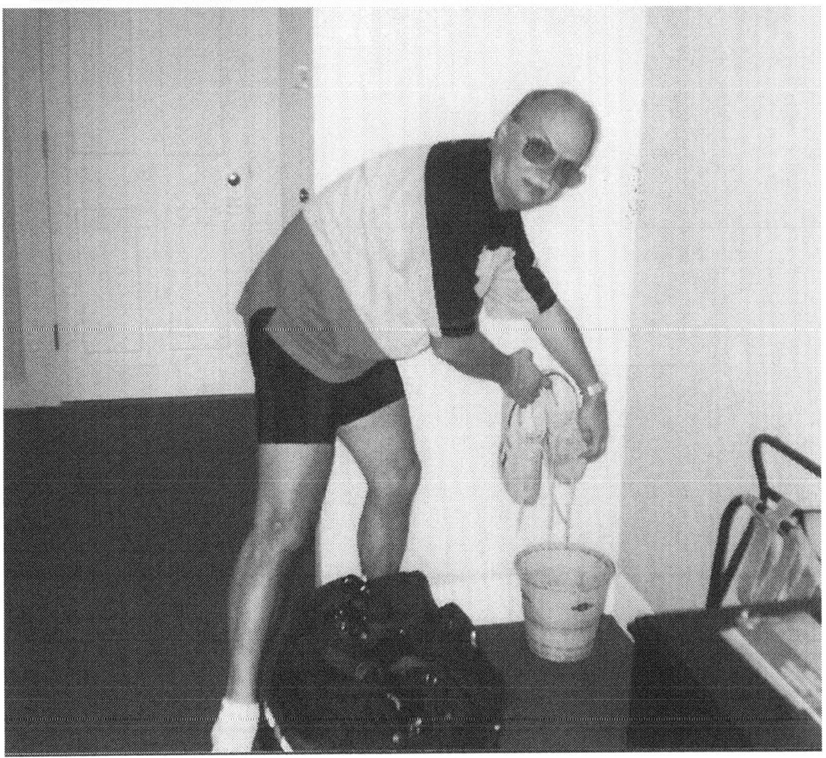

From Michigan to Florida—the Long Way

The flight back to Michigan was not difficult and it was good to be back with things we were familiar with. We had left our motorhome with the RV dealer so that he could put a solar panel on while we were away. They didn't get to it right away so the motorhome sat in their back lot for six weeks while it was nice and hot out. The battery ran down so the refrigerator didn't restart automatically. All the food in our refrigerator spoiled and kept getting worse for the whole six weeks. Luckily, they discovered it before we got back and cleaned up the mess, but we had to buy all new groceries. They said it was a pretty bad mess and I could imagine that it was.

As small as our little house was, it was simply wonderful to be home. Little things meant a lot like having our own bed, and comfortable chair and being able to enjoy our simple breakfast of cereal and toast with butter (English toast is served dry). The best part was being able to make coffee in the morning.

It was good to see the kids and we stayed with Marty, parking in their backyard for a week. We were waiting for Ron's house to close. Ron's son Karl was buying the house from Martha and Ron. While waiting, we decided to go up north, in Michigan, to Traverse City near where our friends, Jim and Norma, had property. We had planned to spend time in the Traverse City area anyway because we wanted to buy property up there after the house sold. Time dragged on and it wasn't till the end of August that they could finally close on the house. But while we were up there we got in a lot of biking and I got to visit with Robert a lot because he was stationed at the Coast Guard base in Traverse.

Ron's new problem was the car. This was especially frustrating after all the bike problems in England. He got new brakes and had the transmission fixed.

Finally, on August 30 we were back in the Lansing area getting ready for the house closing. Ron called and asked his daughter

Marty if we could park the motorhome in the backyard for a day or two again but she said, "No". Martha was going to be there and Martha didn't want to see us. We figured she was really, really mad about having to sell the house. It was no surprise and in fact their divorce stated that when Susie graduated it had to be sold. While we were waiting around for the paper signing we went shopping for a computer. I had planned on taking my typewriter with us in the motorhome right from the beginning, but Ron said we had to have a computer. I didn't want one, mainly because I didn't know anything about them. But he promised he would help me learn all there was to know about computers. As soon as the papers were signed we paid for the computer and took off for the upper Peninsula of Michigan, stopping in Traverse City first to pay for the property we had found. It was fifteen and a half acres of beautiful wooded property. Our plan was when we got tired of RVing we would build a little house there.

We camped in Brimley State Park in the upper Peninsula. It looks out on Lake Superior. At that time of the year it was a little cool during the day and downright cold in the evening. We were tired that first night so I didn't do anything with the computer.

I was anxious to play with my new toy (the computer) but I couldn't make sense of the instructions. The first thing it said to do was "format a diskette". I had no idea what that meant and when I asked Ron he said, "I've never heard of such a thing." Please remember, this was 1989 before Windows. That Toshiba laptop had 20 MB of hard drive and 1 MB of RAM and operated in DOS only. What I learned later was that Ron never had to format his diskettes; his secretaries always did that kind of stuff for him. Well anyway, he was no help at all and before you know it, I had formatted the hard drive. I didn't know any better. By then I was really in trouble and I couldn't get anything to work at all. The nearest payphone was at the ranger station so I walked up in the rain and made a phone call to Toshiba. I had to wait on the phone a long time but when I finally got someone I explained my problem and I don't remember if they laughed at me or not but they did tell me what I needed to do. I tried to write it down but by the time I got back to the motorhome. I couldn't really remember what it was I was supposed to do. It was all like Greek to me. I went back to the pay phone. I called again but this time I had the computer with me except that didn't work either. There was really no place to set it so I could work conveniently. After several trips to the payphone I finally got everything working and was a bit disappointed because there wasn't much in the way of programming in this little laptop. There was something I called a "Mickey Mouse" program which was designed for salesman to keep track of their accounts and their sales. I was able to at least put some addresses in there and use the diary. Ron kept saying something about WordPerfect and Lotus but that was not on the computer. Those were the programs he was familiar with.

Our plans were to head to upstate New York and then go to Vermont then down the coast to Florida. Since I was born in upstate New York, I wanted Ron to see that part of the country and we were both excited about visiting Vermont. As an added bonus. David, who was in the Navy, was stationed in Virginia so we could visit him on our way south.

The trip across Canada and then to New York was very nice. We had both been to Niagara Falls before so we didn't stop there. I still had aunts and uncles in southwestern New York, and we were able to stop and see them all. It was kind of exciting to introduce my aunts and uncles to Ron and vice versa. We played a lot of golf on the rolling hills in New York State. Some were a bit challenging. We checked out the old family cemeteries. We even got to go to the homecoming football game with my uncles at my mother's high school. They all went to the same school; it was the only high school in the town of Hornell.

We loved Western New York because there were lots of farm markets all along the roads we traveled. They had baskets of fresh produce just sitting in little stands by the road. The vegetables were reasonably priced and there was a can where one could place the money. It was all on the honor system and the produce was really good. We visited Lake Placid and even went up to the top of the highest ski jump to get the perspective.

In Vermont we had the very most fun because we biked all over the state. The air was crisp, the leaves brilliant, the people were very friendly, and the hills were alive with color. We had never seen anything so breathtakingly beautiful. We biked over covered bridges, into little towns, and biked to country stores where we had fun browsing.

We slowly moved along at our normal pace and visited both Revolutionary and Civil war sites in Virginia and we visited friends as well. We even biked into DC again and toured a couple of things we hadn't seen the first time. Then before long we were in Norfolk to see David and his new wife, Evelyn.

Soon we were back in Winter Haven, Florida, visiting Ron's mom. We spent a little while with her and treated her to some dinners out. Then we went back over to West Palm Beach and were there for Christmas of 1989.

While we were at my daughter's in West Palm she showed me some tricks with the computer. Up to this point I had been able to write letters with it and we were sending them out to family personalizing the first part of the letter and then making the main body a kind of a travelogue. Although no one ever responded to our computer letters, we hoped they read them. But Ron came up with a brilliant idea. Why not just write a newsletter? We probably weren't fooling anyone anyway. But I had just learned how to type with the computer and had no idea how to do a newsletter. My daughter, Glenda, had a software program that did just that. It was very, very simple to use and it was kind of fun. I thought "Oh, goody, I have a new fun project to work on." The very first Movin' On newsletter was one page on both sides. I was able to make columns and headlines and even included a graphic or two. We folded them and put them in envelopes and addressed them to our families along with a Christmas message, which was also typed on the computer. I really liked computers from that moment on. In fact I was totally hooked.

Robert was in Florida after finishing a month in a Coast Guard Re habilitation center for alcoholism. We guessed he had a problem while we were up in Traverse City and were glad he got mandatory treatment. I am very proud of him because he is celebrating his 22nd year of sobriety as I type this.

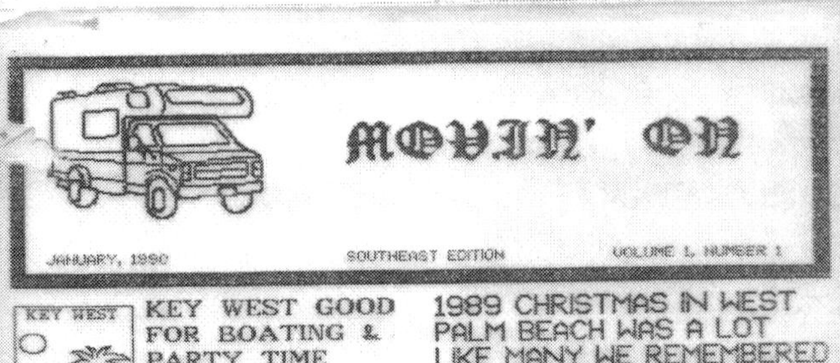

JANUARY, 1990 SOUTHEAST EDITION VOLUME 1, NUMBER 1

KEY WEST GOOD FOR BOATING & PARTY TIME

If you want to party, Key West is the place to be. Don't go there if you want to lay on the beach all day. There is only one rather small area that resembles a beach and the original sand is so bad that sand has to be imported from the Bahamas.

If you like people watching, take a trip to Key West and plan to spend a lot of time on Duval Street. That is where all the action is. The bars and cafes are wide open and music is all around as you walk down the street. ...s of "street people" from all over ...e US spend winters in Kew West because of the mild climate. They are everywhere - young and old. The tour ships arrive daily and deposit a completely different assortment of people for watching.

The wildest scenes we saw were on the docks at sunset time. It was cloudy every evening so we did not get to see the sun do its thing but the show we saw was fun. For about an hour before sunset, carnival type performers do their tricks for whatever donations they can get. We witnessed a sword swallower, a Hungarian balancer, an escape artist, palm readers and even a guy dressed in long red flannel underware and awful face makeup who was trying to sell his jokes for 25 cents each. We didn't buy one. All this reminded us of the Renaissance Festivals that we have attended.

We did enjoy taking the trolly ride around the town and all the historic homes were pointed out to us. If you ever go there, do plan to take the same tour.

1989 CHRISTMAS IN WEST PALM BEACH WAS A LOT LIKE MANY WE REMEMBERED IN THE NORTH COUNTRY

RON BLAMES BARBARA FOR THE COLD SNAP IN FLORIDA. SHE WAS WISHING FOR A WHITE CHRISTMAS.

We did not get to do any swimming in Glenda and Pekka's pool during the holiday but we did have a wonderful time. Pekka fired up the hot tub one night and we kept warm as long as we were under water. It was fun to help Liisa bake Christmas cookies and more fun to eat them.

We each got backpacks and canteens to make our hiking easier and we both acquired some new jewlry and fun computer programs. Ron had wanted some BRIGHT golf pants so Glenda and I shopped all over looking for some that were nice but not too gaudy. We found a nice pair but we were in a silly mood and wanted to get him some really LOUD pants without spending good money for them. We found 2 AWFUL pair at the Jewish relief store in Palm Beach and the price was right- $1.95 per pair. Not only were they Ron's size but they looked like new. We wrapped them up and gave them to Ron before he opened his "nice" pants. Guess what? He likes the gaudy ones and insists that he will wear them often. NOT WHEN I'M WITH HIM.

BAN DESSERTS
That's our New Years resolution for 1990.

MICHIGAN TOURISTS TAKE ON FLORIDA'S TOP BRASS

While touring the Capitol building early in Jan. we noticed that the door to the Governor's office was open and felt that it was an open invitation. We had been getting increasingly upset over the state park fee charged to non Floridians. $20. is a high price for a campground spot for one night. All through the tour of the old capitol building, we kept reading how Florida valued their tourist industry. We felt that they had a strange way of showing it. Most private campgrounds charge less. The secretary was nice but Governor Martinez was not in. We asked to see the Lt. Governor and got his secretary. At least we vented our feelings to some human being and she assured that she would relay our message. OH SURE!! Did you know that as of Jan 1, 1990 Florida's new sales tax is 7%? OH and it is 9-11% for lodging. No wonder Florida likes its tourists. Tallahassee is similar to Lansing - capitol and university town. The weather is better here but Michigan's Capitol building is much prettier.

WATCH YOUR MAILBOX FOR REGULAR ISSUES OF "MOVIN' ON".

How regular? We will print as often as we get around to it and you will get your copy free of charge. To stay on our mailing list, we request that you write us once in a while OR think of us often. In case you have misplaced our address it is:

Ron & Barbara Hofmeister
1616 17th ST Suite 372
Denver, CO 80202

We get mail once a week (usually Fri) so mail that arrives in Denver by Tues will reach us that same week.

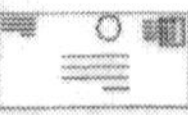

MAIL WARMS OUR HEARTS

POTPOURRI BY RON

Some of our favorite campgrounds:

* Haupt's driveway- E.Brunswic NJ
* Latchworth State Park-a 17 mile park in upper New York
* Peunonen's patio in W. Palm Beach
* Pines Campground - Everglades

Our favorite Lutheran churches:

* St. Paul Lutheran, Proctor, Vermont (a woman pastor - terrific sermons)
* Christ Memorial Lutheran, East Brunswick, NJ (brother-in-law Ken does a great job here as pastor)
* Grace Lutheran, Winter Haven, Fla. (great bible classes)
* Epiphany Lutheran, Tallahassee, Fla (this church has everything, friendly people, dynamic pastor, outstanding music, beautiful facility)

The Elks club in Tallahassee has six camping spaces next to their swimming pool for RV's ($6.00 a night). Too bad we didn't know until we had booked in another spot. I wonder how many other Elks Clubs have the same program. Intend to find out.

We have heard that Gainesville, Fla has hundreds of miles of bike paths within the city -- a must on our next time through Florida.

So far the little Horizon that we tow has proved to be more expensive to maintain than our motorhome. To date: Horizon - $ 450 Motorhome - $0

Did you know that Jewish thrift shops have super buys on your clothes

FOLLOW US THIS WINTER

He's Writing a Book

The second edition of our newsletter briefly covered our visit in Mississippi and New Orleans. We stayed in a couple of national parks. Nearly every Sunday since we started traveling, we visited a church near where we were staying. In Ocean Springs, Mississippi, we attended church and were asked to introduced ourselves at the beginning of the service. At the end of the service many people came up to talk to us and welcomed us to the community. We felt so welcomed we were ready to move there except for the humidity, of course. One couple especially wanted to come out and see our motorhome and wanted to take us on a tour of the town. It was as if we were old friends and we enjoyed our short time with them.

It was Mardi Gras time and in every town we visited in that southeastern coast we heard about a float parade. That was great fun to watch the parade and try to catch the beads. We got right into the swing of things. Since we were heading to New Orleans. We figured we were practicing up for the big event.

We got word that our family was growing with the birth of Kristopher in England. He was our sixth grandchild.

In New Orleans we learned what "po boys" are (they are similar to a subway sandwich but different) and were told the best place to go to get one was at Mother's in downtown New Orleans. We did just that and agreed they were very good. But we had also decided if we kept sampling all the local foods we are never going to lose some of the weight we gained in England. But when visiting local places, eating local foods is part of the charm.

I didn't mention earlier, but shortly after we started full-timing Ron told me that he was going to write a book about it. When we were getting ready to go full-time, we had a hard time finding good information about the lifestyle. We especially didn't know about the cost of full-time RVing. So shortly after we got our computer Ron started working on his book. Our newsletter was growing and when we met new people who were going in the direction we just came from, we gave them one. Our newsletter had grown to three pages already by the March issue. Ron had predicted that it would grow even more.

Ron announced in the March edition of the newsletter that he was writing a book about the lifestyle of living and traveling full-time in an RV. He was using my newsletter to promote his book. That was okay; we were a team.

We reported on our tour of the swamp in Louisiana where we met an old Cajun man's house and he showed us how to skin a nutria (rat-like animal). He also told us how he caught his limit of alligators in hunting season. The swamp was kind of spooky, but it was good to learn how others lived.

I wrote a tiny article in the March newsletter saying that every week was a new adventure in the grocery store. Number one, it was hard to find where everything was and number two, there were new items in each new store which we had never seen before.

We stopped to visit my brother in Kingwood, Texas, which is just north of Houston. Also visited my aunt, Genevieve and my cousin Mary in Austin, Texas. I loved that we were able to visit family along the way. And in both of these visits we got to park in their driveways.

While in that part of the country we visited the LBJ national Park and the lovely little town of Fredericksburg. We also visited San Antonio, which is easy to fall in love with. From there we went to Corpus Christi and South Padre Island, but it was almost spring break time and we didn't want to hang around where all the teeny boppers were.

In February we were at Meadow Creek Country Club and RV Park in Mission, Texas. If we didn't have more country to see we might have stayed there forever. It was a very friendly place with tons of RV parks and all of them were full of happy senior citizens who were having a great time. For the first time since we started this lifestyle we decided to stay three weeks in one place. That gave us a chance to wash the motorhome, check out a slight leak on the roof, and a few other things. Ron was going to work on those projects. Besides, we wanted to play with all the others and there was a lot to do there. This was our first experience in a real RV resort. They had a lovely swimming pool, tennis courts, card games and dances all the time.

We had to keep moving though, because we were heading to California for my son's wedding the end of April. On the way we spent about five days in Big Bend National Park in southern Texas. There was so much to do, we could've stayed two or three weeks. Hiking was great. Big Bend is an amazing national park which is divided into three distinct areas consisting of desert, mountains, and the Rio Grande River.

Since we had done a lot of hiking in Big Bend we decided to tackle a real mountain — Guadalupe Peak, the highest point in Texas. It was on our way to New Mexico anyway. The elevation of the mountain is 8749 feet and we were starting at 5000 feet so it would be a climb of over 3000 feet. We were told that our hike would take us about six to eight hours so we started very early in the morning. We had to sign a log book at the beginning so the Rangers would know who was on the mountain and it was a very spectacular hike starting from the beginning. When we finished the hike about seven o'clock that night, we were so tired that we just simply took off our shoes, plopped down on the bed and went to sleep without even eating dinner.

In New Mexico we briefly visited White Sands National Monument, Carlsbad Caverns, Cliff Dwellings, and my dad and his wife Frankie in Silver City. We didn't stay anywhere very long because we wanted to get to California in time for the April 28th wedding.

We didn't do any touring in California but simply went to the wedding and enjoyed my son, Mark, and his new wife, Ana, and her family. Almost to the day by the time Mark was married we had been on the road for thirteen months and were having a ball. When we thought of all the things we had done in a short time it was mind boggling. We had learned an awful lot about this country and we had enjoyed our bicycle trip in England. We weren't through yet. It was all overwhelming when we thought about it. We had also learned another valuable lesson; don't schedule such long trips where we have to travel freeways. We liked our original plan; move down the road a couple of hundred miles then stay a week.

Top: On the summit of Guadalupe Mountain.

Bottom: White Sands National Monument

Limping all the Way Back to Michigan

We filled up with gas at the Shell station near Mark's house and then headed for Las Vegas. There are big hills and mountains in California and our motorhome wouldn't go up them. We had no idea what the problem was. When we got to Vegas we took it to a Ford dealer and they suggested a tune up so we said, "Do it." When we left Vegas, the motorhome seem to run fine for a little while, then it started sputtering again. It was Saturday and when we got to Gallup, New Mexico, the Ford dealer (Gurley) was still open. They suggested rebuilding the carburetor. So again we said "do it". It took a long time and they stayed open in order to fix it. We were amazed that in that day and age when everything was disposable, they had someone who could actually rebuild it. Then we were off again but we didn't even make it to Albuquerque before the motorhome was sputtering again. There was a campground on the freeway and we checked in. I found the pay phone and started making phone calls. One call was to that Shell station to ask him if anyone else had had problems with their gas. That man was downright nasty and accused me of accusing him of selling bad gas etc.

It was late on Saturday and I wanted to get a hold of someone back at the Gallup Ford dealer. I called information and they gave me the phone numbers of all of the Gurleys in Gallup. I started calling and found the owner, Steve Gurley. I told him our sad story and he suggested that rather than driving all the way back to Gallup which was 180 miles, we should go to Albuquerque. He would call Rich Ford and make arrangements to make good on anything we were overcharged.

We finally got fixed in Albuquerque and the apparent solution was replacing the fuel separator valve, but they did suggest that when we got back to Michigan we have our Ford dealer there drop the fuel tank and clean it. We made it back to Michigan easily from there.

By the time we got to Michigan, Mark told us the Shell gas station closed and was boarded up. We knew we had a load of bad gas. Lesson learned: Only fill up at busy stations on main thoroughfares—preferably truck stops on freeways.

Babies, Blueberries & Big Lake

We originally intended to stay in Michigan for only two months, but changed our minds and stayed for a full three months. Besides lots of family visits there were three family reunions which were lots of fun. The first one was held at my mother's place and attending were Ron's sisters and their children, my sisters and their children and my mom. This was an opportunity for our sisters to meet each other—a kind of blending of our families. They had not met before this occasion. Another reunion was the John Hofmeister reunion which was held in Dearborn Michigan. Attending this reunion were all of Ron's aunts, uncles, cousins, his mom and his sisters and their families. The third reunion was my children. Jim, Sue and new baby Kristopher, came from England, Mark and his wife, Ana came from California, Glenda, Pekka and Liisa, came from Florida and Robert was in Michigan for just a couple days before he had to report to his new base in California. This was the first time they were altogether in eleven years.

One of the real highlights of the summer was camping with our two four year old granddaughters Erika and Mary. We had them for four days and they took to camping like it was an everyday thing. We had campfires, fixed s'mores and campfire pies. We took them for walks, helped them with their bikes and they were as good as gold. We were amazed at how good they were without their parents around. We thought they'd be homesick.

Another special event was the wedding of our good friends, Jim and Norma. It was a very small affair and we were glad to be a part of it.

We did manage to spend a little time by ourselves up in the small town of Grand Marais which is right on Lake superior. It's not on the way to anywhere but it's worth the trip. We picked wild blueberries and visited the Picture Rocks National Park where we did a lot of hiking and learned about the ship wrecks on Lake Superior. All in all we had a fun summer vacation.

Ron had a little article in the October issue of our newsletter which he wrote after our summer in Michigan. He stated that when we started RVing full-time in April of 1989, regular gasoline was around 95.9 cents per gallon and as he was writing it was up to $1.40 per gallon. As you read this, what is the price of gasoline going for in your area? What a difference a few years made.

Glenda looked great. In April she quit drinking and was doing great recovering from alcoholism. Her problem had been living with a Finnish alcoholic. He didn't quit and years later, after their divorce moved back to Finland.

Top Mary, Ron and Erika.
Bottom left: Jim, Sue and Kristopher
Bottom right: Mark and Ana

Pekka,
Liisa
Glenda

Robert
Jim
Mark
Glenda

Bathing in Hot Springs

While we were in Michigan, Susie told us she was engaged to be married and the wedding would be in December. Of course we wanted to be able to go to the wedding, but we could not hang around in the north country while it was freezing. We looked for some way to be nearby so we could simply drive the car back for the wedding. In our travels so far we had met couples who had been campground hosts or worked in national parks in different capacities. I sent out five applications and right away we got a reply from Hot Springs National Park in Arkansas. We agreed to volunteer for the months of October and November.

When we arrived we were given a wonderful campsite with full hookups in a beautiful setting and it didn't cost us a penny. We didn't know exactly what we would be doing for the national park but after meeting with Ranger Paul Sullivan, we were given several choices. Ron kind of liked the idea of working in the bookstore and I like the idea of giving tours of the thermal features area. We also did a few other jobs and it was a neat experience to be in the national park working with the rangers and feeling useful. We only worked thirty three hours a week and none of the work was hard. We also found it quite comfortable living in Hot Springs and even took advantage of taking a hot bath. You see that's what Hot Springs is all about. In the early 1900s there were many bathhouses and that was the thing to do. These baths were supposed to cure everything that ailed anyone. But then when penicillin came along that did more curing than the baths so many went out of fashion. But taking a bath in Hot Springs is still an experience I recommend.

We met ranger Paul Pfennenger at Hot Springs and he was being transferred to Yosemite National Park in California. He said he wanted us to come and work for him and we told him we would. It was exciting to have another national park volunteer position to look forward to. We made plans to be there the coming April through July (1991).

We were able to leave the motorhome parked in Hot Springs while we drove up to Michigan for the December 1 wedding of Susie and Ross. The whole wedding party was in the same motel and I wrote in my diary: "It seemed strange to sleep in a king sized bed in a motel room which has more room than our whole house." It was a beautiful wedding with lots of Christmas decorations. All of Ron's sisters and other family members were there so it was fun to catch up again. We were only there for a couple of days before the wedding and left the morning after to drive back to Hot Springs to get our house and move on.

L to R: David, Karl, Susie, Marty and Kurt.

Round Up

By the end of December in 1990, we were back at Meadow Creek RV Resort in Mission, Texas, and it was like old home week. Instead of just three weeks, we decided to stay there for a whole month. It felt good to be in one place again. I think we had gotten spoiled while we were in Hot Springs not having to move all the time. There are only so many places we could go in the winter because of weather restraints, so there was no point in hurrying along. The bridge group was happy to see us, so were the golfers and the tennis players. We were ready to play. And when our month was up, we hated to leave, but it was time to move on – but not very far. We headed it up to the hill country of Texas which included Austin, San Antonio and a little bit further west.

Back in Michigan we had joined a camping group called Coast to Coast. Membership in that group gave us our home part back in Michigan, and we were able to camp in member campgrounds for as little as a dollar per night. There were three or four Coast to Coast campgrounds in the hill country of Texas and we wanted to check them all out.

At every new campground, we met more people and we became fast friends.. Maybe it was because we were retired and so were they; we had time to be friendly and social.

The newsletter had grown. It was now nine 8.5 x 11 pages. It was no longer something that I could just do in the motorhome. I'd make a master and paste in the pictures, then I take it to a printer and have them printed. When they were all printed Ron and I would pick them up, collate, tri-fold, staple, address and stamp them then send them out. Suddenly we were in business. It looked quite professional with a few pictures that I had taken inserted in the newsletter instead of graphics. And every month when we had the newsletter printed, I had several hundred extra copies made and we handed them out to people we met along the way. It was advertising for Ron's upcoming book.

Just like your local newspaper we had special features in each issue. Some were regular like Ron's Potpourri, my This n That, Letters, Interesting People, and Family News. Later we added a Campground Report, Good Places to Eat and a recipe of the month. Every once in a while we even had a quiz or something fun.

People really liked the newsletter and often asked to be put on our mailing list. Even while our mailing list was growing we wanted to keep in touch. If we had had e-mail back then, it would have been easy to keep in touch that way, but that was a long time coming. I was still using pay phones.

I really enjoyed doing the newsletter although it did take time. And it wasn't just doing the newsletter that took time it was answering the mail, because once a week when our mail came, there were lots of letters. Some people wrote about their progress in getting ready for full timing. Others had questions about the lifestyle that we hadn't answered when we met with them. These types of things made Ron realize that he needed to get that book done; people were really interested in going full-time and they needed our information.

But we still had fun too like the time we got to go round up horses at a ranch in West Texas. The Prude Ranch was a Campground and also a working ranch. When we got to the campground we noticed that they offered horseback riding so we signed up to do that one day. This was a ride like we've never had before. Once on the horses with our guide he asked us where we wanted to go. There was no straight line we had to follow. It was just the two of us and our guide. We pointed in some direction and off we went. It was the most fun ride I'd ever had on a horse. We decided that we'd like to ride the next day also so made our reservation but when we showed up to ride, we were told that it was going to be a free ride. They needed help rounding up the horses that had been out in the far pasture for a long time. We really felt like we had played cowboy for the day and that was the headline story in the March 1991 issue of Movin On.

Me playing cowgirl at the Prude Ranch in West Texas.

When Illness Struck

When it was time to leave the Prude Ranch on Wednesday, February 20, we woke up early, to discover that we had had a hard freeze and the hose was frozen even though we had left water running at a trickle. And I was very sick. I couldn't help Ron get ready to roll so he had to do it all himself. And he forgot a few things that caused him even more problems. When hooking up the car, he forgot to unlock the steering, so we drove the first few miles with the wheels not exactly straight and it ruined a front tire.

I had a bad case of the flu. My chest hurt and I had a fever so I laid on the bed as we traveled. West Texas is a very remote area, but I asked Ron if he came to a town that looked like it had an emergency room to please stop. There was one in Van Horn. When we went to the hospital we were told they had no staff doctors but there were two doctors in town. Very close to the hospital was Dr. Carter's office and I was taken in right away. She felt we ought to stay overnight and told me to get some rest, take the cough syrup and drink lots of fluids. Luckily there was a campground right across the street. I went to sleep and Ron just read, visited with campers and relaxed. The next morning I was not feeling any better and we decided to stay one more day. We left the next morning and I slept all the way to Vado, New Mexico, which is very close to Las Cruces. We stayed at a horrible campground next to a huge feedlot that stunk terribly but it was part of our Coast-to-Coast system and only cost us a dollar a night. I slept another day away and by Saturday morning Ron was sick. We had to move to another camp site and as soon as we were settled we both went back to bed. I finally got up about noon on Friday and left Ron to sleep.

I went to the store to get some more juice and get my film developed for the newsletter. I looked around to see if I could find a Kinko's anywhere. There was one right across the street from the hospital; I made a mental note. I was back home in no time and coughing my fool head off. One time when I coughed, I felt a horrible pain and it was very painful to breathe from that moment on.

By Sunday morning, I felt I needed to go the emergency room. I knew I couldn't drive because I needed to keep a towel tight around my rib cage so it wouldn't hurt so much. Ron was sick himself and I hated to asked him. I tried to talk him into seeing a doctor there too but he said he'd be all right.

The doctors said I had a dislocated rib and gave me some antibiotics because they didn't want me to get pneumonia from not breathing deep enough. We both went to bed when we got home; I was on day five, Ron was on day two. Monday we hibernated, but at four o'clock in the morning, Ron said he had to go the emergency room. I was glad I could finally look forward to getting some medicine in him. He didn't have a fever but he was soaking wet from sweating and said his chest was tight.

Right from day one we carried our medical records with us and I took them to the emergency room with me. Since Ron was a middle-aged man, coming into the ER in the middle of the night, complaining of chest pain and was clammy, they started working on him just as though he was having a heart attack. I couldn't believe it. I said, "He just has the flu". To make a long story short, they admitted him, talked him into having an angiogram, and put him in ICU; I was helpless to defend him. They convinced him he was having a heart attack. When the doctor finished the angiogram, he said that his arteries were all clear, "but he has a terrible cough". I glared at him and said, "What the hell do you think I've been trying to tell you; he just has the flu the same as I did". But that wasn't the end. They insisted on keeping him for three more days putting him through a stress test, which caused me a lot of stress. Lesson learned: know your body and don't let anyone do something to you which you don't need to have done. Ron was bullied into thinking he had a serious heart problem. He knows better now.

Too Much Snow

In March of 1991 we were heading towards Yosemite National Park and we got a message from Kevin, the ranger who would be our boss for two months, asking us to delay our arrival a little bit. They recently had four feet of snow cover their campground and there would be nowhere for us to park until they got the roads cleared. We were almost to Arizona when he called so I started checking around for campgrounds we could stop at on our way. All the campgrounds in southern Arizona were booked full with winter visitors. Not understanding altitude (growing up in Michigan were we had no big mountains) and what happens at high altitudes in the winter, we thought we would travel the northern route. We were coming from my dad's place in Silver City, New Mexico, and went straight across. In Show Low, Arizona, everything was covered with a thick blanket of snow which sparkled in the bright sunlight. It was really breathtaking. Michigan winters are gray and never looked very pretty. I remember thinking that I could live in Show Low.

When we got to Valencia, California, it was raining. We planned on sitting there for a couple days while visiting with Mark and his family before heading up Interstate 5 towards Yosemite. We learned another lesson about altitude there. When it rained at the low elevation, it was snowing up above. Interstate 5 kept closing due to the heavy snow up on "the Grapevine" which is the name given to that part of the freeway which separates southern and northern California.

Yosemite National Park is a huge park (761,757 acres of breathtaking beauty) in the Sierra Nevada Mountains. There are several entrances to the park and they are all miles apart; we were to enter at state Route 41 which enters the park just north of Oakhurst. We planned to stay a night or two at the Coast-to-Coast park in Coarsegold before we headed up to the park, but curiosity got the better of us. As soon as we got set up in camp, we took off in the car to check out this place called Yosemite. There was a big sign as we left Oakhurst saying that we must put chains on our tires to go much further. Ron said, "Chains!! I never heard of such a thing", and when we were stopped along the way, a man came up to the window and said, "Pull over there to put on chains." Ron told him he was a Michigan driver and knew how to drive on snow. But the man told him that they had something in California that we didn't have in Michigan and that was "California drivers." But the reality of it was there was a ton of heavy wet snow; we really needed chains.

We didn't have chains, but a German couple had just gone through the area and turned in their chains that they had purchased earlier, so we were offered those for just $20. The man put the chains on for a fee and we took off. We drove about a mile without seeing any bad snow on the road and suddenly there it was---thick heavy snow. All of the trees were bent down low from the weight of the snow. This was a true winter wonderland and it was beautiful. We drove all around but didn't try to get into the campground. Hardly anything had been plowed so it was hard driving. It was the best winter picture I had ever seen in my life.

It was a couple more days before we heard from Kevin that it was okay to come into the campground. Even then there was still a lot of snow on the ground but the roads were cleared and our campsite had been plowed.

In the application letter we wrote to Kevin, we stipulated our requirements and they were: we needed to have full hookups for our motorhome (water, electric and sewer). The day came for us to pull our house into the campground and Kevin was there to assist us. We were guided to the special campground host pad which was good as it was a nice level cement slab. We easily found the water and sewer hookup and when I asked Kevin where the electric outlet was he said, "There is no electricity anywhere in the campground". Since it was the first of April, I questioned, "April fools?". And he said, "No, I wouldn't kid you." Since we were at an elevation of over 4000 feet we worried if we would be able to keep warm. Kevin assured us they would give us lots of firewood and we thought that maybe with our little generator we could make it. We wanted to stay because we needed to be in Yosemite for the months of April and May so we could yet be in the area to work for Paul Pfenninger in June and July when the Pioneer History Center would open.

Our little generator was useless so we had to develop a routine in order to survive. We had a campfire going day and night and we would stay outside until about 10 p.m. When we came in, we would light a candle for a little warmth, climb on the bed with our clothes on, cover up with the afghan, turn on the light over the bed and read until the cold got unbearable. By then, the bed had been warmed and we blew out the candle, undressed and climbed under the covers. Our down comforter kept us nice and warm and underneath the bottom sheet we had a wool mattress cover which helped too. Only our faces were cold by morning. In fact it got so cold in the house at night that ice in a glass of water was still there in the morning. Before we got out of bed, I jumped up and started the engine then turned on the furnace. We waited for the indoor temperature to get to at least forty degrees before I got up and made coffee. The stove being on helped warm the house also. We had to have Ron's son, Karl, get our "long johns" out of storage and send them to us and we always had several layers of clothing on. We were glad that we had winter coats, hats and gloves with us. We made a game out of keeping warm.

But we got to take a nice brisk walk in the mornings and we got lots of fresh air. And we were serenaded by the sounds of rushing water from the nearby Merced River.

When we volunteered to be camp hosts we thought it would be an easy job. Any hosts we had ever seen looked very relaxed and simply enjoyed meeting the campers and giving helpful information. That was probably true of most smaller parks, but Yosemite had tons of visitors and all the problems that went with that. And perhaps if we were different that could've worked, but both Ron and I have always been very conscientious. We took our jobs seriously. We were given the rules of the campground and we intended to make sure everything ran smoothly. So when someone came in and tried to camp in the handicap spot, because it was closer to the river, we would chase them away. Sometimes we would chase away ten different people in just a few minutes. And we got angry at people, at least inwardly; we didn't actually holler at people. But we got so we just didn't like people anymore. Oh there were some wonderful people we met there in the campground but so many were rude and selfish and just didn't believe they needed to follow the rules.

Most of the time our campground was full of people who had driven a great distance to get there. Because we were full, they would be turned away; of course they would be angry and holler at us. This was our first and last campground hosting experience. But we had agreed to be there for two months so we stuck it out.

We did have time off and we enjoyed our time in town or even touring the park more. One of our first days there we drove to Yosemite Valley and I cried for its awesomeness; it was just too beautiful for words. I remembered the deaf man we met in Kentucky who said he always cried when he saw the valley.

We drove to the big trees which was near our campground. And I went on a tour there with one of the other rangers. She asked me if I would like to do the tours. I jumped at the chance. I even got a uniform. At least once a week, I would go up to the big trees in the Mariposa Grove and either lead a tour of the giant sequoias or wander around the area and answer questions. Because I had a uniform on, people would stop me if they had a question. It was one of the best things I did those two months.

The rangers were overworked and not that organized especially Kevin. He promised us wood so we could keep warm and we had to bug him for weeks to get it. He never hooked up our phone as promised either, we also didn't get the propane we were promised and generally we felt we weren't treated that well. They have too many jobs to do so we didn't blame him entirely. Having been in business like Ron and I had, we could see where the National Park Service made a lot of mistakes. For example we were in a self pay campground. We couldn't collect any monies because we were not bonded and the rangers were so busy that they seldom emptied the money tube. The protection rangers handled the campgrounds and there were other more important things to take care of. Believe me people would come into that park and just become crazy. There were shootings, there were bad accidents, people feeding animals and getting hurt; it was crazy. Campgrounds were low priority. Several times there were payment envelopes sticking out of the tube because it was so full and had not been emptied. I had to go to the office more than once to find Kevin and tell him that anyone could take envelopes out instead of putting any in. Then it took two rangers to empty the tube. That was the rule. We even thought that people camping in our campground could simply stick an envelope in the tube with no money in it; who would know? Ron told Kevin that since he handled a two billion-dollar budget at the Department of Transportation certainly he could collect campground fees.

Here are the park's protection facts for the year 1990:

183 search and rescue operations
343 part l offenses
636 part II offenses
553 motor vehicle accidents
7 fatalities
766 custodial arrests
139 DUI arrests
4.942 case incident records

Every night just before we went to sleep, I would look out the front windows to check on the campground. One night when I looked out, I saw fire on the hill across from the campground. California was in a drought even after all that snow. I yelled at Ron and he was up in a minute putting on his pants and jacket. Several other campers saw it too and were heading up the hill. A couple of Asian boys who were camped in the spot across from us had borrowed matches from Ron. They were up on the hill looking for fire wood and without a flashlight, they were gathering dried grasses and lighting them to help them in their search. When the burning grass got too close to their hands, they simply dropped the burning material and lit another bunch. There were a bunch of those little fires burning. The campers put the fires out and Ron marched those boys back to camp and told them not to move a muscle for the rest of the night. Without a phone there was no way we could call a ranger so we handled it ourselves.

Going Back in Time

Memorial Day weekend in the campground was an absolute zoo and we were glad to be gone on June 4. We went to the coast -to-coast park in Coarsegold for a few days, we vacuumed the motorhome for the first time in two months because we finally had some electricity. I worked on the newsletter; it had grown to 9.5 pages. Ron enjoyed watching ESPN; we were back in civilization and glad of it.

Robert had been stationed in San Francisco for a while and we tried to get there the month before but had car problems (transmission) and had to turn back. For my birthday in May, Robert tried to get into the park to see us, but there was a snow storm raging; the roads were closed. We planned to leave for San Francisco as soon as I finished the newsletter. But as Ron was going back into the park to get our mail, the car quit. We had already spent a fortune on fixing that car from day one and this time it was the transaxle and it was going to take a week to fix. We left the car to be fixed and took the motorhome to San Francisco and I finally got to visit with Robert for a few days. There was a campground downtown so we didn't need a car. We did some touristy things with him, like Alcatraz, Fisherman's Wharf and so on.

Back in Wawona, Paul got us settled in our beautifully secluded campsite. We were all alone in the woods and it was quiet which we enjoyed after the campground. We got fitted for costumes and then went to orientation; we were excited to start playacting. Liisa was coming from Florida to spend two weeks with us and she even had a part to play in the history center. She was going to be the granddaughter (Minnie Hodgdon) to the homesteader and Glenda had made her a beautiful costume to wear.

We didn't have a car yet but we were able to borrow one to pick her up at the airport in Fresno. She was very excited when she saw where we were going to be living. And she was even more excited at the pioneer history center. What an actress she turned out to be. Everyone was so proud of her.

We did have a couple days off but without a car there was nothing left to do but go hiking. One day we hiked to the Chilnualna Falls which was an eleven mile hike (round-trip) from our campsite. Hiking along those falls was a thrill. The river was super fast and the roar was deafening.

Ron and I were the Wells Fargo agents from 1915. All the buildings in The History Center, depicted the history of Yosemite and the unique peoples that came at different times. Everyone who visited the history center was first greeted by a docent who gave them a little spiel about what to expect. I sometimes played that role. We would ask that visitors pretend they're going back in time and ask questions to learn about what went on at each particular time they were visiting. I would suggest they did not ask about whatever was going on in 1991 because those people hadn't lived in that time yet.

We decided that people watch too much television and didn't know how to interact in that situation. They would come into any of the buildings and just stand there waiting for us to tell them whatever. So that's what we sort of ended up doing most of the time. Every once in a while someone really played the game and that was more fun. I liked to tell the people in our office that there's a war going on in Europe and Ron, playing my husband, would tell me, "Don't worry your pretty little head about such things. Leave such affairs to the men." It was fun to watch modern-day women bristle when he said that.

Liisa on the other hand, was portraying a child in 1889 when the homesteaders had settled in Yosemite. She would gather the eggs in the morning and help her "grandmother" make cookies. When people would come into her "house" they would ask her how far she had to walk to school. I loved her answer, "It's only a five mile walk" emphasizing "only". If they asked her if she missed TV, she would look at them with a puzzled look and ask, "What's that?"

On a day off we borrowed a friend's car again and took Liisa to the Bodie Ghost Town which was on the other side of Yosemite.

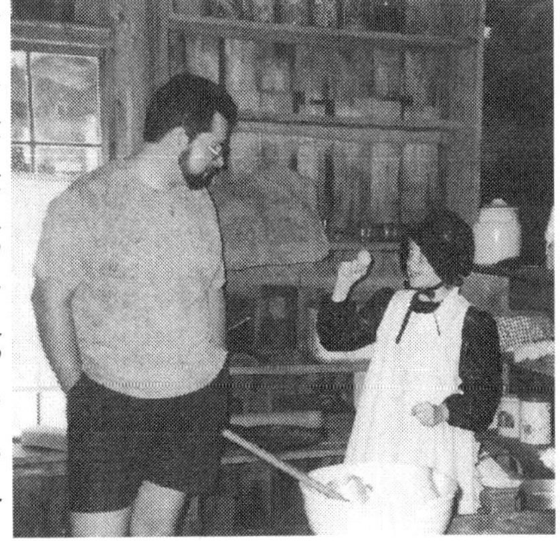

We had to drive over the Tioga Pass which had just recently opened (normally closed from October to June). It is the highest highway pass in California at 9943 feet. As we were driving over, our precious granddaughter from Florida saw falling snow for the first time in her life. She was one excited little girl. Bodie was a wonderful adventure. It's a true ghost town which has been kept in a state of "arrested decay". It is managed by the California State Parks.

We hated to see Liisa leave and all too soon our time in Yosemite was over also. At the end of July we said goodbye to all of the other docents we had grown to love, the rangers and our beautiful park. We felt so privileged to be able to be in Yosemite for four months. Most people can only go for a week at a time, if that.

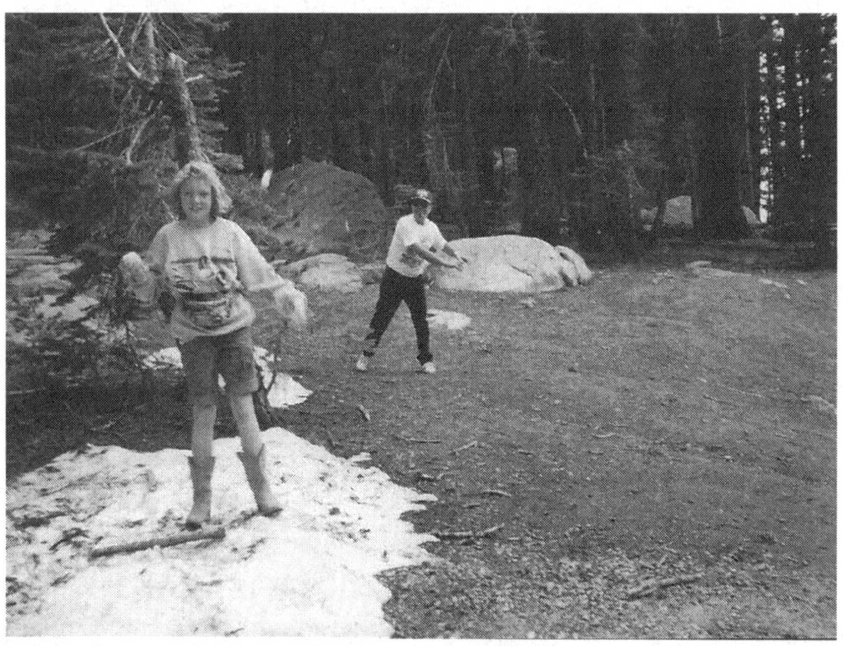

Liisa and Ron with snowballs on the Tioga Pass.

Top: At Glacier Point with half dome in the background.

Bottom: Liisa and Ron at Bodie.

New Pull Toy

Just a little while after the car was fixed in Oakhurst, it died again. We decided to just let it sit for the two weeks we had left, although that meant we couldn't do the kind of touring we wanted to do. We decided to just tow it out of Yosemite and get it fixed in Lodi. We had made an appointment at the Chrysler dealer, got it in on Monday though they couldn't fix it till Wednesday because parts had to be ordered. We really needed a new car. We were on our way to Oregon but in no hurry because there were things we wanted to see along the way. The reason we were waiting for Oregon was there is no sales tax in that state. Once the car was fixed (and it seemed fixed, finally) we went up the coast in a leisurely fashion. First Isleton then San Francisco to see Robert again then the giant redwoods. Napa Valley, Ferndale, and Eureka were also on our list. I loved the last two towns especially with their Victorian homes. The giant redwoods were way different than the Sequoia. They were taller, not as fat and denser in the forests. Both were majestic looking and I don't know which I liked better.

Once we got to Ashland, Oregon, (just inside Oregon), we talked about looking at cars and Ron was toying with the idea of just going with what we had since it appeared to be running okay now. But all of a sudden the transmission slipped. Even though it was Sunday and we thought all the car dealers would be closed, we went to several of the lots and just started looking around. All of a sudden there was a salesman wanting to help us. Most of the Rangers at Yosemite were driving Toyota or Nissan pickups. Some of them had over 300,000 miles on them so we

thought surely those would be good for us also. What we wanted was a little pickup truck with a cap on the back and we found a nice white one.

MOVIN'
ON
volume 2
SEPTEMBER 1991
"The best things in life aren't things"
number 8

It wasn't just a simple process because we had to have the tow bar installed on the new truck, and bike racks put on the truck as well. We had to deal with an RV dealer for the tow bar, a bike shop for the bike racks, and a camper place for the shell which would fit over the bed of the truck. It took a few days but we got it all done and we gladly gave them our brown Horizon which we hoped to never see again.

What we learned later on was that the Horizon which was a Dodge product was not designed for towing. No wonder we had problems with it from the very beginning. We hadn't done our homework. The Toyota standard transmission trucks were guaranteed for towing. We towed that very dependable truck behind three motorhomes and drove it lots of miles without the motorhome.

Volcanos, Ghosts, Glaciers and Geysers

After we brought the truck the middle of August, we did some more touring in Oregon checking out Crater Lake National Park which I could write a book about; it's fantastic and amazing. We also toured LaPine and Bend, Oregon, and found some interesting spots like the High Desert Museum. We had never been in the Northwest before and were having a wonderful time. You may have noticed that we didn't go back to Michigan that summer and we hadn't planned to. We figured that if we went back to Michigan every summer, we could never see the Northwest because those are places you can not go to in the wintertime.

From Oregon we explored Washington state which we found quite interesting. The coast is green and lush while the eastern part of Washington is high desert. They both have their high points. In Washington we visited Mount Saint Helens National Monument, Mount Rainier National Park, and North Cascades National Park plus we explored some neat towns and we enjoyed great campgrounds. Because winter was pushing us on, we couldn't stay as long as we wanted to so we made a mental note to come back.

Sandpoint, Idaho, was delightful and the views were simply spectacular. Driving U.S. Route 2 into Western Montana, I told Ron I wanted to stay there forever. I envisioned us having a cabin there and living in relative isolation surrounded by the magnificent views. The Rocky Mountains are spectacular and they were especially so because of the brilliant fall colors. The next stop was Waterton Glacier National Park which we didn't get to do properly because it was snowing on the main road. We put that on our list of things to do soon. While in Montana we visited the well preserved ghost town of Bannack, but were disappointed as there was not a lot of information on what happened to that town.

While we were in that part of the country we got messages that we had two new grandchildren. Susie and Ross' daughter Taylor was born early in September and Mark and Ana's daughter Robyn was born the end of September. And we heard that Jim and Sue were expecting again.

We included Yellowstone and Grand Teton National Parks in that trip along with many other little towns. Yellowstone reminded us of Yosemite in that it was full of rude, pushy tourists who became terrible drivers once they saw a buffalo. That kind of took away from the enjoyment of the park beside it was getting cold and we had to keep moving south.

Lesson learned: tour the north country in the summer and go slow (two hundred miles and stay a week in each spot).

Ron at Bannack state park

Below: Barb at Yellowstone

Thrills

Arches & Canyonlands National Parks in Moab, Utah, are about 30 miles apart in the southeast corner of Utah. The Rocky Mountains of northern Utah disappear and are replaced with red Navajo sandstone carved by Mother Nature into mountains of interesting shapes. It is desert country and every bit as beautiful as Sedona, Arizona. But we felt more at home in Moab. Visitors were there to hike, not shop and the shops sold moderately priced goods. There was one golf course nestled up against the red rocks with fairways and greens fit for a pro tournament with prices for anyone's pocketbook. We split our time in Moab between golf, hiking, and sightseeing.

The very first hike we took was a "moderately strenuous" ranger led hike into a labyrinth of sandstone fins (narrow walls) called the Fiery Furnace. It was a three hour walk/talk over, under and around two miles of "slickrock" so called because of ever present lose sand on top which made it slippery. Several passages were so narrow that we had to climb up the sides of the walls a little like spiders (one foot on each side) to get to a wider area. Oh it was great fun and we wouldn't have been able to do it without the ranger as there were no trails in the furnace. We did think the hike should have been labeled "strenuous."

We hiked just about every day hike in the park (for a total of 11 miles) and each one took us to new heights and sights. The arches in the park are plentiful and big. We felt so tiny in the presence of them. The other rock formations were also spectacular but too difficult to describe. It was fun to give the shapes our own names reminiscent of naming clouds.

To really explore Canyonlands National Park (85% of which is back country) you must leave your car and proceed on foot, mountain bike, horseback or four-wheel drive vehicle. Some of the roads (if you can call them that) would even be a challenge for the most rugged jeep. For example the nine mile Elephant Hill Trail begins with sharp switchbacks and a 40% grade. The

White Rim trail stays above the inner gorge, always on the edge and runs for more than 80 miles. A hiker on that trail fell to her death the day after we left the park. The Shafer trail winds down into the canyon, twists around above the Colorado River (which carved out the canyon) and exits on the other side of the canyon at river level. The ranger we talked to said it was definitely a four wheel road but some trucks could do okay. Since we owned a truck, we started down the road but it was just too rough. Ever since we had to cancel our rafting trip to the Grand Canyon (because we helped with Susie's wedding), I have been anxious to go into a canyon and see what it was like. We could not drive down so I suggested we bike it. What could be so terrible? It was mostly downhill.

One logistical problem was quickly solved. We were camped 30 miles from the park (all up hill) and if we biked to the Shafer Road (30 miles) then down and thru the canyon (20 Miles) and back to the motor home (20 miles) we would be dead. Okay so some of you younger folks could do it but you must remember this was all high altitude too.

Where there is a will, there is a way and the way was a taxi service for mountain bikes and the Shafer trail was on their list. Every morning at 10 in the morning a taxi delivers anyone and their bikes to the starting point and will even spot a vehicle at the end. We opted for both. After all we were a little out of shape.

Excitement was high Monday morning as we started out. Lunch was packed, we had extra water bottles and comfortable clothes for the predicted 85 degree dry desert day. It was close to noon by the time we were delivered to the start of the trail. The taxi left and it was just Ron and I miles from nowhere. We were totally alone with 20 miles of desert canyon to cross. And we had no way to notify anyone if we got in trouble. The first mile or so was easy. The road was rutted but we went slowly. From the starting point, we could clearly see the road going steeply down and down. This was the area we had attempted in the Toyota several days before. The trail (little more than one car width wide, high up above the canyon floor) started around the rim and was fairly level. On the left, it was a sheer drop down and on

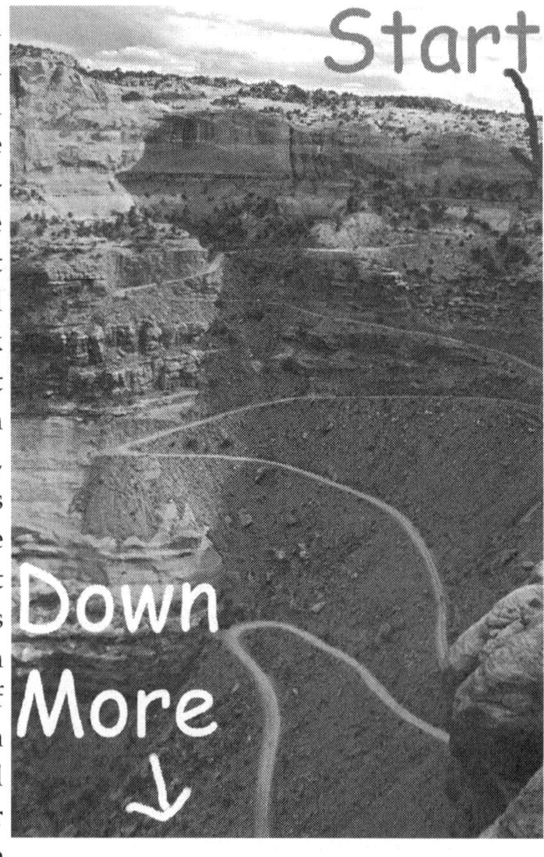

the right, a sheer wall up. Just past the area where we had stopped with the Toyota the trail suddenly went down. We were very happy that we hadn't ventured further with the truck and wondered what we were doing on bikes. Steep, rocky, rutted, switchbacks took us down. There was no pedaling just braking. Our knuckles were white from both fright and might. If we went fast and hit a rock or a rut, it would have been curtains for sure. I didn't feel like flying so I clenched the brakes with all my strength. It was difficult to even take a rest break. It would have been easier to start on an uphill than on such a rocky downhill. Always the fear of going over the handlebars was with us. Good thing Mark had advised lowering our seats to lower the center of gravity. After five miles we finally entered the canyon floor and thought the going would be easy. It was hot, dusty and now we either had a tough uphill grade or another downhill one. Also there was no escaping the sun or the rocks. We just kept on. Oh sure, the views were magnificent but after a while, I'd have given anything for a nice asphalt road, even one going uphill. All day long we saw only five vehicles. They were only going five miles an hour and all stopped to talk a moment. Four out of the five were going up the switchbacks (not down) and I imagined that if I was driving a four wheel drive vehicle, it would be more fun to go up rather than ride down on brakes. On a bike though it was a different story.

We sat on a big rock to eat lunch. As soon as we took our sandwiches out of the Tupperware sandwich boxes, the bread dried out. It was like eating toasted sandwiches. Ron's banana was black from the bouncing it received. Imagine what we were like. We moved slowly onward, crossing rutted and steep washes; maneuvering was difficult. I wondered how any vehicles could get through and imagined the torrent of water that would rush through after a rain.

Five hours and tons of dust later, we finally exited the canyon. I am glad we did it but we were cured of ever wanting to ride a bike on any such trail again. I much prefer the smoothness of pavement or asphalt.

Capitol Reef National Park is southwest of Moab and near the village of Torrey, Utah. Its main attraction is petrified sand dunes and the giant sinuous wrinkle in the Earth's crust that stretches for 100 miles across south central Utah. This wrinkle which is called the Water Pocket Fold can be seen from a distance, but as in most parks, the best way to see it is up close. There is one road which runs along the Fold but after just a few miles we gave up on it. It was of the washboard variety suitable for jeeps or other such vehicles. We did some hiking in the park and drove the "scenic drive" which was a passable dirt road. At the end of that drive, we hiked into the Grand Wash to see the water pockets and the names of the early Mormon pioneers who first entered the area. They are etched in the walls of the wash.

Bryce Canyon National Park is southwest of Capitol Reef and much higher in elevation. It is not really a canyon like one carved by water but it has the appearance of one. Carved by wind and rain, the phantom-like rock spires jut out of the earth creating a maze like never seen before. Entering the park reminded me of the Grand Canyon in that it is heavily forested, unlike the red rock desert we had spent several weeks exploring. We could have been driving into Yosemite, that is until you walk over to the overlooks and look down.

We really wanted to get down into this canyon but opted to try

horseback over hiking. When we awoke the morning of the ride there was one inch of snow on the ground and much more on the trees. We headed for the barn and in no time we were off. As we descended into the canyon, the views were indeed breathtaking. Names like Thor's Hammer, Silent City, Queen's Garden and Fairyland Point are just a few which aptly describe the sandstone sculptures. They were all the more fairy-like with the fresh white snow (the first of the season).

Sadly though, our visit was cut one day short when both our heater and furnace decided to quit working. We headed for Zion which is at a lower elevation and in the part of the state that is called "Dixie."

Zion National Park is the western most of the parks in Utah. From Bryce we drove scenic route 89 to 9 knowing that it would take us through Zion for a quick peek on our way to our coast to coast campground. As we turned on route nine, we saw large warning signs. "Tunnel in park clearance 11' 4"" We were OK with four inches to spare so we continued on. But when we stopped at the entrance station, we were informed that we were too wide to travel through the tunnel safely. For a ten dollar fee, they would stop traffic so we could travel through the center of the 1.1 mile tunnel. We had no choice but to go on. To reach our destination any other way would mean over 100 additional miles.

The drive through the park was just as spectacular as Yosemite Valley except instead of granite, the vividly colored cliffs towering above us were Navajo sandstone. Set aside in 1919, Zion is one of the early national parks. The scale is immense -- sheer cliffs dropping 3,000 feet, massive buttresses, and deep alcoves. Again, I felt very small.

Flowers and Football

I was in the laundromat in the Hurricane RV park in St. George, Utah, and struck up a conversation with the gal who was also doing her laundry. We became fast friends. Esther was traveling with her husband Jack (from Washington state), in an Airstream trailer. Jack had just retired as a logging truck driver and the two were on their way to California for the winter. They were first going to stop in Las Vegas and so were we. We were both members of the Coast-to-Coast system so we knew we'd be in the same campground in Vegas and made plans to look each other up. This was another one of those chance meetings and friendships that continued for many, many years. Esther's birthday is in the middle of May (the same as mine) so we quite often met and spent time together on our birthdays. Jack and Ron had a lot in common too – love of sports.

We were also on our way to California because a friend of Ron's whom he worked with (Chuck Fischer) had invited us to go to the Rose Bowl with him. He was a big fan of the University of Michigan in Ann Arbor, and we were fans of Michigan State in East Lansing. There's a big rivalry between these two colleges. Michigan had earned a chance to go to the Rose Bowl and play against the University of Washington. Because Chuck donated a lot of money to the U of M sports department he had a bunch of really good seats. He had also rented a big and beautiful condo in San Diego and invited his kids and other friends to come as well. He was really doing it up big. He even made sure that Ron had a U of M sweatshirt to wear which was really against Ron's liking. But what could we do as guests? He even made arrangements that we all got good seats for the Rose Bowl parade. This was a once-in-a-lifetime thing for us so we grabbed it.

One of the best highlights of this event was New Year's Eve. We got to wander around where they were decorating the floats to see them up close and talk to the people who were doing the decorating. That was most amazing. The ball game was a disaster– no, an embarrassment and I think Ron was secretly tickled that U of M lost.

We spent a little time with Esther and Jack in their campground in Hot Springs, California, before moving back to Texas. They showed us all around the area and we had a great time.

I wrote in my newsletter that we were not on vacation and I think I was trying to get that through our heads because we were eating like we had been on vacation. And while that would be okay for a short vacation, a vacation that goes on for months and months is not healthy. We were trying to ignore all the temptations and eat healthier but it was not easy. We started eating vegetables, eating at home and passing up all the temptations. We were heading to a new volunteer assignment at the LBJ Ranch in Stonewall, Texas, and hoped we'd be busy enough working at the ranch, on the newsletter and book that we wouldn't be going out to eat all the time.

Esther and I at the top of the mountain in
Palm Springs, California.

Oops—Big Time

By this time in our life on the road, our newsletter had grown tremendously. We had so many subscribers we had to start asking them to please give us stamps and we would apply them to their "account". I kept track, with a neat software program. This was becoming a big business and somewhat exciting. Ron was still working on the book and everyone was anxious to get it so when we got to the LBJ (Lyndon Baines Johnson) Ranch National Historic Site in Texas, the first part of February (1992), I asked him to finish the book while we were there. We would be there for three months and I thought that was time enough.

Upon checking into the LBJ Ranch we were directed to a very private little campground. There were two other RV's in the fenced area right on the ranch. It used to be the helicopter pad when LBJ was president. There was a cattle guard at the entrance so the cattle wouldn't bother us. It was a very lovely setting with big Live Oak trees.

We were going to be tour bus drivers so right away Ron and I

spent the first weekend taking tours which the other Rangers did. Each of the rangers and volunteers giving tours had to make up their own tour based on facts about the LBJ Ranch and even LBJ himself. We did not have to memorize a "canned" talk; we had to write our own. Listening to other rangers give the tour, gave us more information on the ranch and things we might want to include in our tour. It was really quite interesting.

We were trained in handling the buses early on. The buses were tandem in that they were comprised of two rigid sections linked by a pivoting joint. All totaled we would be carrying 59 passengers. The tour route was about 10 miles long starting at the State Park Visitor Center then crossing the bridge into the National Park which included the LBJ birthplace, the first school he attended, the family cemetery which is where LBJ is laid to rest, his grandfather's house, the Texas White House and the working part of the ranch.

Since the driver was the tour giver we had to prepare a talk and coordinate it with our choice of audio tapes that were available. The tapes I liked to play were the ones where either Mrs., or President Johnson spoke. Each tour would take one and a half hours to complete and there would be two stops along the way. During the busy season which is when we would be there (February, March and April), we understood that tour buses would run every 15 minutes all day long and we might be doing three or four a day.

After I told Ron to get to work on the book, I sent out inquiries to publishers in the area and Ron spent all his free time writing and editing. Early in February, he had typed all day and rewrote chapter 13 then started on the final chapter. I suggested that we print all the chapters which were done so far and throw out the old copies.

At the time I was using WordPerfect 5.0 software. We had access to the bus barn on the ranch with new computers which had WordPerfect 5.1. I thought it'd be neat to put the newest version on my computer borrowing their diskettes, but before installing the new version, I wanted to take my personalized macros off of our computer and save them. Our computer was so small it couldn't hold both. So after the hard copies were printed and I had removed the old version, I put the new version on the computer. To save the macros, I simply put them on the diskette that held Ron's book because it was handy. Once the new program was installed, and I put the macros back on, I wanted to delete them from his diskette. I had read somewhere that a neat trick to remove several things at once was this command that started with asterisk dot asterisk. Remember this was in the DOS days. So very confidently I did just that and promptly removed Ron's book from the diskette. The macros were still there but the book was totally gone. I tried everything to restore them then felt like dying. It was rather late in the evening and Ron was sitting right across from me reading (everything was right across from everything in that motorhome). I tried not to show my panic and kept trying to get his book back. Nothing worked.

So I was still working on the computer when Ron said he was going to go to bed. I calmly said, "I think I'll stay up a while and work on the new program." As soon as he was in bed, with the curtain pulled, I started typing in desperation, using the hard copy to recapture his book. By one or two o'clock in the morning I gave up, having only typed a couple chapters. In the morning I swallowed hard and confessed to losing his book.

Surprisingly he was very calm. It had probably helped that we had hard copy. And right away I promised to retype the whole thing up at the bus barn on their faster computer and promised it would be done in a short period of time.

Retyping his book was the best thing that could have happen. It was a forced editing and I found quite a few things that were repetitive and things that perhaps he hadn't described fully enough in my opinion. He is a man of few words and I am a woman of many (as you may have observed). I suggested adding stories from our newsletters to selected chapters which would accentuate what he wrote about. He liked the idea. We've always been a great team and working on this book made us an even better team.

During the week when I was retyping the book, we finished our training. We took our driving test, were audited and got our uniforms. We both did a great job with our tours on the auditing run. We drove those buses 60 miles each day in practice.

I got a good price on our tickets to England. We were to leave May 26, and return June 24. We are going to take the bikes again and as before we would visit Jim, Sue, Kris and new baby, James, then bike around the eastern part of England and maybe Scotland.

We also saw another publisher that week but decided to do it ourselves. We planned to deliver camera-ready copy to the printer by April 1 so we could have our books before we left. But I had a lot of work to do first. I was on the phone with WordPerfect on my days off and was thankful we could use the WATS line in the bus barn. I had to do all the typesetting (on my computer). The printer was simply going to print it. Yes I had learned how to do the newsletter and it looked pretty professional but I didn't know beans about formatting a book complete with table of contents, index, headers, and more. The people at WordPerfect walked me through it step-by-step. It was good to know we would have the book before we left the LBJ Ranch.

We really enjoyed giving the tours and meeting our passengers except for the days when we had a bunch of school kids that were wild. Ron did a super job of handling wild kids. He would tell them he was a volunteer and he didn't have to put up with their "crap". He promised to let them off in the middle of the field if they were wild and let them try to find their way back.

The buses were very old and were always breaking down and they leaked when it rained. I had the power steering go out on my bus one day just as I was turning up the main road to cross the bridge. I thought I would never get it turned. It took all of my strength. I radioed my problem and they had another bus there right away so my passengers and I could change buses. It was all part of the fun. Another time, the rear axel broke just as I was crossing the low water bridge. I didn't feel it (because I was in the front section) until I looked in the rear view mirror and saw my rear passengers waving frantically at me. Not wanting to stop right on the narrow bridge, I dragged them up the hill then stopped. I left a huge groove in the asphalt that was a reminder to me every time I crossed that bridge thereafter.

Ron at his tandem bus (two sections hitched together.)

Hot off the Press

The headline in the May/June newsletter was "Hot off the Press". We titled our book innocently, "An Alternative Lifestyle". In 1992 we didn't think anything about what that title conveyed other than a different way to live.

As I mentioned earlier it wasn't easy putting this book together. Writing it was easy; formatting it in WordPerfect was another story. Since we weren't using a publisher but were, in fact, self publishing it, I had to use WordPerfect to format it exactly as it would be in book form. Each page needed to have headers, footers, exact margins and page numbering. I also had to learn how to make the table of contents and the index (which was a real bear). We were not professional writers or editors and now when I look back at that first edition I am embarrassed. The editing of the text wasn't that bad, it was the headings and the captions under the photos that just didn't look proper. It doesn't look professional but we were proud of it nevertheless. And we started promoting it like it was a New York Times bestseller. What did we know?

My mother was a terrific salesperson and I learned even more sales techniques and PR from Tupperware so I went to work right away promoting our masterpiece. I sent out an advance notice to all who we had addresses for giving them the option of pre ordering the book at a discount price. We got over 50 orders right away. I also made a list of important people I wanted to send a book to hoping they would promote it. I had even written the cover letter ahead of having the books.

While we were yet working on the book and working at the ranch we had a visitor. Mom Hofmeister had made arrangements to attend an Elder hostel in Austin, Texas, when she knew we would be there. Part of her Elder hostel week included a visit and tour of the LBJ Ranch. We were excited and made arrangements with our supervisor that we would be giving the tours for her group. Ron was her tour bus driver, and I was the docent at the birthplace. What a fun time that was. When her hostel was over, Ron drove into Austin to bring her back to stay with us for a couple nights. We had arranged to get a couple of days off and took her to a nearby campground where we rented a cabin for all of us. She had a real good time.

One of the other volunteer couples with us at the ranch, were Liz and Don Ryding. We had met them one Sunday morning a year before, in a church in Arkansas. At the beginning of the service, the pastor asked if there were any visitors and Don stood up introducing themselves. Right away Ron said to me, "I know a pastor by the name of Eugene Ryding; I wonder if they are related." After church we talked and yes he was Eugene's brother; Pastor Eugene had been Ron's pastor when he was growing up. They were traveling in a fifth wheel trailer and he mentioned they would be volunteering at the LBJ Ranch and told us all about it. That's exactly why we chose to go there also. We and Mom Hofmeister enjoyed visiting with them when we would sit around outside in the evenings on the ranch.

We left the ranch on May 8 with lots of hugs and tears. We were glad that we were coming back the next year. It was something we really looked forward to.

Revisiting England, But First...

We left the ranch on May 8 and headed towards Missouri where we had made arrangements to give a seminar at a campground on our way to Michigan. Since we had ordered 1,000 books, I had been thinking of ways to promote it and doing seminars came to mind. I also had contacted our favorite radio station in Detroit which was WJR to see if we could get on their noon interview show. J.P. McCarthy was the morning man at the station which I had listened to for years. I felt he was my buddy although I never met him. I loved him in the morning but especially loved the noon interview show, Focus. One of the things we missed while living on the road and not being in Michigan was listening to our beloved WJR station.

We found out right away that people were interested in learning more about the full timing lifestyle because it was unique. In fact, most of the workers at the LBJ ranch bought a copy right away. It was a fantasy and people wanted to know how to accomplish that. So we were going to be on the Focus program as soon as we got back from England. We couldn't do a seminar at the Missouri campground like I wanted but they let us leave some books in their bookstore and eventually they sold. I was still thinking of ways to move the books because boxes of books filled the back of our pick up truck and really weighed it down.

Our trip to England was much easier than the first time. We still had to go through the packing of the bikes at the airport and then putting them back together but we didn't have to ride on the subway because my son, Jim, had purchased a bike rack for his car and was at the airport in Gatwick to pick us up. That was a piece of cake. He had reserved a bed-and-breakfast in the little village of Grundsburgh for us for the days before we started riding and it was very charming–lovely in fact. Every morning and

evening a farmer would walk through town with his herd of cows. In the morning he took them out to the pasture; in the evening he brought them back for milking. It was a treat to watch him every day as he walked through the middle of town.

We had a wonderful visit with Jim, Sue, and children. Jim made the most elaborate, wonderful meals while we were there which was a treat. When our week was up and we started biking we had a whole different attitude than the first time. Number one we weren't planning a long trip; we were just going to go here and there as the spirit moved us.

The very first day we rode was a killer and we didn't even go

far. We had both gained weight and were badly out of shape. It was painful. We didn't quit but just went along at a fairly leisurely pace.

When we were at Yosemite, we met several people from Britain who invited us to come and stay with them when we went back to England. One family, the Mc Cambe's (Janet, Brian, Helen and Ana), lived near Cambridge. When they were in Yosemite they camped in the campground we were hosting and asked how they could see the big trees but it had snowed so heavily their rented motorhome couldn't get up to that part of the Park. I had been so impressed with the sequoia trees that I thought they should see them. I offered to drive them up myself in our car and I gave them a personal tour of the trees. They had appreciated that and told us we must stay with them the next time we came to England. He was a professor at Cambridge University and she was a medical doctor. So when we had our plans for England solidified we let them know and made plans to spend a night with them. We enjoyed our short visit with them and gave them a copy of our book.

Of course we wanted to see George and Ann again in their bed -and-breakfast and the couple we met on the Ferry to Ireland as well as Ron and Rose Eldridge and their two children whom we met when we were working at the History Center.

On the way to Thetford, I got sick and could hardly breathe. We were at a very nice bed-and-breakfast and our hostess, Maggie, took me to her doctor who gave me some prednisone; my asthma had flared up. They didn't charge us a penny and I couldn't help but know it wouldn't have been free for them if they were visiting the United States and had to see a doctor. We stayed a couple extra days at that bed-and-breakfast till I felt better then we took off. And then I started feeling bad again maybe because of the trees; It was a very wooded area. We had to have Jim come and pick us up and take us back to their area. Then after I felt better, we took off again this time taking a train first then biking some more for a few more days but didn't wander too far and decided to go back to Jim's and just enjoy being grandparents.

We left England on June 24 and the flight was uneventful. But when we got home we had an ugly surprise in that our refrigerator had gone out again. This time we were parked in mother's backyard. I had given her the key but she'd never bothered to check. There had been a storm and the power went out. When the power came back on, the refrigerator didn't go on because it had flipped the breaker. So we had a whole refrigerator full of moldy smelly food. I said I would never leave home again. Although I had emptied everything out of the refrigerator (filling several garbage bags) and deodorized the motorhome it still stunk and it was hard to sleep with that smell.

A post script to the story about my getting sick is that two years later I would be diagnosed with severe acid reflux and hiatal hernia all because of a medicine prescribed for me way back in Oregon by the pulmonologist. Theophylline was bad medicine. I personally think it wasn't asthma that got me when I was in England, it was reflux. I had gained weight; no wonder I had a problem.

Business, Family and Friends in Michigan

We were able to do several seminars while in Michigan. Our home coast-to-coast Park let us do three and we did a seminar for the Michigan Department of Transportation. They were all well received. Plus we sold books.

Our interview on the J.P. McCarthy show was terrific but I was disappointed that JP had left for vacation after his morning show that day. Joan Siefert, from the news department, did a good job asking great questions and admitted that it was her dream to travel full-time like we did. Also on the show was a former Miss America and the actress/dancer, Mitzi Gaynor who was a favorite of mine. It turned out she lived right near where I had lived is a young girl. We had even attended the same school at different times so after the show we shared memories of the candy store and a few other things.

Right away we discovered we made a mistake with the book; we didn't have an ISBN number which would've allowed people to find our book easily. On the interview at WJR they did give an address where the book could be ordered but most people wouldn't go to that trouble. And our mail service meant a delay in getting to us. Of course this was before the internet places like Amazon.com. Miraculously we did get a few orders from the show.

Before we left the LBJ Ranch, we had changed our address. We had heard about an organization called Escapees which had a very efficient mail forwarding service in Livingston, Texas. They were used to full timers. Our old address in Colorado had not been working. Yes, it was a pain to notify everyone of our new address even though we weren't actually moving (or were we?) but it had to be done. The Escapees billed themselves as an organization of serious RVers and they were. We even licensed our motorhome and car in Texas and it was a lot cheaper than in Michigan.

We were starting to talk more and more about getting rid of all that stuff that we had put in storage. It was looking more and more like we weren't going to settle down on our property up north either. So when Jim and Norma's house was finished, I asked her if she would be interested in buying my organ. She had an older organ and had liked mine. She said she would think about it and we were at Mother's when the phone call came from Norma. We had been sitting in the living room and when the phone rang I got up and went all the way into the kitchen to answer it. It was Norma saying that they would like the organ and they would meet us in Lansing to pick it up in a few days. I told her I was happy that I would be able to visit it once in a while. But by the time I got to the living room to tell Ron and Mom the good news, I started bawling like a baby. I couldn't talk and they thought that someone had died. It took me a while to settle down. To me the organ represented the last vestiges of good times with my kids; we had so many happy hours playing as a group — all of us.

During the rest of the summer there were many family visits. We had a base at Smoke Rise, our home Coast to Coast park in Davison, Michigan, (near Flint) which was centrally located between my family in Waterford and Ron's kids in Lansing. The Park had lots of facilities which appealed to our families and included cabins that could be rented, lovely indoor pools, tennis courts, volleyball, biking trails, and much more. We took off a couple times to visit Jim and Norma, our friends in Northport. I was not only excited to see them but to be able to visit my organ. It was no longer mine and I was able to let go of it.

During the summer I was busy thinking up promotions to sell the book, and mapping out our fall travels so I would know where we could plan seminars, and I was working on the newsletter too. Our subscription base had grown so tremendously that we had to charge $1.50 for each issue. It was becoming a full-time job — not only doing the newsletter but keeping track of the subscriptions. And we had to keep moving to have good things to write about; it was a vicious circle. But a big benefit of the newsletter is that we could promote the book. As we traveled we freely handed out copies of our newsletter and we kept getting new subscribers. We were always happy to find a few book orders with every package of mail we received.

I had been able to contact a few places that would sell some of our books. One such organization was WorkKamper News. They ordered 50 books and paid for them at the proper publishing discount (forty percent off). WorkKamper News was a publication geared toward people who want to work and camp at the same time. Some of the positions they advertised were campground hosts while others were looking for help in a business. Meanwhile I kept trying to get more people interested in selling our book. As a funny side note, we couldn't cash the WorkKamper News' check because it was made out to R & B Publications, a name we chose to make our book look more professional. Our credit union in Michigan had never heard of that business so they wouldn't cash our check. We called the Escapees and they sent us a form to fill out so we could register our business in Texas. They took care of the details for us.

It was a good summer but we were so happy to be back to just the two of us and our style of living when we left Michigan on August 13.

First Lobster

This is an article I wrote for the September 1992 issue of Movin On; the title is It's so Good to Be Home:

"Don't you agree that even after the most exciting vacation in paradise, it's good to get home and back to your old routine? Somehow it's like a comfy old chair — good to curl up in with a book. And now that you're home, you might have time to read. Remember how you thought you'd read on your vacation? Even though eating out is fun, a steady diet of it isn't. Home again, you can fix that favorite dish that only you can fix and you can have your coffee the way you like it when you like. Even if your routine means getting up early and going to work, there is comfort in knowing the job and coworkers are there, the mail is in the mailbox and life can get back to normal.

We carry our house with us so we are really always home but to us "being home" means being back in our chosen lifestyle — on the road and doing our thing. And even though we had a marvelous vacation in England and six delightful weeks at our home park with lots of family around, it's good to be back home, in our routine and on the road again.

We like our house, small as it is, our bed, our cooking, time to read, time to work on the computer, listening to a new radio station, driving a new road, visiting a new restaurant, seeing new sights, talking to fellow campers, studying the map and plotting the next stop and picking up and moving down the road. It is our normal routine and after we sit a while, we are ready to get back to normal. This is hard for most people to understand.

When we were at the LBJ Ranch last spring, Mary Helen, a fellow volunteer and coworker, was quite sick. The staff was concerned and wanted to make her comforta-

> ble. Ranger, Sandy Hodges, offered her her house and a "real bed", but as we would've predicted, it was turned down. The four of us (RVers) discussed this phenomenon: non-RVers have a difficult time comprehending anyone feeling "at home" in an RV. We understand their caring concern, but we are as comfortable in our home and lifestyle as they are in theirs.
>
> As I write this we are in a campground in upstate New York. We are publishing a little early to finish the chapter on Michigan then we will get busy seeing the sights in the east and report on all of our adventures. We plan to do some biking around the finger Lakes, visit the wineries around Hammondsport, check out the White Mountains in New Hampshire, see, hike and bike Acadia National Park, eat seafood in Maine (I had never eaten lobster), check out the coast of Connecticut and visit the historic spots in Boston before the next newsletter is printed. But there will be lots of time to be at home in our house too. We don't go out every day. That's the beauty of this lifestyle. Since we have our house and all its comforts with us, we are home, no matter where we are, but it's especially good to be Movin' On again."

Some of our family news headlines in that same issue were that I had another grandson on the way. Mark and Ana announced their son would be born in January, 1993. Also in the news my son-in-law, Pekka, had become a US citizen.

I loved all the big houses in New York and Massachusetts and Maine. I didn't much care for lobster at first, but my second try at it was better. Since lobster is generally so expensive and apparently one needs to develop a taste for it, I decided not to try it anymore. We didn't care for New Hampshire at all, mainly because we got kicked out of a campground. The campground was one of the Coast-to-Coast campgrounds and they didn't want us in there for the cheap rate when they could get much more from the regular tourists. It had been a very bad summer weather wise and they had missed a lot of good business because of that. Since we were there on a weekend they felt they didn't have to give us what we deserved; they found a way to kick us out. It was a Yogi Bear Campground so my headline was "Yogi Nasty in New Hampshire". I made sure I sent a copy of the newsletter to the campground so that they knew I was spreading the bad news about their unfriendliness.

Ron and his lobster.

We especially enjoyed our visit to two historic homes in New York. The FDR Home and Presidential Museum in Hyde Park was excellent. It was very homey and comfortable; there was nothing pretentious in that home. What a garish contrast was their next-door neighbor's Gilded Age home. It belonged to Frederick and Louise Vanderbilt who died childless and left their home to a niece. She already had several mansions. When the niece heard that FDR had donated his house to the National Park Service she did the same. I can understand FDR leaving his home to the park service but why a Vanderbilt Mansion? And why would the park service want it? It has been a ward of the National Park Service in 1940 and a big white elephant.

While in New York we visited West Point Academy and learned some interesting facts about a couple people who attended that school. Did you know that Edgar Allen Poe was expelled from the school? But while he was there one of his duties was to guard the mortuary. It figures! He was kicked out because he refused to conform to standards – like dress rules. The last straw was when ordered to wear a certain part of the uniform, he showed up with only that part on. Apparently West Point does not approve of nakedness. Another ex-cadet was the painter Whistler, (you know, Whistler's Mother). One of the required classes at the school was bridge design. He submitted his drawing of a bridge which included three children fishing off the bridge. Rebuked for adding children to a military situation, he was ordered to re-do it. He did but this time he had the kids fishing from the bank of the river. Again he was admonished and ordered to "get rid of those kids". The last drawing he submitted showed three small tombstones along the bank of the river. He was gone from then on.

We wanted to include a short visit with Ron's sister, Linda and her husband Ken, in New Jersey, which we did and from there we went to Cape May also in New Jersey so we could take a ferry down to Norfolk, Virginia. We wanted to visit David again before he went off for a three-year stint in Spain. But we were really hurrying on to Florida because Ron's mom needed us after her recent bunion surgery. Of all the family members we were the most foot loose and fancy free—and able to go.

Our book report in the September issue of the newsletter said that we had quite a few newspaper articles written about us and they were bringing in orders. Since we were heading to Florida, I had called ahead to some newspapers and they promised to do stories on us when we got there. It was wonderful free advertising and it really did the trick. We were a human interest story and that suited us just fine.

We Grew and Moved Up.

As always our time spent in Florida was great. We were celebrating our 3 ½ years on the road, life was wonderful and we were growing business wise. Clarence and Kay Elliott started *The Full-Time RVers Newsletter* about the same time we started *Movin' On*. The stress of their business was causing health issues so they talked to us and asked if we would be willing to take over their business for a fee. They gave their customers a choice of a refund or switching the number of issues remaining on their subscription to our newsletter. We ended up getting about 250 new customers by January 1.

Another thing that was changing was that we were buying a new motorhome. Since we were going to stay out for an indefinite amount of years, we thought it was about time we moved up about 10-feet. While in Florida, we visited one of the largest RV dealers in the U.S. which was Lazy Days RV Sales in Tampa, Florida, and looked at the motorhome we had already decided we would want. It was a 34 foot Bounder. It had so many things that we wanted including couch, microwave oven, a place for a big computer, queen-size bed (separate from the bathroom), a nice bathroom with a shower, dinette, extra chairs and a side entry. Lazy days was so easy to deal with because they sold tons of motorhomes and other RVs too. The owner Don Wallace was nice to talk to and I decided to interview him for the newsletter and in doing so mentioned our book. He was very interested and I suggested that each of his salesman, since they dealt with a lot of full time RVers, should have a copy of our book. He purchased 30 on the spot. We got a good deal on the motorhome too.

When it was time to move in it was a piece of cake. We parked the Mallard next to the Bounder so that their entry doors were opposite each other. Not that it was easy to carry everything from one to the other but being so close made it quite simple. We spent all of one day moving. We got up early the next morning and worked the whole day again with a little interruption to go through the walk-through which was something they like to do with each new sale.

Their "move in coordinator," Bill, spent about 1½ hours doing the walk-through. We learned about the two furnaces, two air conditioners, the hydraulic leveling jacks, awnings (1 patio & 4 window), two televisions, built in VCR, microwave, water filter system, back up camera, water and sewer hookups, 7000 Onan generator and all the storage compartments. That was good because we got to learn more about the motorhome, where everything was and what to do with what. It was oh so exciting. They didn't rush as we were told to stay as long as it would take which we did. Then when we were through they gave us a place to park in their campground for free.

One of the first things I did was call our furniture dealer in Lansing where we had ordered the mattress for the Mallard. For that motorhome we had a custom-made super firm foam mattress which was very, very comfortable. In fact it was still comfortable in the Mallard and we hated to leave it but it wouldn't fit in the new motorhome. The mattress in the Bounder wasn't all that comfortable but we knew it would be okay until we got back to Michigan and could pick up the new mattress.

Our first night in the motorhome was wonderful. We enjoyed the big TV up front, and we were going to put the new computer up on the passenger side of the dashboard where it would fit nicely. It was something we were going to go shopping for soon as well as a new printer. I don't know which I was more excited about, a new computer and printer or the motorhome itself; I think it was a combination of the two.

I hadn't remembered how much I had liked our microwave oven from before we went on the road and to have one back again was pure heaven. Fitting everything in the motorhome was fairly easy because we had so many compartments. The Bounder even had a large basement which we easily filled with some of the things from the back of the pickup (like cases of books). We got it easily organized and it was easy to get to everything.

When it was time to leave, Ron did a remarkable job of driving.

He drove it just like a pro. We were on our way to Winter Haven and there were a lot of curvy roads; we got a little lost and it was getting dark but we made it safely. When we pulled into our favorite campground he gave us a drive-through spot so we didn't have to back up, which was very nice especially since it was dark.

We had several visitors while in Winter Haven. Ron's mom of course came and then Glenda, Erkki and Lisa from West Palm Beach. They had a new pop-up trailer so they camped with us for a night.

We had to go back to Lazy Days about a week or so later for a few bugs we found. One of the furnaces wasn't working and I forget what else but we got it all fixed in one of their 48 service bays.

When we left Lazy Days we were headed to Texas with stops in Pensacola, Florida, Alabama and Mississippi. We spent Christmas at Rainbows End which was the main headquarters for the Escapees' organization in Livingston, Texas. We opened a business checking account in Livingston, got our Texas license plates, and I checked out their mail service which we already knew was great. I even worked in the mail service room one day to get the real feel of it.

We were in Trinity, Texas, by New Year's Eve. It was an almost deserted campground but it was a nice one. It was warm and humid until about 3 PM then it got real cold. They had a nice hot tub and after dinner in our beautiful new home, since it was New Year's Eve and no one else was around, we went skinny dipping in the hot tub late at night.

LOTS OF ROOM IN NEW HOUSE

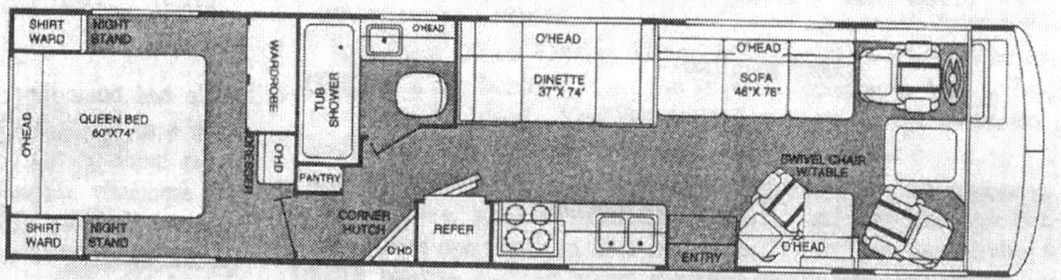

MOVIN' ON

volume 4 JANUARY 1993 number 1

Home on the Range Again

We were due to start back to work at the LBJ Ranch the first of February in 1993 and we were there in plenty of time. It was good to be back with all the rangers and the other volunteers. We had our same spot but we looked a little different with our bigger motorhome. We had a bigger window in which to see all of the cattle on the ranch.

We started right away doing the tours again and I really loved that job. I met so many nice people on my tour, many who I will remember for a long, long time. Our tour consisted of one-stop (LBJs birthplace) where the people were actually allowed to get off the bus so they could tour the little house in which he was born then walk across to the cemetery and pay their respects there. On one tour, a gentleman sitting up front didn't get off the bus like everyone else. He stayed with me as I drove across the street and parked at the cemetery where LBJ was buried. Once I was parked he got off the bus, walked to the area where LBJ's grave was, and stood there for quite a while. When he got back on the bus he said, "It looks just as I remembered". I had time to chat while I was waiting for the rest of the passengers to get back on the bus so I questioned when he was there before. It turned out he was a Secret Service agent who had been assigned to work for LBJ shortly after he became president. He said he remembered the day like it was yesterday when he was out by the flight line with LBJ and some other people and someone came out to give LBJ a message from former president Eisenhower. It was the president's wife Mamie. She wanted to think LBJ for the fact that Ike had Secret Service protection. She went on to say that when Ike had his heart attack, he would have died if it had not been for the secret service people who were right there to take care of him. My passenger went on to say that LBJ questioned the fact that Ike had Secret Service protection because he knew Truman didn't. It turned out that former president Truman didn't want Secret Service protection. Right then and there LBJ broadcast loud and clear (in his own brusk style) that from then on Truman would have Secret Service protection whether he wanted it or not. And shortly after, my passenger had been reassigned to guard the Trumans until the two of them died. He added more: as they aged and their friends died off, the only real friends they had were the agents who played cards with them, took them shopping and were their constant companions. We could see that that was happening with Mrs. Johnson who still lived at the ranch half of the time. I thanked him for the story which gave me a little insight into the kinds of things that went on between the agents and the former presidents.

When preparing our tours we were given carte blanche (to an extent) on the slant of our tour. One tour guide, a ranger, talked more about LBJ as a rancher than a president. After reading about him (pros and cons) and listening to other's tours, I decided to build my tour around LBJ—the man. And because our tour started at the school house where he first started school, I started with his upbringing and told about how he was taunted and teased and really didn't have any friends. Because he was an only child and his mother was a teacher he was smart but he had a lousy personality. He always wanted to have friends and strove for that almost at all costs. When he first entered politics it's well-known that he lost to a contender who stuffed the ballot boxes so the next time he ran he did the exact same thing and won. Yes he did some very shady things but as one man said to me when he got off the tour, "They'll never be another like LBJ. He would grab a senator by the shirt collar and tell him he better do this or that." He got his way a lot. But when Kennedy was elected and LBJ became a vice president, he was shunned more than ever. All of Kennedy's friends laughed behind LBJ's back and called him a "*country bumpkin* and a bore." They really had no use for him. When Kennedy was assassinated, LBJ tried to buy their friendship in a way. He would invite them all down to his ranch for a barbecue, get them drunk and tell them what they had to do; it was a little like coercion. He got advice from the wrong people (like Defense Secretary McNamara) regarding the Vietnam situation. Kennedy had sent troops, so when Kennedy was assassinated LBJ thought the best thing to do was follow Kennedy's beginning. Towards the end of his presidency when things were so bad in Vietnam all he heard outside the White House every day were hordes of young people chanting, "Hey hey LBJ how many kids did you kill today", it broke his heart. He knew he was a beaten man.

I was not a fan of President Johnson before working at the ranch, but I surprised my self by liking the guy after talking about him so much. Well maybe not necessarily liking him, but feeling a little sorry for him.

We did have some fun times at the ranch; it wasn't all work. One fun time was when we were invited to have dinner with Lady Bird. The dinner was for the three of us RV couples who were volunteers at the ranch. Mrs. Johnson had her Secret Service Agent drive her to our little compound where she knocked on one door and invited us to dinner. That was a real treat and dinner with her was charming; what a sharp lady. The inside of the home was very cozy and comfortable and not one bit pretentious. Our meal was delightful, but the conversation was even more special. She made sure she asked each of us a little about ourselves and then allowed time for us to ask her questions.

A New Book

We were running out of books which was a good thing. But because I didn't want to reprint our first book again (I didn't like the look or mistakes), we embarked on a new book with a new title, new cover and some new things inside. We were so naive when we named the first book and didn't have a clue about other meanings. But we knew we were in trouble when a gay/lesbian bookstore in San Francisco, California, ordered six copies of An Alternative Lifestyle right away.

Ron still liked the title, so for clarification we added, *Living and Traveling Full-Time in a Recreational Vehicle*. It was nice to have a new computer that had Windows on it. Many evenings and some off-hours were spent working on the new book. I didn't advertise it yet because I wanted to make sure we sold all of the old ones first. We talked to our printer and set up the date for reprinting —August.

It had been easy to promote our book because of the uniqueness of the lifestyle and I had been busy. We had had many interviews at local newspapers in the past year and even some big city newspapers. Being on that radio show in Detroit had helped and I was actively looking to find other media places that would be interested in what we had to say. Austin, Texas, had a nice daily paper—the Austin Statesman, and they came out and did a beautiful story on us about working at the ranch, our lifestyle and our book. When the paper came out, we were amazed. It was two full pages with pictures in the Sunday Lifestyle section. I mean we were plastered all over that paper and it was fantastically, wonderful, free advertising. I vowed to do as much of that as possible and while working on the new book even planned our route and where we could use newspaper stories on our way to wherever we were going.

We talked to our printer and found out how to get an ISBN number which we discovered was very important, and we found an artist to draw a cover picture. Also the cover was going to be full-color this time. We vowed to have a very professional looking book. I was even searching for an editor because one of the reviews of our first book said something like, it's a great book with the bad title and it needs editing badly. So we vowed to fix all that; our goal was to produce a masterpiece.

Another thing we were planning for the new book was that we wouldn't have to distribute them all ourselves; we made arrangement with an organization with an 800 number that would store our books and take care of all orders. With this service, anyone could order the book and the company would ship them out, take a percentage then send us a check once a month.

On May 1 we finished our last tours and left the ranch, from there we went just a short distance to a campground in Spicewood, Texas, where we planned to stay for one month to work nonstop getting the book ready to print. We purposely did not strike up any conversations with other campers. We were disciplining ourselves to get the work done. But one day a Bounder motorhome pulled in across from us. The next morning we were just finishing our walk when the couple from the Bounder came out. The "Hi" we started with turned into a nice half-hour conversation with Bette and Clyde Salter. The outcome was most amazing. Fate, I called it. We mentioned our struggles editing the book; Betty, a retired schoolteacher offered to do it for us. We agreed on a price and over the next three days, she read everything we had ready and did a super job. It made a big difference when someone else looked over the material.

We left the campground early in June and dropped off the hard copy for the book at the printer in Austin, Texas, and then we took off slowly for Michigan, stopping to visit Jim and Sue in their new home in Warrensburg, Missouri. Their move from England was smooth and I was so glad that they were safely settled in the US. And because their home was in the middle of the United States, they were almost always on our way to and from anywhere.

Since we were sure we had a winner this time we ordered 2000 copies of the book and asked that several hundred be shipped directly to us from the printer so we could use them for PR and for sale during seminars. We planned to be in Michigan by early June. The remainder of the books would be shipped to our distributor. Always in anything we did, I was thinking about possible PR opportunities. We were very proud of this edition with its 45 new pages, some covering topics we hadn't covered before like traveling with pets, single full-timers and security.

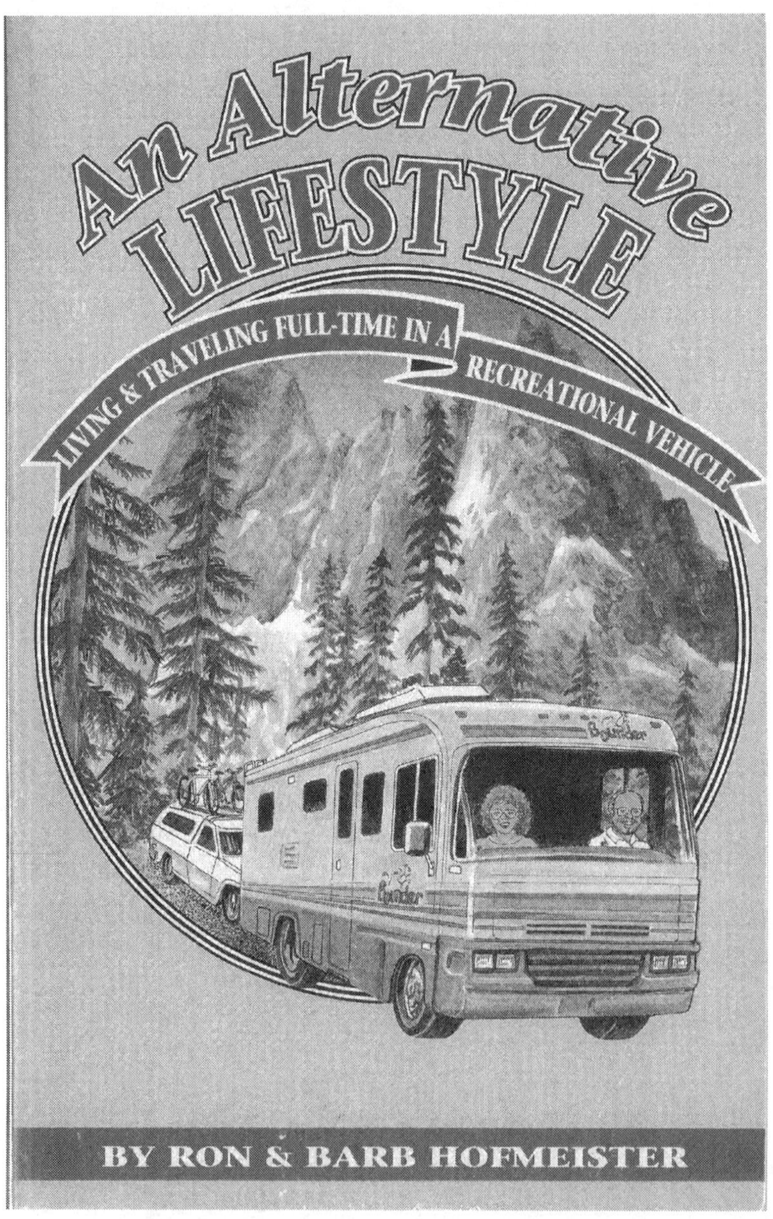

Frustration then Excitement

About mid June, just after we got back to Michigan, I flew to Florida for a week because my daughter had had a new baby boy and I wanted to see him. Erkki Christian was a beautiful baby and it was fun to be with the family. While I was gone, Ron spent Father's Day with his kids and there was a large blow-up. I was glad I wasn't there. Apparently Ron's son, Karl, gave him a Rush Limbaugh book for his birthday. Ron was insulted with it so he gave it back to Karl, and thus ensued a lot of harsh words. Ron thought his son should have known him well enough to know that a book about Limbaugh would not be welcomed. They didn't speak for many months after that.

After I got back from Florida we prepared to have the garage sale. We had made plans well in advance to have our garage sale immediately after the July 4 weekend and we were offered the use of Jim and Norma's small garage at their old home in Haslett. They were up in Northport but we had the keys. In preparation for the garage sale I had contacted a reporter at the State Journal and explained our situation so they could do a story on us and the lifestyle while mentioning the garage sale. They had done a story on us before so it was easy to get them to do a follow-up. We were staying at our Coast-to-Coast campground in Davidson and it was an hour's drive from there to Jim and Norma's. We had to get up early in the morning for a week, work all day then drive back to the campground. It was a tough week.

First thing we had to do was arrange for a U-Haul truck and Ron and I worked by ourselves all day on Monday, July 5, in extreme heat and humidity, loading everything from our storage unit into the truck. It was backbreaking work. When we got to Jim and Norma's place, we unloaded it into their garage which was much smaller than our storage unit. We spent all of Tuesday and Wednesday pricing things and the sale was to be on Thursday, Friday and Saturday.

As we unpacked boxes we looked to see if there was anything the kids wanted. Ron's son Karl had asked for the German steins and my sons wanted my cookie sheets, recipes and other things used in cooking. Jim wanted the Christmas decorations but none of the rest wanted anything. But as we opened boxes I said to myself, "Why had I saved this?" None of the things that had been carefully packed away for 3 ½ years meant a darn thing to me. It was easy to price them cheaply for sale. I had a beautiful fox jacket for example which I sold for five dollars. Who would want a fox jacket when the temperature was 95 degrees? I had a lot of sexy nightgowns and things like that which I priced cheaply too.

We were selling everything: dishes, pots and pans, TVs, stereos, beds and dressers and tons of clothing. Ron had lots of suits and I had beautiful dresses, shoes and boots. It didn't bother me a bit to get rid of a thing ---even our wedding presents. I did save out for myself some of my microwave dishes now that I had a microwave. And as you can imagine I had tons of Tupperware that had been carefully packed away. I sold most of it easily only saving a tiny bit for the motorhome.

We had big crowds for the sale and everyone commented that it was a good sale because it wasn't the typical garage sale stuff. It was all of our good stuff. We collected $2500 and that is about what we had paid for the three years rent on the storage unit.

With that over with, we felt unburdened and headed to the West coast of Michigan, where we had some work done on the motorhome and I printed up another newsletter. From there we headed up to Jim and Norma's new home in Northport.

We had the books by the end of July while we were there in Northport, Michigan. Immediately we went to the post office and got a bunch of priority envelopes and prepared to ship books out as PR to radio and TV stations, newspapers and other RVing publications, or anything else I could think of. I had already printed the cover letters with the help of a mail merge program and was prepared to make follow-up phone calls a short time after I figured everyone got their books.

When we left Jim and Norma's we went to Interlochen, where

Good friends Jim and Norma with us.

we had made arrangements to be interviewed by a nearby radio station. They were going to come out to the campground to interview us, but as we were backing in to our narrow spot at the State Park, Ron decided not to pay attention to my directions. With a motorhome as long as the Bounder, even though there was a backup camera, the driver was supposed to depend upon the person in the back directing the motorhome for directions. As he was backing he brushed up against a tree and ignored my signals to stop and just kept going further then abruptly pulled forward which really finished the job. That little maneuver tour off the side awning and put a big hole in the fiberglass. And goody-goody rain was predicted. To make matters worse the interviewer was told we weren't there so he left without doing the interview. Surprisingly Ron was calm although I wasn't. It really bothered me that he wouldn't watch and pay attention to me. Luckily, just up the road from the campground was an RV repair facility and our house was fixed up good as new with only $100 out of our pocket. Insurance covered the rest.

But Ron and I were having problems. We had been fighting a lot. He seemed supersensitive, and angry. It seemed we weren't friends anymore. I surmised it must be all the pressure we put on ourselves. We talked about it and we agreed we would work on it. We were together 24/7 so we had to.

We were getting busy and mail day (usually Monday) was a whole day's job. People who ordered books and newsletters always sent a letter with information about themselves, what they hope to do, questions, and so on. They wrote like we were old friends. I tried to be a good business person and answer them personally. I even designed some forms in which I could basically just fill in the blanks. That saved a little time but they still looked personal. And I had a file on everyone who subscribed or ordered a book. That file contained notes that reminded me of who they were, how they heard about us and any notes that gave me information which I could use in a letter back to them. For example if the woman had mentioned that her husband had had surgery and they are waiting for him to recover completely, I could see my note and make sure I asked how he was doing. My motto was: "little things mean a lot."

While we were visiting Ron's cousin near the Twin Cities of Minnesota, I used their phone to place some follow-up calls from the PR books we sent out. One of the calls I made was to Tyler Matheson, the money guy from Good Morning America. Several times a week on that show he did a segment on finances. And I had pitched the book to him because of Ron's data on the cost of the lifestyle. I almost fell over when he personally answered his telephone. I asked if he had received the book and he said, "Yes it's on my desk right now." I could hardly contain myself when he said that they were going to do a piece on us and our book and added his producer would get back to us soon. Things were really rolling.

Important Phone Call

We left Michigan from the southwestern edge of the upper Peninsula and visited Wisconsin for the first time before going on to Minnesota. From Minnesota we went to Fargo, North Dakota, and then gradually worked our way south. Most of these were places we had never been before so it was fun to explore and we did a lot of that while we were working along the way. When I say "working along the way" I mean I was always working on the next newsletter, we were always getting mail that had to be answered, we were always working on something.

The newsletter had grown in a different direction; it had more and different articles. It was still just 9 ½ pages and couldn't get any bigger without costing more in postage. When it was tri folded, the top and bottom section of that last page still had information or pictures. I crammed in as much as I could. Ron was by then doing a column on "Finances on the Road", he still did his "Potpourri", and his "Campground Update" columns. I usually did the travel articles, a new column called "Coffee Break" where we answered questions from our readers, a page or two with letters from our readers, and my page which was titled "This 'n That". On the top third of the back page, I generally had a quiz and on the bottom third we had some extra pictures. Inside I sometimes had a column titled "Signs along the Way" which featured funny signs we saw and we had a column titled "Family News". Everyone thought it was very professional looking and it was now that we had our laser printer to go with new computer.

On our trip south we spent a little time in each of the following – South Dakota, Iowa and Nebraska and were planning to be in Oklahoma City by October so we could attend a regional Family Motor Coach Association rally. We hadn't heard any more from Good Morning America so we just kept on going.

I still remember the really fun time we had in Iowa. The Iowa Great Lakes in the northwestern part of the state include West and East Okoboji and Big Spirit Lakes. All are glacier made and

boast great fishing. It was fall when we were there (my favorite time of the year). There was a rail trail (old railroad track converted to a hiking/biking trail) that went between the towns of Milford and Spirit Lake. As we started to ride, we enjoyed the warmth of the sun but a cool northerly breeze made us keep our jackets on. We hadn't been on our bikes in a long time and it felt really great to ride. We were all alone on the trail most of the time as I remember; it was just us and the birds, the cornfields, and woolly caterpillars. The only sounds were the rustle of leaves trying to hang on one more day and the crunches as our tires ran over the dry crisp leaves lost to the season. It was a sensory paradise. Occasionally we heard the scratch and ping of a metal rake being pulled somewhere nearby, and heard the leaves squish together. Brilliant marigolds and mum's graced the edges of yards and flower gardens and the smell of fall was in the air. Leaves were burning somewhere and fireplace chimneys were sending fragrant smoke signals. We rode several days in a row just for the sheer joy of it.

Would you believe that former president George HW Bush, and Ron and I have something in common. We are all graduates of Okoboji University. We had heard about this University. Several people snickered that we really needed to get a university sweatshirt. So figuring that any T-shirt shop in that touristy area would sell university T-shirts, we went looking for one. Any time we asked, we were told that we could only get them at the Three Sons store in Milford.

We made a special trip to Milford and found it as directed. It was a typical looking sporting-goods store so I asked where I

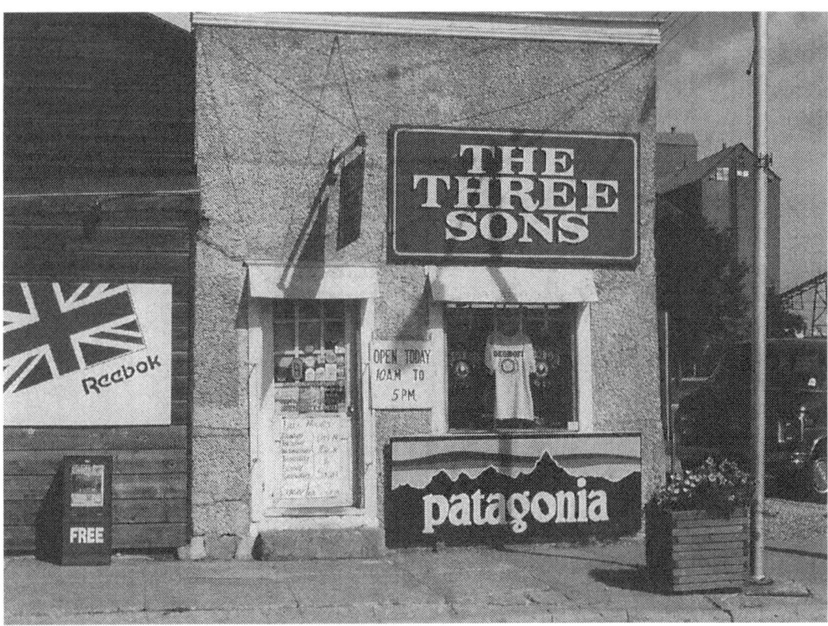

could find the university shirts and was directed to the back of the store. It was way back; the store was huge. As I walked back I recognized top quality merchandise in this old, unpretentious, creaky floored building. There were names like Polo, Patagonia, the Esprit, Nautica, Calvin Klein and Nike. Besides all that, there was an upstairs full of marked down brand-name clothing but that's not what was so interesting.

In the back part of the store they had all sorts of university clothing—everything from jogging shorts, football jerseys, tennis shorts etc., to expensive sweaters. All sported the university emblem. It looked like a college bookstore minus the books. There were Okoboji University cups, mugs, beach towels, playing cards and more.

I remember getting a little suspicious when I was being helped by a nice woman who wore a name badge that gave her the title of "Director of Economics". After picking out my T-shirt, I meandered the 10,000 square foot building reading some of the posters. They heralded the university's mascot, the "Fighting Phantoms" which seemed a bit strange to me. Then it hit me. There was no university. It was all tongue-in-cheek.

As I was still browsing, Herman Richter, Director of Student Affairs, offered to help me. I recognized him from some of the newspaper stories displayed in the store. I asked him if I could write about him and he armed me with all sorts of good stuff for reporting. The Wall Street Journal wrote in 1977, "the University of Okoboji, located somewhere on the boundary line between the Big Ten and the Big Eight, has everything you would expect of a top-flight institution of higher learning. Everything, that is, except dormitories, classrooms, a curriculum, students and a faculty. That leaves bumper stickers, pendants, and sweatshirts…"

When asked to describe the University of Okoboji, Herman Richter replied, "It is an attitude. If Walter Mitty were alive today, that's where he'd be going to school. Believing in the University of Okoboji has become a bit like believing in Santa Claus." The three brothers who opened the store added the university clothing as a lark and it's been going strong ever since. We were proud to be graduates and made sure we had a decal on the back of our little pickup truck proclaiming we were Okoboji University alumni. We have met other graduates along the way which was part of the fun and I still have my T-shirt.

Another thing we did in that area which I still remember fondly, is we discovered a drug store with an ice cream soda fountain. What nostalgia that was. Then I remembered reading that in that particular area in Iowa/Nebraska there were many little towns with soda fountains. I talked Ron into taking a ride with me so I could report on this nostalgia. The towns were very close to each other so it didn't take long to find each town, go to the drugstore order an ice cream soda, drink it and then go on to the next one. Except after we each downed one, we weren't in the mood to try another one; it was too sweet and filling. But I felt I had to order one at each place just so I could write on the experience. At the other two stops, I ordered one and we each took a sip. It was a fun day.

By December, we were almost out of books so we quickly had the printer print 2,000 more. We corrected the few typos we found first, but didn't change anything else.

With our travel map almost filled in.

We hadn't been to Colorado yet.

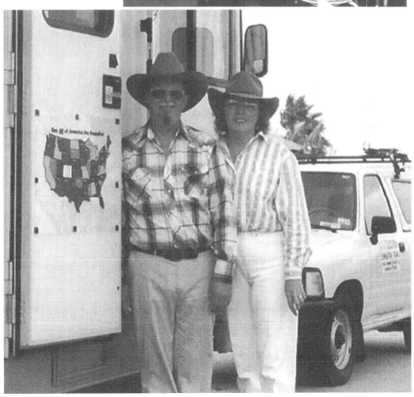

Haunted by an Old Ghost

In December of 1993 Bob was still haunting me. I don't think I had written that a couple years before, in the spring, Bob was still operating the studio successfully, and in fact had just finished taking pictures at a wedding when he returned the film to the studio as well as his equipment and went home. No sooner had he gotten home when he got a call from someone in town saying that his studio was on fire. It was a total loss and he also lost precious wedding pictures and his equipment. The fire department (even though they were all good friends of Bob's) decided that it was a suspicious fire. I thought I knew Bob pretty well and felt fairly sure that even in his most desperate situation, he would never start a fire in which it would ultimately cost someone their precious wedding pictures. But the fire department investigated thoroughly and thought sure that they had proof of fire accelerates. I wasn't there of course but if I had been I would've defended him. The fire started in a basement of the studio which had been the old Grange Hall building. A dry cleaners had operated a cleaning company in that building before we bought it. Linoleum was under the carpeting and it had dry cleaning stuff spilled into it. That was the fire accelerate. He tried to tell them that but the end result was he was prosecuted for arson and found guilty. Poor guy! I felt so sorry for him and even wrote to the judge and told him what I knew. Bob was careless and a procrastinator. He knew the furnace needed cleaning yet he ignored it because it was spring. I suggested to the judge that Bob was probably thinking summer was just around the corner when he wouldn't need the furnace. I knew that would be his thinking. Why fix it now; wait till fall. Anyway, because of the fire, he lost all his business and he defaulted on the second mortgage on the building that he and I had both signed a long time ago.

Now back to December 1993. We were very comfortably settled

in Outdoor Resorts in South Padre Island, Texas, when I got a telegram from HUD telling me (just me) that I owed over $9000 and when I called they were downright nasty. Bob and I had been divorced for over 10 years; they had a hard time finding me because I got married and moved. But now that they found me they wanted their money. I called the lawyer that handled our divorce and Bob. Neither one was any help. I talked to the gal at HUD again she said she'd take $3500. Ron assured me that since she had already lowered the amount, she would even take less. I started by telling her that we lived on the road because we had no other home and so on. I can't remember how much I had to pay or how I did it but somehow $1200 sticks in my mind. It still makes me mad to this day.

Just a little footnote — we had had our second mortgage with the local Savings and Loan in Ortonville, Michigan. When they went belly-up during the S & L crisis of the late 80's and early 90's, HUD took over. So that's the end of that story.

Hitting the Big Time

We thought it would never happen because it had been five months since we first heard that we were going to be taped for a segment on Good Morning America. Finally on January 20, 1994, I got a message from Kathleen Friary, the producer for Mr. Matheson. She wanted to set a time for the taping. I returned her call and we talked several times before their scheduled arrival on January 27. She explained that she and her crew of two (cameraman and soundman) would spend two days filming us at Outdoor Resorts in Port Isabel, Texas, where we were staying. Tyler Matheson would not be coming since he was scheduled to go to Hong Kong for three weeks; they would film his part separately.

I thought it was funny when she called a day later and said she needed another copy of the book and asked if I would have the publisher send a courier with one across town. I figured she thought we had a New York publisher; I shipped her one overnight express. She had also asked if we could find a couple of couples who would be willing to be filmed. We immediately thought of the new full-timing couple who we enjoyed. Don and Kay Slattery were excited to be asked. The day before the film crew was to arrive, Kay had her hair done and they washed their motorhome. But at 4 AM on the day the film crew was arriving, there was a knock on our door. The security guard came to tell us that Don was just taken to the hospital by ambulance; he was apparently having a heart attack. Ron was concerned because Kay had left her car there so he took it to the hospital and waited a while to bring her back. Don was in ICU but would be okay.

Preparations were made for the interview part right away. We had miniature microphones attached to us with tape and we were positioned so we were seated a little ways from the motorhome but with the full view of our surroundings. Kathleen began asking questions. "How did you decide to go full-time?" I started by explaining Ron's heart attack, our trip to San Diego, and the realization that this country was so big and we could never see it all even in long trips. Kathleen said that it was good, but she wanted it shorter so they did it again and again and again and again until it was just right for her. We had to do that with each question until we got the hang of "short and sweet" answers.

She explained that the entire spot would only be three or four minutes long and they wanted to get a lot in; short, precise, answers were a must. The whole interview process took almost 2 hours by the time everything was set up and all. Neighbors watched from across the street. Every time there was a distraction—even seagulls coming too close with their screeching call, the shot had to be re-done. It was amazing how much those small microphones picked up. One time the scene had to be re-done because someone way far away was using a power saw.

Once the interview part was done, we had to do a few things in and out of doors. They shot us coming out of the motorhome and going for a short walk. They had Ron open a compartment, put down an awning and I had to open a compartment to get a book. Inside, they had Ron on the couch reading, they had me at the computer, they shot us making the bed, frosting a cake that was sitting out and several other things. The cameraman wanted to show how long the motorhome was so he had me sitting on the bed and reading, while the camera was rolling he turned around and walked to Ron positioned on the couch. But he was a big guy (6'3" tall) with a big camera and kept bumping into things so that had to be shot many times. That never did use that in the piece but it was a good try.

They did a lot of things: Jerry, the cameraman, got up on the roof and panned the whole campground. Another time he sat on the hood of their car filming as Dave drove through the whole length of one loop (about a mile). They filmed the clubhouse, people playing golf, people on the tennis court, swimming and so on. They finished filming about 5:30 that day with us arriving at the potluck with our cake and sitting down to have dinner with our friends. Before they left, they gave us instructions for the next day. They wanted to film us moving the motorhome and wanted to start early.

The next day's filming began with me driving the motorhome out of its slot then Ron hooked up the car under the watchful eye of Jerry's camera. He got close-ups of us going into the motorhome, taking our seats, and pressing in the tape of Willie Nelson singing "On the Road Again". As we slowly drove out of the campground he filmed us from inside and out and then did it all again. Traffic got tied up a little with all the stopping and starting. Once out of the park itself we were given the driving sequences. We were to cross the causeway to South Padre Island several times. Each trip was filmed from a different angle culminating with Jerry actually sitting in the trunk of their rental car just in front of the motorhome. He kept motioning for us to come closer and closer. At one point there wasn't three feet between us. Another time he was sitting out of the passenger window of the car, riding along to film the side of the motorhome while moving. It was easy for us, we just had to keep making the loop. I think we crossed the bridge six to eight times. Then we drove the length of the island several times. All the while the camera was in different spots. Before they finished, they did some filming of Ron using the ATM in the shopping center and me checking voice mail by using a pay phone. They were done filming by about two o'clock in the afternoon then packed up and were gone to catch a four o'clock plane from Brownsville.

The segment was supposed to air February 9 between 7:30 and 8 a.m. and was announced at the beginning of that half-hour. But the live interview on prostate cancer with the doctor at the Mayo clinic was not good. Robert Goulet was next and was only supposed to be on for a minute or so, but he was so good talking about his bout with prostate cancer the producer canned the full-timing spot and kept Goulet on. Kathleen called and said it could be on any day and to just keep watching. Our friends and family didn't know what happened. On February 15 at 7:43 a.m., it was on without being announced at the beginning of the half-hour. Just as Kathleen had said, they like to have taped segments that they can throw in "just in case" and that is what happened.

It cost them a bundle to film that piece. They had to fly the crew to us, rent cars, and so on. The short shots of Tyler were filmed in Virginia; Tyler and Kathleen flew there just for that "stand up" part. Add to that all the time spent in editing. Out of the 43,000 books published that year, very few made it to GMA. We really felt honored that they thought enough of our book to spend that kind of money helping to promote it. And we were excited because it opened a lot of doors. All we had to mention was that we were on Good Morning America and like magic doors were opened.

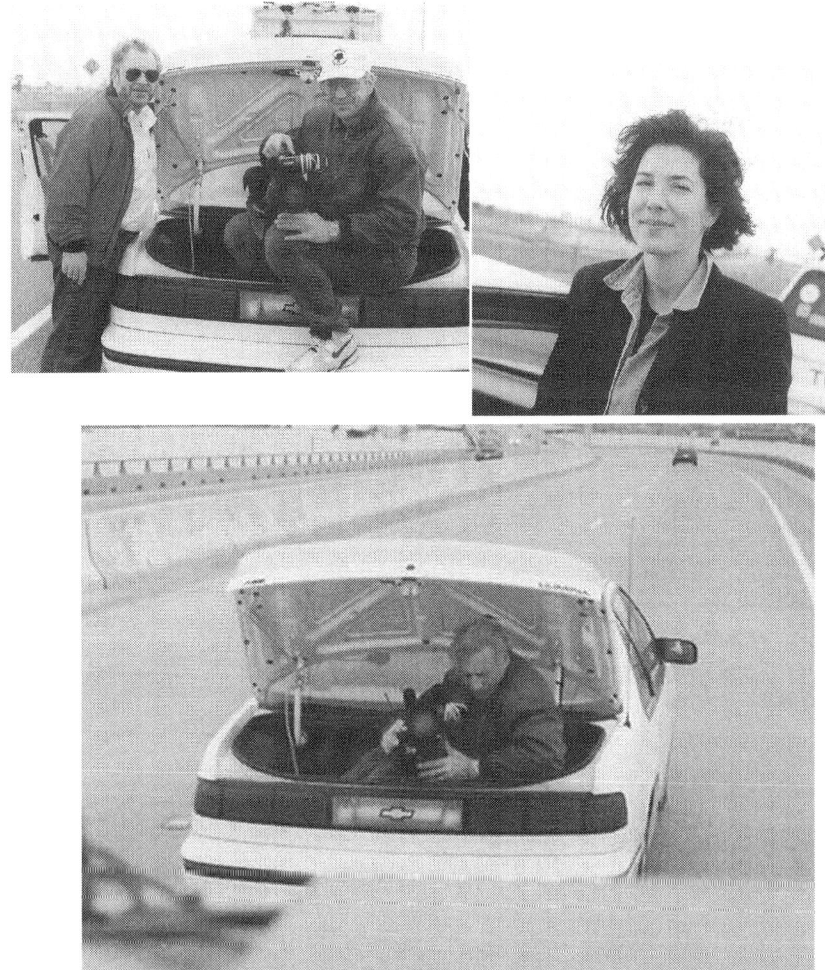

Jerry on the road and filming three feet in front of us.

Busy, Busy, Busy

Early in March we left South Padre Island and headed to San Antonio where we had made arrangements to attend a national Coast-To-Coast rally. There were to be thousands there so we had decided to rent a booth in the trade show. We had made arrangements to rent a television with a tape player also so we could play a tape of our appearance on GMA in our booth. Besides having a space at the trade show we were scheduled to do a seminar that had been well publicized.

After the three day rally we were exhausted. Yes it was good for business but we vowed we would never do such again. We sold a lot of books and got a lot of subscriptions for the newsletter but it was too much work. We did get to meet a lot of new and old friends which was nice.

It was an easy drive to Big Bend National Park and we settled in to relax for a few days. I really needed to rest my voice as I was hoarse. While there we had a chance to talk about our experience at the rally. Ron came up with a fantastic idea. Even though his ideas always caused me more work they were usually good. He suggested that our seminars might best be performed at an RV dealer and after we finished our presentation those attending could buy our book and pick out their new home. Ron thought RV dealers would go for it and we wouldn't have to promote ourselves—"They'll do it for us".

I took the ball and ran with it first calling an RV dealer in New Mexico. He was excited about the idea even though they didn't have a lot of space to work with. They came up with a terrific idea to put chairs in one of the service bays and open it up. He arranged for us to be on a radio show early on the morning of the seminar. We went to a truck stop so we could have a phone at our table. I had a little gadget that allowed us to put the suction cup on the telephone we were talking on and we could both hear what was going on. That way we could both hear the question that was being asked and decide which of us would answer it. At

5 AM as requested, I called the radio station. In late morning (as I remember) we went to the RV dealer for the seminar. They had it set up with a lot of chairs but by seminar time it was standing room only. They scrambled around to find more chairs and we had a great seminar selling a ton of books. Everyone was excited.

Because that worked so well I started making calls to RV dealers in Colorado because we were heading that way. We picked one in Colorado Springs which sold Bounders and they were excited to schedule a seminar. It was tremendously well attended and we had fun meeting all who wanted to hit the road as we had. There was no advance publicity. They had come on just a couple of hours notice (from a radio show) to hear our seminar. Ron always had great ideas.

Stumbling Blocks in Colorado

By mid-May we were in Colorado and I absolutely fell in love. The mountains were bigger than any I'd seen before. It was awesome. But I couldn't breathe. But there again we were one mile high or more. The main reason we moved to Colorado besides wanting to visit it was Ron had seen an article about the world renowned National Jewish Center for Respiratory Diseases which was an outpatient hospital dedicated to treat breathing problems. I had called and made an appointment. I've been having breathing problems since we were at Yosemite breathing campfires day and night for two months. Doctors in Oregon and Texas tried to help me but nothing was working. So I was hopeful they could do something for me at National Jewish. Because my appointment wasn't until little later in the month we had time to do a little touring. Several things we enjoyed were Colorado Springs, the Air Force Academy, Salida, a Rockies ball game, and we even took the cog railway up to Pike's Peak.

It was hard to find campgrounds near Denver which was where the hospital was. We did find a pretty city campground in Golden (home of Coors Brewery) but were only able to stay there for a couple weeks because they have a limit on the amount of time one could stay. But that short time there was delightful. Then we moved to an okay park in Wheatridge.

At the hospital they ran tests and determined that the valve from my esophagus to my stomach never closed. That condition was probably caused by Theophylline (a medicine prescribed to help my breathing). It caused the weakening of the lower esophageal sphincter. Plus they discovered I had a large hiatal hernia. I was also diagnosed with GERD (gastroesophageal reflux disease) for which there is no cure but can be controlled by diet. They recommended surgery to fix the sphincter and the hernia. When I asked the question I had rehearsed many times (where in the United States is the best place to go for that?) they suggested nearby at University Hospital in Denver. They set up an appointment for me to meet with the pulmonary surgeon they thought would best do the job. If I hadn't had so many surgeries in my life the operation could have been simple. Instead the surgeon had to cut from under my left breast all the way around the side to the middle of my back. Yes, I was in a lot of pain after surgery. But they promised me I'd feel better soon. I was in the hospital about seven days.

In preparation for surgery, Ron and I both began walking daily and dieted. I had lost 15 pounds prior to surgery and more after because it was difficult to eat. Anytime you tamper with the esophagus things slow down a little bit. I had to eat small bites slowly and chew thoroughly.

Before I went into the hospital, knowing that we would be there for a while, I looked in the Yellow Pages under physicians to find a doctor that Ron could go to for his annual physical. I found one early in the B's and made an appointment for Ron with Dr. Baumgarten for July 13. Ron wanted to cancel the appointment when it turned out to be the day after I got home from my surgery but I convinced him to keep the appointment, "After all," I said, "it was just a routine physical." In preparation for the appointment he had already had the fasting blood work done.

After his physical, he came home to share very bad news. The doctor told Ron he had an irregular heartbeat, was a diabetic, and probably had prostate cancer. I dearly wished that I could have gone with him. I felt so bad that he had to drive home alone without me and with that dark cloud hanging over him. It was almost impossible to deal with all three bad things at once so we picked the worst—the prostate problem.

The PSA blood test which screens for prostate cancer was not only positive but very high (37). Dr. Baumgarten made an appointment for Ron to see Dr. Abernathy, a urologist at nearby Lutheran Medical Center.

Dr. Abernathy did a biopsy and reported that four of the six samples were malignant. Right away he ordered a bone scan and another blood test to see if the cancer had spread then surgery was scheduled for September 1.

I woke up that morning feeling great. At least we would know what we were dealing with and how to fight it. It was the "not knowing" that was so horrible. The doctor had explained it would take about one hour from the start of surgery to get the results on the lymph nodes, if negative they would continue with the operation. It would be about three hours total before Ron was in recovery. I remember looking at my watch and noted it had been one hour and 10 minutes and breathed a little easier thinking that the surgery was continuing which meant that the cancer had not spread. At just that moment, Dr. Abernathy entered the waiting room and motioned for me to come with him to a private room. I told him that I didn't want to see him yet and he understood.

The doctor explained that the cancer had spread and it was evident to the naked eye. One lymph node was very large, hard and the lab reported it was totally consumed with cancer. The doctor went on to say, That there is no cure for prostate cancer once it has metastasized; radiation or chemotherapy do not work". But it can be slowed down by hormone therapy (decreasing the production of testosterone). I felt like I had been kicked in the stomach, but the doctor went on to reassure me that since Ron was symptom free, we should continue with our life on the road, get checkups every three or four months and we should have some good years yet. I asked him how many years and he answered with "two."

When I went back out to the waiting room, I was surprised and delighted to see that the pastor from the church we had been attending was at the counter asking where he could find me. He was just the person I needed to see. I remember thinking that was great timing but he assured me it was more than that. He got lost on the way there which he assured me was exactly what God had in mind. I told him I needed to make some phone calls and he asked me if I'd like him to come with me and I said, "Yes". My first call was to Ron's mom who took the news bravely. Next on my list was Ron's oldest daughter, Marty and I knew that would be difficult. It was. It was so frustrating for them to be so far away and not able to be near. I assured them I would give them a phone number once he was back in a room.

After he got home and was recovering Ron and I talked at great length about what to do. We decided we needed a second opinion and it would be good if it was somewhere other than Colorado since it had snowed once already. We decided on the Mayo Clinic in Arizona and made appointments there as well as reservations at an upscale RV Park (Valle del Oro) in Mesa, Arizona.

What originally started as a three-week stay in Colorado had turned into three months plus. We really liked Colorado, but we were becoming too familiar. It was like grass was growing under our feet and so on September 30 we pulled up stakes and headed South.

Liisa, Erkki and Glenda came to visit after my surgery and Dave came after Ron's surgery .

A Phone in My Home

Arizona was great for the two month's we were there. The Mayo Clinic was wonderful too. They confirmed what Dr. Abernathy had said, the only treatment for Ron was hormone therapy. He got his first shot of Lupron before we left Colorado and already his PSA was almost zero. That shot would last for several months then we would get the next shot somewhere along whatever road we took.

We had been in Arizona for a little while one April which was nice but October and November seemed even better weather wise. Valle del Oro was a wonderful place to have to sit for two months. It was centrally located to shopping malls and anything one would need but the best part was the activities in that park. I was so impressed that I did a whole newsletter on all the activities and goings on there. One could learn such things as lapidary, sewing, quilting, tennis, pool, painting, sculpturing, and any kind of card game all the while enjoying dances, parties, potlucks and whatever else you could think of.

We met a whole bunch of wonderful people while we were either playing cards or at the pool and I decided that I could live there but Ron just laughed; he said that I say that all the time. I must have been easily impressed.

The thing I liked best about being in that park was we had a real phone in our motorhome. It was an honest-to-goodness phone. After over five years without one of my own I had forgotten how nice they were. Since we were going to be in one spot for two months and they had a good deal on the phone, we opted to take it. Right away the kids started calling and we felt very normal. We even had a phone book which to us was a little like heaven because any of the phone books we ever found in a pay phone were torn and tattered and attached to a cable that wouldn't allow them to be looked at easily. When in a strange place, trying to find a business was hard without a phone book.

Our time there went fast and we had several visitors. Ron's

mom flew to spend a little while with on us as did Ron's daughter, Marty. We had time to show them around a little and I think they enjoyed it. Some of our subscribers stopped by and that was also a joy.

Business had been very good too. We had just ordered our fourth printing of the book and more and more bookstores were carrying it. The Arizona Republic interviewed us and we did a book signing at Camping World (they finally agreed to stock our books). We did a radio show interview from our in-home telephone, for a station in Salina, Kansas. We also did a seminar at an RV dealer in Mesa and we were on live TV (Channel 10) as a remote from our motorhome which was really good. It not only promoted our book but it promoted the seminar as well.

We had promised Ron's kids and our sisters we would fly back to Michigan for Christmas. We hated to leave the beautiful weather in Arizona but everyone had been so worried about both of us that it was the least we could do. We wanted them to see that we were okay. We put the motorhome in storage (with the refrigerator empty) and had the shuttle take us to the airport in Phoenix. When we landed in Detroit, Ron slipped because it was icy and I heard him say, "What are we doing here?" We had a great time with family though so it was a very worthwhile trip.

In heaven with a phone

After the plane landed back in Arizona, we took the shuttle to our motorhome, got in and drove to a little shopping area where the Applebee's restaurant was. We got out jumping up and down like we were kids just let out of school for summer break. It was that good to be back on our own and with wheels on our house. After a nice dinner at the restaurant we took the motorhome to a small campground nearby and stayed for just a couple days before taking off for California. Life was great.

Our Christmas Picture 1994

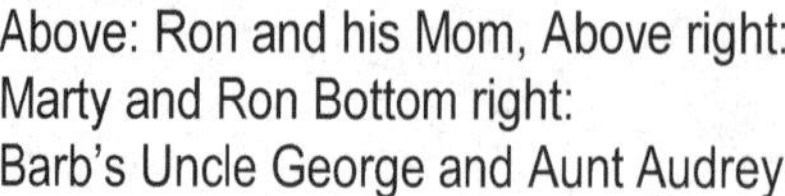
Above: Ron and his Mom, Above right: Marty and Ron Bottom right: Barb's Uncle George and Aunt Audrey

A Big Circle

We spent a wonderful couple weeks in the Palm Springs area of California which was filled with visits with lots of friends who wintered there. Esther and I discovered the fun of shopping in resale shops in Palm Springs. They were full of designer outfits at good prices. Ron and I drove up to see my son, Mark, for a couple days, drove over to the coast to see Ron's cousin, Hollis, and just plain enjoyed being in the area.

We had a little bit of difficulty there when it was time for Ron to get his Lupron shot. We couldn't find a doctor who was willing to do it. We finally had to go to an emergency room which seemed totally ridiculous. After waiting for hours and being checked over by a doctor for all of two seconds, he got his shot. The nurse saw how stupid the situation was and showed me how to do it. She said I should get a prescription for the medicine, have it sent by way of our mail-order pharmacy and do it myself. That was a wonderful idea because during those two hours Ron was very frustrated and he kept thinking that to stay alive we were going to have to pull off the road. From that time on I did it for him and it was a whole lot cheaper for Medicare that way.

We were in death Valley by early in February and had a good time camping there. We didn't have any hookups so we got out the Coleman stove and my old coffee pot and enjoyed being rustic. We had never been there before and it was fun exploring that mind-boggling area. From there we spent several days in Vegas with our good friends, Jim and Norma from Michigan, and visited the Hoover Dam before going back to Arizona. In Arizona we investigated the old town of Jerome as well as the Tuzigoot National Monument. That was a very enjoyable circle trip. And I had stories I could use in the next newsletter. It seemed we had to keep playing tourist to sell all the books we had on hand. It was a large investment. Since we were the publishers of the book, we had all the expense. We wondered if the tail was wagging the dog. It was.

We had to go back to Arizona because early in March we were doing a seminar at the Coast-to-Coast rally there. We were not going to have a booth though. We found an RV dealer who had a booth and agreed to take care of our books sales for us.

Our seminar at the rally was terrific and was fully attended. Everyone was enthusiastic and loved what we did. Our seminars were very polished. We always took turns talking and we each had our own subjects that we talked about much like we did when writing the book. Ron talked about choosing the right motorhome and finances where I talked about organization and where we go and what we do. I also talked about family and medical and Ron would talk about insurance and so forth. We had well rehearsed seminars that looked spontaneous and very professional — at least that's what everyone always said.

Right: Cooking outside at Death Valley

Below:
Me, Ron, Jack and Esther

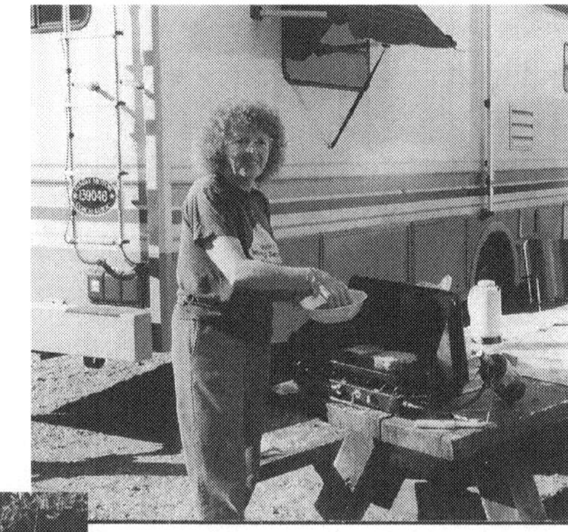

Up the Coast and...

From that rally in Phoenix we headed back to California and then eventually all the way up the coast with stops in lots of fun places. We were meeting new people all the time. Book sales were great. Most of the major bookstores carried our book, libraries all across the United States had our book and we were doing seminars regularly. We had to reprint the book again. Because we had gone through five printings already, we decided to print 5000 at one time hoping that maybe we wouldn't have to print every year.

We had been scheduled to do a seminar at the Camping World store in Saugus, California. We showed up but they weren't ready for us. Either they had the wrong date or we did. They expected us on February 25, our readers and we thought it was on March 25. But we stayed around anyway in case some of our readers showed up and they did. We met a couple of gals, Judy and Cec, who had driven a long way to get there so we were glad we stayed. That lesbian couple went on the road shortly after we met them. They became one of our best friends on the road and they were always there when we needed them. More about them later.

I wish I could share all the wonderful news stories printed about us. I have most of the articles saved on big poster boards but there's no way I could include them. It would have cost us millions of dollars to get the kind of publicity those articles gave us. We were even in USA Today which really generated a lot of books sales. But it only worked because we finally got our book in bookstores so that people could run out and buy the book after they read about it. If they had to write a letter, include a check and send it off to order a book by mail they probably wouldn't have bothered. Now with the Internet it would've been a piece of cake too but we didn't have Internet back then.

On this trip we went back to Yosemite just for a couple nights, visited Sequoia National Park, Morro Bay, Sacramento, Reno, the

Oregon coast, Portland, Seattle, and the Olympic Peninsula of Washington and took 3 months to do it.

My son Robert was stationed at Port Townsend in Washington and we were excited to be able to spend a month in that town so we could see him once in a while. While there we were corresponding with Ron's oldest son, Karl, and oldest daughter, Marty, because we were planning a nice vacation for their two daughters (our granddaughters). Because we had my granddaughter Liisa with us at Yosemite for two weeks, it made us think about having other grandchildren come and join us as they got to an appropriate age. That way we would get to know them better and vice versa. We had decided that when grandchildren were between nine and 12 we would invite them to join us. Because we were limited on space in the motorhome, I tried to impress upon them to limit their packing to absolute necessities. I planned menus and an itinerary because we were going to be going on essentially a three-week vacation with these girls. We were looking forward to Mary and Erika's (nine-year-old cousins) visit and we were heading east to Spokane, Washington, where we would pick them up. We chose that town as the arrival place for the girls because it wasn't a huge airport and it was fairly close to places we intended to go. We wanted to take them to Glacier National Park in Montana and Yellowstone in Wyoming then back to Spokane. We had planned lots of stops along the way and I had actually made reservations which was something we almost never did in our regular traveling. They and we were looking forward to our fun vacation.

After conferring with their parents, we bought the plane tickets from a travel agent in Morro Bay, California, and she did a terrific job of coordinating two different planes to come at the same time. Mary flew from Tulsa, Oklahoma, and Erika flew from Detroit. They arrived on July 11, within a half hour of each other and at two different gates in the same airport. They were so excited to see each other because it had been a little while since they had been together. Mary moved from Michigan to Kansas a year of so before. From the airport, we made the short drive back to the motorhome, got them settled and the next morning we took off on our vacation. It was fun from the very first moment. We taught them how to read a map and had them take turns following along on the map. We also taught them to play dominoes and pinochle and enjoyed many evenings of playing games. Besides taking them on lots of hikes, I had them keep a journal. I encouraged them to read all the signs in the national parks and even gave them little quizzes. They became Junior Rangers in the parks we visited and that was another learning experience for them. They were excited about everything we showed them from wild flowers in Glacier to buffalo, mud pots, and hot springs in Yellowstone. We went to Ranger programs and at our campfire we roasted marshmallows. It was a wonderful vacation. Best of all, we got to know them better and visa versa.

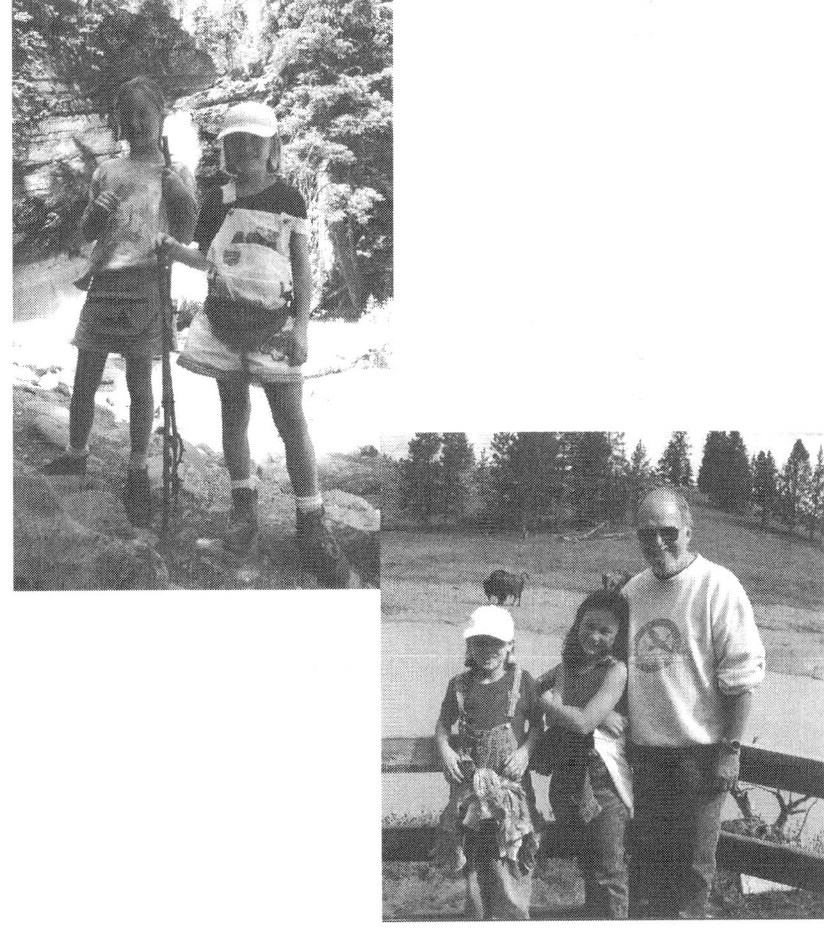

Rafting the Salmon River

The girls left on August 1 and we headed south into Idaho. I had been wanting to go rafting on a fast River. Since it was August none of the rivers were that fast but the Salmon River promised to be exciting and we decided on an overnight trip. Tourist information on the River said that it flowed through the largest wilderness area in the lower 48 states so that sounded interesting. The rafting company provided the tents, sleeping bags, "keep dry bags" and all the food. Our guide, Skip, was our cook and captain. We were the only ones on the trip.

We had to take a van ride to the put-in point which was just under two hours away on a narrow, rough, national forest road. The road which was nearly level with the river wound along the Salmon as it made its way through the canyons and open areas. There was not another soul around. We were full of anticipation especially when we saw some of the famous white water. Indians learned early on that the river will not let you paddle back upstream thus its nickname — *the River of No Return*.

It was about 10:30 in the morning when we entered the river. We didn't even have to paddle; our competent guide, Skip, did all the work. There were no other rafts on the river; it was very peaceful. This was the trip of my dreams. We had been rafting many times before and I always had to paddle. That was too much like work. This was just plain relaxing. When we started Skip made sure we knew that we were guests and we were to simply enjoy the whole trip.

After about an hour on the river, Skip brought the raft to shore at a sand bank and said he wanted to show us something special. We walked and talked about the area as he took us on a path along a foundation of an old home. From early on it was obvious that someone had lived there long ago. There was a whole row of Irises along what was left of a stone wall. Now completely overgrown, it seemed sad that someone had loved them once but no more. Then came the blackberries. They too had been lovingly planted but were now overgrown. The bushes were loaded with big, bulging berries. We picked as we walked along, sometimes standing a little longer to pick a bunch more. There were millions, but the bushes were so thick that it was nearly impossible to get to a lot of them. We were having so much fun picking berries that for a while we didn't even realize we were climbing. We kept following Skip as he slowly led the way up; the river below us kept getting smaller and smaller. Near the top, was a small log building with windows and curtains. Inside was a hollowed out log into which hot spring water flowed constantly filling the log. There was a bench for sitting and a nice wooden floor. Skip left us there to soak while he went just a little ways down the hill to another hot spring in a cave.

After our soak Skip went on ahead to fix lunch which was really excellent. We had pita bread, and turkey salad, tuna salad, cheese slices, grapes, cold soda, small bags of chips and fresh chocolate chip cookies. Best of all was the turkey salad which had finely chopped apples and raisins added to the turkey and blended with Miracle Whip. Maybe it all tasted better because we didn't have to do anything to fix it and we were in God's country.

After lunch we continued rafting. Although the scenery was breathtaking, Skip kept us entertained with tales of different people and events in history. We later learned that most of his stories were made up. He was a great storyteller. At about 4:30 in the afternoon we reached the place where we would camp for the night—a nice long, wide, sandy beach. Immediately he put up our tents (ours and his) and gave us our bags so we could get out our sleeping bags and so on. While we were doing that, he set up the kitchen shelter. Dinner was baked potatoes, perfectly

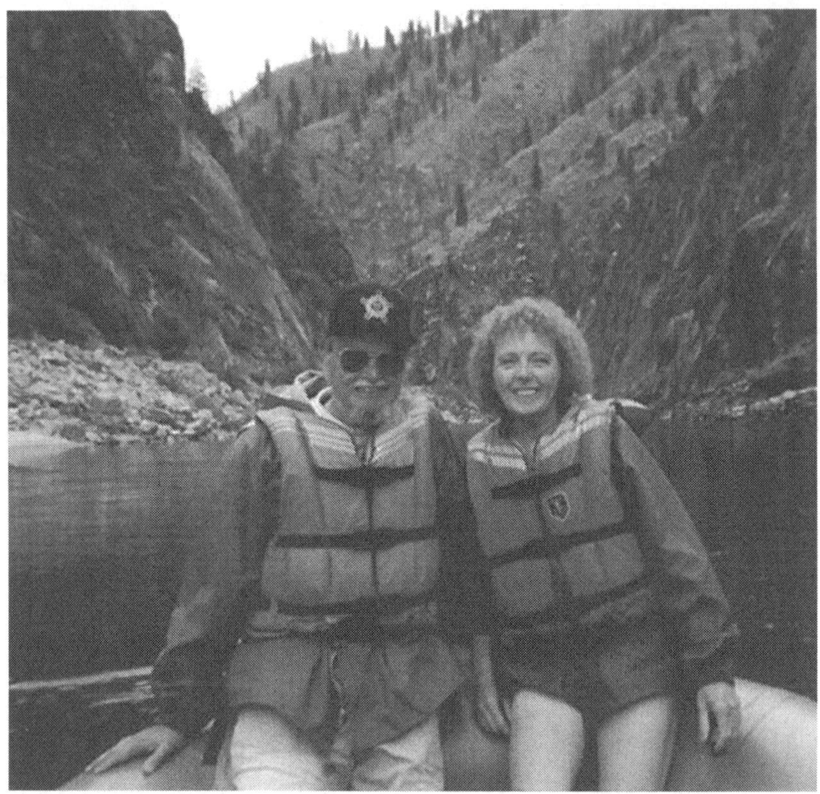

done steak, fresh salad, dinner rolls and drinks. We even had strawberry shortcake for dessert. All were served on real plates with real silverware. Nothing plastic on this trip. This was a first class operation. Skip still wouldn't let us do anything. It started raining and we wished we had brought a book to read but we hadn't thought of that.

We went to bed when the sun went down and tried to get comfortable. I wished for a small pillow. Shortly after we got in bed, it rained harder. Loud crashes of thunder and lightning that lit up the sky continued all night. It was scary. We stayed nice and dry, but my concern was that it would never stop. I certainly did not want to be on a raft in that kind of weather. I prayed hard. But Ron had a different concern. He gets up a lot to go to the bathroom and we didn't have a "pee" can so he had to get wet.

Thankfully the rain did stop just before we got up in the morning. The River had risen a few inches due to the deluge. But Skip was in control; he was busy making breakfast and packing up.

He fixed blueberry pancakes, eggs, sausage, coffee, juice, melon and grapes for breakfast and it was delicious. The sun was promising to come out by 10:30 a.m., as we headed down the river again for the most exciting part of the trip.

Rivers are rated on a scale of one to six with six being unnavigable. We were going to go through 10 rapids which were rated three and four at that time of the year. In the spring they are rated even higher. They were as exciting as I had dreamed. It was like a soft roller coaster ride. Skip skillfully steered us through the heart of some of the largest waves. He was good! He made sure we got real wet more than once. More people raft (day trips) on the second half of that river trip so we had company. In fact at our lunch stop, Skip unloaded our gear and a second couple was added for the final stretch. We were glad that we had had the two days; they were as different as night and day and we loved both.

Good News

After the river trip we stayed in Idaho for a while traveling south enjoying state parks, touring and discovering new things. One of the interesting campgrounds was Craters of the Moon. It was full of lava formed spires and shapes. This very desolate area was created not by a volcano but fissure vents, volcanic cones which began erupting 15,000 years ago. What a contrast when compared to Idaho's Ponderosa State Park a short distance away. It was a beautifully wooded campground. Idaho is certainly an interesting and beautiful state.

From there we played in Western Colorado which was another favorite of ours and explored such places as Silverton, Ouray, Telluride, and Durango. We even added the train trip from Durango to Silverton. And we visited Mesa Verde National Park.

From there we were back in New Mexico and on our way to Texas where we had planned to present a seminar and attend the bounder rally which was being held near San Antonio the middle of October. And as long as we were going to be in Texas, we decided to go back to Outdoor Resorts on South Padre Island. We even made our reservation for four months and ordered our telephone.

The rally was excellent and we met a lot of new friends as well as reconnected with old friends. Here's a funny little note which was in my This 'n That column in October 1995 newsletter.

> "My son, Robert, who has a new computer was looking through the Good Morning America menu on the Internet, found us and got excited. Did you know we were there and that you can also order our book on the Internet? I have never seen what the Internet looks like so don't know for sure what this means."

It was good to be back at Outdoor Resorts and see all our old friends and get back into a routine. Ron fished, I took watercolor classes, we golfed, played cards and dominoes, ate out, I cooked in and we just lived a fairly normal life for the four months we were there. The thing I didn't like about South Padre was the wind which always blew. Sometimes I felt like I was getting beaten up. I was campaigning to go Arizona the next winter.

We gave our newsletter readers a Christmas present. The January issue was 14 pages long. I must've been crazy. We had a couple of guest articles that made it longer. Because we weren't traveling, we didn't have any travelogue to include of our own. One of the guest articles was about Alaska written by Betty the gal who edited our book. We had no intention of going to Alaska and people kept asking us when we were going to write about it so to satisfy them we let Betty and Clyde tell their story. They had a Bounder motorhome also.

While in Texas Ron kept saying he wanted to take the motorhome to Mexico, but I put my foot down. I didn't mind going to the little border towns for a few hours but had heard too many horror stories about what happened to people in RVs in Mexico. So we decided to take a seven day bus tour to Mexico City. It was okay but I really didn't like the regimentation of the tour schedule. Getting up early with the suitcases packed was not my mode of travel. And Mexico City with guards carrying submachine guns everywhere was not very appealing either. I was glad when we got back home.

Ron's checkups had been wonderful; his PSA's were zero and we felt that cancer was no longer a problem. Praise the Lord.

On April 1 we left Texas and headed up the road. Our immediate destinations were Missouri, Illinois and Michigan.

"I Can't See"

It was fun to have family to visit along the way. Karl had recently moved to Kansas, Jim lived in Missouri and David happened to be living in Illinois so we visited all three on our way to Michigan. We were on our way to attend a regional Family Motorcoach rally in southern Michigan the end of May. We had several good seminars there. Just before we were about to leave Ron said that he was having a hard time seeing; his glasses bothered him. He had had new nose pads put on his glasses in Kansas on our way up from Texas (we were visiting Ron's son Karl and his wife worked in an optometrist's office). There was a long line of motorhomes leaving the exit of the campground and once out of the park, the road was narrow and without a shoulder. Suddenly Ron said that he couldn't see. I got up from the passenger seat, stood behind him and told him to slow down, carefully brake by tapping them first (to let those behind know he was stopping) then stop the motorhome, put it in park then quickly get up. I immediately jumped into the driver seat, shifted into gear and took off.

As soon as we got to our home park in Davison, Ron jumped out of the motorhome to unhook the truck and in backing up, he crashed into the huge water station near the office. There was an immediate geyser and our whole back end was bashed in.

I took Ron to the mall to see the optometrist. The optometrist examined him and said the problem wasn't with his glasses; he needed to see an ophthalmologist. So we did that the same day. The doctor diagnosed him with having ocular myasthenia gravis. He told him it would take about three months for the double vision to go away and gave him some medicine. In the meantime I was it, as far as driving went. That was bad news because I had always been the navigator and Ron didn't do a good job reading a map even when he could see clearly. I did both for a while (not at the same time). The doctor was right; his eyes cleared up nicely by the time we got to Tennessee three months later.

We enjoyed our summer in Michigan mainly visiting family. I announced in the July issue that we were going to have to have another printing of the book but that we would first update a few things to make it up to date before we did.

We purchased new bicycles while we were in Michigan because the ones we had were very rusted from setting out in the salt air of South Padre island. Several big city papers like The Detroit News did stories on us so we were still getting lots of publicity. My son, Robert, made a web page for us but I wasn't even online yet. It was very basic but at least we had one. We did a seminar at a Barnes & Noble store in our old hometown which was well attended. And I had decals made for our readers and included them in one newsletter so they could put them on their RV. We were that well known by then that we thought it would be fun for others to be able to find fellow subscribers to Movin' On while on the road.

This was in the May issue of the newsletter.

Important Information

...We love the mail and I want to answer each and every letter personally, but we may have gotten too big for that anymore. I really am torn by this, but it seems we work all the time lately..... Although I am afraid of losing the family feeling I simply won't be able to answer all of the letters and renewals anymore.

.... It takes us the better part of two days to collate, fold, label, staple and stamp your newsletters. We can't even move inside the motorhome with newsletters all over the place. We need to pay to have this service done and we cannot do that at the price we charge you. In fact these printing places actually charge more for folding etc. Our price of $1.50 has not changed since we started charging for the newsletter in 1991 and there have been two big postage increases since then and paper prices have gone out of sight.

Starting July 1 our per issue price will be $2 ($2.25 Canada). We will honor all prepaid subscriptions at the old rate as long as they are postmarked before July 1. Having someone prepare our newsletters for mailing also means that after this issue there will be no personal notes tucked inside. Thank you for understanding our dilemma.

We attended the Escapees rally in Elkhart, Indiana, in September of that year. We enjoyed our best seminar to date. We had a large room and it was packed full. We had even planned (advertised on a bulletin board) a happy hour we were hosting at our campsite so we could meet them all personally. That was a lot of fun.

When we were finished with the rally we slowly headed south (it took us two months) as we took red roads (US routes) all the way. We visited such places as Louisville, Kentucky, Nashville, McMinnville with a visit to get some of Jane's pies, and Lynchburg, Tennessee, home of Jack Daniels bourbon. We tried to visit Fort Knox but they wouldn't let us near the place.

I had been talking with Don Wallace (owner of Lazy Days) in Tampa, Florida, since our new book came. Right away he had ordered 100 copies to give to his employees. I had suggested that we do seminars there during the month of January. He liked the idea a lot and agreed to allow us to have a full hook-up space for free. We thought we could sell a lot of books this way and we did but I'll tell you that story in the next chapter. Our first seminar was to be just a sample on December 7 and in January we would do one on each Tuesday and Saturday at 10:30 AM for the whole month of January.

The decal we had made for everyone on our newsletter mailing list.

The American Dream

We arrived at Lazy Days early in December for our December 7 seminar. We were there for a week and during that time we did a lot of walking around their huge compound looking at hundreds of motorhomes. That part was fun but I was upset: they weren't ready for our seminar. They hadn't advertised and there were no signs up. Way in advance of our arrival I had been talking with Tony, their PR guy. I had been told that he was **the** one who made things happen. We had the feeling that he felt he did all of the advertising Lazy Days ever needed and didn't want us. They hadn't even set up a room for us. They put us out on the noisy patio which was not acceptable but we did the seminar as best we could while competing with loudspeaker announcements and so on. A lot of people had showed up because I had mentioned it in our newsletter. They were completely surprised at the number of people we drew.

I had long talk with Tony after and told him that the Tampa Tribune newspaper would be doing a story on us because I had already contacted them and their local television channel was coming out to interview us live. I added that we deserved to be treated like we were somebody. I remember him looking at me like "who the hell are you". Reluctantly he agreed to let me show him what we did. So we scheduled another seminar for December 19.

In our walks there we had seen one motorhome which really impressed us. It was too beautiful for words. But we weren't sure it was for us, because we still felt comfortable in the Bounder. It had been a terrific coach and was almost as good as new. In fact it only had 28,000 miles on it and everything inside was working perfectly. Because of those things we didn't have to move; I think our success had gone to our head and we just felt we deserved it. But the American Dream was quite pricey (listed at over $200,000). Yet it was so lovely that I wanted it. The color and the options were perfect. The real problem was that for the week we

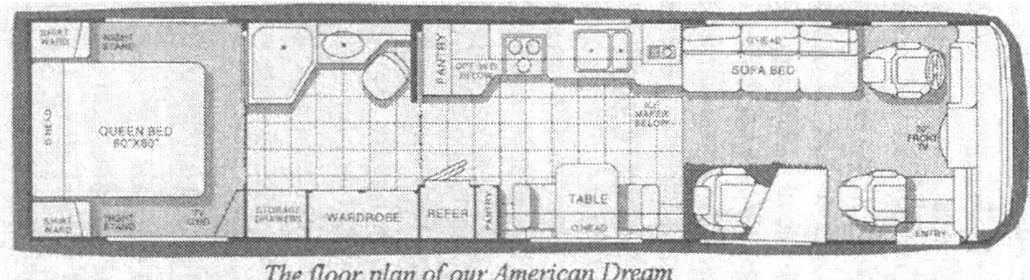

The floor plan of our American Dream

were in Tampa, I looked at that Dream every day. We were too close to it so we left Tampa knowing we would be back in a couple of weeks and went to West Palm Beach to visit my daughter.

I had to call Lazy Days to talk about the December 19 seminar and I just happened to ask if "our" Dream was still on the lot. It was. Ron and I talked and decided then and there to go for it and had them get it ready so we could move in when we were back in Tampa.

Exactly four years prior to that was when we had purchased the Bounder. At 10 feet longer than our Mallard sprinter (the cocoon we started out with) that was like heaven and we called it the mansion. The American Dream was beautiful, luxurious, and exciting and we called that our “castle”. Besides that it had a diesel engine which Ron wanted. It seemed all men wanted a big diesel engine.

Another thing that swayed us in our decision was that we were at Lazy Days the biggest and best RV dealer in the country. We

Ceramic tile floors, Corian© countertops, and luxurious burgundy leather furniture. The exterior was burgundy and white. It was striking.

had been in enough RV dealers across the country to know that no other had customer service or inventory like Lazy Days. Their new place was so large that each of the 50 plus salespeople had their own golf cart. There were over 120 service bays including special carpentry bays, paint booths and everything one could want.

But back to the seminar. I had arranged for the TV station to come out and interview us live for their morning show a couple of days before we actually did our seminar. I had also made arrangements with our salesman to park the Dream next to our Bounder in their campground so when we were on TV we could talk about both motorhomes. We hadn't actually moved into the dream yet because they were going to make some adjustments for us in their specialized carpentry shop. The computer desk had to be modified to fit the printer and the keyboard tray lowered; that was in our deal. The desk actually had to be rebuilt and they had the people to do it. It was beautiful when finished and just perfect for my needs. Also in the deal was to take out the washer and dryer (in the kitchen area) and put in three huge drawers in its place. I also wanted the mattress from our Bounder (because it had been custom made for us) instead of the new mattress but it was six inches too short so they cut a piece of firm foam, covered it then added it to the head of our mattress with Velcro. Once a sheet was on nobody would notice; it was perfect.

Good Day Tampa Bay is on from 7 to 9 every morning. We were on intermittently for the whole show. And we were able to announce the date and time of our upcoming seminar. So on the day of the seminar we overwhelmed Lazy Days by the amount of people who showed up to hear us talk. And after the seminar we overwhelmed them again with the number of people who went out looking at RVs. We knew it worked because we had been doing seminars at RV dealers for a couple of years. Tony was impressed. So we went ahead with the planning for all the seminars in January.

As before, it took us a couple days to move in and it was a bit of an adjustment to know where to put everything. The Dream had less room inside as far as cupboards went and a lot more room outside in those big Greyhound type days. I really loved the kitchen with its microwave/convection oven. And when we were pretty well set we went back to West Palm Beach to spend Christmas with my daughter. I drove the Dream into West Palm Beach and was pretty proud of myself. It was a dream to drive. We parked it in her driveway even though we blocked the sidewalk because we were so long. Christmas was wonderful.

Plans Change Quick

When we were at Lazy Days when we purchased the Bounder, Don Wallace bought 30 copies of our old book and I remembered him telling me that he really valued full-time RVers. He had said something like when the economy was bad families who had to cut back on something cut back on recreational things but full timers would always be in the market for a new house. That's why I knew Don Wallace would like having us do the seminars.

Our first seminars were great and they got better as we went along as far as attendance went. The Tampa Bay/St. Petersburg newspaper article about us (Sunday paper) was gigantic. It was two full pages with pictures and included detailed information about the seminar times and place. After that came out our seminars were standing room only. Both Don and Tony loved us even more than ever and they really understood the draw that we had. I even remember seeing different important people from the staff sitting in on some of our seminars. And at the end of each seminar we suggested that people go out and pick out their new home which they often did. At least they looked. Don told me later that he wished he had a nickel for everyone who bought an RV after hearing our seminars. We knew many who bought and they weren't shopping for used RVs either. Most bought new, expensive motorhomes similar to ours.

At our last seminar in January Tony presented us with a huge bouquet of 12 of the most perfect blush roses I had ever seen in my life and a gigantic fruit and cheese basket with a bottle of Dom Perignon champagne (with two champagne glasses) in the middle of it and invited us to come back any time. We told them we would like that. They were happy and so were we.

We had everything planned so we could take a nice leisurely trip to Colorado. Stops from Tampa would include, Titusville, Jacksonville, Savannah, Macon, Columbus (GA), Montgomery, Mobile, (Al), Jackson (MS), Memphis, Little Rock, St. Louis, Wichita, Amarillo, Silver City, and finally Coaldale, Colorado.

We didn't need to be in Coaldale, Colorado, until May 19 (we were planning my 60th birthday party) so we would've had plenty of time.

We were in Jacksonville, Florida, when we checked our voice mail and there was a message from the Escapees organization asking if we could please present our full timing seminar at the escapade in Chico, California, towards the end of April. We felt so honored to be asked (founders Joe and Kay had always done that seminar) that we said, "Yes." As long as we were going to be in California, we thought it would be fun to attend the FMCA (Family Motor Coach Association) National Convention which would be held March 20 in Pomona, California. So we tossed aside the first plan and we mapped out a new route (mostly interstate) which would help us move along at a good clip. On the way we stopped in Atlanta for a while and then went to Hot Springs, Arkansas. We even took one of those special baths again in Hot Springs. We made a short stop at White Sands National Park in New Mexico and I stopped in to see my dad and Frankie at their assisted living place in Silver City.

The FMCA rally was terrific; they had a lot of people there but the Escapade was the best yet. Our seminar was in a very large room which was filled to the brim and everyone listened very attentively. I would guess there were 7 to 800 in attendance. Prior to our seminar we had a happy hour for our readers and that was very well attended also. We had so many friends and we loved them all.

Together at last

In 18 years my children had only been together once and that was for only part of a day. They lived in vastly different parts of the country and have at different times even lived overseas. For my 60th birthday I asked Ron if we could get them all together at one of my favorite places, Cutty's Resort (a coast-to-coast park) in Coaldale, Colorado. The logistics of getting them together in that miles-from-anywhere place was interesting. First of all we had to make sure they could all get time off from their busy schedules. They could. Plans began. Then the Air Force decided Jim should go to Bosnia for a while. The party was canceled. Then his trip to Bosnia was canceled so my birthday party was back on.

The first obstacle was that Cutty's Resort was heavily wooded and suggested that rigs be no longer than 34 feet. We were 39.2 feet long and a wide body at that. I called Cutty's ahead of time and asked if we would be able to fit in and they assured us they had a spot for us. We reserved that spot and four of their darling but rustic cabins—one for each family. Then we sought out a travel agent to purchase the plane tickets.

Glenda and her son, Erkki, lived in West Palm Beach, Florida. She was divorced from her husband. She owned a bead and jewelry shop and had to arrange for help in the store. Glenda's daughter (my oldest granddaughter), Liisa, lived in Finland and sadly had to be left out of the reunion.

Mark, Ana, Robyn and Jonn, lived in Saugus, California, (just north of LA) and he worked for the Secret Service. We worked around Ana's daughter's prom night.

Robert and Kristen lived in Poulsbo, Washington. He was a chef in the Coast Guard. We held our breath as we weren't sure his ship would be back in time. He did make it okay but had to leave a day early because of short staffing.

Jim, Sue, Kristopher and James, were driving from their home in Warrensburg, Missouri. He was an air traffic controller in the Air Force at the time. Sue had no trouble getting off from her job.

We rented a van for the trips to the airport and since Jim was driving we'd be able to use his van also. I had made arrangements for the cook at the campground to fix breakfast for us every morning. He was terrific. The kids loved Colorado, the campground, the indoor pool, the drives we took and just meeting each other. Most of the cousins had never met. Erkki had never seen snow before but because it was old crusty snow on the mountains he would not believe that it really was snow. I think he thought snow should always be falling; since it wasn't snowing he wouldn't believe us.

For lunches I had plenty of lunch meat and fixings for sandwiches. For dinner one night I had made a big kettle of sloppy

Joes. I don't remember what I made for the next night but we all ate good and in the evenings we had a big campfire near the four cabins and we talked the night away. It was the best birthday I ever had in my entire life and I still remember it fondly.

Robert left the day before everyone else and the rest all left early on a rainy, dreary morning. Jim, Sue and the boys were heading east after saying goodbye to everyone at the airport. Kristen left early. Mark, Ana and the kids flew out at 9:30 then we had an hour to wait for Glenda and Erkki's flight to leave. We talked over a cup of coffee while Ron returned the van. After they left, we drove that long lonesome drive back to the resort; I was so sad. When we got back the sun was shining beautifully, but Cutty's seemed completely empty. The cabins were there but the kids weren't. I was glad we were leaving the next day and heading to new territory because there were too many memories there and I missed the kids a lot.

All Things Must End

After doing scheduled seminars along the way, we were back in Michigan by summer. But first we had a five day detour in Decatur, Indiana, for warranty work on the motorhome. This wasn't the first time nor would it be the last—more about that later.

We had to reprint our book again. That made the seventh printing and the books were still selling good. It was amazing to us that it was still gaining in popularity.

Our summer was terrific and when we left Michigan we headed to Toronto to visit Paivi (she was my exchange student from Finland in the late 70s) then towards Virginia (for an Escapade where we would do several seminars) by way of Ohio where we did seminars at an RV show. And we settled for the winter in Mesa, Arizona, at the same RV Park we had stayed when we first discovered the area in 1994 after Ron was diagnosed with prostate cancer.

It was so good to sit still and we got involved with the activities in that huge park. Our book was outdated again and we thought about revising it and made a feeble attempt but gave up. We decided we would simply write a new book but not for a little while. Both of us were tired; we wanted to play.

I didn't even want to do newsletters the three or four months we were there. The real nail on the coffin had been when a reader sent an order for 52 issues of the newsletter and included a check for $104. At that moment I knew I was going to end the newsletter by the end of the year. It had become nearly a full-time job. We had over 800 subscribers at the time and the subscriptions were growing by 25 or more a week. I even started talking about pulling off the road, but we had a big expensive motorhome to pay for so we decided to just change our course a bit.

I did think it would be fun to have a "camp out" with some of our readers though. So I had put a blurb about that in one of the newsletters and there was great response. Nearby, Lost Dutchman State Park was the perfect location and they had a wonder-

ful place for group camping so I made the reservation.

The camp-out was January 13, 14 & 15, 1998 and we had space for 25 RVs. We had picked up a cord of wood so we could have a campfire morning and night. And on the 14th we had scheduled a potluck picnic for those who just wanted to come for the day and join the rest of us. It was a fun time. I had planned some get-acquainted games so we could get to know one another. I delighted in playing camper hostess and even cooked breakfast outside for everyone on Saturday morning. It was just pancakes and sausage but it was yummy. Everyone had a great time.

I didn't have the heart to make the announcement that the newsletter was ending during the camp-out. I chickened out and put a news article in the last newsletter which went out in February. All the monies that had been paid us had been in a dedicated account and Ron started writing checks in March. In our newsletter we offered this option. "If you would rather not have a check sent to you, we will donate your refund to the Escapees CARE program. We would total the amount of those who want to donate to that and write one check to CARE giving you credit for your share of the donation."

Some of the 800 subscribers had paid for as many as 12 issues of the newsletter while others were down to two or three. Those who had only a few issues remaining on their subscription generally opted to donate their refund. Ron wrote a check to CARE in the amount of $2.046.75. He also wrote individual checks for varying amounts which totaled about $4.000.00.

After we sent out that last newsletter we got a slug of mail. Most of it was supportive but many were literally crying in their letters saying how much they would miss us. That was sad and tugged at my heart strings.

What a Mess

It was the end of May and we were planning to leave our home for the winter and head out. After having a telephone and being able to be on the Internet any time, I wasn't sure I wanted to be on the road without means of communication. But we had places to go and things to do.

First off we were heading up to Salt Lake City, Utah. It was time for two more grandchildren to join us for two weeks. These two were boys, in fact these boys were the brothers of the two girls we had had a couple years before. Richard and Ryan were nine and 10 and very excited about the trip we had planned for them. We were taking them to the five national parks in Utah. We thought they would enjoy the ruggedness of these parks and we had them prepared to do a lot of hiking.

They were good kids and got little homesick but only at night. During the day they were both fine. We first visited Zion National Park, then Bryce National Park, Capitol Reef, Canyonlands and Arches National Parks. We also included the north rim of the Grand Canyon in our trip. It was one of our most fun grandchild trips. And like the girls we taught them to play pinochle and dominoes and also had them write in journals and become Junior Rangers. And we had campfires with s'mores. We flew them in and out of Salt Lake City.

We spent our summer in Montana, Wyoming and Alberta, Canada. We did enjoyed playing a little bit especially at Banff and Lake Louise National Parks. We did a lot of hiking and that was invigorating. The Canadian Rockies are beautiful beyond words and just being in the presence of them refreshed us. But being able to hike in the presence of such majesty was even more rewarding. The last month we hibernated in a small town in Wyoming and worked a minimum of 10 hours a day on our new book.

Early in September we wrote in our new electronic newsletter: "...the good news is that today the new book, *Movin' On---Living and Traveling Full-time in a Recreational Vehicle* went off to the editor. When she is through with it in a few weeks, I will have a couple more weeks worth of work correcting all that she suggests then I will do all the final typesetting and get it ready for the printer. We expect to have books by late November or early December."

We were glad we were heading back to Valle Del Oro (VDO) so we could rest up from our vacation. I was anxious for a phone and Internet in the motorhome. But on our way we had another incident with the air bags. Several times they hadn't aired up but there was no damage done. When leaving this particular campground, we didn't notice the coach hadn't aired up. It twisted when we pulled out from the campground. Everything inside opened up which cost me most of my Corelle dishes. They flew out of the cupboard and broke into smithereens on the ceramic tile floor. But that wasn't the worst part, the town we had stayed in was so small there was no one who could fix it. We were stranded in the middle of nowhere and it wouldn't be the last time this happened. We called Spartan chassis in Michigan and they talked to some little mechanic who understood and was able to follow the directions to bypass the system to get us going. It didn't get fixed correctly until after we got back to Arizona. They had to order parts and send them to a truck repair facility there.

Ryan and Richard at Delicate Arch in Arches National Park.

New Book

Our shipment of Movin' On (the special advance orders) came in on Wednesday afternoon and we had a shipping party. Friends who were in the park joined us. While Ron and I signed books, they stuffed them into mailers, stapled them shut, licked stamps (four on each regular envelope) and labeled them with the mailing labels I had printed. After the work was done we enjoyed lots of pizza before we finished up with special orders. Then the guys stacked and carried them to cars to wait for the caravan to the post office Thursday morning.

We were overwhelmed with the response. We had well over 600 advance orders and reports from our fulfillment service were that orders were pouring in. Never in our wildest dreams did we ever envision the success we enjoyed with An Alternative Lifestyle, the newsletter and Movin' On, the new book. Just a few months after our first printing of 5,000 books, we had to order another 5,000.

I have decided that I must not have learned to play when I was a child because as an adult I seem to have to be doing something productive all the time. It's true that if my mother caught me doing something idle like reading a book, she would often say, "Don't you have something to do?" The reason I mention this is because the newsletter was gone, the book was done and printed, yet I immediately got involved with three big projects at VDO. I started teaching a couple communication class which met once a week for 8 weeks, I was teaching several different computer classes several times a week and I produced and directed a variety show called the Fools Follies which took a lot of time and organization. I was now busier than I had been with the newsletter and the book. I figured that at least I was working with people instead of sitting at the computer.

We also had a constant flow of visitors drop in and Jim and Norma came for a whole month. They didn't stay with us but rented a park model in the park so they were there the whole time and we tried to do things with them.

Ron was busy also. He was happily volunteering at a local elementary school by working one-on-one with second graders who needed help with math or reading. He loved it and the school loved him as well.

We also decided to have a second camp-out and this one got booked solid right away. So getting organized for that took time. We had to order wood and pick it up then take it out to the campground in time for the camp-out.

While we were in Mesa we looked into getting a cell phone although the roaming part was very expensive. They wanted to charge big bucks for roaming all the time, but if we had a "home" somewhere, that charge would be eliminated.

We decided to rent our site at VDO RV resort (Valle del Oro) for a whole year. A plus was it would give us a little bit of a break on the monthly rate and we could come back any time we wanted. We figured we could truthfully say that our home was Mesa, Arizona. It might be hard to explain why we were licensed in Texas, and our mail went there too but we were going to do it. I had to have a phone.

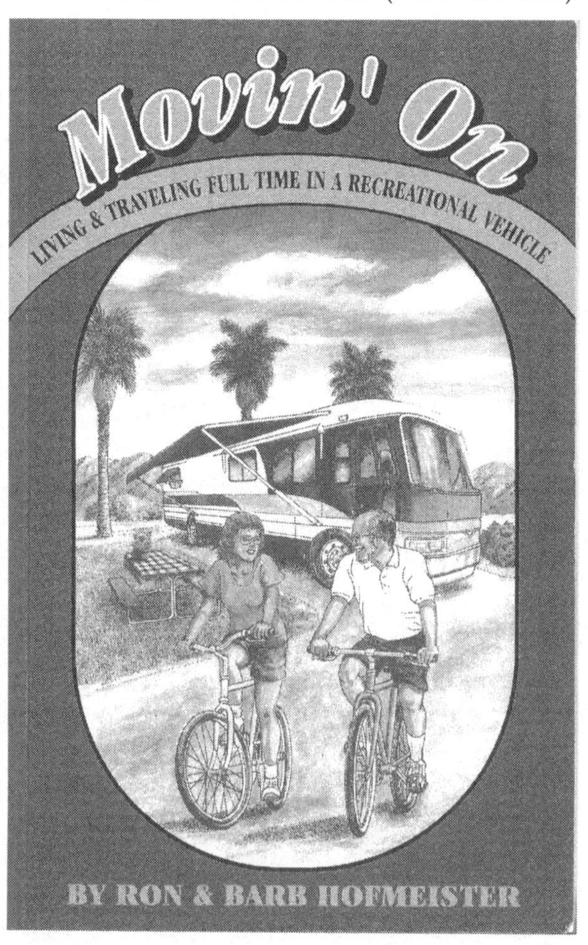

Implants, Tornados and Talks

I had been having trouble eating because of my lower denture; my gum had worn down and couldn't support a regular denture after all I had been chewing on dentures for 37 years. I saw lots of ads about implants and shuddered at the prices. Ron convinced me that I had to do something so we made an appointment to talk to Dr. Dane Robinson who advertised heavily. That was mistake number one. He gave us two options: the new kind of implants or the kind that fit on top of the jawbone which was called subperiosteal. The regular implants were $20,000 and the subperiosteal were only about $10,000. We swallowed hard and decided to go for the subperiosteal without researching it any further. That was mistake number two. What we didn't know was it was outdated technology and only lasted about 10 years as compared to the titanium kind. We would've been better off with the regular implants. But quite frankly they worked wonderfully for 11 years—more about that later. We went ahead and scheduled the surgery but since I was going to be without teeth for more than a week (Ron had never seen me without my teeth), I talked Ron into going to Michigan for his son, David's, second wedding. My girlfriend, Karen, promised to help me during the time he was away.

There were two surgeries involved. The first was to open my gum and take an impression of the jawbone. They sewed up my gum and sent me home to wait a week then I was opened up again and a metal implant was placed directly over my jawbone with the posts protruding through my gum. Those posts were where the denture would snap on. I had to wait a few days before I had teeth but in the meantime since the second surgery was far worse than the first, Karen had called Ron in Michigan and told him that I wasn't doing well so he flew back even before the wedding. I did feel better with him there and shouldn't have sent him away. So he was home for a day or two and then he went back for the wedding. That made it all very expensive.

Once the sutures were out we were able to leave and head to Michigan in the motorhome.

Ron's kids were very unhappy with me because I didn't come to the wedding. Ron explained to them that having that surgery done would take quite a while for recovery and the doctor was going to be leaving town in June like a lot of dentists did in Arizona. The bulk of our population (winter visitors) were all gone so they didn't have as much business in the summer. If I didn't have it done then, it would have been another year before I could have the surgery. In hindsight maybe I should've waited and learned more, but we did what we did. I planned to have a talk with Susie and Marty once we got to Michigan and hoped that I could clear up the problems.

Meanwhile in Oklahoma City, they had had many horrific tornadoes that devastated the area near where were Jim, Sue and the boys lived. Thankfully they were okay. They hid in their bathroom (huddled inside the tub) for several hours while the tornadoes destroyed everything around them.

On our way to Michigan we stopped to visit them and we took the boys camping with us for a couple days. We went to a campground east of where they lived. It was a nothing kind of park but Jim and Sue were going to join us for the weekend just for an opportunity to get away. The first night we were in that campground there were tornado warnings which shook up those poor boys terribly. Thank God none materialized because we were not very well protected in the tiny little shelter (laundry room open on three sides) the campground people sent us to. We would not have been at all safe in the motorhome which was one of the hazards of being on the road. Generally we steered clear of the Midwest in the spring for that very reason.

Clearing the Air

Ron and I had been married for 15 years and in that time I had never felt like I was part of his family. There were many times when I wished Ron would have spoken to them about things they did or didn't do. I had shared my feelings with Ron, but most of the time he just flipped it off as my "supersensitive feelings". I always felt he was afraid to ruffle his kids because he was still dealing with guilt about divorcing their mother. Regarding the kids, he walked on eggs many times.

I felt I had proof of my feelings. For example none of his kids ever sent me a birthday card and when they sent a Christmas card it was addressed to "Mr. Ronald Hofmeister". Ron didn't see it that way. My kids always addressed cards to both of us when they sent cards; they remembered his birthday also.

So his kids (especially his daughters) were upset that I wasn't at David's wedding. Frankly I thought they'd be glad I wasn't there. And Ron told me when Karen had called him in Michigan to tell him that he should come back to Arizona the girls (Marty especially) were furious. They didn't think he should come back. To Ron's credit, he did have words with Marty over that.

I figured the girls and I needed to talk and I had planned my "speech" on the way back to Michigan. Susie wanted us to park in her driveway so we did and immediately I went in and asked her if we could talk—just her and I. I hadn't told Ron of my plan.

Understandably she was on the defensive and quite cool but I kept my calm and used my best powers of persuasion and communication (without attacking) to map out what I saw as the problem. After all I had been teaching communication classes during the winter. I told her that I honestly believed the family would not miss me because I had never been treated like part of the family. I mentioned her wedding when I was not told the color theme and I stuck out like a sore thumb with my orange/red dress. I dearly wished that I had brought another dress with me so I could change quickly. And I mentioned that just before the wedding started I had overheard her and her mother saying, "Oh, we forgot Barb" speaking about the flowers. They offered me a red boutonniere but I did not take it. Susie remembered that and felt bad. Then I asked her if she knew when my birthday was. She didn't. I reminded her that I always send her a birthday card and then I asked about Christmas cards addressed to her father only. She agreed that wasn't right.

We made great progress that day. I also asked her if being moderately nice to me would make her feel she was being disloyal to her mother. She denied that. I assured her I had no intention of taking her mother's place and at the same time I did not want to be the wicked stepmother. I added that I dearly loved her father and I felt that I had made him happy. I had to point out that I didn't break up the marriage; we met nearly three years after they separated.

I also had a chance to listen to things she was concerned about and we promised to make things better. We agreed to communicate better from that point on. I felt better about our relationship after that day and I think Susie did too and as a plus I get a birthday card every year from both Susie and Marty.

Guess Who Came for Dinner

For something different when we were finished visiting with family we went North into the upper Peninsula of Michigan and went East for a little while crossing into Canada then North then West so we could travel along the northern part of Lake superior. It was an area we had never covered before. It was nice traveling except we were disappointed in being too big to fit into the rustic provincial campgrounds but we did enjoy the scenery. We stayed for a little while in the town of Wawa and found a nice restaurant to go to for Ron's birthday.

The Cedarhof restaurant in Wawa was highly recommended. The cute little restaurant could only seat 37 at the various tables which were all covered with pretty sunflower tablecloths. We arrived at a good time and took a table set for two near a window. There were fresh flowers on all the tables and we started with some wine. The fresh Lake Superior trout that Ron had was "something to die for," he said. He just couldn't get over how well it had been prepared. I chose a delicious peach chicken dish with wild rice. Even though I was full, I ordered a piece of homemade lemon meringue pie which was huge. Ron took a fancy to the wild berry torte. Our waitress had heard me mention that it was Ron's birthday so she delivered his dessert with a candle on top.

The restaurant was full and when the waitress started to sing "Happy Birthday", everyone joined in. It was neat. Shortly after the singing, a lady near the center of the restaurant said, "Excuse me" in a kind of excitedly urgent voice, and we all looked up to see her pointing toward the glass entry door. With our eyes, we followed her finger. Imagine our surprise to see a black bear pressing his nose and paws right into the glass. The young and beautiful waitress went to the door (now mind you she was dressed in a long black skirt and high heals) and from the inside shooed it away then opened the door to further holler at it. Everyone was like one big family talking about the bear and what excitement it was. The waitress said that one has been around a lot and told about a day the summer before when she went out to the shed to get desserts. She had left the door open and when she turned around there were three bears in the shed with her. She screamed and the owner came to her rescue. We were really in the North country.

We came back to the US from Thunder Bay then went West in the US. We visited lots of places in both North and South Dakota and then spent time in Wyoming, Colorado and finally back to Arizona by the middle of September. One of the highlights was being in Sturgis, South Dakota, during the annual motorcycle rally. We had no idea what went on there; it was just mind-boggling. We walked downtown with all the motorcycles and biker babes. It was quite wild. One can get quite an education traveling around the country.

While we were traveling I was able to be in communication with our new cell phone. I was able to make arrangements with Lazy Days in Tampa, Florida for our January seminars. We were scheduled to do 14 seminars there from January 7 to January 29 and I posted the schedule on our website. We had made an agreement with Lazy Days that since we were doing so many seminars they would not only give us our free campsite but they would pay us a fee for being there for the whole month. I promised to get good publicity and Tony said he would work on it too.

More Than a Crunch

We had just ordered another printing of 5000 books and we decided to head East in November slowly heading to Florida. We hoped we could get some newspapers interested in doing a story about us or TV and/or radio publicity to help sell the new books. We weren't carrying very many books because we hadn't had to take care of orders anymore. We were going to be having quite a few cases of the books sent to Lazy Days early in January so we could have them to sell during our seminars.

We had just left our friends in Canyon Lake, Texas, on Friday morning (November 19) and were looking forward to the short drive to Austin for a visit with my Aunt Genevieve and cousins. We were on Texas state route 306 heading to I-35 and it was a good road. Although only two lanes, the shoulders were paved and each was as wide as a lane, plus there was a wide grass shoulder on each side beyond that. As we were starting a wide sweeping curve to the left, we saw a van heading straight for us on our side of the road. Ron swerved off the highway avoiding a head on but she got us good. It almost seemed like she didn't know she was on our side because she didn't correct at all until the split second before she hit us and we were already on the grassy shoulder. Because she turned the wheel of her car just as she hit us, she kept going thereby taking out the rear half of motorhome on the driver's side and the Toyota truck too. Her vehicle impacted the motorhome one bay behind the propane tank and continued on taking out the rest of the bays pulling the back of the motorhome from the side wall then continued on crunching our Toyota from the hood to the back quarter panel. She was going so fast that she wasn't able to stop until she was almost through the curve and her correction was so severe she ended up on her side of the road well into the grassy area.

Thank God for lots of friendly Texans who stopped by to witness to the police, and help clean up lots of debris. Thank goodness for our cell phone too.

Amazingly we were able to drive the motorhome the short distance to the town of Seguin where there was a very good RV shop by the name of ProTech. At first we were going to do like we did any time we had service on the motorhome and that was to just be gone during the day while they worked on it and go back into the house at night when they were finished for the day. We tried that for a couple days and it just wasn't going to work. One day I wanted to take a nap and there was nowhere I could nap. We were tired of driving around and being homeless which is what we felt like. Since we were going to be hung up for six weeks I just couldn't do it like that anymore. We talked to the insurance company and were told to find a hotel or apartment—whatever we wanted and get a monthly rate. They would take care of it. They had already given us a loaner for the car so we did have transportation.

We found a nice condo in New Braunfels which was really quite reasonable; the insurance company was happy. Once we moved our stuff in it was very comfortable. There were two bedrooms so we even invited my son Jim and his family who lived in Oklahoma to come on down for Christmas which they did.

The problem with being in that condo was I liked it. I liked having more room and more than one chair to sit in and a bigger kitchen and shower—the whole nine yards.

But the accident did something to me. I felt violated. We had just paid for all those books and made commitments to Lazy

Days and also to the Life on Wheels Conference (Moscow, Idaho) where we had agreed to do dozens of seminars the middle of July in 2000. I did some strong talking to myself and felt I would be okay once we were back on the road and working.

I had been doing a small electronic newsletter and the headline on the last issue that went out was about the accident, but none of our friends tried to contact us to find out more. That really made me feel bad. I called some of our closest friends and they hadn't even opened the newsletter. I felt even worse then but bit my lip and carried on promising to quit that newsletter also.

We didn't get the motorhome back until about five o'clock on New Year's Eve. Then we had to move everything back in. That was New Year's Eve 1999 going on 2000 when everyone thought the world was going to end or something because computers weren't set for the 2000s. But midnight rolled around and everything was still working. Our only break that night was to pick up some Taco Bell tacos for our dinner. Much later we would laugh about it but not that night. It was an exhausting night.

ProTek had a few more things to do on the motorhome but they were mainly cosmetic. We had simply run out of time so we

agreed we would come back when we were finished in Florida. The truck looked great too. We laugh now at how many times different parts of that truck had been damaged and rebuilt. And all the accidents except for the first one, when Ron backed into that water stanchion, were caused by other people.

We left early New Year's Day and drove pretty much straight through to Tampa, Florida, with stops just to sleep and get fuel.

The Beginning of the End – Again

We had a great time at Lazy Days and our seminars were very well attended. We also sold a ton of books which was what we hoped for.

Since we didn't get to go for our planned vacation in Disney World on the way to Lazy Days we did that right after our seminars. That was early in February and we spent seven days in Disney World then went to West Palm Beach to visit my daughter before heading West again.

We had planned early in April to go house boating on Lake Powell in Arizona for a week. There were four of us couples (all bridge players) and during the day we did some sightseeing; at night we played bridge. It was a was a fun week and we enjoyed the sights of Lake Powell.

After our houseboat trip we took off again heading to the Northwest mainly because we needed to be in the area anyway as we were scheduled to do seminars at the Life on Wheels conference in Idaho early in July.

We had developed about five different seminars for that Life on Wheels conference and each one of them was on a specific area of the lifestyle. I even had one about how to pack an RV and it was presented with a PowerPoint slide show which I had spent months working on. Ron did one on finances and we did another on medical care on the road. All were well attended. Life on Wheels was something we actually got paid for and since it was only one week long it was very profitable.

From there we went to Gillette, Wyoming, where we presented seminars at the great North American Rally where the attendance at our seminars was well over 800. We didn't get paid for rallies but our payment was in publicity and book sales.

After that rally we made a beeline towards Michigan with a stop in Missouri to visit Jim and Sue. We were in Michigan by early August and visited both of our mothers who were in poor health. We wondered if we would ever see them alive again.

While we were visiting Ron's mom we got a phone call from a man named Rich who was with an advertising agency. He explained that they were in the process of making a documentary for Homestore.com about how people lived and they wanted to include us. Ron was excited about it. I don't think I was because I didn't want to work that hard. But they sent a guy to do a kind of a sample interview and if the powers that be liked it they would arrange to meet us on the road somewhere to shoot.

We got a call from Dominic, the producer, who said that they wanted to film us as soon as possible. We told him where we were going and when. Soon we all agreed on meeting in Tucumcari, New Mexico, and the plan was to travel to Corizozo, New Mexico, and the Valley of Fires National Recreation area and from there we would travel to Las Cruces with a stop at White Sands National Monument. We were really on our way to a rally in Tucson, Arizona. They told us they would be spending two days with us. We thought we knew what it would entail because Good Morning America spent two days taping us for that four minute spot five years before, but we were about to learn that making movies is a lot different than making a tape for TV. I had been sick and rather run down from a cold but we got ready and moved West.

We pulled in to Tucumcari two days before the crew was to arrive so we could wash our motorhome and get ready for the cameras. We were in constant contact with Dominic, and knew that the crew was flying to Albuquerque (from both Los Angeles and New York) then driving to Tucumcari. When they arrived in Tucumcari, he called and asked if they could come over for a short visit before filming started the next morning. Besides finally meeting Dominic, we met the very creative cinematographer, Chris Smith, who had recently won a prestigious award at the Sundance Film Festival for his documentary American Movie. We also met the lighting man, Fritz, and another cinematographer, Hubert. They all seemed very nice and basically all they wanted to do with this first visit was to see what obstacles they might have in filming in our motorhome. After this brief visit they told us that they would arrive at 7:45 and start filming by 8 a.m., the next morning. We were excited and I did not sleep well. I had not fully recovered from my flu/cold/bug or whatever it was.

The van arrived right on time with the guys we had met the night before. Behind them were three more cars/vans and a large truck plus a rented Bounder motorhome which we learned later was the place for snacks and drinks and the rest room for the crew. The first person we met was Fabiola, the make up artist. Dominic had said that making a film was a lot different than taping for TV and we were beginning to see what he meant. Soon we met Janet, the sound person, Agnes the script writer (she writes in long hand everything that is said on camera), Rudy the focus puller (he is always next to the cinematographer and keeps the camera in focus), Rodrigo, the director and his two assistants, the guys in the production truck who kept the film magazines loaded, John the caterer who made sure there were plenty of snacks and drinks for the crew, Barb, Rich and several others from the advertising agency, Steve from homestore.com and others that I can't remember right now. All in all there were 26 people who traveled with us most of the time. Just imagine that. I get a headache again just remembering it.

We didn't leave that campground in Tucumcari until 11 in the morning because they were filming Ron and I doing various things. It was only 150 miles or so to the campground at the Valley of Fires in Corizozo so even leaving that late did not worry us. But shortly it was clear that it would be very slow going.

Chris, Rudy, Fritz, Janet and Agnes rode with us all of the time. Chris wasn't always filming but when he was he was up front filming us (asking questions as we were rolling), Rudy had to scrunch on the floor at my feet to do his job while the others had to hide by lying on the floor beside the bed. One time Chris was filming out the bedroom window.

Hubert and his crew filmed us going down the road and several times after he filmed us radioed that he would like us to stop while they got set then take off again. Three times we were asked to turn around so they could redo the shot and that was not always easy since we were on two lane roads with no cross roads or places to turn. Those times we had to unhook the car, turn around, re hook the car then do what they wanted. They filmed us from the side, the back and even from the front (Hubert was anchored in the back of the van with the door open shooting straight up at us from just a few feet away). By the way, everyone in the crew was always in radio contact so communication was good.

We could see that it was going to be dark by the time we arrived at the campground and were worried that we would not be able to get a camping spot. Dominic took care of that for us and had an assistant call ahead and save a spot for us. Dominic had a good contact at the park because they had had to pay a hefty fee in order to film there. To us it seemed like an expensive project and there were lots of complications.

The next morning at Valley of Fires we were again filmed doing lots of things. Ron was filmed visiting with the neighbor, Wyatt. We had wondered what he and his wife must have thought when late at night we pulled in accompanied by the Bounder, the white truck and the other vehicles. The crew left shortly to stay in a motel and went over to apologize to Wyatt and Donna for disturbing their peace. They got a kick out of the whole situation especially when Wyatt was included in the film the next morning. We didn't get to explore the park as we would have liked but did take part of a walk on the nature trail so it could be filmed. Again we got a late start and had to exit the park twice for the benefit of the camera. Always Fabiola was handy to do a little touch up and Fritz was often asked to take a light meter reading. They all worked well together.

At White Sands National Monument, we ran up the sand hills while the camera was rolling again and again. Before we got to the campground in Las Cruces, they had us pull into a truck stop and fill up with diesel so that could be filmed. They generously paid the bill which was a nice treat. The campground was just around the corner and they filmed us setting up camp then having a cocktail outside as the sun was setting. Then good byes were said; they had been a part of our life for two whole days.

We were told we would get a copy of the movie when they finished. We were the fifth couple they had filmed and they had one more to do. Two of the others who will be in this documentary are a couple who live in an old missile silo and a couple who live in a house boat on a bayou in Louisiana. The ad slogan will be something like ---"This is their dream home; what's yours?"

Mainly because I hadn't been well, I was totally exhausted and I hated the whole thing. I think Ron kind of liked it but my patience wore out with all those people in the motorhome. And the worst part was we ended up on the cutting room floor. We were too normal; they wanted odd people like the lady who lived with several hundred cats. I am glad we weren't lumped with the odd balls.

To rest up we went to Sierra Vista, Arizona, which was fairly close to Tucson. I think I slept for two days and then while driving around town we happened upon a new subdivision. I wanted to go look at the model homes just for something fun to do. But when I did I knew I was through full timing. I wanted a house and I wanted to settle down as soon as possible. Ron and I talked. I think he knew that between the accident and all the seminars then this movie fiasco I was about ready for a nervous breakdown. He promised me that in two years, if I could hold out that long, we could get a house. He needed to stockpile some money and selling books would help with that. Just knowing that there might be an end, I mustered all my strength and got to work. We were going to be coming off the road. I couldn't wait.

I had really loved the first three years on the road, but lately we were so busy and so noticeable we couldn't just have fun. And our motorhome was too big and too much trouble to be enjoyable. I longed for our little motorhome and no books. "Oh, my," I often thought, "what did we get ourselves into?"

Remember when Ron couldn't see and backed into the water stanchion? When the truck had been repaired, the bump shop didn't have a Toyota decal. Bryan, our son-in-law suggested we put Movin' On on the back. At the time it a great idea but all of a sudden it was like a neon sign. We couldn't go anywhere without being recognized. Even as we were going down the highway, people recognized us and waved. In campgrounds people would knock on our door and want to visit. They felt like they knew us personally even though we had never met.

Accidentally House Hunting

The winter of 2001 was busy. I directed Fools Follies II in February which was a roaring success and we were busy getting ready for our third annual camp out which was already booked solid when Ron's mother died (March 3). I had just been diagnosed with having pneumonia so Ron wouldn't let me go back to Michigan with him. And it was a good thing because it was very cold and stormy the whole time he was there.

In April we were invited to put on a seminar in an RV park in Gold Canyon which was only 14 miles east of where we had been staying at VDO. Immediately I fell in love with the mountains there. I had seen them before because we had our camp outs on the other side of the mountain in the state park. But the thing that made these even more beautiful to me, which might be hard to understand, was there were new houses there in a senior community named Mountain Brook Village.

We had a little extra time one day so we decided to look at the models. I loved them, the location, the whole community and all of the facilities. I especially loved one model which was called the Saguaro. It had two bedrooms a den/office and the main living area was big. The living room dining room kitchen was one big lovely area. I especially loved the den/office and could even envision my desk in there. I made a mental note: when we are ready to buy that's the house I wanted and that's where I wanted it to be.

We had made arrangements to volunteer at Three Island Crossing State Park in Idaho from mid May to mid June. It turned out to be a kind of boring assignment. We worked in the visitor center a little bit then on a couple evenings a week we led the campfire program in the campground. It was interesting though as it was on the Oregon Trail and we had to learn about that in order to talk about it and it was a very lovely setting. On our days off we took nice long drives up into the high country and discovered a ghost town or two.

We were scheduled to present seminars at the Life on Wheels Conference in Moscow, Idaho, from July 8-13 which was fun as well as work. My seminar on packing an RV was very well received and I thought I did a good job. Basically I am a very organized person.

Next on the agenda was another trip with grandchildren. We flew Jim and Sue's sons, Kristopher and James from their home in Kansas City, Missouri, (they used to live in Oklahoma) to Spokane, Washington, like we had done for Mary and Erika. And like the girls we took them to Glacier and Yellowstone National Parks. Our weather was good but the motorhome wasn't.

From Glacier, we were supposed to leave for Yellowstone on Saturday. We were all packed and ready to leave. The last thing I always did was turn on the engine to warm it up and then I would put up the jacks. When I turned the key nothing happened. We had never had that problem before; in fact it had always started like a gem with never a hesitation. There was no way to get help on a Saturday morning. We called Good Sam Road Service, but they couldn't find anyone who could come out and fix our problem what ever it was. We couldn't be towed anywhere because our jacks were down and they didn't go up until the engine started. So we paid for two extra days and hoped someone could come out on Monday morning. There was a truck repair facility in Kalispell. I had moved up our reservations at Yellowstone and we hoped to get there by Tuesday or Wednesday. Meanwhile we were comfortable and we just played a little longer in God's country. Northwest Truck Repair came out to our site early on Monday and he worked for several hours trying to find out what the problem was. We called American Coach and they gave him all the help they could and suggested we call Spartan (the chassis manufacturer). When we finally got through to them they helped our mechanic to troubleshoot. It turned out that Spartan had a hidden solenoid which was no where near the ignition; it was defective but a few hits and we were able to start the engine. To be sure it wouldn't happen again we drove to the Truck Repair place in Kalispell and they put in a new solenoid.

We were on the road by 2 p.m. and drove until about 6:30. On Tuesday we arrived in Yellowstone and had a great time.

Instead of flying the boys back to Kansas City we drove them and that was uneventful except for the bear who was ready to cross the road as we neared it. He saw us at the last moment and decided to go back into the woods.

It was just a long boring trip and from Kansas City after staying only a couple of days, we went on to Michigan. In August, we had to order another 5,000 copies of our newest book. Sales were good from every source.

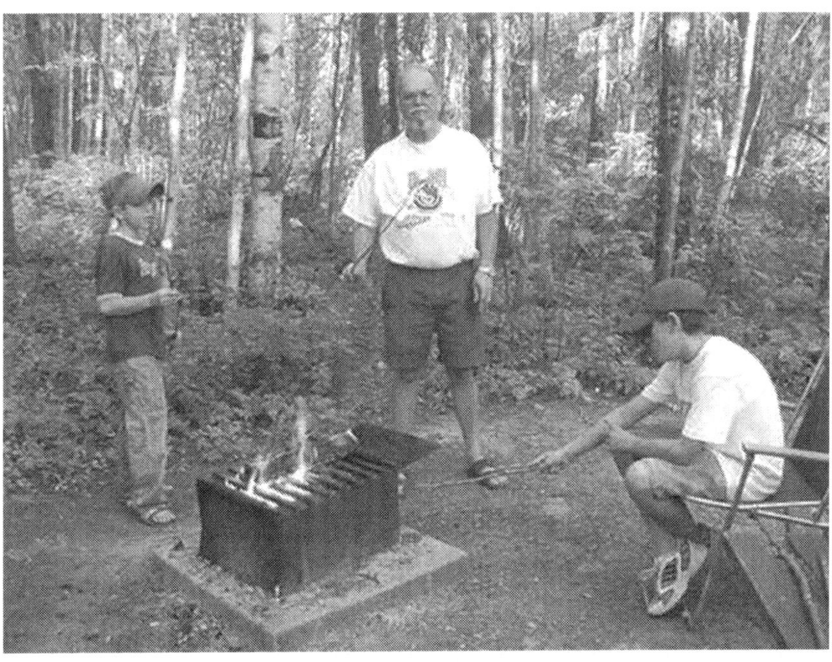

James, Ron and Kristopher in Glacier.

Frustration and More Frustration

We met Cec and Judy in the spring of 1994 and had met them on the road many times. But they mostly stayed in the West. Being natives of California they just stayed close to what used to be home. I didn't blame them because the whole West Coast was so beautiful. We talked often and were really great friends. They had checked our website frequently so they knew we were going to be going to Michigan then in Florida to do seminars. They had never been to Michigan so they decided to join us there and since there were other places in the East they wanted to visit we could follow each other to Florida.

Since they were entering Michigan from the Northwest (Wisconsin) we agreed to meet in Mackinaw City. We wanted to show them some of the Upper Peninsula of Michigan and had fun taking them such places as Mackinaw Island, Whitefish Point and the Shipwreck Museum also Tahquamenon Falls. South of the bridge we took them to the sand dunes on the West coast of lower Michigan. What fun we had. We camped for a while near Bryan and Marty' s cottage at Crystal Lake and enjoyed being in the woods yet close enough to the water that we could bike there from our campground. Cec and I biked while Judy and Ron rode in the car. We had fun introducing our friends to Ron's kids and they fit right in. While we were in the area the girls got us to join Weight Watchers. Judy had been going and had lost quite a bit and we were complaining about our weight

so she convinced us to go with her. Once a week, all the way down to Florida we weighed in at a Weight Watcher meeting and kept losing. It was easy. By the time we got to Florida we each lost over 20 pounds.

After spending a few weeks up north we went back to Lansing. I don't remember where Judy and Cec went but we would catch up with them later. We visited both my mom and dad who were in the same assisted living home but didn't know each other. It was so sad. I would tell mother who I was but I don't think she really got it, neither did dad. When dad had left mom back in the 60s she pined away for him the rest of her life yet there he was living in the same home she was and she didn't know him and vice versa.

We had to go to Decatur, Indiana, to the factory where our motorhome was made. We were having problems with it — lots of problems but we also wanted something done with our dinette chairs. They were permanently attached to the floor. They were comfortable swivel chairs that never moved from their position. The factory found a freelance furniture maker for us who would rebuild the chairs (putting regular legs on them) while they replaced the tiles that had to be removed in order to get the chairs up off the floor. They had been bolted to the floor.

While we were there we got a phone call that my mother had died. We were glad that she died while we were so close to Michigan. Instead of waiting for the chairs to be finished, we went back to Michigan for her funeral which was quite nice. She had suffered long enough and we were glad she was finally at peace.

We finished up at the factory and headed south to meet up with Judy and Cec. It was a Thursday and we were all ready to leave Lexington for the Cumberland Gap National Park in Southeastern Kentucky. We were unhooked and I had started the engine so it could warm up. Then I turned on the inverter (as suggested by the factory so I could keep the ice maker going while traveling); it didn't go on. I called the factory and read them the code that the inverter's panel was displaying. That code indicated a wiring problem. While on the phone with the factory, he had me start the generator to see if we had power; we did. Then as directed I tried the inverter again; sparks flew and the microwave started smoking. I smelled the odor of a burnt motor. Instead of heading south on I-75 we went north and arrived back in Decatur, Indiana, about 3:30 in the afternoon. We were number 20 on a list of drop in customers (who did not have appointments). We sat and waited with a cold rain making the day unpleasant.

They didn't work on our unit until Monday afternoon and again Tuesday morning. They replaced the burned out inverter and some other parts and proclaimed us fixed. We decided to stay the night to keep checking the inverter. We unplugged the coach three or four times and turned on the inverter. All did seem to be working. We slept in a bit the next morning instead of getting up at 5:30 like all who were there for service had to do. At 10 a.m., we were ready to leave and unplugged the coach. The inverter wouldn't go on—the same old problem again. I walked in and told the guys who had worked on it what had happened. Scratching their heads, they immediately brought the motorhome inside the building and after a while found another loose wire. They told us it was fixed, but we stayed one more night. This was the third time in one year that our inverter had blown and taken other appliances with it. We weren't leaving until we were sure that they had totally solved the problem. I wrote in my journal: "We may be shoveling snow this winter."

The rest of the trip to Florida with lots of stops along the way was uneventful. We enjoyed our times with our good friends playing tourist in Charleston, South Carolina, and Savannah, Georgia, and arrived in West Palm Beach, Florida, by the day before Thanksgiving so I could fix dinner for Glenda and Erkki. Judy and Cec went on to Key West for a while.

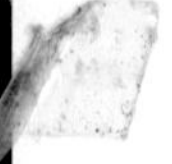

Don't Faint

We spent a wonderful month in West Palm Beach. I played grandma mostly and also worked in the bead shop and at home sorting, counting and repackaging beads. We would pick Erkki up from school and bring him back to the motorhome then help with his homework. Later on Glenda would pick him up. She worked long hours and we were glad to help her out.

On January 27, 2002, we left West Palm Beach and drove to Lazy Days in Tampa. If I remember right we were doing about 17 seminars the month of January. I had called the TV station (Good Day Tampa Bay) that had us on for a whole morning several years before and they came out on January 2. Like the last time, they had us on the whole morning which resulted in a big promotion for the seminars. Tony was ready for us and couldn't do enough for us and Judy and Cec were camped nearby in another RV Park that they had affiliation with. They were planning on coming to our seminars every day to help with the book sales at the break time (half way through the seminar). They were terrific help and so enthusiastic that it made it more fun for us. With them taking care of the book orders we could rest at break time. At every seminar we sold lots of books (30-50). It was really smooth. We only gave them five minutes for their stretch break and had set the price of the book at only $15 rather than $16.95 so making change was simple. Judy and Cec were mobbed, took care of business then we went on with the seminar.

I think I mentioned before that we divided the subjects up with Ron and I taking turns speaking. One time when I was talking (Ron was behind me drinking some coffee) and Judy and Cec were in the back of the room, I saw Judy stand up and look worried and about the same time I caught Ron out of the corner of my eye. He had just passed out. Judy (a retired nurse) could tell that he was going to faint before he did. After an ambulance ride and a little time in the emergency room he was fine. His blood pressure had dipped too low for two reasons. Number one was his doctor back in Arizona had upped his blood pressure medicine way back in the winter of 2001 before he lost weight. And secondly he wasn't drinking enough water.

The rest of our time in Tampa was very profitable and fun. Meeting all the people who wanted to go full-time or already were but wanted to meet us and being able to take little day trips with Judy and Cec to explore more of the area was fun. When we were about to leave the staff at Lazy Days asked us to please come back the next January and we agreed to do that. Judy and Cec said they wanted to join us again also.

The four of us were going to be traveling along the south coast hitting Alabama, Mississippi, and New Orleans. We were leaving Ocean Springs, Mississippi, one morning for the short 90 mile

We treated by hiring a limo and taking Judy & Cec, out to dinner at the end of January.

drive to New Orleans and we were going to drive together as we had been doing (one motorhome behind the other). Just after we hooked up and were driving out of the campground, we realized that our rear end (air bags) hadn't aired up. It had happened before and Ron had been able to fix it with the help of someone at Spartan Motors on the other end of the cell phone. So the four of us drove to the visitor center which had large parking spots for RVs. We unhooked the car and I put the rear jacks down so Ron could get under the motorhome. Cec was right under there with him, but they couldn't find anything out of place. We called Spartan and tried a few things they suggested, but still nothing worked. We sent Judy and Cec on to New Orleans, and told them we would get there "whenever" then we called our Good Sam road service. They found Glenn's Auto and Marine Repair in Pascagoula, Mississippi. Glenn came and after a quick phone call to Spartan and a look at the schematics from our Spartan book, was able to identify and fix the problem. We were aired up and on the road again. An hour and a half later we were with the girls in the campground in New Orleans.

Unfortunately we took turns being sick. First it was Judy then me and finally Ron. It was just some sort of a bug. But Ron spent a whole day and part of the night in bed and didn't eat nor did he drink much water. He finally woke up around 9 PM. I asked him to check his sugar. He did and reported it was normal. Immediately after he went down. This time he fell flat on his face hitting the tile floor from a standing position. It was loud and sounded awful. I thought he was dead. I couldn't turn him over or rouse him so I reached for the cell phone and called Judy who was parked next to us. A simply said, "Hurry". She and I together couldn't turn him over. We called 911 and an ambulance was there in no time—just as Ron was starting to come to.

It was the same thing (low blood pressure) but this time he got a broken front tooth and a big cut on his lip. Rather than try and get his tooth fixed in New Orleans, we decided to just head on back to Mesa. The next day I made appointments with both his dentist and doctor. But we stayed one more day in New Orleans to make sure he was feeling okay. We drove straight through to Texas where we both needed to get some work done at ProTech RV (the company that fixed us after the accident). From there we went straight onto Mesa; the girls went to California.

Death, Dying and Rebirth

We did not go back to Valle del Oro. We thought we would try Venture Out RV Resort also in Mesa for something different; we chose them primarily because they had instant telephone hookups at each site. We really liked it there.

Keeping in touch with Ron's kids as we did, we learned quite a while before that his former wife, Martha, was dying from metastasized breast cancer. We really thought that Ron would get a call any day saying she had died and we had planned that he would go back for her funeral to be with the kids. Instead of getting a phone call about Martha we got a most shocking phone call from one of my sisters. My darling niece Kathleen, had committed suicide on Saturday, March 2. She was in her early 20s and it was very sad. We flew out immediately for the funeral and stayed a couple extra days to go visit with Ron's kids and see how Martha was doing. She wasn't going to be dying real soon so we went back to Arizona.

After we finished with all of the doctor appointments, lab tests and so on we headed out to the Palm Springs area of California. When we had been at the factory in Indiana we asked about the paint on our motorhome which was cracked and bubbling. They agreed that it was covered under the warranty. We were told there were two places we could take the motorhome to be painted—one was in Chino, California, the other was there in Decatur, Indiana. We didn't like the idea of being in Michigan in the winter so we picked California. Our appointment was for the middle of April and they would need it for four to six weeks. We would, of course, have to move out of the motorhome again and Judy and Cec, knowing that area well, found a Park model we could rent in a nice RV resort in Cathedral City, California.

Shortly after we got to the Palm Springs area we got word that Martha died. Ron's son, Kurt, sent him a ticket so he could fly back for the funeral which he did, flying from Palm Springs.

Moving into the park model was fairly easy because Judy and

Cec were there to help; it was done in no time. Then the next morning we (Ron and I) drove the motorhome to Chino (about an hour and a half away) and left it. They explained that they would be stripping everything off the motorhome—windows and all and starting from scratch. We couldn't believe all that the motorhome was costing Fleetwood, the manufacturer. When I asked Ron if he remembered how much the paint job cost he said, "$30,000 sticks in my head". It was beautiful when finished. It was like our motorhome had been reborn. And instead of putting decals on for the striping they actually painted the stripes on. It was better than new.

Spur of the Moment Decision

After we moved back into the motorhome, we slowly made our way north through California and when we got to Oregon we basically followed the coast and enjoyed a nice leisurely trip. We were heading to the very tip of the Washington's Olympic Peninsula where Robert was stationed. He was in the small village of La Push.

I wrote on our website, "We are at the end of the earth. At least that is what it feels like. If you'd look at your map of Washington and follow U. S. 101 north until you see Forks then go west on Washington Route 110 stopping only when you reach the ocean at the little community of La Push. There is a small Coast Guard base here (search and rescue) and a small community of Native Americans. There is a tiny store at the rustic campground which conveniently has full hook ups. The guests in the campground are either here to surf or fish. There is no cell service here, a single gas pump at the campground store and we are 16 miles from the nearest town of Forks which has restaurants, a grocery store and most basic needs. The view here is terrific when it isn't fogged in. By the way the fog horn serenades us all day and night."

When we left La Push we continued east along the northern part of the Olympic Peninsula, until we got to Port Townsend where we took the ferry which would take us across to the mainland. We were slowly heading to Leavenworth, Washington, which is a German town, and where we planned to celebrate Ron's 70th birthday with Judy and Cec who would join us. We had a lot of fun there and ate in a good German restaurant. From there it was a short trip to Moscow, Idaho, for the Life on Wheels conference. Although it was work it was also fun.

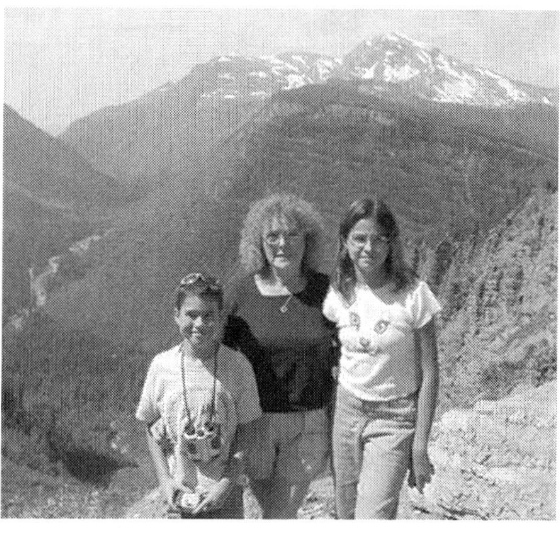

Immediately after the conference we went to Spokane, Washington, where we picked up two more grandchildren. Robyn and Jonn (Mark and Ana's children) came to us from Southern California (just north of LA) and they only had 10 days to be with us because of school so we only took them to Glacier National Park then back to Spokane. Even though the time was short we had a good time and they seemed to enjoy it also. The weather was perfect for hiking, game playing and just getting to know them better.

We originally planned to stay West and were thrilled to be just sitting in a nice campground in Spokane. We had been there a couple days and were really relaxing. I was shopping in one of the nicest grocery stores I'd ever been in and saw fresh corn which I couldn't resist. But it certainly left a lot to be desired. While we were eating it I looked at Ron, he looked at me, and I said, "You know if we left tomorrow we could be in Michigan in no time and have some good corn." He said, "but we just drove to Montana and back on the same road we'd have to drive to Michigan on." I replied, "So?" We left the next morning.

As we were traveling I thought we could even go further than Michigan, after we had our fill of corn and tomatoes of course. When we had first visited upstate New York and points east we were not doing our newsletter or website and I wanted to write about those places. As soon as I proposed it to Ron he agreed saying, "Why not?" I loved that he was usually so agreeable to my crazy ideas. So that's what we did. It was a wonderfully, brilliant (fall colors) summer and fall.

Foot Loose and Fancy Free

For the first time in a long time we felt completely footloose and fancy free. We didn't have to be anywhere for five whole months and by changing course suddenly with no one knowing ahead of time what we were doing, we were as free as butterflies. It was a wonderful feeling. It turned out to be the most fun we had had in a very long time.

So we left Spokane on August 7 traveling fairly slow. We were in Hackensack, Minnesota, by August 15 with a short stop to visit old friends and we were in Michigan by August 18. We only stayed in Michigan for a couple of weeks leaving September 5. In that short time, we got to visit with everyone. Oh yes, and the sweet corn and tomatoes were delicious. We went through Canada staying only one night in a rest stop and were in Western New York by September 7. Then we slowed down a little almost going from one farm market vegetable stand to another along the way.

We had a glorious time in the Adirondacks and Lake George, New York. By September 17 we were in Vermont. The colors were in their prime and we remembered the first time we were in Vermont and how we enjoyed biking so very much. This time was different though. Because we had the big motorhome, it was harder to get into campgrounds, over bridges that had low weight limits and under bridges with low clearance. But we did find a couple of campgrounds that were big and wonderful and we did our touring with the truck.

On October 1 we left Vermont. After a short visit to a Coast to Coast campground in the Catskills, we were in New Brunswick, New Jersey, to visit Ron's sister Linda. There we actually parked the motorhome in the church's parking lot where Linda's husband was the pastor. Linda, talked us into going into New York City one day (in her car) where we delighted in the play Aida after a short prayerful stop at "Ground Zero".

By October 11 we were in Philadelphia (a place we'd never

been before) but the only campground close to the city was booked solid. We did get two nights so we only had one cold rainy day to visit the sites of our nation's beginning. That left us hungering to see more of that city because it was so interesting.

We had always wanted to visit Shenandoah National Park so we were glad we finally had the time and the opportunity. The Blue Ridge Parkway begins where the Skyline Drive of Shennendoah National Park ends. It was specifically created to bridge Shenandoah Park with Smoky Mountain National Park and was a way to employ thousands of Conservation Corps workers during the 30's. We drove part of the northern part. I liked that a lot, because it contained a history of the people who once lived there. I happen to like history and people better than nature, I guess. When Shenandoah was made a national park, the park service moved every one who lived there and tried to restore it to its original wilderness. That's nice, but we had seen so much beauty and hiked in almost every national park that I wasn't that excited about getting on yet another trail. That may have been a result of being on the road so long. I did get real excited at our first stop on the Blue Ridge Parkway though. There was a dwelling—a place where real people had lived and struggled to eke out a living and life. The air was crisp and the smell of a wood fire coming out of the cabin made me want to go back in time for a little while. It seemed so serene and quiet, like heaven for the soul.

We were ready to leave Virginia. Although the days were pretty, the nights were cold and the mornings were heavy with fog. Rain was predicted for three out of four days and quite frankly we were also tired of touring; we had planned on spending a week or two in Georgia then slowly meandering to Florida. But Ron (while eating popcorn) broke two teeth from his bridge. We tried to find a dentist in Wytheville (and would have stayed longer) but they were booked solid. We called the Chamber of Commerce in several different places in Georgia where we had wanted to go and got phone numbers of dentists. We thought that calling ahead of time would enable him to get an appointment, but that didn't work either. Everyone was too busy to squeeze him in. We decided that we needed to be near a big city to find dentists with labs nearby. Jacksonville, Florida, seemed a good location and the first dentist we called (again with the help of the Chamber of Commerce) gave Ron an appointment. So we went to Hanna Park (a Jacksonville city park on the ocean) with 20 miles of bike paths and many miles of hiking trails not to mention the beach. While there (two weeks) we did not plan to do any touring; we just wanted to walk the beach, enjoy the park and read.

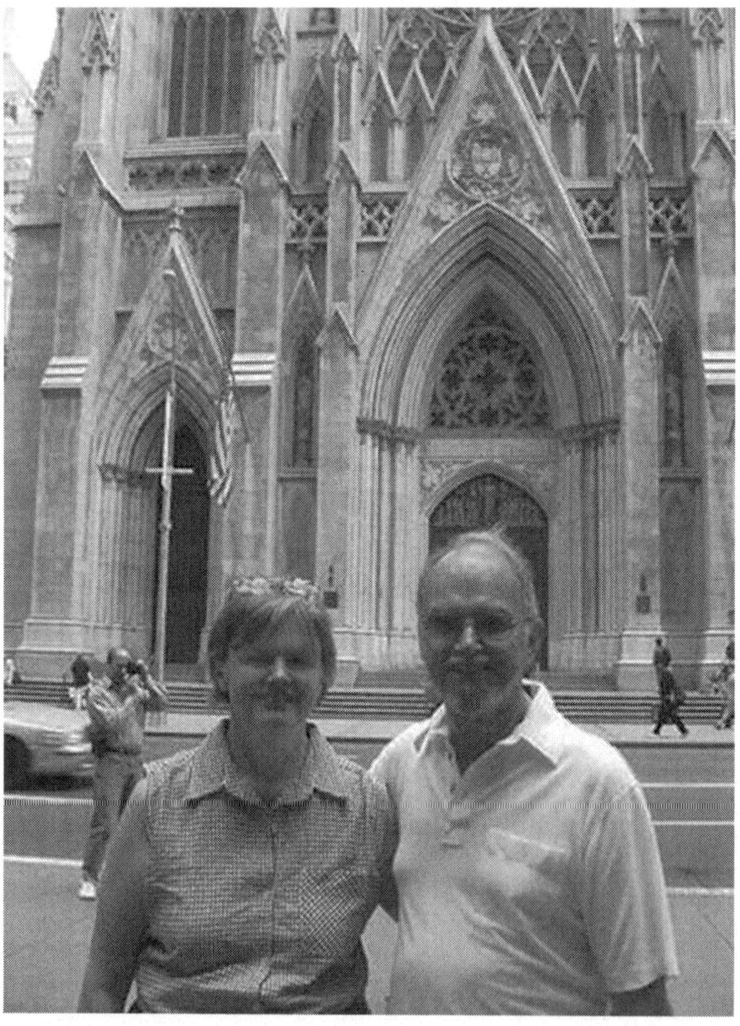

Linda and Ron at St. Patrick's Cathedral in NYC

Look What I Found On-line.

On one of our walks while we were at Hannah Beach Park, we were talking about what we would do after our seminars at Lazy Days. Out of the blue one day. Ron said, "When we get back, we can start looking for that house." I was excited.

We couldn't get online at the county park so I had to go into town to the library any time I wanted to go online for anything. I usually went once a day since it wasn't far. Shortly after Ron talked about looking for a house, I was at the library. I had gotten e-mail and had a little time on my hands so just for fun I did a search for "houses for sale" in Gold Canyon, Arizona. At the time I did not know that Mountain Brook Village was not Gold Canyon but was in fact **in** Gold Canyon. There were a lot of very expensive homes in Gold Canyon. Mountain Brook Village had more moderately priced houses and in an active adult community where Gold Canyon is more stratified. I also learned that Mountain Brook village was sold out. My only hope of finding the house of my dreams there would be to buy a pre-owned one. Once I figured that out, I narrowed down my search and found several houses that kind of looked like "my" house.

Some of the houses I found didn't show the square footage or number of bedrooms so I wasn't sure. About that time a pop-up window appeared and it was from a realtor who offered to help me. I responded telling her of our situation and that we would be looking for a house in the spring when we got back in Arizona. I told her that I was looking for the Saguaro model in Mountain-Brook Village. It turned out that she lived in Tempe which was about 45 minutes from Gold Canyon and she didn't know anything about the homes there but being a good salesperson, Margaret White was quick to find out as much as she could.

She got back to me fast with links to some of the houses for sale in Mountain Brook Village based on my preference for price and square footage. I printed them off and went home to show Ron. I didn't have detailed pictures to show him— just the exterior and the little bits of detail about each house like square footage, rooms, etc.. Knowing that the community was sold out and we only had the pre-owned homes to choose from we thought maybe it was good to act sooner rather than wait until spring.

From my memory of the day we visited Mountain Brook I picked the house that I thought looked like the Saguaro model and got back to the realtor and asked if she would check that one out specifically. I also added that if in fact it was the Saguaro model we would probably make an offer on it right then but first we needed more information. There were no pictures of the interior of the house, no information on square footage or number of rooms and of course, we needed to know those things.

The home was in fact a Saguaro and it was only about a year old. Margaret immediately made a special trip out to Mountain Brook with her camera and took pictures of the interior, checking out everything so she get could get back to us soon which she did. Those pictures, and what she told us prompted us to ask a few more questions and back and forth we went until we felt we had a good picture in our minds of what we would be buying. She went so far as to check out how clean things were such as the oven; we really appreciated that. After Ron and I talked about it, discussing all the ramifications of buying a house on line and the money we would spend furnishing it, we decided to put an offer on the house. It was accepted right away.

By the time we left Jacksonville we were actively buying a house. Of course paperwork had to be completed by fax and we were glad we were in West Palm Beach by then so we could use my daughter's fax and phone in her bead store. We asked friends in Arizona, Tom and Carol Vind, to be our long distance helpers as we would need them. We wanted him to be the one to witness the inspection of the house and when the sale was final to get the key for us and hold it until we got back. If the closing was on time it would be January 4 but we wouldn't be arriving back in Gold Canyon until February 5 after we finished our seminars at Lazy Days.

We had a good December in West Palm Beach enjoying the weather, Glenda, Erkki and being able to help out in the bead store. In my spare time I was trying to figure out what kind of furniture I would want and I made lists of all the things we would need to buy. The list was overwhelming.

Since we were keeping the motorhome to use for summer travel, I didn't want to take things out of it like dinnerware or linens. If and when we felt like going somewhere I didn't want to have to load it all up again.

For 14 years I hadn't been in many houses and hadn't paid attention to such things as household furnishings. I found myself needing to go to stores just to look and see what was available especially in the way of kitchen appliances. It was fun but scary at the same time.

Section Ten

Home Sweet Home

2003—2012

Going Crazy With Decisions

Our seminars at Lazy Days that year were very good and we were glad that Judy and Cec came in their motorhome and camped nearby again. They were there to help every single day we did a seminar. This was our last time to work at Lazy Days and everyone there was sad we wouldn't be coming back. They sold a lot of RVs because of our seminars.

When the last seminar was over we packed up to go to Arizona. Judy and Cec were going to be traveling with us. They were anxious to see the new house too and Arizona was on the way to California.

We drove pretty much straight through stopping for the nights in Wal-Marts or other such shopping center parking lots or where we could safely park without pulling into a campground. They were long days but full of excitement about what our house would be like. As we were driving through Houston we heard on the radio that the Challenger had exploded upon take off and parts of it were falling in the Houston area. We had walkie-talkies so talking with Judy and Cec was easy. We talked a little bit about how sad we felt at that tragedy.

When we got back to Gold Canyon we checked into Canyon Vistas RV resort which was less than a mile from our new house. Once we got checked in and settled we drove over to the house. It was an odd feeling trying to find our house which we had never seen before. Driving down the street looking at house numbers to see which one was ours seemed bizarre to say the least. I mean if we were looking for a place we had rented and we needed to find it that would've been the same way but we were looking for the house that belonged to us. The one we had just purchased.

Our good friend Tom had hidden the key for us. Once we got to the front door I looked at Ron and he looked at me. Judy and Cec were behind us watching. Then we put the key in the door and unlocked it. I actually shed a few tears of joy. The house was so beautifully big and with very high ceilings. There was a long hall with two nice rooms and a bathroom off to the left. At the end of the hall was another hall (to the right) that led to the master bedroom. But straight ahead at the end of the hall was a huge great room which included kitchen, dining area and living room. It was awesome especially with the high ceiling and large picture windows. The master bedroom was also huge. I had never seen a bedroom so big except in mansions. Well, I exaggerated, but it certainly was big compared to our big motorhome. The master bathroom was also gigantic as was the walk-in closet. It looked to me like I could never fill it in a million years.

From there I started opening closets and drawers and doors. I had the same feeling of spaciousness with everything I opened and again I wondered how I would ever even begin to fill those spaces. Then I was suddenly overwhelmed. I didn't know how I could decide what I needed and what would go where and as I looked around I had more questions than answers. I knew where the dining area would be, just off of the kitchen, and talked to the girls. "So this is where the table would go, then what should go in this cupboard or in this drawer..." And so on.

The couple who owned the house had it built and had moved in in November. Sadly he died on Christmas Eve. They had spent extra money to have ramps put at all entrances because the husband was in a wheelchair. They also spent extra money to have a large handicapped accessible shower in the master bathroom. It was lovely and included a marble bench inside.

But as we looked at the walls we realized they needed painting badly. Most of the walls had not been painted other than by the builder and they were marred from the wheelchair. Ron and I discussed that it would be easier to have the house completely repainted before we moved a single thing in. By talking with neighbors we found and hired a painter right away. We got a special price on painting because they didn’t have to dodge any furniture. In two days he and his partners had completely painted the inside of the house. Since I didn't have a clue on what colors I would use in buying furniture I felt that going with white would give me a lot of options and we could paint again sometime down the road.

Think of everything that's in your house and imagine having to shop for it all at once. We had to buy everything from a toilet brush (in fact two, one for each bathroom) to drapes, furniture, sheets, pillows and towels. Add to that all the cooking utensils, pots and pans, glassware, silverware and on and on it went.

Right away we started shopping. We lived out of the motorhome for almost a month, but it was so close to the house that we could make trips over anytime we wanted.

From the time we knew we were buying the house I had been looking in malls and on the Internet trying to decide what kind of dishes I would want among other things. I knew I wanted a particular design which I had fallen in love with. So one of the first places we went to was Mikasa. I think Ron was sweating because the dishes were pricy but he had promised to be a good guy when it came to shopping. And he said he wouldn't argue with prices if it was something I wanted. I knew the budget so I wasn't going overboard. What a sweetheart he was.

We shopped for the furniture next and had that on order ready to come within a week or so. We shopped for and bought two TVs, one for the living room and one for the bedroom. One phone call to DirecTV and we were scheduled for installation. We ordered the telephone installation (after I bought telephones), office furniture which Ron had to put together (we saved a little money that way) and Internet.

Once we had the bedroom, living room TV, couch and recliner as well as the table and chairs for the kitchen we moved in. We brought the motorhome over to the house parking it in front so we could empty out our clothing and personal items, the important things out of cupboards like our business records, books, computer stuff, food from the refrigerator and cupboards, along with several special pieces of Tupperware. Once that was done we took the motorhome back over to the RV park and put it in their storage lot where it would be safe from vandals. We would not be living in it for a while.

How Many Square Feet?

I was on my knees washing the kitchen floor when I looked to my left and saw what looked like an open sea of floor. I wanted to cry. I thought, "What did we get ourselves into?" When I cleaned the motorhome it took all of 10 maybe 15 minutes at the most. Suddenly I was chained to being a housewife again and it took quite a while to get the job done. So that was the downside of buying a house. The good part was that I liked having all the room.

I didn't like all the shopping though and was glad when we were finished with that. One day we were in Home Depot, buying such things as a rake, shovel, gloves, and other tools when my son, Jim, happened to call on the cell phone and asked what we were doing. He laughed so hard when we told him and I wanted to hit him. He was very familiar with that particular downside of being a homeowner.

We found out early on that we made some mistakes. We picked out a nice round glass dinette table which only seated six. And the chairs for that set had casters on them. When we went to sit down they rolled backward. Ron actually fell on his butt once when the chair kept going and he didn't. We kept them for a while and eventually sold the set and bought a regular wooden table with the leaf and regular chairs. We had not made too many mistakes.

We loved the community we had moved into. There were things going on all the time and right away we got involved a little bit by going to a few dinners and events and met more people and suddenly it was like being with a wonderful family. There are three different pinochle groups which play weekly and there's bridge, bingo, classes and more than I could mention here. Right away we signed up to play pinochle and bridge, two of our favorite card games.

MountainBrook Village publishes a monthly newsletter and I read in there that they were starting a theater group —

MountainBrook Village Players. Because they had a wonderful stage in the biggest room which was called the Superstition Center this new group was going to put on annual plays. "Wow", I thought "This is right up my alley." I went to the first meeting and then I tried out for a play, got a part and met the other actors. I was in my glory and it made mopping the floor on my hands and knees worthwhile.

But we had also made plans to bring the motorhome over, load it up and take off for a few months in the summer. Even thinking about going back on the road for just a little while was tough. I did not want to leave my house. During our seminars when people would ask us if they should sell the house, we always said, "If you keep the house it will be a magnet to draw you back." We were so right.

Our plans for the summer included the Life on Wheels conference in Idaho which would be held in July, my bicycle trip with Cec the beginning of September, a seminar in Texas the last part of September, and we had three grandchildren we wanted to take on their "trip". Sadly that would leave five grandchildren who were still too young and would never be able to go on a trip in the motorhome with us. It was just a fact of life.

The Last Trip in the Dream

Erkki came in June by himself because there was no one else in his age group at the time and we made a special trip just for him. We took off from our house here and took him up to the Grand Canyon and planned to go to the Zion National Park and then back here. He loved camping in the Grand Canyon. It was very peaceful and nice. We camped right in the national park. The only problem was he and I had an accidental fight. Oh it wasn't a mean fight. Nobody was mad. We were looking at the Canyon with the binoculars and we both had to take our glasses off in order to see. He was holding his glasses in his hand while looking through the binoculars and he was ready to hand the binoculars to me when I reached; our wrists hit each other and his glasses went flying way down into the Grand Canyon. Poor kid. I felt so bad. He really needed his glasses too. When we got to St. George, Utah, I had his mother fax the prescription to an optometrist in town and Erkki happily picked out a new set of glasses; we had them in an hour so all was well. Even with that we had a really great time. After we brought him back and got him on a plane to go back to Florida we reloaded the motorhome for what we would need for the whole summer, closed up the house, and took off again.

We headed up towards Utah again when we left and Ron and I spent a couple of days biking. I needed to get back in shape for my bike trip with Cec. From there we went right up to the Life on Wheels conference in Idaho which was good and then moved to Spokane to get ready to pick up two 12 year old granddaughters. Taylor (Susie's daughter) and Kailee (Marty's daughter) had camped with us from the time they were about four years old. But having them as 12-year-old silly girls was another thing. They were 12 going on 20; they thought they were bigger than they were and didn't want to do kid things. Writing journals and going on hikes was not to their liking. They spent a lot of their time complaining "it's too hot" or "I'm tired". All they really wanted to do is play pinochle and pick on me. Ron was oblivious to most of it; he just tuned them out.

We were only in Glacier for a day when the park caught on fire and we were evicted. It was really hot there even before the fire. We had heard reports that Yellowstone was heating up also and the staff was worried about earthquakes. So all in all it was a bad summer weather wise. When we got kicked out of Glacier we went to Missoula, Montana, and did a rafting trip but the river was way down so it was just a mediocre trip at best. Another day we went to a movie. It was a different summer with different grandchildren who we love but I think we loved them better when they were little and more manageable.

In August we were in Missouri to be in attendance when Sue became a United States citizen. That was a joy to witness. We had planned to go to Missouri to visit them anyway but we were really there for another reason at the time.

Right after we started out in the summer I got an e-mail from an old friend I used to walk with at Valle Del Oro. Shirley and Mike had been full-time RVers in a motorhome very similar to ours until they decided to settle down again and buy a house in Texas (Dallas I believe). Her e-mail said they wanted to go back on the road again and that they didn't like living in a "stick house". I wrote back and asked her if they wanted to buy our motorhome. She wrote back and said, “yes”. Well it wasn't that easy but close. They did want to see the motorhome so we had made arrangements for them to see it when we were in Missouri because that was the closest we would be to their home. We had told them that we had commitments that would take us to the end of September and then they could have the motorhome if they wanted it. As promised they came and met with us in Missouri and we agreed on a price and a date and shook hands.

On September 3 we met up with Judy and Cec in Akron, Iowa. I was excited because I always wanted to just bike from somewhere to somewhere in the U.S. And checking out the road it looked to be fairly rural. We wouldn't have much traffic to deal with and pretty much thought that wind wouldn't be a problem because at that time of year the wind blew from West to East and we hoped it would give us a push. What we didn't count on was a strong southerly wind that would beat us daily. And the other thing we didn't count on was the scenery which was boring. The only thing to see was corn and bean fields and few towns which would have made the trip a little bit more interesting.

Every morning Cec and I got ready and started pedaling and left Ron and Judy to pack up the motorhomes, hook up the cars and go down the road. We had planned the stops all along our trip in Iowa so that Cec and I would bike about 30 miles each day. Ron and Judy were in no hurry to take off daily but they did want be in the new campground early enough that they could get the motorhomes set up with the hot water heater heating so we could take showers when we got to the campground. And each day the four of us had time to do a little touring once we got to where we were going. It was okay but I didn't like it and I quit two days before getting to the end of our journey. I left Cec to finish on her own which she did much to her credit. My excuse was we needed to get to a rally in Texas to do our last seminar and then get home. Judy and Cec were going to meet us at the rally them follow us home to help us unload the motorhome and get it ready for the new owners. But the truth was, I was just tired of the wind, hills and boring farmland. I had had enough.

Trouble, Trouble, Trouble

I was not at all sad about selling the motorhome. Neither was Ron. And to reinforce that, our lovely motorhome gave us problems on the summer trip. I don't remember were the first trouble was---maybe Idaho or Washington but it was early on and I don't even remember what the problem was. I do know we spent time in a service bay instead of having fun. But after our seminar as we were rolling down the road in New Mexico heading for the barn it happened again.

I was driving on what looked like a new road but it was as rough as could be. It was worse than a washboard road. Then suddenly I got the bright idea that maybe it wasn't the road. I stopped the motorhome on the shoulder. The road was smooth. It was our air bags again. I called road service and they came out from Lourdsburg, New Mexico, and jury rigged something to get us going back to their garage. A bracket or something had broken off but he said he could make a new part.

We had a deadline though. Shirley and Mike were coming the next day and we had made arrangements to have a carpet cleaning company clean the carpeting in the motorhome and we needed to move our personnel things out of the motorhome. We were losing time and in fact had to cancel the carpet cleaning. I decided that we would just give Shirley and Mike the money to do it on their own rather than holding them up.

It wasn't as easy as that even because it still rode rough. We did get home and Ron took the motorhome up to the RV repair facility nearby and had them work on it but it was still rough. We felt so bad. It wasn't anything we did or didn't do. It was the $#%&*# Dream.

Again Judy and Cec were a big help unloading the motorhome and when Shirley and Mike came we told them right off that we expected them to get the motorhome fixed in Tucson at a certified RV dealer and we would pay for it. They were satisfied with that, hooked up their truck to the motorhome then we waved them goodbye. I was just glad it was gone. Even though it was beautiful, it was a nightmare.

Top: Erkki in Utah and Kailee, Taylor and Ron in Glacier.
Bottom: Cec and I beginning our bike trip.

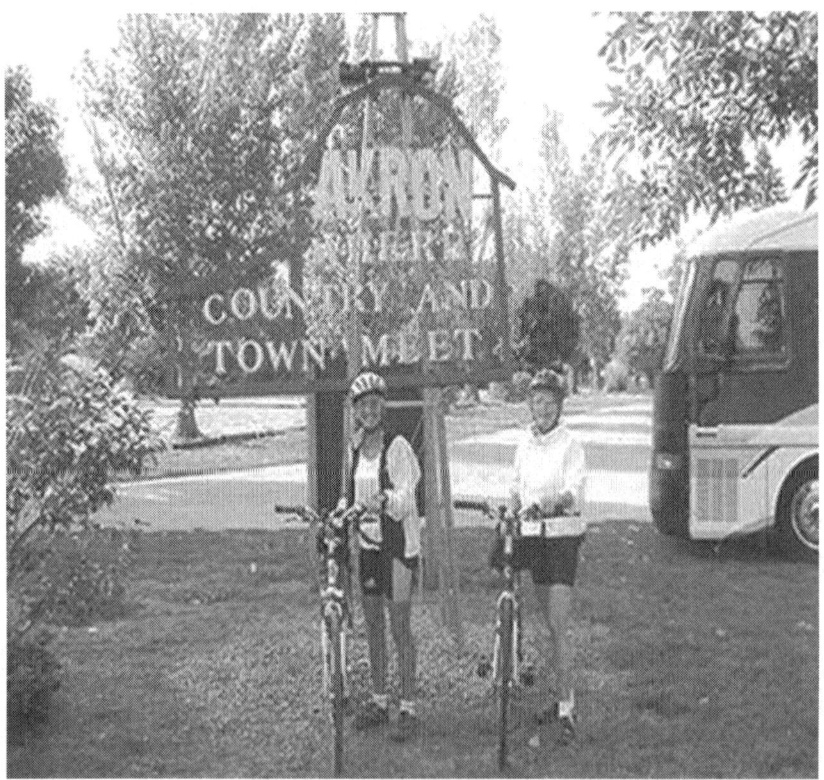

Ups and Downs of Life

The title of this book, My Rocky Road to the Good Life would lead one to believe that once Ron and I found each other life would be all good and nothing bad would happen. Of course that's unrealistic. We have had our share of bad times like the bad time when Ron was diagnosed with prostate cancer but we still continued with our lifestyle and had good times on the road. We just added dealing with the disease. Our life in our new house is no different. We have lots of good times but there have been some bad times. At our ages we expect that.

One of the worst bad times was September 23, 2011 when we got word that our gifted grandson, Jonn Flath, dropped dead while on an easy run with his ROTC group. He was an honor student and a devout Christian, but we miss him terribly. I can still hear my son's voice on the phone when he tearfully said, "Mom, I've lost my son." There were over 800 (mostly young people) at his funeral which is a testament to his love of life. He touched a lot of lives.

Some of the other bad times were difficult as well. I've been hospitalized several times since we settled down. But we are thankful for good hospitals and doctors and all is well in the end.

But another incident began with Ron just being in a hurry. So I say it was all his fault. We were going to have a rehearsal here at our house for an upcoming Follies and people were coming over so he took out the trash and coming back in he stumbled over a rock that was right where he knew it always was. He just wasn't paying attention. Poor guy flew up then came down hard really smashing his hip. It was a bad break. Of course the paramedics and the ambulance were here right away and took him to the hospital. Surgery was delayed a day or two while they tried to remove the effects of the Coumadin (blood thinner) he was on. The surgeon decided to put screws in which was a mistake because Ron's bone density was low due to the Lupron injections he regularly got for his prostate cancer. But we didn't know that was a problem right away. After his stay in the hospital he was transferred to a rehab facility so they could teach him how to walk and help them with exercise and therapy. At home and months later he was still in pain and having problems even after going to the local physical therapist that was highly regarded. We decided to get a second opinion. I took him to the orthopedic doctor that had repaired my rotator cuff. After looking at x-rays he could tell that the pins the first doctor had put in were backing out. So after about a year of pain Dr. Schenk said he would take the pins out and do a total hip replacement. That meant he had to spend three weeks in rehab again and then go through a lot of physical therapy. After all that, Ron was just about worn out. But he's okay now with his hip.

In the meantime I knew I had an infection in my mouth. I talked to my prosthodontist about it and he recommended I see an oral surgeon. The oral surgeon and the prosthodontist agreed that my (what had been wonderful) sub periosteal implant had gone bad (10 years is max and I was at 11 years). The recommendation was that I have the old implant taken out and new implants put in. Imagine how much I looked forward to that—not. I knew I needed the surgery but I had to keep postponing it because of Ron's hip. But finally on May 17, 2010 I had surgery. They took the old out then put four new implants in. But I got a bad infection and the doctor did not understand infections very well. It went wild and the antibiotics weren't working. Penicillin might have worked but after that one episode of anaphylactic shock when I got Penicillin in the 60s, I was warned to never take Penicillin, ever. With the infection raging, I demanded the doctor put me in the hospital and there the infectious disease doctor assigned to me said that antibiotics would not work until the infection was scraped off of the bone. But my doctor disagreed with the hospital doctor so nothing was done except keep me on antibiotics while the infection was eating away at my jaw. Finally early in August, all of my implants fell out when the oral surgeon was just checking to see if they were okay. He looked shocked and seemed dumbfounded. He simply said, "We will wait a while and see" and let me go. I went running right away to the infectious disease doctor. He wasn't surprised. He called the oral surgeon and told him the bone needed to be scraped immediately. The oral surgeon did that which was a lot of fun for me. As I was waking up from the anesthesia, he came to talk to me. He was rather white and looked a bit scared. He admitted later that he thought I must've had bone cancer for the way my jaw looked; it was eaten up through the bone marrow. I personally think he knew he goofed at that time. From that time on I knew I could never have implants and my dentures didn't fit on my gums that were almost nonexistent. For two years, I visited different doctors to see what they had to say and finally found my hero—Dr. Fish. I now have mini implants which screw in and were put in by Dr. Fish and they seem to be working okay although there's no guarantee. I tried to sue the first surgeon but the lawyers said I didn't really have a case. They all stick together in my opinion. One thing good that came out of that was the first surgeon gave me all my money back which I thought was pretty decent. We put it in a savings account in case a miracle happened. The little mini implants were much cheaper so I'm money ahead. But I can never catch up with the pain and discomfort I suffered.

While I was waiting to get the mini implants there was a whole year that I was doing fairly well even without teeth. I couldn't eat meat or salad and a lot of things except ice cream and cake and wine of course which meant that I gained weight. But I was lucky to be cast as the hippie in a play which I loved. That was really up my alley because I think I'm a hippie at heart. And I was able to do that with those ill-fitting dentures. I had so much fun playing Crystal and I hope the audience enjoyed it. I had spent two months going through rehearsals and was excited for the opening night (our plays run four nights). But leading up to that Ron had been having difficulty swallowing. We had gone to about five different doctors during the time I was rehearsing for the play so that would have been over a period of two months at least. No one could come up with any reason for his problem but it kept getting worse. He couldn't even drink liquids. I don't know how we got through the four nights of the play. I do know we spent all day Saturday in the emergency room and I barely got back in time to go on stage but it didn't do him any good at all. The last day of the play was Sunday, February 27 and on Monday and Tuesday I took Ron to different doctors. Finally on Wednesday his general doctor suggested that he see a neurologist and made arrangements for Ron to see her the next day. Our appointment was at 4:30 on Friday, March 4 and she sent him to the hospital right away. His diagnosis: myasthenia gravis. It's not curable but it's controllable and we are doing just that. We've had some ups and downs with that but currently we are both doing just fine.

Regarding Ron's prostate cancer: In 1994 we were told he had maybe two years but now every doctor says he will die of something else. We are so fortunate and thank God every day.

But now the good times which have been many. Since we've moved into the house we've been on at least four cruises which have been wonderful. I really love cruising. We also did a home exchange with a couple in England. They came to our house and while they were in our house we lived in their house for six whole weeks. We also exchanged cars. I'd like to do more home exchanges but the problem is very few want to come to Arizona in our summer because it's so hot and I don't blame them. We can't exchange houses in the winter because I'm usually busy with my plays at that time. We like summer here because we simply hibernate. Our home is very comfortable so we watch movies and it's a nice slow time for us. There isn't much going on in the community because most go up north for the summer.

Another fun time we took a train from Flagstaff to Chicago, stayed overnight and then took another train to Michigan. We came back the same way. It was a lovely way to travel and much more comfortable than flying. One time we drove the car to Michigan but hated that. After having a motorhome to travel in, traveling in a car for a long distance is no fun—there is no comparison.

Other good times are just what we do here. I have become extremely active with our Village Players. I have directed six full-length plays, acted in two, served on the board of directors as president twice. I've also produced and directed three Follies (our variety show) for this community which has been well received. Besides the plays and Follies I have organized and directed several Murder Mystery Parties primarily for our actors so they can have fun just ad-libbing and playing. And I regularly teach classes on life story writing. The stories people write and the way they've grown in their writing make me feel proud. I feel I've helped them do something good for their families. And we are busy in our church. Ron helps by feeding the homeless one day a week and I help by making the PowerPoint slides for a lot of our services.

Me as Crystal in Ghost of a Chance smoking a fake cigar.
Ron in his drunk airline pilot act for the Follies.
Ron and I in Holland.

Pantomiming
In different
shows

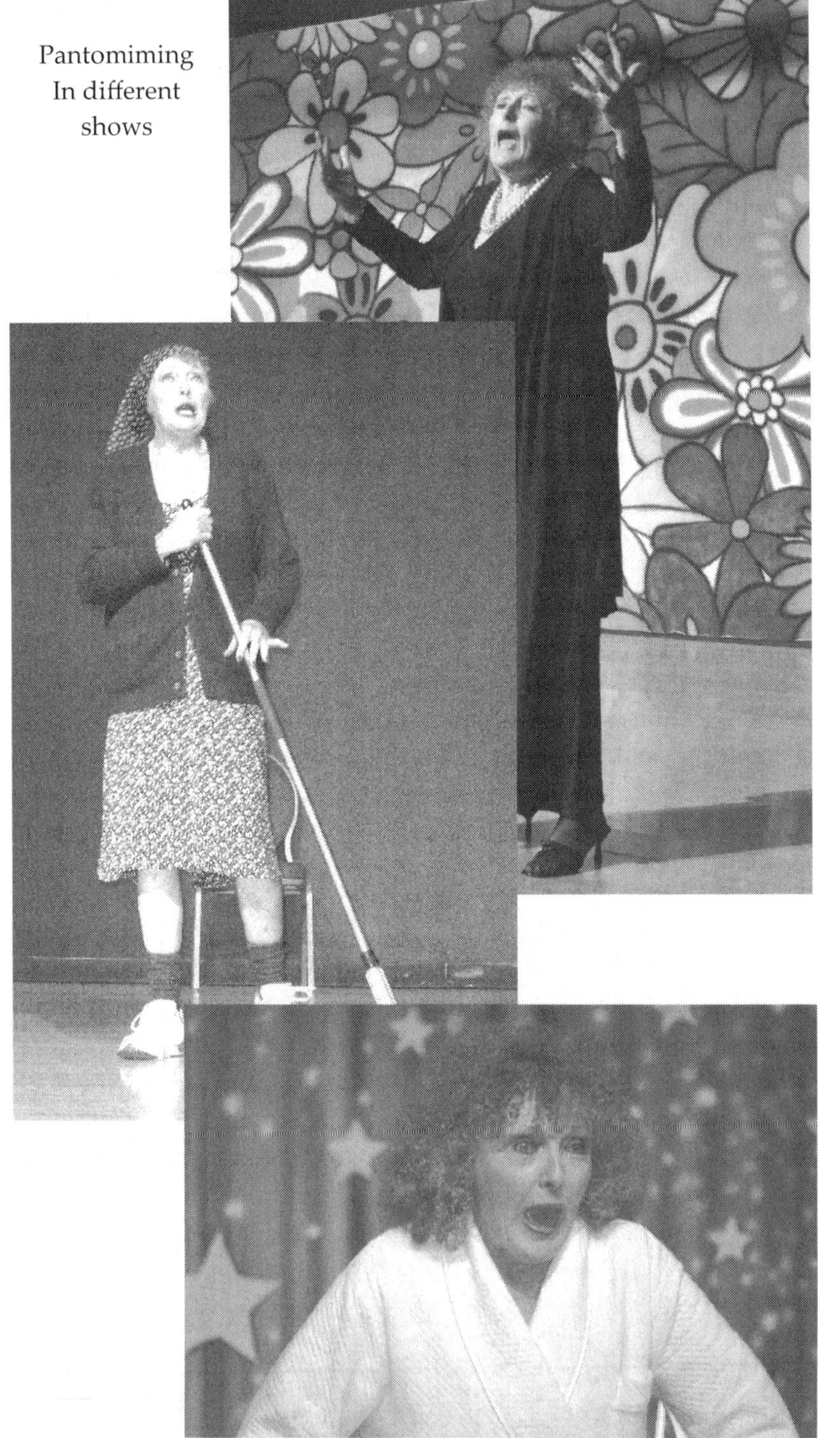

We are Not Finished Yet

In May of this year I celebrated my 75th birthday simply by just going out to dinner with good friends. In July Ron had his 80th birthday and I heard from his daughter, Susie that three of his kids and two husbands wanted to come here and surprise him. So I got going on that but it was difficult to surprise him and get the house ready for company. Ron is easy to surprise because he's not curious about different things that may or may not happen.

I had already purchased his birthday present long before I heard from the girls. I had to be able to go pick them up at the airport so I told him I was going shopping for his present the day before his birthday. I had his present hiding in my closet underneath my long dresses but when he wasn't in the house I hid the present in a cupboard in the garage that he never went to. Then the morning it was time to go to the airport to pick them up I simply transferred the package to the trunk. When we got home from the airport I dropped them off at the corner and told them to walk slowly toward the house while I drove into the garage. I ran into the house saying I had to go to the bathroom so I had an excuse to get out of Ron's way and also that would make him answer the door. And in a few minutes the doorbell rang and there they were. He was so excited to see them standing there singing happy birthday with party hats and noisemakers. It was a fun surprise. I didn't really think I had room to put up five people but we managed because I had borrowed the big air mattress from my neighbor, Laura and had that stashed in the garage too.

I had made reservations at a nice restaurant for after church on Sunday and had a limousine hired for the afternoon and evening. After dinner, we went to two different casinos and I gave everyone money to play with. I loved being in on the surprise.

We are going on another cruise in March after I finish the play I am directing this year. We are finally getting a chance to go to Hawaii. We had to cancel two other times because of Ron's different problems but will get to go this time. Life is good.

Out on His Own Terms

Ron had to have open heart surgery (triple bypass and aortic valve) the end of August 2013. He was in rehab for a full month and we were finally got to take that cruise to Hawaii in January of 2014. It was very relaxing and I loved the tours we took on the islands.

We kept busy the rest of 2014 with the things we always loved doing. Once a month we went to a local casino with a couple of bus loads from our community. We always looked forward to the people and happy hours. Twice Ron got a full house playing video poker while I generally lost money. He was always so lucky with video poker. He won four times in his life.

Each month was busy with his Tuesdays working at Genesis (feeding the hungry at lunch), doctors' appointments, playing cards and visiting. Every time we made an appointment for a doctor's visit we would try to make the appointment around when we could eat lunch out. Our favorite lunch spots were Olive Garden (for soup and salad) or On the Border and once in a while we would do Applebee's. If the appointment was late in the day we would go to dinner at our very favorite place which was Carrabba's. We always sat in a booth in the bar and got to know the waiters; they became friends.

On December 18, 2014, Ron had an appointment with Dr. Grossklaus (Dr. G) , his urologist, for his routine Lupron shot for his prostate cancer. He had been getting the shot every four months for years. Just the month before, Ron's GP got some out -of-whack numbers from his routine blood work showing problems with the kidneys. Right away Dr. G. said the PSA was up and we told him about the kidney numbers. He gave us that look which spoke volumes. Trouble. Ron had been incontinent for some time but it had gotten worse. He also was not peeing much. Dr. G. left the room to get a Foley catheter, and Ron and I looked at each other with a look we had had before in doctor's offices. Ron said, "Is this it?" I just shrugged my shoulders but inside I was afraid. When the doctor inserted the Foley, he got so much urine out he was surprised. So having a Foley all the time would be the new norm. Ron was a little down at first but on the bright side, it was a lot less trouble, he didn't have to get up at night and there were no more accidents. Dr. G. suggested that we see an oncologist to see what else might be done so in January of 2015 we saw Dr. Bacharach. He took all sorts of Xrays and tests and suggested we try one other medicine which Ron took, but it didn't make any difference. Our new routine became to see Dr. G monthly for a catheter exchange.

By October of 2015 Dr. G. had a hard time getting the new catheter in and each successive month it was even harder. I knew in my heart that the end was coming but said nothing. On Tuesday, January 12, 2016 it took Dr. G. longer than ever before and there was blood all over the table. When he finished he looked so sorry and said, "It is time for hospice or more chemo." It was the last time we saw Dr. G.

We did make an appointment with the oncologist and saw him two days later, but neither Ron nor I liked what he was proposing. After he did a rectal exam, I asked what it felt like, he said "lumpy and bumpy and full of cancer." Ron said, "Hospice". He had made his decision and it was mine as well. He had suffered enough.

Over the weekend we made phone calls. Ron called his kids and sisters. I notified my children and siblings. Jean and Linda (Ron's sisters) suggested I join Caringbridge so I could post updates that everyone could read which I did. Meanwhile last fall I had signed up to do two more Life Story Writing Classes at the college and was looking forward to them. I was especially excited about the advanced class for 17 who were in my beginning classes in the fall. They were so enthusiastic and eager to actually put their stories in book form. So I didn't cancel the classes because Ron had been good by himself for the five hours I was gone last semester.

By Thursday, January 21 Ron was officially under Hospice care and we happily learned that they took care of everything. No more doctors' appointments, no more calls to the pharmacy, everything we would need would be provided even a hospital bed and wheel chair.

We always played pinochle on Thursday evenings but Ron didn't want to go that night. He said he had wanted to watch the Republican Debate so I went alone. But when I came home I learned that he had not watched the debate. He said he couldn't find it and there were unanswered phone calls on the answering machine. I knew I'd need to find a nurse for my class times on Tuesday and got busy finding a gal who could care for him. Helen worked out beautifully.

Ron's youngest daughter flew in Friday evening. I was so happy to have her here. Her job as a closed captioning technician for Michigan State University allowed her to work from our house. Shortly after David arrived then Marty and her husband Brian, and over the weekend of the 30th Ron's oldest sons, Karl and Kurt along with granddaughter Mary got to say good bye to Ron. Yes, we had a house full but it was good for them to be with their father. By that weekend he was bedridden. So all the visiting was done in our bedroom which was good. It limited the confusion.

Susie left on January 31 and Marty and Brian left on February 2 and David left the next Friday, February 5. While I had appreciated Susie and David's helpful visit it got a bit much with so many here. I am used to a quiet life. Early in the day before David left Cherie, the social worker from Hospice came and spent quite a while with Ron and I. Cheri told Ron and I we should do 4 things:

1. Forgive each other.
2. Apologize to each other.
3. Thank each other.
4. Express our love.

So after she left we were alone and did just that. When David left, I was glad to be alone with Ron. I had neighbors and hospice I could count on if I needed anything. Ron was pretty quiet that last week. I would sit with him and read to him from our newsletters. After I read the story of our hike up Guadalupe Peak in Texas, I said, "Boy I really got us into some tough situations" and he responded with a smile, "More than once." That was very true. That was just about the last time he responded to anything.

Ron loved baseball so much and was looking forward to spring training but they weren't playing yet. Thanks to my sister who suggested looking for ball games on YouTube, I found a Detroit Tiger game from 1984 when they won the World Series. I am not sure he really heard much of that.

Helen stayed with him on Tuesday the 9th and when I came home she said Good-bye to him. I think she knew he was near the end. That day and the next couple of days, I wanted to stay in the bedroom but I needed something to do so I took his clothes out of the closet a few at a time and folded them then placed them in large plastic bags. His bed was on the opposite side of the room and he couldn't see what I was doing. It wasn't emotional, but I knew he would never need clothes again. I would never see him dressed up for church or dinner out.

All night Thursday Ron's breathing was so labored I didn't get any sleep. Friday he quieted down and he wasn't putting out any urine so I knew I needed to be with him. About dinner time I was hungry so I warmed up some macaroni and cheese, but couldn't eat much. I went back to the bedroom to sit with Ron and I kept telling him, "I loved you very much but it is okay to go home. God is waiting for you and I will be okay, I promise". I had been telling him that all along, but I just said it over and over while holding his hand. Suddenly he licked his lips so very lightly and took his very last breath. It was just before 6 p.m. on February 12, 2016. I stayed with him a minute then called Hospice.

They said a nurse would be coming but it would be a while since she was across the valley in Phoenix and would have rush hour to deal with. Then I called David because I promised him I would let me know right away. All I could do was cry when he answered the phone. I then called my two best friends, Barb and Kay and they came right away and stayed with me until the nurse came. We cried a bunch and pastor came. He and I went in to Ron and he prayed while we held Ron's lifeless hand. That was one prayer Ron would never hear. I encouraged Pastor to leave for an event he was supposed to attend. And when the nurse finally arrived I encouraged Barb and Kay to go home. The mortician came next and I went next door to the Dave and Ronette's while Ron was prepared to be moved. We watched until they were both gone then I went home to my empty house. The hospital bed was still in the bedroom but it was empty. It didn't bother me to be in the room where Ron died and from exhaustion I slept well.

Ron was the best thing in my whole life and now that he is gone life is very empty. I loved him and our life together more than anything else in my life. We were best friends, my very best friend ever. We made such a good team and helped so many people learn about full-time RVing and even in the plays, follies and anything we did, we made people happy and had fun.

Ron's memorial service was at 10 a.m. on Friday, February 19. Glenda, Jim and Sue came on Thursday, my sister Bunnie and her husband Jerry and Mark and Ana arrived on Friday. Cec and Judy drove from California and there were a lot of local people at the memorial. So many friends were there; some of my writers came, bridge friends, pinochle friends, church friends, neighbors, and some of the actors were there. I am so fortunate to have so many friends here.

I will keep busy with more Life Story Writing classes and in fact added another class just after he died and plan to do four or five at three different campuses starting in October. The college loves my classes and students. Just like I told Ron, I will be fine. We had such wonderful experiences that all I have to do is go back in my mind and I am with Ron again. No regrets.

This picture and sentiment was in the thank you notes I made for everyone following his death. This picture was taken on that Hawaiian cruise.

Ronald Richard Hofmeister
July 8, 1932 - February 12, 2016

"I was supposed to spend the rest of my life with you - and then I realized...you spent the rest of your life with me. I smile because I know you loved me till the day you went away and will keep loving me...till the day we're together again..."

What Did I Do?

I had just returned from a wonderful trip to Michigan where I drove over 800 miles visiting friends and relatives while celebrating my 80th birthday. I felt terrific, independent and alive.

I had been back in Arizona only a few days and quickly got into my routine. I play bridge on Mondays with the ladies of Mountainbrook and on Thursday, August 3rd, I had been asked to sub at Barb Lembke's house for her bridge game. We had fun although the cards weren't hot for me. Shortly before 4 pm we all started to head home. My car was parked in front of Barb's house facing the direction I needed to go. My 2010 Lincoln MKS is my pride and joy and I felt so lucky to have such a luxurious car as I pressed the push button start. As soon as I pressed the start my seat moved into position and the AC came on full blast because I had had it on when I arrived. After all it was August in southern Arizona and the temperature was well over 100 degrees.

I did not put the seat belt on because our community has very little traffic and we drive slowly. I was only three blocks or so from home. I am not sure what happened next. The car was in drive but it didn't seem to want to go anywhere. Maybe I didn't press too hard on the gas pedal but I thought that the car hadn't actually started. I joke that maybe I had used too much brain power playing bridge and I might have left common sense fly out the door. I remember thinking I needed to restart the car. But I cannot figure out why I didn't put the car in park before pressing the start button. Did I have a "brain fart"? So when I pressed the start button again, I actually abruptly stopped the car which was running and because the car was in drive, it lurched forward about maybe two feet then rocked back again. Barb who was still at the gate heard the commotion and looked at me with a very concerned look. I felt so foolish and calmly put the car in gear and restarted it properly and waved to her that I was okay as I slowly moved down the street.

When I got to Rugged Ironwood for my left turn, I reached up and pressed the garage door opener button rather than putting on the turn signal. What was wrong with my brain? Once home I felt a tightness in my shoulders. My solution was to take my bra off and put on a more comfortable top then I took two Tylenol before starting to fix my dinner. The tightness was getting worse so I grabbed the ice pack out of the freezer and tried that but it didn't help. Next I tried the heating pad. That didn't seem to do anything. I saw my neighbor Mathie out back so I went to him and asked him to massage my shoulders a little. That didn't help. I called Jim McCann who is a retired chiropractor and asked him what I should do. He told me to go to the emergency room.

I drove the short distance to the ER in Apache Junction and they were not busy. Right away I was given a very strong muscle relaxer shot in my left arm. That helped almost immediately. They did a CT scan and Xray and while I was waiting for the doctor to tell me what was wrong, I went to the restroom which was right across from my room. I had no trouble peeing but when finished I could not pull up my pants. My arms wouldn't work to pull up.

I told the nurse of the situation and immediately she put a cervical collar on me and told me they would transport me to Banner Desert which has a trauma unit. While waiting I called Guy and Mathie and asked if they would please come and get my car and take it home. They arrived just before the transport people came for me.

At Banner Desert I was taken into a huge room where at least 12 nurses, doctors, and technicians were waiting for me. I was surrounded by these angels who knew what to do and did it. One gal cut off my top, others were hooking up IVs or electrodes. What a team they were. I was told I would have an MRI and that happened soon. Basically I was feeling okay but a bit overwhelmed. I knew everything would be okay but I was feeling the loss of that very favorite top of mine. I had had it for many years.

The MRI is an awful test and it seems to take forever. After I was taken to the Intensive Care Unit (ICU). Shortly after I was taken there my friends came to see me. Barb, Kay, Jaquie, Carol and Bonny were there when the neurologist came in to tell me the MRI results. **I was a quadriplegic.** When the car threw me forward it caused a whip lash injury with complications. Apparently I had two bone spurs in my neck. One punctured the spinal column when I went forward and the other got the spinal column on the way back.

Changing My Attitude

I did not want to be a quadriplegic. I wanted to die but other than my damaged spinal cord, I was not going to die. I briefly thought of suicide, but what could I do in the hospital. And what could I do anyway. My left arm and leg would barely move. The doctors would come in and ask me to raise my leg. I could not make the left leg lift up even a fraction of an inch. I couldn't even wiggle my toes. The right leg was better and I could lift it a bit. My left arm was helpless. I could not move my fingers or raise the arm up off the bed. When they grabbed my hand and asked me to squeeze, I couldn't. I had to be fed which was so very humbling. I was helpless.

I talked with the kids and told them the situation. When I told them I wanted to die, they all said the same thing. "You never ever let us give up that easily. Come on, you can do anything." I was told I would be transferred to the spinal cord rehab at Banner University in Phoenix and would be there for more than six weeks getting extensive physical therapy. I really didn't think that would help but I did promise the kids that I would give it my best shot for two months. But I let them know that I did not want to live in a wheelchair. After all at 80 years of age, it was almost time to die. I had had a great life.

I told all of my friends not to come to Phoenix to visit. It was a long drive and I was really going to be concentrating on getting mobile. I promised I would keep in touch and encouraged them to think that I was going to a health farm or something like that.

Banner University was wonderful. For three hours every day I was put through some pretty tough paces. First there was occupational therapy which included being showered, learning how to get dressed (almost impossible at first). PT concentrated on trying to get my legs to work. Before long I was actually taking a few steps and actually pedaling a stationary bike for a short while. Yes, I was going to be able to walk. Getting my arms to work properly was a lot harder but I could see the progress.

When it was time to leave University, I was transferred to Sante` in Mesa for two weeks and the best part of being there was that I was able to have visitors. Therapy was okay but not nearly as intensive as it had been at University. I was walking with a walker and able to eat but still needed help getting showered and dressed.

My daughter Glenda, was fighting a battle of her own in West Palm Beach, Florida, as hurricanes promised havoc. She flew to Arizona to be here when I was released from Sante`. Together we looked for a nurse I could hire at affordable rates and luckily found Cheri, an aid who lived in Mountainbrook. With her help three mornings a week for showers and reaching things I can't reach, I do fine. I live alone, but I am fairly independent. I cannot cook because pans are too heavy for me to lift so I depend on TV dinners and sometimes eating out. I do drive and right now I am teaching three classes on Life Story Writing. I feel lucky that I can do what I do and that I am not a quadriplegic. Life is good.

Thank You

Writing this book has been quite an effort. I started it because I was teaching adults how to write their life story and I wanted to set an example. Once I got going, I didn't want to stop until it was finished. I have spent all of this summer (2012) sitting at the computer until my butt is totally flat and tired. I felt that I was in a marathon and just kept plugging along. Our life has been so full of adventure and I wanted to put even more in, but in the interest of your eyes, I cut out a lot.

I have had the most wonderfully supportive husband in Ron. First of all he went along with all of my hair-brained ideas. Consider that he grew up very conservative, but followed me into a canyon and to the top of a mountain. Neither one were much fun but we are glad for the experience. He says it even beat sitting on a beach in Florida which was his plan before he met me. And he says he isn't sorry for his choices. That is a true friend.

We have had a very full life but we didn't do it alone. First and foremost God was always there guiding us and our family and friends have cheered us on.

It is hard to end a book when life isn't over yet but you can be assured that I will still be teaching for a couple of years and enjoying bridge and pinochle. Thanks for sharing my life.

Our web site is still up although not active any longer. Please feel welcome to browse it for fun and recipes. There are a lot more stories and pictures on there about our life on wheels.

www.movinon.net
canyongal03@gmail.com

Made in the USA
San Bernardino, CA
04 March 2018